Brent,
I'm glad our
lives intersected at
christ church!

peace, Geoff

ENDORSEMENTS

I love this devotional! It is the *My Utmost* for this generation. The Word is made clear and the Difference Maker challenge sticks with me throughout the day. I look forward to it every morning.

ROB McCLELAND, PhD
President, John Maxwell Leadership Foundation

Our deepest longing as human beings is for significance. *Make a Difference* isn't a luxury—it's at the core of our lives. Here, author and Bible scholar Ken Castor serves as an expert guide into a life of significance. Every day is a surprising exploration into a deep truth about Jesus, a reflection on his impact in the world, an intimate connection-point with him, and a simple challenge to live in his Spirit. Don't just read this book—do this book.

RICK LAWRENCE
Author of *The Jesus-Centered Life* and editor of the *Jesus-Centered Bible,* simplyyouthministry.com

We're surrounded by a generation of emerging young leaders who are tired of watching, waiting for permission, and wondering when they will be called on to make a difference in this world for Jesus. Ken Castor understands their cry and provides a clear formula for daily empowerment and mobilization through this habit-forming devotional.

TIMOTHY ELDRED
President, Endeavor Ministries, endeavorministries.org

Ken continues to caringly but honestly encourage and drive people to grow deeper into what it means to follow Jesus. *Make a Difference* is another fantastic resource for anyone who desires a daily push to learn, grow, and live out their faith in a new way.

CHRIS THEULE-VANDAM
Regional Director, Young Life's Western Great Lakes Region, westerngreatlakes.younglife.org

Too often our lives become so cluttered with selfish pursuits that we miss the opportunities right in front of our eyes to help people and change the world around us. In *Make a Difference*, Ken Castor reminds us every day what is good and what priority we ought to set first: to act justly, to love mercy, and to walk humbly with our God.

JOSHUA BECKER
Wall Street Journal best-selling author, Founder of Becoming Minimalist (becomingminimalist.com) and The Hope Effect (hopeeffect.com)

My favorite devotionals for forty-plus years have been crisply written hybrids, blending biblical encouragement and challenge. Their authors are word chefs, cooking up sweet swallows for the soul with lingering, satisfying aftertastes. Ken Castor uses this same tasty style with daily doable adventures for a year's worth of nourishment.

DAVE RAHN, PhD
Senior Vice President, Chief Ministry Officer, YOUTH FOR CHRIST®, yfc.org

I've learned from twenty-five-plus years of caring for orphans, the most valuable investment we can make is to give God the freshest (and the best) part of our day. It is harder for the enemy to sabotage our mind with irrelevant thoughts when we are committed to doing what God wants us to do. Ken's book is an extremely useful discipline in guiding us through a meaningful conversation with God, laying the foundation for a successful day.

THEA JARVIS
Founder and Director, The Love of Christ (TLC) Orphanage, South Africa, tlc.org.za

Do you want to be a positive force for good in this world? Form the simple practice of walking with Jesus—every. Single. Day. Grow in your faith and be challenged to take action. *Make a Difference* concisely yet brilliantly nourishes you with God's truth and then invites you to participate in what God is doing in the world.

KATHERINE WELCH, M.D.
Founder and Director, Relentless, gorelentless.org

MAKE

A

Difference

KEN CASTOR

BroadStreet

P U B L I S H I N G

BroadStreet Publishing Group, LLC
Savage, MInnesota, USA
BroadStreetPublishing.com

Make a Difference

978-1-4245-5841-4 (faux)
978-1-4245-5234-4 (e-book)

Cover by Chris Garborg at garborgdesign.com
Typesetting by Kjell Garborg at garborgdesign.com

Printed in China
19 20 21 22 23   5 4 3 2 1

The life breath of our day should be spending time with Jesus so that we can make a difference in this world in which we live. Too many times, though, we push Jesus off like he's a vagrant: *Maybe I'll see you on Sunday and throw some money your way, Jesus.* Our attitude stems from an apathetic belief that displaced and broken people don't really matter, and a lethargic belief that Jesus is passive.

However, Jesus is not passive. He's passionate and he's proactive. And he doesn't want us to be lethargic about him or apathetic about people any longer. He wants to change us, and he wants to change the world through us.

Since I was a kid, Jesus has been active in my life. That doesn't mean I always noticed it. In fact, there were several moments where my focus was distracted and my steps were jumbled and my actions made the wrong kind of impact. But I've come to learn that Jesus has been intentionally seeking to change me every single day so that I can intentionally make a difference in this world through him.

I don't want to be a blob. Human blobs, who only think about doing something if they feel like it, are letting the world down. A disciple, however, is a learner. Our world needs fewer blobs and more learners of Jesus—people who are actively seeking him in a catalytic relationship, searching for his life around every corner and in every person.

My prayer is that this book will help kick you into that world-changing gear where God operates. This earth needs more people pursuing their radical God-created potential. People like you. It's a mess out there. And you have been called by God to take initiative, to do something about it.

Make a Difference helps you walk with Jesus and gives you encouragement to see the opportunities you have to deliver restoration where there is desperation. Through daily reflections (sometimes quirky, sometimes serious, hopefully always deep), verses, prayers, and "Difference Maker" challenges, I want you to discover ways to daily grow closer to Jesus and be spurred to make a difference in others as a result.

Oh, and note this: Many times when the Bible verses in this book say "you," it is plural. So even though this is a personal devotional book, remember that you are a part of a larger "you," a network of others who actively follow Jesus. In fact, you can go to my website (where, over the years, some of these daily entries originated) to find organizations and people who can help you follow through with many of the Difference Maker challenges in this book: kencastor.com.

It's your calling. It's your turn. It's your time. You can do it. Make a difference.

Ken Castor

January

Jesus,

Remind me that your eyes are on me.

And then help me to see what you see.

Amen.

START FRESH

Jesus wants you to have a fresh start in this world. In fact, he made this world with you in mind. He made it so that you could breathe in its air, marvel in its sunsets, surf in its waves, and wander in its paths with him. Be confident today in the one who made this world. While most people get caught up in their hectic schedules and busy lives, pause throughout this day to treasure what Jesus created for you and for me.

> The LORD merely spoke,
> and the heavens were created.
> He breathed the word,
> and all the stars were born.
> He gave the sea its boundaries
> and locked the oceans in vast reservoirs.
> Let everyone in the world fear the LORD,
> and let everyone stand in awe of him.
> For when he spoke, the world began!
> It appeared at his command.
>
> PSALM 33:6–9

Lord Jesus, let me see this world as you intended it to be. Thank you for making this world to be the place where I can be with you. Let me breathe in your creative power today. Amen.

DIFFERENCE MAKER

Notice something about this world that you may not have spotted before. Then tell somebody about it.

IN A MESS

There are some troubles that are massive in scale—like war, terror, disease, and death. And some of the troubles we see appear to be less intense, but they are the seeds that spawn disruption in our lives, such as hate, pride, jealousy, and selfishness. These things interfere with the amazing vision God has for his creation.

This is where you come in to play. First, God wants you to know something powerfully life changing: the problems of this world will one day fade away. Jesus is taking care of them. And second, God wants your words and actions to stand in contrast to the disruptive troubles of this world.

Live today in the freedom and power of Jesus. Don't allow the troubles around you to control your mind or your heart. Turn yourself toward your Creator today, knowing that he is taking care of all things.

For sin is the sting that results in death, and the law gives sin
its power. But thank God! He gives us victory over sin and
death through our Lord Jesus Christ.
So, my dear brothers and sisters, be strong and immovable.
Always work enthusiastically for the Lord, for you know that
nothing you do for the Lord is ever useless.

1 CORINTHIANS 15:56–58

Almighty Jesus, give me the strength today to stand against those destructive forces that seek to disrupt your plans in this world. And let me invite others into your victorious life. Amen.

DIFFERENCE MAKER

Here's a simple challenge that makes a big impact. If you see a mess today, clean it up. Just do it, whether someone notices or not.

GOD LOVES YOU SO MUCH

God has a track record of not giving up on his people. When they got lost, he pursued them. When they sinned, he made a plan to rescue them. When they ran away, he actively looked for them. When they were in trouble, he fought for them. When they continued to wander, he continued to seek them. When they cried out, he gave them a Savior. And when they turned to him, he embraced them with his creative, unlimited life.

You are a person, are you not? The good news for you today is this: You are so loved by God, the very one who created this world so that he could be in relationship with you. He sent Jesus to find you, to pursue you, to search for you. He will never give up on you. In fact, he is thinking about you right now. He is calling out your name, and he wants you to call out his.

> "For this is how God loved the world: He gave his one and only Son, so that everyone who believes in him will not perish but have eternal life."
>
> JOHN 3:16

Lord Jesus, thank you for chasing after me. Let me be found by you. Here I am, Lord. I put my life in your hands. Use me to find others in your love. Amen.

DIFFERENCE MAKER

Look for someone who needs an extra chance today and find a way (through words or through actions) to share God's love with him or her.

DO SOMETHING

This world needs you to make a difference. This good world has veered a long way from what God created it to be. God did something about it, and he called you to do something about it with him.

Jesus, the Light of the world, calls you the light of the world too. You are a partner with Jesus in his mission on this earth. He wants everyone to see him, and he wants you to help shed some light for them. Jesus wants people to know the way to him. He wants you to offer to light the path. Jesus shines in brilliance. He wants you to shine his radiance upon your family, your friends, and all those you will encounter today.

Jesus spoke to the people once more and said, "I am the light of the world. If you follow me, you won't have to walk in darkness, because you will have the light that leads to life."

JOHN 8:12

Lord Jesus, Light of the world, let me reveal your life and light to others. Let me not be afraid. Let me stand tall in the confidence of your good news so that those around me would be blessed. Amen.

DIFFERENCE MAKER

Think of someone who is clouded by darkness today. Then take time right now to pray for them. And as you do, ask God to let you be a light in their life.

SPREADING IMPACT

You can't always see the impact you are having on those around you. The little things you do for Jesus that don't make you famous, and that seem to go unnoticed, may actually be a catalyst for something greater than you could ever imagine. Making a difference in this world sometimes means simply living every day in the creative light of Jesus. By doing this, people begin to be changed by the authentic truth and life that is evident in your integrity, in your joy, in your peace, in your words, and in your acts of kindness.

And here's a cool thing: While you are living out your faith in Jesus, there are millions of others who are also living out theirs. Millions of little actions become a gigantic world-changing movement. You are a part of something huge—the good news of Jesus transforming this world, one by one, little by little, person by person.

This same Good News that came to you is going out all over the world. It is bearing fruit everywhere by changing lives, just as it changed your lives from the day you first heard and understood the truth about God's wonderful grace.

COLOSSIANS 1:6

Jesus, let me be consistent in the little things of my life so that over time it will have a huge impact on others. Amen.

DIFFERENCE MAKER

Through either a message, a phone call, or a visit, share with someone a simple thing that God is doing in your life.

JESUS SHAPES YOU

Jesus shapes and tinkers and molds and forms. It's what he's good at. He walked the earth as a carpenter—trimming edges, nailing boards, and constructing treasured and useful items.

Jesus shapes people too. For instance, he radically changed a stuffy, murderous religious type named Saul. Jesus knocked his egotistical, self-righteous butt to the ground. He then healed the hatred and hurt that was in his heart. So deep was the transformation, in fact, that Jesus was able to use Saul (also called Paul) to shape others. He formed him into a life-giving example for people to follow.

You too can be changed by Jesus to become someone who changes others.

Keep putting into practice all you learned and received from me—everything you heard from me and saw me doing. Then the God of peace will be with you.

PHILIPPIANS 4:9

Lord Jesus, trim from me everything that gets in the way of your work in my life. Let me be transformed as your agent in this world.

DIFFERENCE MAKER

Think of a habit in your life that is holding you back from fully serving God. Give it up to Jesus. Make a plan of action and let Jesus change you so that you can change others.

YOU ARE IN GOD'S PLANS

Even when things around you, or in you, are messed up, there is a remarkable truth that still reigns: Jesus created this world so that he could hang out with you. There is also a second truth that is just as remarkable: God doesn't give up on his plans. And no matter what you are experiencing today, no matter what you are facing in this moment, it just so happens that you are in the blueprint of God's plans for this planet. That is good news indeed. And good news is what Jesus is all about.

So turn to the Lord today. Call on his name. Ask him to re-create things around you and in you. This is what he wants for your life—it's why he created you in the first place. It is why he came for you, and it is why he called out on your behalf on the cross. It is why he conquered sin and death. Jesus made you, he loves you, and he plans to do great things through you. Call on Jesus today.

For "Everyone who calls on the name of the Lord
will be saved."
ROMANS 10:13

Jesus, I call on your name today. Be with me in a renewed way. Make me right in your eyes. Make me mighty for your plans. And make me a light for this world that you love so much. Amen.

DIFFERENCE MAKER

Without placing any limits on yourself for a moment, imagine all that God wants for you. What desires has he placed on your heart that can make a positive impact on this world?

IMAGO DEI

An image is a reflection of the original. It has traits that resemble another, much like a mirror, a recording, or a picture. For instance, some people will look at a child and say, "You look and act just like your parents. It's like you're a spitting image of them."

So we can understand that it is an amazing announcement when the Bible declares that humans were created in God's image. *Imago Dei* is an old Latin term that describes how men and women were made in the image and likeness of God. Humans were made as reflections of the Creator. All of God's characteristics, desires, and abilities are on display in each and every one of us. His compassion, strength, wisdom, love, creativity, joy, and wonder are embedded in who we are. He endowed us with world-changing authority and entrusted us with life-giving responsibility. God made us to be his very representatives on the earth.

> Then God said, "Let us make human beings in our image, to be like us. They will reign over the fish in the sea, the birds in the sky, the livestock, all the wild animals on the earth, and the small animals that scurry along the ground."
>
> GENESIS 1:26

Dear Jesus, let everything I do today represent you. Let me not be a distraction, but let my words and actions reveal who you are. Amen.

DIFFERENCE MAKER

As you go throughout your day, make a note of how you, as a human being created in the *imago Dei*, look and act like a representative of God.

IMAGO EGO

Self-image problems began the moment humans rejected the *imago Dei* (image of God). Insecurity, embarrassment, frustration, confusion, self-hatred, shame, false thoughts, and self-harm—none of these things were characteristics humans were ever supposed to experience. In the beginning God created us with confidence, joy, clarity, innocence, and love. We were created with all of the great attributes of God embedded within us.

Instead of being people who represented God, we chose to be creatures who represented ourselves. And ever since we have suffered with our self-image. We stopped giving attention to God and we started focusing on ourselves instead. The result, of course, is a broken world—humans who are self-absorbed and self-destructive. Our world needs people who are brave enough to drop their ego and be re-created by Jesus again in the very image of God.

> Then he said to the crowd, "If any of you wants to be my follower, you must turn from your selfish ways, take up your cross daily, and follow me."
>
> LUKE 9:23

Lord Jesus, for the next twenty-four hours, help me take my attention off myself and place it on you. I give up my "self" so that you can use me to impact this world. Amen.

DIFFERENCE MAKER

Look in the mirror and ask yourself, "Whom will others see reflected in me? Whom will I represent today—myself or God?"

JESUS GAVE UP

To say that Jesus gave up is alarming. But it is also true. Jesus had everything. As the Creator, he owned everything—he was in charge of everything—but then he simply gave up. He gave himself up so that we can capture him. He surrendered his greatness so that we can embrace him. He let down his power so that we can enclose around him. Because we were unable to see him in all of his brilliant glory, he chose to lay aside his power so that we can know him personally once again.

Jesus doesn't ask us to do anything that he is unwilling to do himself. Rather, he asks us to follow his example, to do what he does, to be reflections of his attitude and actions on the earth today. He loves others so much that he willingly gave himself up so they—and we—could have life.

> You must have the same attitude that Christ Jesus had.
> Though he was God,
> he did not think of equality with God
> as something to cling to.
> Instead, he gave up his divine privileges;
> he took the humble position of a slave
> and was born as a human being.
> When he appeared in human form,
> he humbled himself in obedience to God
> and died a criminal's death on a cross.
>
> PHILIPPIANS 2:5–8

Lord Jesus, thank you for giving yourself up on the cross. Thank you for thinking of us as you did that day. And thank you for inviting me to follow your heart.
Amen.

DIFFERENCE MAKER

What could you give up today that is more about you than God?

OTHERS FOCUSED

The first person on our mind in the morning is often ourselves, and the last person in our thoughts at the end of each night is often ourselves too. The primary person we're concerned about throughout the events of each day is often ourselves. Do you see a pattern here?

Do you want to change the world? Then try to think less of yourself and more about others. Consider what a friend is thinking about. Put yourself in your parents' shoes. Look at a situation through a hurting person's eyes. You see, Jesus calls us to be others focused. He doesn't want us to be so self-absorbed that we miss what is happening in the lives of our friends and family. He created us to be like him and to follow his example. Because he loves others and gave himself up for others, so should we.

But we don't need to write to you about the importance of loving each other, for God himself has taught you to love one another.

1 THESSALONIANS 4:9

Lord Jesus, let me be more like you today by noticing the feelings and needs of others. Push me to do things for others that will give them encouragement and hope. Amen.

DIFFERENCE MAKER

Pick an important person in your life and, before you do anything else, call or text that person with a note of encouragement.

MIMIC

As a kid, did you ever play that fun but annoying game where you repeated everything someone said and did? If they moved an arm, then you would move your arm in the same way. If they spoke, you would repeat what they said verbatim. If they said, "Hey, stop it!" then you would say, "Hey, stop it!" too. It was funny (for a while, or unless you were the one being copied), and then it eventually got on everyone's nerves.

Imitating God is a lot different than that game. It's more like the moment when a little boy, after watching his dad shaving in the mirror, puts shaving cream on his face, picks up a razor (with the cap still on, of course!), and begins to practice the strokes up and down his face. Every father who has experienced this moment can't help but smile.

When we imitate God, we aren't playing a game where we merely repeat him like a robot responding to a command. When people copy God like that it can become really annoying really quickly. Instead, as we watch God, we learn to do what he does. When we follow his actions, his words, and his heart, we tend to put his movements into practice. In this way, when we mimic God, a smile spreads across his face, for we are becoming more and more like him.

Imitate God, therefore, in everything you do,
because you are his dear children.

EPHESIANS 5:1

Lord Jesus, so much of my life doesn't imitate you. Align my thoughts,
my words, and my actions with yours. Amen.

DIFFERENCE MAKER

Think about your favorite characteristic of God. Then think of a way you can put that same characteristic into practical action today.

AMBASSADOR

An ambassador is a person who is sent by the leader of a kingdom to live in another kingdom as an official representative of the kingdom from which he or she was sent. In other words, what the ambassador speaks and does tells everyone, *This is what my leader is all about.* So it is important that the ambassador do and say only what their leader would want them to do and say.

Now imagine that Jesus has asked you to be his ambassador. He wants you to represent him where you live. As you interact with others, Jesus has given you his authority to share his words and customs with those with whom you live. It's as if you are a citizen of heaven and have been sent to your family, your friends, your career, and your community in order let others know what God is like. It's a lot of responsibility.

Unfortunately, throughout history, some people who have claimed to represent Jesus have done some terrible things, and, in the process, Jesus' message was misrepresented. Don't let the poor example of some people stop you from being a true ambassador for Jesus. Choose today to restore what it means to represent Jesus purely and share his message clearly.

So we are Christ's ambassadors; God is making his appeal
through us. We speak for Christ when we plead,
"Come back to God!"

2 CORINTHIANS 5:20

Lord Jesus, let me represent you today in everything I say and everything I do.
Amen.

DIFFERENCE MAKER

What can you speak on God's behalf today? What message has God given you the authority to share? And what would be the best way to share that message with someone else today?

MAKE ME LIKE YOU

Jesus celebrates when you follow him. In fact, it's his greatest joy. He came to this earth so that you could hear what he says and see what he does. He spoke with power so that you could see he is the source of all truth. He healed people so that you could know he is a God of restoration and love. He died on the cross so that you could have your sins forgiven and have a relationship with God. He gave you his Spirit so that you could be renewed every day and change this world with his authority. And he called you to follow in his steps, to walk in his ways, and to encourage others to become his followers too.

Heaven rejoices when you begin to look like Jesus in the way you live your life. This is God's original intent: making humans in his image, to be close to him in every moment. If you want to make a true difference in this world, one that matters forever, then today is a day to embrace God's re-creating work in your own life.

You made me; you created me.
Now give me the sense to follow your commands.

PSALM 119:73

Jesus, teach me to follow you in the little things of my life so that I can be entrusted to follow you in the big things too. Change me so that I can change the world for you. Amen.

DIFFERENCE MAKER

Pick something in your life that does not reflect God's image in you and give it over to Jesus today. Then use your new freedom to do something that gives life or joy to others.

GOD KNOWS YOU

Remember this truth: You are not forgotten. You are not alone. You are not unseen. You are not insignificant. You are not untested. You are not unknown. God has taken a remarkable interest in you. He examines you. Like a precision specialist finely tuned to your every joy or fear, God listens and searches and understands what is happening in you and to you. No matter what you are going through today, God knows and he is close.

David, the writer of Psalm 139, had incredible moments of victory, gut-wrenching moments of failure, endless hours of loneliness, and countless repetitions of everyday routines. Through his experiences, he grew to understand that everything he did throughout each day—every motion and emotion—was known by the Lord. Whatever your life is like today, know that God knows all about it. His attention is turned toward you in this very moment.

> O LORD, you have examined my heart
> and know everything about me.
> You know when I sit down or stand up.
> You know my thoughts even when I'm far away.
>
> PSALM 139:1–2

Lord Jesus, let me know that you know me. Let me not forget that I am not forgotten. Let me stand up and sit down in that confidence today. Amen.

DIFFERENCE MAKER

Every time you sit down and stand up today, make a note in your mind that God's attention is on you in that very moment. And let that knowledge transform everything you think about and do.

GOD SEES YOU

Where are you going in the next twenty-four hours? Think about all of the places, near or far, that you will pass through. How will you get there? Will the travel be nerve racking? Whom will you meet? Will the locations be familiar or adventurous? Are you going to a classroom, coffee shop, or office? Gas station, highway, or sidewalk? Hallway, couch, or bathroom? Conversation, speech, or game?

Maybe you have trouble noticing God during a typical day. But God has no problem focusing on you, whether you are a moving blur or a still picture. God sees you when you are far away as clearly as he sees when you are at home. God also has no problem knowing what you're doing or what you're going to do when you are near or far. Jesus knew the thoughts of people (Matthew 9:4) even before they spoke them and even when he wasn't visibly near them (John 2:47–48).

You see me when I travel
and when I rest at home.
You know everything I do.
You know what I am going to say
even before I say it, LORD.

PSALM 139:3–4

Lord Jesus, remind me today that your eyes are always on me. And then help me to see what you see. Amen.

DIFFERENCE MAKER

Realizing that God sees you, choose one positive action to accomplish today that you wouldn't have otherwise done. Then choose one negative habit to avoid.

GOD IS WITH YOU

If you could create a high-pressure diving suit and descend to the deepest underwater caves submerged several miles under the most remote surfaces of the ocean, you would still be as near to God as if you were at home asleep in your own bed. You are not alone. *Omnipresent* is the fancy word that smart people use to state a profound theological reality: God is everywhere.

If you feel alone, maybe this comforts you. Or, if you are trying to hide something, perhaps this gives you the shivers. Even if you rode a rocket past Pluto or if you ran away to the darkest recesses of your soul—still you would find God looking for you there because he is everywhere at all times. There is no place you can go to escape his presence. This is a profound and terrifying truth.

> I could ask the darkness to hide me
> and the light around me to become night—
> but even in darkness I cannot hide from you.
> To you the night shines as bright as day.
> Darkness and light are the same to you.
>
> PSALM 139:11–12

Lord Jesus, give me the sense to be aware of your presence today,
wherever I may be and in whatever I may be doing. Amen.

DIFFERENCE MAKER

Jesus goes to great lengths to reach you. Think of someone you know who either feels all alone or is trying to hide. Be bold and make the effort to let them know Jesus is there for them too.

GOD MADE YOU

It has been said that every stitch of a quilt is made with love. Actually, a quilt is made out of thread and fabric, with scissors and needles and sewing machines. But the sentiment is still there. The time and effort that, say, a grandmother puts into making a quilt for her new grandchild is evidence of love. Every stitch is another thought, another prayer, another action of care and compassion for the one she loves.

In the same way, the Lord took the time and effort to stitch you together. In the seclusion of your mother's womb, even before the day you gasped your first breath, the Lord's heart and hands were forming you. Every time he patiently wove a sinew or precisely measured a cell or miraculously gave beat to your heart, he thought about you, planned for you, and couldn't help but be consumed with love for you. Every fiber of your being was uniquely patterned and intimately sewn with God's hands. From before you were born, God committed himself to you and loved you.

You made all the delicate, inner parts of my body
and knit me together in my mother's womb.
Thank you for making me so wonderfully complex!
Your workmanship is marvelous—how well I know it.

PSALM 139:13–14

Dear Jesus, thank you for investing so much in me. Keep creating my heart to beat with yours so that I will know how marvelous you truly are. Amen.

DIFFERENCE MAKER

Through a prayer, donation, or by volunteering, take a moment to support agencies that celebrate the precious created nature of each individual person (such as a crisis pregnancy center or an orphanage).

GOD PLANNED FOR YOU

You are not a mistake. God knew you would show up. You didn't surprise him. He was ready for you. And he was looking forward to your arrival. God also was looking forward to how you would live the life he has given to you. He has planned your days with purpose. He has things for you to do and people for you to reach.

Ephesians 2:10 says that you, along with others who follow God, are his masterpiece, created in Christ Jesus to do the good things he planned long ago. He shaped you with incredible attention to detail and with immeasurable value so that you could join him in his good work in this world. You are not a mistake—God made you into a beautiful masterpiece.

> You watched me as I was being formed in utter seclusion,
> as I was woven together in the dark of the womb.
> You saw me before I was born.
> Every day of my life was recorded in your book.
> Every moment was laid out
> before a single day had passed.
>
> PSALM 139:15–16

Jesus, I am not an accident, but a treasure in your eyes. Let that thought filter what I do and how I interact with others today. Amen.

DIFFERENCE MAKER

What is something God created you to do? And what step can you take today to pursue that purpose?

GOD CHERISHES YOU

"The very hairs on your head are all numbered," Jesus said. "So don't be afraid" (Luke 12:7). Jesus wants you, just like his first followers, to be empowered by the fact that you are incredibly valuable to God. He wants you to stand with awe-inspiring confidence—a confidence that comes from learning how precious you are in his sight—and to declare with life-changing assurance that God loves you.

In other words, God puts your drawing on his fridge, not because it's perfect but because it came from you. His heart sparkles when you smile, sing, and serve. His hands clap when you create beauty and when you copy his character. His knees bend when you fall, his healing cleanses your wounds, and his power sets you on course to go and play again. He doesn't stop thinking about you—ever.

> How precious are your thoughts about me, O God.
> They cannot be numbered!
> I can't even count them;
> they outnumber the grains of sand!
> And when I wake up,
> you are still with me!
>
> PSALM 139:17–18

Lord Jesus, let me be bold in my steps today, knowing that you won't stop thinking about me. Amen.

DIFFERENCE MAKER

Think of a creative way that would bring joy to God's heart and let others know how much love he has for them.

GOD SEARCHES YOU

That cute little magnifying glass icon has tremendous power. Anything that is typed next to it is searched and, as long as it is connected to the Internet, returns millions of hits. The information transfer of the world is being driven by a little icon's algorithms.

Imagine now that the cute magnifying glass icon was ruled not by some little Internet search engine like Google, but instead was owned and operated by God. Then imagine typing your name next to it and hitting Enter. What would God's algorithms return on you? Are there any results that might worry you?

The good news about this search process is that Jesus celebrates everyone who comes to him with an open heart. He forgives and cleanses and heals and restores the life of those who seek him. Come to him today and let his cleansing take effect in your life.

> Search me, O God, and know my heart;
> test me and know my anxious thoughts.
> Point out anything in me that offends you,
> and lead me along the path of everlasting life.
>
> PSALM 139:23–24

Jesus, you know me better than I know myself. Reveal those things in me that shouldn't be showing up but keep returning to the top of the list. Thank you for your forgiveness. Please lead me to walk with you through every result. Amen.

DIFFERENCE MAKER

Type your name in a search engine and pray this question:
Jesus, what results would you like to show up here?

GOD'S PATTERNS

Many people look at the commandments in the Bible as a negative list of don'ts—what they are not supposed to do. But God's patterns are more about living according to his original blueprint for life on this earth. Like a good parent trying to raise children for successful living, God's instructions provide the right framework for relationship with him, relationship with others, and responsibility on the earth.

It's as if God noticed his kids couldn't figure out how to build the coolest LEGO set ever (#483 Alpha-1 Rocket Base for those classic space LEGO fans out there!). God didn't want to derail the whole creative experiment called humanity, so he gave his children an instruction manual by which they were to live. And these commands are only tough for those who struggle with God.

> Loving God means keeping his commandments, and his commandments are not burdensome.
>
> 1 JOHN 5:3

Lord Jesus, teach me to love your commands. As I follow your ways, your Spirit will help me become more free to make this world the place you created it to be. Amen.

DIFFERENCE MAKER

Read the Ten Commandments in Exodus 20:1–17, not from a mind-set of don'ts, but from a perspective of potential: What if people followed these commands? How would things improve? What damage could be avoided? What good could be done?

I LOST ON JEOPARDY

One of the great tortures of life is receiving grades on papers and tests. Sometimes those all-night cram sessions just don't cut it. Those practice questions and study groups might help a bit, but they don't solve every problem. The standard is 100 percent—and we all know that no one gets 100 percent all of the time.

Even Ken Jennings, the winningest contestant in *Jeopardy* game show history, eventually lost. Oh, he was pretty good. In fact, one could say he was amazing. For seventy-four *Jeopardy* shows in a row, Jennings outdueled other trivia wizards. But on appearance number seventy-five, he answered some important questions incorrectly and he lost.

The greatest achievements are not enough to sustain any human being forever. Eventually everyone succumbs to a less than perfect score. Often by mistake, and regularly even by deliberate choice, humans fail to measure up to God's pattern. We never hit the 100 percent mark.

> For everyone has sinned;
> we all fall short of God's glorious standard.
>
> ROMANS 3:23

Lord Jesus, I am humbled in the face of your greatness.
Help me admit my failure to completely keep your commands.
Forgive me and restore me to your side. Amen.

DIFFERENCE MAKER

Any time some pride creeps into your judgment today, keep it in check.
A humble heart is an essential characteristic for a person God wants
to use to serve others.

EMERGENCY RESCUE EFFORT

God created humanity to walk with him in a close relationship. *Sin* is defined as anything that lets go of his hand and steps away from him. Sin is a "work" of our heart that leads us away from the life God created humans to have. Since God is the author of all life, the consequence of the refusal to walk with God is to miss out on God's life. We all get paid for our work. If the work is sin, however, then the paycheck is nasty.

Even after humans walked away and found themselves in serious peril, God went on a dramatic rescue mission. He sent his Son, Jesus, the greatest emergency response expert the world has ever seen, to save people who wandered away from life. He reaches out to those who got lost, extends his arms just as their lives hang in the balance, and urges them, *Grab my hand!*

For the wages of sin is death, but the free gift of God is
eternal life through Christ Jesus our Lord.

ROMANS 6:23

Lord Jesus, thank you for dying on the cross and saving me from my sin.
Please help me live the life you have given me. Amen.

DIFFERENCE MAKER

Accept the rescuing arms of Jesus Christ today. Accept his free gift of life and reject sin. Restore yourself to a full walking relationship with God.

DON'T PRETEND

Have you unwrapped a present only to discover you didn't actually want it? Perhaps it was a hideous sweater or last year's trendy item or a gift card to a store you didn't like. When you unwrapped those sorts of presents (and I know you have), have you pretended to be thankful? Perhaps you said, "Oh, thank you! That was so thoughtful. I love it."

Many people have been hurt by others who say they love them but who actually are pretending, wishing for someone else to love. Jesus wants you to be honest, but not in a "Oh, I can't stand you" sort of way. He wants to reshape your heart so that you can receive people and truly say to them, "I am thankful for you in my life and I want to care for you." After all, he received you and rejoiced in the process.

> Don't just pretend to love others. Really love them. Hate what is wrong. Hold tightly to what is good.
>
> ROMANS 12:9

Lord Jesus, help me grow closer to you and become authentically true. As much as it might cost me, don't allow me to get away with being fake today. Help me to truly love people like you do. Amen.

DIFFERENCE MAKER

Think of someone you judge inappropriately and take a practical step to love them today.

BEAUTIFUL FEET

Feet can be really ugly. Bunions and calluses, hair and veins, nails and knobs—these things can combine to make feet look pretty gross. Add athlete's foot or some dank odor to the equation, and you might need some pretty strong spray to just get through the day.

There might be a chance even for the stinkiest, nastiest feet. The Bible mentions, both in the Old Testament and in the New Testament, that there is a way to make even the lowest part of a person's life look gorgeous. Feet look good when they are used for their proper purpose, which is to carry God's good message to this world. In other words, when you hear that Jesus saves people from sin through his work on the cross, you use your feet to run around and proclaim that good news. This has happened for thousands of years, and God wants you to be a part of his news team.

How beautiful on the mountains
are the feet of the messenger who brings good news,
the good news of peace and salvation,
the news that the God of Israel reigns!
ISAIAH 52:7

Lord Jesus, help me be so changed by your good news that I can't help but share it with others. Amen.

DIFFERENCE MAKER

In order to share the good news about what Jesus has done, where do your feet need to go today? (If you need ideas on how to share Jesus with others, go online and check out some ministries that share Jesus.)

TRANSPLANTED

Trees are meant to be rooted in fertile, well-watered soil. But many trees find themselves stuck in pots that are too small, too shallow, and too dry. What's needed is for someone to purchase that tree, bring it home, take it out of the pot, and replant it in ground where it can grow.

People need to be planted in a place where they can flourish. They don't need a restricted basin, superficial soil, or bare ground. The good news is that people who are stuck, who are struggling to grow, can be transplanted by Jesus to become strong and flourishing. This process is not always easy, and it most certainly costs the planter. But it also provides freedom for those with constrained hearts, release for the imprisoned, and beautiful joy for those who yearn for abundant life. It is a powerful message—and it takes root when those who were once stuck begin to find their freedom and identity in Christ.

> To all who mourn in Israel,
> he will give a crown of beauty for ashes,
> a joyous blessing instead of mourning,
> festive praise instead of despair.
> In their righteousness, they will be like great oaks
> that the Lord has planted for his own glory.
>
> ISAIAH 61:3

Lord Jesus, let me become an oak replanted by you to flourish with your life. And, as a result, let me become a source of shade, oxygen, and seeds so that others can grow. Amen.

DIFFERENCE MAKER

Purchase a small plant in a pot. Place it in a window. Take care of it for a few months, making sure it gets adequate water and sunlight. Then, in the spring, plant it in fertile soil.

PAUSE

You must pause. Life has been running. Your breath has been flying and you need to catch it. The last few weeks have been incredibly rich—full of all the dramatic ups and downs that life has to offer—tragedies, victories, eateries, friendlies, and frenzies. You cannot complain about being bored, but at times you have been tempted to drift toward mind-numbing laziness. You have thought to yourself, *I'll just play one more round of this game…or maybe twenty more rounds.*

You know that a numbing of the mind leads to a dumbing of the mind, which then leads to a frustration of the soul. The effort you sometimes take to become an automaton is both surprising and exhausting. Between the busyness and the weariness, you are left to gasp on fumes, losing vitality, clarity, and aspiration. What you truly need is a rest. Not just sleep. You need a Sabbath. A restoration. A peace. A pause. A still. A capturing of time. A moment to shut your eyes and dream of what could be, what should be. A reflection of God's image at work and at rest within you. You must pause.

Then Jesus said, "Come to me, all of you who are weary and
carry heavy burdens, and I will give you rest."

MATTHEW 11:28

*Lord Jesus, let me rest—truly rest. Let me seek you, trust you, and take a…
deep…breath. Amen.*

DIFFERENCE MAKER

At a certain point today, put everything you have planned off to the side
and take time off. Get away and get alone with God, letting him restore
your soul with his peace and rest.

BE NEEDY

People need God. Every person needs a relationship with his or her Creator. People need the daily breath and long-term purpose that only God provides. When things fall apart, they cry out to the Lord because he is who they need during those time. And when people have God, they have everything they need.

But people have also been known to fail to recognize their need for God. Instead of finding their dependency in their Creator, they have tried to go at it alone. While independence from God might puff up the ego and build up a bank account, any get-rich-quick schemes or quick-fix solutions that avoid God are bound to end in ruin.

Being "poor of heart" is an important posture for humans to take. Pride is a false sense of having everything, while poverty is the desperation of not having enough. Those who realize they need God, that they are desperate without him, will be rewarded with the relationship and royal status only God can provide.

> "God blesses those who are poor
> and realize their need for him,
> for the Kingdom of Heaven is theirs."
>
> MATTHEW 5:3

Lord Jesus, let me admit my need for you throughout the day.
Let me rely on you rather than myself. Amen.

DIFFERENCE MAKER

Think of something you have in your life that supplants your need for God and discard it.

BE SAD

One of the signs of a good heart is a sad heart. In other words, those who don't care don't mourn. But those who care are willing to feel the pain of loss. There is a remarkable amount of hurt in this world. And while it would be great to avoid pain, the only alternatives are to become abusive or to become numb to it. And, lest you're confused, neither of those are a good way to exist.

Jesus understands this. One of the shortest verses in the Bible, and one of the most significant, says this: "Jesus wept." At a funeral, Jesus mourned the loss of his friend and he carried the heartache of the situation, precisely because he was willing to love deeply. He didn't have to care. But he did. Jesus cries with his friends. He wears their burdens. He tends to their wounds. And then he raises them to life once again.

> "God blesses those who mourn,
> for they will be comforted."
>
> MATTHEW 5:4

Jesus, give me a heart big enough to mourn and a soul big enough to take the risk. Amen.

DIFFERENCE MAKER

Grab coffee with or write a note to someone you know who has recently experienced loss, expressing your sorrow.

BE HUMBLE

If anyone ever had a reason to brag, it was Jesus. After listening to some simpleton humans boast about conquering nations or building coliseums or inventing aqueducts, Jesus could have interrupted their grandiosity with a snap of his fingers. "Be still, morons! You don't know squat. Those nations you defeated—I made them. And you! You call those tiny buildings 'coliseums'? Ha! I made asteroids bigger than that. And what's so great about an aqueduct? So you can move a little bit of water from one place to the other. Have you ever heard of rivers? Seas? How about oceans? Oh, and have you ever noticed how your heart is beating right now? Yep, that's me. I sustain your life."

If he wanted to, Jesus could have put humans in their place pretty quickly. If he was tired of conceited humans claiming to be the greatest, he could have snuffed out their puffed-up arrogance with one breath. But instead he serves. He listens. He embraces. He heals. He saves. He treasures. All because he wants people to share with him all that he has made.

"God blesses those who are humble,
for they will inherit the whole earth. "

MATTHEW 5:5

Jesus, you are greater than I realize, and yet you put my life ahead of your own.
In humility, I fall to me knees and find that you already there serving me.
Thank you, Jesus. Amen.

DIFFERENCE MAKER

Be humble like Jesus today. Try to make it through the entire day without using the word *I*. Instead of talking about yourself, take that effort to focus on others.

February

Jesus,

You have asked me to be like you.

Please lead me to be radically open handed.

Amen.

BE HUNGRY

Jesus wants you to make a difference in the community in which you live. It isn't enough just to feel like people shouldn't be treated unfairly, for instance, or to think that people shouldn't be oppressed. He actually wants you to figure out something to do that will help these people and address the terrible situations they are in.

Jesus hungered and thirsted for justice. He hated it when people were pushed down or overrun. His vision for the world did not include oppression and violence. In one of the most famous and countercultural messages the world has ever heard, Jesus' Sermon on the Mount, he made it clear that God values human life, and he expects people to fight for those whose life is being stolen. Does your heart break over the wrongs that are committed against the innocent? Does your soul cry for those whose voice has been taken from them? God's does.

"God blesses those who hunger and thirst for justice,
for they will be satisfied."

MATTHEW 5:6

Lord Jesus, don't let me settle for a fast-food life. Let me be hungry for the nourishment and fulfillment that you have for this world. Amen.

DIFFERENCE MAKER

Connect with a local organization or church that seeks to defend those who are being wronged. Ask what kind of support they need, and choose a way to respond.

BE MERCIFUL

Martin Luther King Jr. was countercultural. In the face of hostility, he upheld mercy. He had every right to retaliate against those who hurled threats, insults, and physical harm. Yet he chose a different path, one that changed the trajectory of a powerful nation, not to mention the hearts of millions upon millions of people.

When you are in a position of power, when you are justified to dispense wrath, when you have the opportunity to absolutely let loose your fury, what would happen if you chose to withhold it? What if you extended a hand of grace and restoration instead? Mercy recognizes that God is in control, and it acknowledges that the person who deserves judgment is both a fellow child of God and in need of restoration.

Not everyone who is offered mercy accepts it or reorients to it. But someone else's response is not your responsibility. Mercy doesn't dictate a person's future; it simply opens it up.

> "God blesses those who are merciful,
> for they will be shown mercy."
> MATTHEW 5:7

*Lord Jesus, give me your authority to forgive and offer a hope
to those who need it. Amen.*

DIFFERENCE MAKER

Gut check. Whom do you judge too easily?
Who needs another chance today?

BE PURE

To "adulterate" a product is to add an inferior or polluted substance to what may have once been a spotless, good-hearted item. It is like secretly adding chemical ingredients to all-natural skin lotion, or adding an affair to a marriage.

Purity doesn't imply naiveté. To be pure doesn't mean you are inexperienced or ignorant. The world mocks purity because it doesn't understand it and doesn't believe it has survival power. Eventually, the world believes, purity has to be corrupted, right?

Jesus doesn't think so. He believes purity can be lived out practically. Jesus believes purity begins in the nature of a person's focus upon God, and then it extends into everyday action. He suggests that purity opens the eyes to see in ways that others cannot. In fact, purity actually expands the paradigm and adventure of life.

> "God blesses those whose hearts are pure,
> for they will see God."
>
> MATTHEW 5:8

Lord Jesus, re-create my heart to seek you in everything. Find anything impure in me, point it out, and begin the process to restore me to a pure vision for you. Amen.

DIFFERENCE MAKER

Pick a glaring struggle you have with impurity, then find a friend who struggles with the same issues so you can hold each other faithful in your pursuit of purity.

BE PEACEFUL

Peace is not passive. Where did that idea originate from anyway? Peace comes about through incredible strain and sacrifice. Ask the millions of people throughout history who have given their lives so that peace could stand.

There is a war in the world today against peace—ideologically, geographically, culturally, physically, emotionally, and spiritually. There are powers and movements whose goal is the disruption and deterioration and destruction of true peace. It is into this fray that Jesus jumps. Like a vigilante of justice, Jesus disarms evil. His effort costs him his life. But it is a cost he decided was worth the outcome.

Jesus is the "Prince of Peace" (Isaiah 9:6), and he exerts himself so that people can have "peace with God" (Romans 5:1). Jesus fought and died to give this world a powerful, proactive peace. When people embrace him, and when they choose to become peacemakers themselves, all of heaven celebrates.

> "God blesses those who work for peace,
> for they will be called the children of God."
>
> MATTHEW 5:9

Lord Jesus, don't let me cheat the steps. Challenge me to become a peacemaker.
Amen.

DIFFERENCE MAKER

Take a moment to pray. Find something in your relationships or
circumstances today, either big or small, that agitates you.
Then ask God to show you what steps you need to take
to fight for peace in that area of your life.

TREAT PEOPLE WELL

Imagine a religious dude entering the room, sweat beading down his brow, feverish "fainthood" (false + sainthood = fainthood) in his eyes, declaring dramatically in a dry, raspy voice, "Oh, I am so burdened because I am fasting for the Lord."

Well, isn't that special. God goes to great lengths in the Bible to make it clear that he doesn't want people to give up food in order to look more spiritual in the eyes of others. God doesn't think it's awesome for people to intentionally malnourish themselves in order to get attention. He actually looks away in disgust from that kind of theater.

God created you to live altruistically in the patterns of your life. If someone is wronged, give up your own interests to pursue freedom for them. If someone is working too hard on your behalf, take their extra burden upon yourself. If someone needs something that you have in abundance, then give it to them. The bottom line is that we are to treat people well because Jesus treated people well.

"No, this is the kind of fasting I want:
Free those who are wrongly imprisoned;
lighten the burden of those who work for you.
Let the oppressed go free,
and remove the chains that bind people."

ISAIAH 58:6

Jesus, show me what I can give up in order to give life to someone else. Amen.

DIFFERENCE MAKER

Think of somebody in one of the categories listed in Isaiah 58:6.
What can you give up today that would help their cause?

SHARE WITH OTHERS

What an amazing calling you and I have. You have been asked by the living God to tackle some of the biggest challenges this world has ever faced. In large scale, they are massive issues. But on a very personal scale, they are intimately and effectively addressed.

If you see someone who is hungry, do you think Jesus wants you to stuff your face and belch? If you see a family sleeping in a car, do you think Jesus wants you to judge them? If you see a kid who doesn't have clothes that fit, do you think Jesus wants you to do nothing? I'm guessing probably not.

"Share your food with the hungry,
and give shelter to the homeless.
Give clothes to those who need them,
and do not hide from relatives who need your help."
ISAIAH 58:7

Lord Jesus, use me in service for others today. Amen.

DIFFERENCE MAKER

You can give your lunch to someone who needs it more than you do; you can ask the local elementary school what size gym shoes they need donated; or you can send a family member a care package in the mail. Do something for someone else today.

FEED THE HUNGRY

Not here, really? Not now, right? Sure, I know there are problems around the world—out *there*—but not around me. Kids don't go hungry in *this* nation. People aren't cast aside *here*. Families have everything they need to be successful in my community, don't they?

Jesus is on mission. That means you had better be too. He listens for the cry of the hungry and leans into the mess of those who are in trouble. He looks for darkness and pierces it with his brilliance. He searches the rubble for signs of those who are trapped. He works with precision to remove the concrete and rebar and beams crushing them. He attends to wounds and orchestrates restoration efforts. He patiently heals and persistently rejoices when he sees people find life through his hands.

There is plenty of rescue work to do. What a privileged calling you and I have.

"Feed the hungry,
and help those in trouble.
Then your light will shine out from the darkness,
and the darkness around you will be as bright as noon."

ISAIAH 58:10

Lord Jesus, thank you for blessing me in my needs. Please use me to share your blessing with others. Amen.

DIFFERENCE MAKER

Make arrangements for some friends to join you at a food-packing agency.

SABBATH

Followers of Jesus are asked to do a lot of good things, like treating people well, caring for those in need, and feeding those who are hungry. But there is one task that, at first glance, seems out of sync with the rest. Like the others, it's a task that requires great effort, but it is not an exertion of work. It is the pursuit of rest.

Rest is too often overlooked in this busy achievement-based culture of our time. Rest might be a neglected practice in your own life, as it is for many people around you. People make up for missing rest by binging on naps, hangovers, or laziness. That's not what God wants for us. God wants us to observe the Sabbath, a day set aside in the rhythm of each week, that focuses the heart and mind on God and others. The Sabbath is a type of restoration that reorients the soul to be ready to serve in the good work of following Jesus in the six days that follow.

> "Keep the Sabbath day holy.
> Don't pursue your own interests on that day,
> but enjoy the Sabbath
> and speak of it with delight as the LORD's holy day.
> Honor the Sabbath in everything you do on that day,
> and don't follow your own desires or talk idly."
>
> ISAIAH 58:13

Dear Jesus, help me rest in your interests instead of my own.
Amen.

DIFFERENCE MAKER

Ask God to reveal his interests for you and your community. As God shapes your heart, begin sketching plans to impact others the way God wants.

SING PRAISE

David didn't have Beats by Dre or an iPhone packed with the latest songs by Imagine Dragons. How did he even survive? Seriously, how did this guy function without the constant stimulation of media continually rewiring his brain?

Well, David spent some time alone (note: time = days, weeks, months) shepherding flocks in the countryside. To pass his hours he learned to write songs, play compact instruments, and talk to God. He had sheep. And they made only one genre of music. (Except when they ate too much grass, then they made a second genre of music. A symphonic movement, you could say.)

David wrote songs of praise—dozens, and perhaps hundreds, of them. Even while he sheered wool and killed bears that attacked his flock, he became an accomplished poet, theologian, musician, and composer. He used his growing skills to turn his heart, again and again, to the Lord.

Sing a new song to the Lord!
Let the whole earth sing to the Lord!
Sing to the Lord; praise his name.
Each day proclaim the good news that he saves.

PSALM 96:1-2

Lord Jesus, help my mind and heart sing for you. Amen.

DIFFERENCE MAKER

Either write a song of praise to God or listen to a song of praise to God. Get that song stuck in your heart and mind and refer back to it throughout the day.

REAPING

Sometimes the difference you make in this world is immediate. Perhaps you called someone on their birthday and they were greatly encouraged. Good job—you made a difference in their life. Quick response. Lives changed. Keep doing it! But other times the difference you make in this world isn't always immediately evident. Perhaps you have started getting rid of some bad habits in your life, but they keep rearing their ugly head and trying to drag you down. The battle is still there. It isn't fixed and it isn't clear if anything good is coming out of it.

But God's Word encourages us again and again to persist. Keep going. Don't give up pursuing Jesus and the life he has for you. Don't quit doing what he wants you to do. Don't stop changing the patterns of your life and the lives of those around you in the long-term direction of Jesus. You will reap a harvest if you don't give up.

So let's not get tired of doing what is good. At just the right time we will reap a harvest of blessing if we don't give up.

GALATIANS 6:9

Jesus, help me keep pressing on for those things you have asked me to do.
Amen.

DIFFERENCE MAKER

Write down five goals for your life that you would like to have accomplished five years from now. Put this somewhere that you will occasionally revisit to remind yourself to not give up.

PUBLISH

Let's say for a moment that in the future you discovered the permanent cure for cancer. But then, let's imagine, that instead of publishing that cure, instead of sharing it and making the cure known, you decided that you would keep it to yourself. Then, let's say, you were able to meet yourself in the future and have a blunt conversation. What would you say to yourself?

What if a group of people were to discover God? And what if they came to know about the great things God had done and the great things he had plans yet to do? What if they knew that God offered salvation and healing and peace and life for the world? And what if they kept all of that information to themselves? If you were able to meet these people and have a blunt conversation, what would you say to them?

The Psalms urge people who have discovered the good news about God to make him known to those around them. And this is what God has called each one of us to do as well—we are to publish what he has done to those around us.

Publish his glorious deeds among the nations.
Tell everyone about the amazing things he does.

PSALM 96:3

Dear Jesus, help me grow in my boldness for sharing what I know about you with others. Amen.

DIFFERENCE MAKER

Brainstorm for a moment: What do you personally know about Jesus? Do you know anyone who needs to know these things too?

WHAT IF?

What if for Valentine's Day a husband bought a card and some roses and gave them to his wife? What if he told his wife he loved her and that she was the only one for him? Nice, right? Well, what if that same husband didn't do much else for his wife for most of the rest of the year? What if he only spent effort on his wife on occasions like her birthday or a special holiday? What if he expected constant adoration and blessing from his wife in return? And what if he looked at other women from time to time, or spent time with pornography, or imagined being with another woman, or acted upon those desires secretively? He's not so nice now, right?

Now try this. What if on Sundays a person went to church and put some money in the offering plate? What if this person told God he or she loved him and that God was the only one for them? Nice, right? Well, what if that same person didn't do much else for God most the rest of the year? What if he or she only spent effort on God on special occasions like Christmas or tax season? What if she expected constant adoration and blessing from God? What if that same person looked at other objects from time to time, or spent time with other desires, or imagined being with another god, or acted upon those desires secretively? Not so nice now, right?

> Come close to God, and God will come close to you. Wash
> your hands, you sinners; purify your hearts, for your loyalty
> is divided between God and the world.
>
> JAMES 4:8

Lord Jesus, thank you for creating me to have relationship with you.
Turn my eyes from worthless things. Amen.

DIFFERENCE MAKER

Get rid of one thing that could compromise your commitment to God today.

UNFORTUNATE EVENTS

In the Lemony Snicket book series by Daniel Handler, a malevolent character named Count Olaf takes in three orphans—Violet, Klaus, and Sunny Baudelaire. In the process he disguises himself as a loving uncle, but it isn't long before the children realize that Olaf is a conniving, lying, twisted, and murderous criminal who is mercilessly trying to get his hands on the Baudelaire fortune. If it wasn't for the purity and determination of the children, their heartbreaking story would have been soul destroying as well.

Sadly, this "series of unfortunate events" is all too common in our world today. The Bible describes the presence of evil in this world, spurred on by Satan, to wreak havoc and destruction upon those whom God loves. One glance at a news site confirms that evil and unfortunate events seem to run rampant. And yet, in contrast to the evil that has invaded our world, Jesus rises to protect and to save.

"The thief's purpose is to steal and kill and destroy. My purpose is to give them a rich and satisfying life."

JOHN 10:10

Lord Jesus, you are so good. Let me live in the satisfaction and power of your life. Let me be pure and determined to stand against evil, in all of its varied forms. Amen.

DIFFERENCE MAKER

Take a sobering note today. What conniving events are at work to erode the life that God wants to give your community? Take time to pray for ways to help people be rescued by Jesus instead.

TRUE LOVE

Today is the big day of love, that fancy day where half-naked flying babies shoot people with arrows. Nothing says I love you like some kid sending projectiles into your backside in order to manipulate how you feel about someone else. Seriously, nothing says I love you like that. Some people treasure this day for the chocolaty-sugary romance, while other people can't wait until tomorrow.

At the risk of being sappy, perhaps this is a good day to remember how much Jesus loves you. He doesn't love you in some consumeristic way. He doesn't run to the store in a last-minute panic after realizing that he forgot to buy you a huge Power Ranger Valentine candy heart. No, Jesus actually loves you. He isn't fickle about it either. And he isn't cheap. He is in this relationship for good, and he wants his love for you to change the way you love others.

> "This is my commandment: Love each other in the same
> way I have loved you. There is no greater love than to lay
> down one's life for one's friends."
>
> JOHN 15:12–13

Lord Jesus, let it sink in how much you truly love me. And let that make a difference in the way that I learn to love others. Amen.

DIFFERENCE MAKER

Because of what Jesus has done for you, what genuine action could you take today to show your friends they are loved?

THE WRONG KIND OF DIFFERENCE

Jesus wants you to make a difference in the world. A good difference—not a mixed-up, mangled, messed-up difference. Unfortunately, all too often, people who say they follow Jesus end up making the wrong kind of difference in this world. Jesus said to his disciples that their love for each other would prove to the world that they were his followers (John 13:35).

So it would be a terrible thing if those who claimed to follow Jesus demonstrated tempers, idiocy, and conspiracy. People who are quick to anger inevitably do really stupid things, which in turn causes them to scheme and worm and twist things for their own protection and gain. It would be terrible for the reputation of Christians to suffer because people who claimed to follow Jesus failed to live with love. Christians are supposed to be a light to the world, reflecting Jesus into the darkness. They are not supposed to be dispensers of darkness themselves.

Don't make the wrong kind of difference.

Short-tempered people do foolish things,
and schemers are hated.
PROVERBS 14:17

Lord Jesus, don't let me mess up in anger today. Keep my heart cooled by your love. Amen.

DIFFERENCE MAKER

What do you see around the corner that is going to trigger your temper? How could you prepare yourself to respond in love?

WORTHMORE (THE OPPOSITE OF WORTHLESS)

Rare is the day when people are aware of what God wants them to do with their lives. Perhaps that is one of the underlying reasons for this devotional book, a simple reminder that God calls people to make a difference in this world every day they are alive.

People don't always check in with Jesus to get their daily assignments. As a result, they toil and labor, but their work is in vain when it's not something Jesus has set before them. People can play and laze, but their happiness is shallow and empty when it's not on God's radar.

Perhaps much of human dissatisfaction in life comes from not doing the work Jesus has assigned people to do. What would change in human hearts if people were to present themselves to Jesus ready for work? What if people checked in with him each morning and asked, "Sir, what do you want me to do today?" This world would be a much different place.

"But my life is worth nothing to me unless I use it for finishing the work assigned me by the Lord Jesus—the work of telling others the Good News about the wonderful grace of God."

ACTS 20:24

Lord Jesus, what do you want me to do today? Amen.

DIFFERENCE MAKER

Strive to align all of your actions today with the work that Jesus has called you to do.

HOT SEATS OF LOVE

Pop culture tries to trick you into thinking that love is often seated in your emotions: "How does that make you feel?" But what if it weren't true that love is seated in your emotions? Some people probably engage in their relationships this way and make some incredible mistakes of judgment. Emotional love without wisdom or a rooted foundation can get people into codependent situations or abusive influences or financial trouble or manic-panic roller-coaster rides of life.

It is really interesting that the apostle Paul refers to three seats of love in Philippians 1. First, Paul said that the Philippians held a special place in his *heart*. Second, he said that he loved the Philippians in the *bowels* of Christ Jesus, which is an awkward phrase nowadays, but it referred to the very core of his being. Third, Paul prays that their love would abound more and more in knowledge and depth of insight so that they would be able to discern what was best and be pure and blameless. In other words, he wants them to love with their *brain*. Each seat comes together to form a beautiful union—each distinct and yet each together—each encouraging and maturing and directing the other.

Paul's desire was for the Philippians to develop a smart, passionate, and, um, moving love.

God knows how much I love you and long for you with the
tender compassion of Christ Jesus.

PHILIPPIANS 1:8

Lord Jesus, mature my ability to love others today. Amen.

DIFFERENCE MAKER

Which "seat" of love do you need to develop and practice more deeply?
What can you do today to act upon this "seat" of love?

RESTLESS

Humans are restless creatures. They are busy carrying busy burdens and are afraid to stop, because, if they stop, they might have to think. And if they think, they might have to wrestle with their burdens and what is going on inside of them. And if they have to wrestle with their burdens, they might get tired. And if they get tired, they might need to rest.

Because of this, humans don't stop. Instead, they pride themselves in activity. They are the most productive least productive creatures in all of history. They overschedule, overcommit, and overextend themselves and then wish they had time to enjoy themselves. Even God stopped the activity of creation to pause and rest. But not humans. No. They are so over that pattern. Instead they choose pace over peace. They are restless creatures. But Jesus, the Lord of the Sabbath, is restful. He asks us to stop our scurry long enough to sit down at the table together for a meal.

Then Jesus said, "Let's go off by ourselves to a quiet place and rest awhile." He said this because there were so many people coming and going that Jesus and his apostles didn't even have time to eat.

MARK 6:31

Lord Jesus, help me rest today. Amen.

DIFFERENCE MAKER

Schedule time today to rest. Do something that will rejuvenate your soul. Invite along others who will be refreshing for you. And be sure to enjoy God's presence as you pause your pace.

PROVOCATIVE

You were created to live a radical life. You were made to be deeply alive, to be stretched to your fullest, and to be passionately involved in this world. So it is no wonder you are attracted to the provocative.

Provocative simply means to "call forward." It recognizes your God-created thirst for activity and purpose. You were created to be called and called to be creative. You were formed so that you could step forward in the shaping of how life is lived on this planet. Jesus didn't make you to squander your days; rather, he made you to live them.

Both Jesus and Satan employ the provocative. But let your ninja-like reflexes be aware that Satan calls you forward, but his is an enticement to eat from a cornucopia of carnage, scheming plans to use you for his own self-serving survival. On the other hand, Jesus calls you forward, and his is an invitation to dinner, shared with friends, empowering you as his partner to give life to others.

Jesus says, "Look! I stand at the door and knock. If you hear my voice and open the door, I will come in, and we will share a meal together as friends."
REVELATION 3:20

Jesus, help me reject the alluring trap of evil and respond to your life-giving call.
Amen.

DIFFERENCE MAKER

Pray for someone who could use a positive nudge. Then call that person on the phone. Invite them to take a step forward in life with you today.

WHATEVER

Do you have a love-hate relationship with your snooze button? Without your alarm you might wake up in a panic because you missed the beginning of the *Phineas and Ferb* all-day marathon. And yet those nine extra minutes of sleep sure would be nice. But do those 540 seconds actually help your grumpy attitude? Some people claim to be even crankier after each smack of their snooze button.

What if, instead of the next time you hit the snooze button, you stopped to pray? Knowing that you have nine more minutes to ask Jesus to get you into the right frame of mind could transform everything about your day. Perhaps that extra slumber could be used to reorient your entire way of thinking. Instead of letting the problems of the world, including your own flaws, failings, and festering worries, muck your mind, choose in those snooze minutes to see whatever is good. Choose to trust God enough to consider, to pursue, and to place your hope in whatever is true.

Since you have been raised to new life with Christ, set your
sights on the realities of heaven, where Christ sits in the
place of honor at God's right hand. Think about the things of
heaven, not the things of earth.

COLOSSIANS 3:1–2

Lord Jesus, let me take every opportunity today to fix my thoughts on what is
right in your eyes. Amen.

DIFFERENCE MAKER

Seriously, try this out: The next time you hit your snooze button, or get some other kind of extra time, focus your thoughts on good things and see what happens.

SPRING IS COMING

Winter can be a cold, harsh drag. But spring is coming.

Near the back of the Bible is a little book named Jude. This little book, which is only twenty-five verses, has an underlying intensity of hope. It begins in love and joy, addresses a frigid concern, and then springs back to love and joy at the end.

The last couple verses of Jude thaw the cold and blooms freshness into the soul. Arms once huddled close to the chest are suddenly spread wide open! God's Word sings hope. When the season seems most somber, the eternal song of Jesus brings out the Bermuda shorts and points to the refreshing life that is to come.

Now all glory to God, who is able to keep you from falling away and will bring you with great joy into his glorious presence without a single fault. All glory to him who alone is God, our Savior through Jesus Christ our Lord. All glory, majesty, power, and authority are his before all time, and in the present, and beyond all time! Amen.

JUDE 24–25

Dear Jesus, let me see the new life that you have for me just ahead. Embolden my faith and keep my heart warm. Amen.

DIFFERENCE MAKER

Do something whimsical that will give you, and others around you, a glimpse of hope.

PROVERB

The book of Proverbs is all about wisdom, but not just the sort of wisdom that helps you do well on a test. This wisdom is proactive, or maybe better said, it is pro-action. Stationary, nondescript living is not an acceptable posture for this type of wisdom. Proverbs does not allow for generic living, or just going with the flow, or being what culture says you should be, or limiting yourself because someone placed a ceiling on you.

This book is not called Pronouns. It is called Proverbs. As you read this book, you are the subject who acts with the wisdom that you learn through its teachings. Wisdom is not slothful, lazy, inactive, or dead. Wisdom is productive. Wisdom flashes like Usain Bolt. In the right moment, it makes its way through the race and realigns things to the way God patterned.

My child, listen to what I say,
and treasure my commands.
Tune your ears to wisdom,
and concentrate on understanding.
Cry out for insight,
and ask for understanding.
Search for them as you would for silver;
seek them like hidden treasures.
Then you will understand what it means to fear the Lord,
and you will gain knowledge of God.

PROVERBS 2:1–5

Lord Jesus, kick my mind into gear. Give me wisdom that will be relevant and active for everything I will face today. Amen.

DIFFERENCE MAKER

Practice one of the action steps in Proverbs 2:1–5 again and again today: listen, treasure, tune, concentrate, cry out, and search.

POCKET PROTECTORS

People can be a lot like pocket protectors. They can be tight-fisted, tight-minded tightwads. Even if they were to see another person in need, they might seize the grip on their wallets, their time, their appearance, their performance, and their stuff. They can desperately keep for themselves whatever precious item they have treasured in their pockets. To let their guard down would be to relinquish control—so without thinking they might find themselves standing defensively against others who simply need the smallest helping hand.

But Jesus lives with wide-open arms. He shares his life, kingdom, mercy, and salvation. He offers himself sacrificially, generously, and even scandalously in concern. He reaches his hands out in an invitation for the poor and downcast to join him in communion. People were never meant to be stingy, stuffy, or stuck. They were created to treasure Jesus, and, as a result, to generously treasure others.

> "Wherever your treasure is, there the desires of your heart
> will also be."
> MATTHEW 6:21

Lord Jesus, you have asked me to be like you, radically committed to open-handedness. Lead me to an opportunity to practice generous living today.
Amen.

DIFFERENCE MAKER

Offer to buy something for someone in need, or leave a larger tip than normal, or send a donation to a charity, or go get your hands dirty at a soup kitchen. Do something generous today that loosens up your comfort zone.

ROT

Three thousand years ago there was a chart-topping pop song that must have gotten stuck in King Saul's mind and driven him mad. The lyrics weren't too deep really, just regular boy-band type of stuff. But they must have irritated Saul over and over and over again. The words from 1 Samuel 18 went like this: "Saul has killed his thousands, and David his tens thousands." Saul didn't like that song.

King Saul began to envy this young warrior named David. What David had (faith, fame, adoration, potential, promise, good looks, magazine covers?), Saul once had, but had lost. And so Saul thought, *Well, if I can't have it, then David can't have it anymore either.*

In fact, the Bible says that the song was "bad in the eyes of Saul." He looked at the song, he looked at David, and he looked at himself, and his eyes made his heart malignant. Jealousy, not God, took control of the way he looked at his life, and so he "kept a jealous eye on David."

A peaceful heart leads to a healthy body;
jealousy is like cancer in the bones.
PROVERBS 14:30

Lord Jesus, rid my heart of jealousy today. Let me find my peace in you alone.
Amen.

DIFFERENCE MAKER

Choose something that you have acquired out of jealousy and figure out a way to give it up.

TAKE A DEEP BREATH

Take a deep breath. You really should do this more often. It's cleansing. Oxygen refreshes your brain and strengthens your heart, not to mention all of your other organs as well. Pause. Breathe in. Hold. Breathe out. Right now, before tackling any more work, or before allowing yourself to fall into an endless loop of laziness, remember to breathe. It is what makes you alive.

A new creation. That's what you are in Jesus.

Take a moment to breathe. Remember what makes you alive. Don't try to manipulate the events of your life. It was God who first breathed life into you. He now gives you the ability to do the same. With deep yearning, find the rhythm God composed for you. Give all of the rises and falls, the notes and beats, the crescendos and melodies of your life to him.

Be still in the presence of the LORD,
and wait patiently for him to act.
Don't worry about evil people who prosper
or fret about their wicked schemes.
PSALM 37:7

Dear Jesus, don't let the wind get knocked out of me today. Teach me to breathe in rhythm with your breath. Amen.

DIFFERENCE MAKER

Commit yourself to silence for at least ten minutes. During that time lay out your thoughts to God. Then, shut up for a while, take a deep breath, and just try to be still before God.

THE FRESH MAKER

God's breath is fresh. Always fresh. It's like he has a constant eternal supply of Mentos, those mints with cheesy commercials and a great slogan. God is like the ultimate "Fresh Maker" of heaven and earth. Everything he breathes upon flourishes with life. When he starts the day, his breath is not like yours after a night of snoring. When you wake up and breathe, things wilt and coil back. But when God breathes, everything draws closer and opens up for even more. God's breath gives abundant life and incredible power.

When he created Adam, he stood there as a lump of molded sinew, until God breathed into him the breath of life. Then he blossomed with relationship and had a lively time naming things like the platypus and the manatee. When God gave Ezekiel a vision of dry bones, they stood there as lumps of reformed sinew until God breathed on them the breath of life. Then they lived again. When Jesus commissioned his followers, they stood there as speechless lumps of confused sinew, until he breathed on them and gave them the Holy Spirit, the breath of God. Then they ran through the world changing the air of history.

Then he breathed on them and said,
"Receive the Holy Spirit."

JOHN 20:22

Lord Jesus, breathe in me today, this unworthy soul. Take this lump of sinew and breathe in me, expand my lungs and revive my soul. Amen.

DIFFERENCE MAKER

Brush your teeth, chew some Mentos, and go around breathing on people all day, but be ready to tell them why you're doing it.

SKUBALA

You could say it is "dog dung," or maybe you would rather call it "garbage," or, if you're British, perhaps you'd like to call it "rubbish." And maybe you have a more profane word for it. Literally, when he wrote it in Greek, the word the apostle Paul used is σκύβαλα, or written in English it looks like *skubala*. It means "excrement." Did you just read that correctly? Yep. Paul wrote it. It's in the Bible. Offal. Dookie. Cow pies thrown on the top of a dump. *Skubala*. That's what Paul wrote.

Why did he drop the boys off at the pool like this? Well, he came to a point in his life where the things that he once held as most important he now considered *skubala*. All of his ambitions and work, all of his pride and achievements, all of it he says was worth a pile of poop when compared to the surpassing greatness of knowing Jesus. Compared to knowing Jesus, everything else is *skubala*.

Yes, everything else is worthless when compared with the
infinite value of knowing Christ Jesus my Lord. For his sake
I have discarded everything else, counting it all as garbage,
so that I could gain Christ.

PHILIPPIANS 3:8

Dear Jesus, help me get my priorities straight. Amen.

DIFFERENCE MAKER

The next time you go to the bathroom, think about those things that have more value in your life than Jesus, and, in manner of speaking, flush them down the toilet.

ADVOCATE

There are situations, unfortunately, where people do wrong, stupid things. Sometimes these people realize what they have done, feel terrible, and strive to turn their lives around. But the problem is that they have still committed harmful mistakes. Eventually, those foolish acts come around to haunt them and they stand judged.

In that moment, they could try to plead their own case. They could pour out their heart with apologies and ask the court to compassion. But the judge, as benevolent and caring as he might be, is in a no-win situation. That stupid thing still happened, damage was done, and someone still needs to pay for it and restore it.

At the end of their life, people will appear before God. They will plead and pour out. The Judge will want to forgive. He will want to grant mercy. But who then will pay for the damage that has been done? That's when Jesus will stand up, look at his Father, and declare, "I will take the punishment. I will pay for the damage. I will stand in judgment in this person's place."

> My dear children, I am writing this to you so that you will
> not sin. But if anyone does sin, we have an advocate who
> pleads our case before the Father. He is Jesus Christ, the one
> who is truly righteous.
>
> 1 JOHN 2:1

Jesus, I need you. You are my advocate. Thank you for standing for me and taking the consequences for me. How could I ever repay you? Amen.

DIFFERENCE MAKER

The biggest difference you could ever make is to accept Jesus Christ as your Savior. With a sense of overwhelmed gratitude, receive what he has done on your behalf.

March

Jesus,

Strengthen me to stand tall in you.

Amen.

ORPHANS BROUGHT HOME

One the places on this planet where God can most be understood is in a loving orphanage. The sickness of the world has left too many children alone. But there are places—homes—where orphaned babies are bathed in water, wrapped in blankets, nourished to health, sung to sleep, and cherished as precious people with a great destiny.

The Love of Christ orphanage, also known as TLC, is a place like this. Babies in South Africa who have been left to fend for themselves, because of conditions like HIV/AIDS, are lovingly accepted in a home like TLC. It's not easy for those who dedicate their lives to this work. It is a nonstop restorative mission. But those who care for orphans are living in the heartbeat of God himself.

Those who care for orphans are reflections of God's heart. He is a God who rescues. Jesus came to this earth just so that people could be brought home into the family of God.

God decided in advance to adopt us into his own family by
bringing us to himself through Jesus Christ. This is what he
wanted to do, and it gave him great pleasure.

EPHESIANS 1:5

Dear Jesus, thank you for treasuring me and giving me a home with you. Amen.

DIFFERENCE MAKER

How could you use your career to support an orphanage
or adoption ministry?

KINDNESS

What makes you feel the best about *you*? What is it that gives you hope about the direction of your life? What is it that fills you with confidence? What makes you laugh without worry? What helps you look in the mirror and see someone who has something good to offer?

One thing that most certainly impacts how anyone feels about themselves is how they treat others. Ironically, by focusing on treating others with kindness, people usually feel built up within themselves. Kindness causes people to stop turning inward and to start living outward. It expands their freedom, their creativity, their joy, and their optimism.

The opposite is also a reality. Cruel treatment of others echoes back to the attacker. Heated anger thrown at another burns more than one person. Hurtful words, despicable harm, shameful acts—they ricochet like shrapnel, rend the hearts of those nearby, and poison the soul of the aggressor. The world hesitates at this thought, but the truth is that kindness has the power to change the world for good.

> Your kindness will reward you,
> but your cruelty will destroy you.
>
> PROVERBS 11:17

Lord Jesus, let your kindness change me. Let me overflow with kind action for others today. Amen.

DIFFERENCE MAKER

Do as many random acts of kindness for others today as you can possibly think of doing. Then rest with confidence and a smile at the end of the day.

WILLINGLY

Have you ever been asked to do a job that you didn't want to do? Of course you have. Perhaps it was mowing the lawn while your friends played outside. Perhaps it was finishing your homework while your favorite show was on. Or perhaps it was cleaning up someone else's mess, or picking up your clothes, or acting polite when you were actually seething with frustration inside.

Whatever it was that you had to do, it didn't kill you. (You're reading this right now today because you are probably still alive.) It may have bugged you and made you feel a wee bit justified in letting whoever told you to do it that you were just a wee bit upset with them. Perhaps you huffed and puffed, perhaps you grumbled and complained, or perhaps you devised ways to get even. Unless the person or job was evil, the work you were asked to do was likely some sort of responsible service in one way or another. It probably served a purpose, even if mundane or routine, or unknown to you. It is God's desire that we work willingly, as if we are working for God, not for people.

> Work willingly at whatever you do, as though you were
> working for the Lord rather than for people.
>
> COLOSSIANS 3:23

Lord Jesus, give me a bigger capacity to serve than I have been known to show in the past. Let me see the work that I do, whatever it may be, as a service to you. Amen.

DIFFERENCE MAKER

Stretch yourself. Find something to do today that will be helpful for somebody else, but that will give you no glory.

MOTIVATE GOOD

Jesus celebrates when we spur one another on to do things he wants us to do. When you give a sudden display of kindness to someone, others notice and eventually do likewise. Your good works can "pay it forward" to someone else.

And when you are creative about your good deeds, your impact increases even more. Your creativity in serving others shows your commitment to love others. It shows that you are thinking of the unique needs and personalities of other people. When you take the time to care uniquely for someone, you display God's love by treasuring and cherishing who they are. Keep doing good. Keep making a difference. Keep blessing this world with the blessing of Jesus.

> Let us think of ways to motivate one another to acts of love and good works.
>
> HEBREWS 10:24

Jesus, help me to keep serving you by serving others. Surround me with a group of people who will sustain and motivate me to be a source of life. Amen.

DIFFERENCE MAKER

Think of two new "acts of love" or "good works." Practice one of these ways yourself and encourage someone else to practice the other. Then be sure to connect in the next twenty-four hours to celebrate what happened.

WHAT TO DO

Do you know what to do today? Did you know that God has already told you? He's already told everybody, in fact. Actually, he's made it pretty clear. God has let the world know what he believes is good. And not good as in "I guess that's cool," but good as in "God looked at all he had made and he saw that it was good" kind of good. Got that?

Well, what is good in God's eyes? He tells us to do what is right, love mercy, and walk humbly with him. That's pretty simple, huh? There's nothing confusing about that. This was why God created people. Oh man, how far from "good" has humanity fallen? What would happen if people set their efforts on restoring these patterns to the earth once again? Since God has already told you what to do, then I'd encourage you to start doing it.

> No, O people, the LORD has told you what is good,
> and this is what he requires of you:
> to do what is right, to love mercy,
> and to walk humbly with your God.
>
> MICAH 6:8

Dear Jesus, today, challenge me to make the right moves, to love being merciful to others, and to walk with your arm wrapped around my shoulders. Amen.

DIFFERENCE MAKER

Which of the three "requirements" do you most need to focus on today? What is one action you can take to pursue that focus?

CREATED TO PRAY

Three thousand years ago King Solomon was finishing one of the wonders of the world. The temple in Jerusalem was an architectural masterpiece. People would travel from around the world to visit this structure and worship the God of Israel. As it was being completed, the Lord wanted to put things into perspective for King Solomon and the people of Israel. As great as the building was, he knew that they would struggle to keep their focus on him. God told them that he would do certain things (or, better said, withhold from doing things) to get back their attention. And if they turned their eyes once again to him, he promised to restore their grandeur. When you find yourself losing focus on God, do not forget that he will try to get your attention. And when he does, turn your eyes to him.

"Then if my people who are called by my name will humble themselves and pray and seek my face and turn from their wicked ways, I will hear from heaven and will forgive their sins and restore their land."

2 CHRONICLES 7:14

Lord Jesus, turn my eyes to you today. I pray that you will not hide your face from me, but let me see you clearly working in my life. Amen.

DIFFERENCE MAKER

Attend to God. Pray to him today. Repent, asking him to forgive your sins.

SO

If you had all the power in the world, what would you do with it? Would you make life comfortable for yourself, hire people to bring you a burrito whenever you felt hungry, or try to become pals with someone famous? The Bible says that Jesus had all the power in the world. But he didn't use his power to serve himself. In fact, right before he was betrayed and arrested, right before he was beaten and ridiculed, right before he had nails driven into his hands and feet, Jesus did something that you wouldn't expect from the most powerful being on earth. John, in his eye-witness account, describes the moment like this:

> Jesus knew that the Father had given him authority over everything and that he had come from God and would return to God. So he got up from the table, took off his robe, wrapped a towel around his waist, and poured water into a basin. Then he began to wash the disciples' feet, drying them with the towel he had around him.
>
> JOHN 13:3–5

Dear Jesus, I'm so thankful that it is you, and not someone else, who has all the power. Thank you for serving me, even though I should be the one serving you. Amen.

DIFFERENCE MAKER

Think of a way to bless someone
with whatever authority God has blessed you.

WALK

Considering that humans were created to walk with God, they have sure spent a lot of time and energy trying to blaze trails without him. It's remarkable that people are so quick to step off the path that God is on. Like people who rely on GPS for direction, when they walk away from God they inevitably get disoriented and lost.

But what's even more astonishing, perhaps, is that if these lost people were to stop and listen, they would see God's steps and hear his voice. If they had the sense to look for him, they would discover that God had followed them down that rough trail and had been calling out their name. God leaves his stroll in the garden in order to save people from the minefield they wandered into.

Thomas, a worried wanderer, once asked Jesus, "How can we know the way, Lord?" Jesus, preparing to save the lost who had walked away, replied:

> "I am the way, the truth, and the life. No one can come to
> the Father except through me."

JOHN 14:6

Jesus, I want to walk with you today. Thank you for coming to find me. Thank you for the chance to take steps with you. Amen.

DIFFERENCE MAKER

Go for a walk. With each step, talk to Jesus about your life, your passions, your goals, and your worries. Confide yourself in him and he will direct your path to the Father.

BENIGN NEGLECT

Are you one of the growing number of people who need a swift kick in the backside to get you going today? There is a mentality in society today known as "benign neglect." Basically, it means that people feel like they can put the normal responsibilities of life off until some other time in the future. They feel like they can extend their adolescence for years, even into their thirties or forties, and that "real life" begins later when they feel more ready.

It is "benign" because it doesn't "feel" bad (at first), but over time it can be neglectful of a person's potential and gifts and calling in life. Now is not the time to put off doing what you need to do. Don't fall into the pit of this off-putting chronic illness. Don't give in to "benign neglect." Rather, work hard to prove that God has made you alive by his Spirit.

So, dear brothers and sisters, work hard to prove that you really are among those God has called and chosen. Do these things, and you will never fall away.

2 PETER 1:10

Dear Jesus, give me the guts to get rid of any benign neglect. What you have called me to do, motivate me to do it. Amen.

DIFFERENCE MAKER

What is something that you should strive to accomplish, but have been putting off? What do you need to do to get going once again?

FOR HE GAVE

If you could buy anything, what would it be? A sports car? Wireless Beats headphones? College tuition? Good grades? Love? Respect? What you would buy?

Jesus had the same question posed to him. His answer? "Well, here's what I'd buy: freedom for people enslaved to sin. That's what I'd want to purchase." And so he did. But not with money. He gave over all that he had to purchase freedom for humanity. He gave over his status, his glory, and his very blood to purchase freedom for the very people who took his life from him.

If you want, Jesus will free you from your bondage to sin, for he gave himself to forgive people of their sin.

> For he has rescued us from the kingdom of darkness and
> transferred us into the Kingdom of his dear Son, who
> purchased our freedom and forgave our sins.
>
> COLOSSIANS 1:13–14

Lord Jesus, I don't deserve what you have done for me. Thank you for your forgiveness. Let me live in the freedom you have purchased for me today. Amen.

DIFFERENCE MAKER

Do you know anybody stuck in a pattern of sin or weighed down by the effects of sin? Buy them a coffee, a card, or a creative gift. Find a way to encourage them with the freedom that comes only through Jesus.

RUN

Life is a lot like a marathon. Learning how to run over a long distance is the key to finishing well. You can't just wake up one day and go out and run a marathon—you need stamina for long-distance running. You need training and discipline to stay focused on the big picture, especially while being tempted to grab a dozen caramel-glazed, chocolate-filled donuts.

Many runners have gotten derailed over the years. Sadly, they have missed the opportunity to pursue their full potential. They have missed the chance to change people's lives, to give hope where it was needed, and to rejoice at the finish line with others who have faithfully put one foot ahead of the next for an entire lifetime. Jesus created you to run the marathon of life. So run as if it was the only thing you had to do. Run from the things that mess you up, and run toward the things that build you up.

> Run from anything that stimulates youthful lusts. Instead,
> pursue righteous living, faithfulness, love, and peace.
> Enjoy the companionship of those who call on the Lord
> with pure hearts.
>
> 2 TIMOTHY 2:22

Dear Jesus, I don't always feel like exercising my faith, but I pray that you will push me like my trainer today so that I can learn to run for you. Amen.

DIFFERENCE MAKER

Go for a run today. Find others who will celebrate the steps that you are taking in your life.

INSTEAD

Worry creeps everywhere. What I mean is that it gets around. When the future is unknown or circumstances are fearful, worry tosses people around. Instead of giving worry power and letting stress steal life from you, twist the intent of worry to your advantage. Every time apprehension hits your heart, take the opportunity to deflect it over to God. He created you to depend upon him. So use your anxiousness to help you trust Jesus more and more today.

The more worry tries to tear you down, lift it up to God. The more you worry, the more opportunity you have to ask him for help. Take the energy that your anxiety is taking from you and focus it on prayer. The sweat and sleeplessness, the panic and pace, dedicate it all to Jesus. Give it to him today. And thank him when he lifts it off your shoulders.

Don't worry about anything; instead, pray about everything.
Tell God what you need, and thank him for all he has done.
Then you will experience God's peace, which exceeds
anything we can understand. His peace will guard your
hearts and minds as you live in Christ Jesus.

PHILIPPIANS 4:6–7

Lord Jesus, I lift my worries to you today. Thank you for guarding me. Amen.

DIFFERENCE MAKER

Write the verses for today on a piece of paper and tape it somewhere you'll see throughout the day. Try to commit it to memory. Each time worry comes after you, pray about it and entrust it to Jesus.

PERSEVERE

Perseverance. What a terrible word. *Per* means "through," while *severance* means "to get cut off." So perseverance means going through a time of getting cut off. Those who have had to persevere through terrible circumstances understand the near-devastating process of longsuffering, especially when the suffering is caused by someone else, or, perhaps, especially when it means saying no to a tempting desire or cheap escape.

The first Christians were persecuted for simply following Jesus. They had to learn to persevere through some terrible treatment, some harsh realities. They had to face fear and threat and loss and pain. It must have been tempting at times to wonder about giving up and pursuing a path that would help them fit in better with the world around them. And yet they endured. Their trials proved their perseverance, displaying miraculous character that changed the world.

Perseverance for following Jesus does not come from a mild commitment to faith. It comes only from a daily practice of deep devotion, of learning how to live for Christ.

God blesses those who patiently endure testing and
temptation. Afterward they will receive the crown of life that
God has promised to those who love him.

JAMES 1:12

Lord Jesus, I don't have the strength in me, unless you enable it. Please give me the motivation to never quit. Amen.

DIFFERENCE MAKER

What testing or temptation do you need to patiently endure today?

EXTRAORDINARY

Jesus thinks people are extraordinary. Even those who feel like their lives are far from glorious, Jesus thinks they're remarkable. Even those who feel like they could never get close to the glamourous grandeur of stardom, Jesus lifts them up on his shoulders and cheers them on. Even those who dream of hanging out with somebody famous, Jesus longs to hang out with them.

The truth is that Jesus came to those who didn't feel like they had a shot at glory. He came to walk with them in the ordinary moments of their lives; he came to sit in their homes, eat dinner with them, talk politics and religion, and laugh at their jokes. Jesus came to cry with them in times of loss and encourage them to do greater things than they could have ever imagined. He came to heal their wounds and their hearts. He came to challenge their despair and their cynicism. He came because he thought ordinary people were worth far more than they could ever realize.

No one is more amazing than Jesus. And yet he came to be with you.

So the Word became human and made his home among us.
He was full of unfailing love and faithfulness. And we have
seen his glory, the glory of the Father's one and only Son.

JOHN 1:14

Dear Jesus, you are the living God, and yet you came to me. Thank you for wanting me to be in the presence of your glory. Amen.

DIFFERENCE MAKER

See the extraordinary in someone you would dismiss as ordinary today. Jesus thinks they are worth his attention, so perhaps they should be worth yours too.

MUSTACHE MARCH

This is the middle of Mustache March. Maybe you have already been braiding your lip hair for the last two weeks, or maybe you haven't…but you certainly cannot deny the countercultural power of the mustache. People simply look at it and are changed by its mesmerizing audacity.

Jesus has called you to be a radical person. He wants to empower you to stand rooted in him against the winds of culture that try to make everybody look the same. Too many people conform to the patterns of this world, giving in to pursuits that are not good for them. Jesus wants you to be an example of a more audacious path.

The apostle Paul told a young leader this very same thing a long time ago. While culture expected him to conform, Paul challenged him to rise to the occasion and make a difference with the people around him.

Don't let anyone think less of you because you are young.
Be an example to all believers in what you say, in the way
you live, in your love, your faith, and your purity.

1 TIMOTHY 4:12

Dear Jesus, strengthen me to stand tall in you today. Amen.

DIFFERENCE MAKER

What kind of a role model could you be for those around you? What could you do as an example of countercultural living that would encourage others to make the right decisions too?

TREASURE

It is in your broken heart where God has room to walk around and restore. It is in the midst of your weakness that God's light and strength and power can do its glorious work. When you embrace the treasure of Jesus in your life, you quickly recognize that you cannot contain him. You are much too fragile to be the living container of Almighty God. And yet in you is precisely where Jesus wants to live. He wants to take up residence in your life and use you to bring his light to others.

True followers of Jesus admit that their power does not come from their own stature of greatness. Rather, those who invite Jesus to live within them are the first to say that they don't deserve such marvelous company. The church, where fragile people are being empowered through Jesus, is a community where real people with real concerns will find real restoration.

We now have this light shining in our hearts, but we ourselves are like fragile clay jars containing this great treasure. This makes it clear that our great power is from God, not from ourselves.

2 CORINTHIANS 4:7

Dear Jesus, what I have to offer is not perfect,
but please make yourself at home in me. Amen.

DIFFERENCE MAKER

Find a church community that displays a humble gratitude for what Jesus has done, and a resilient and confident strength that comes from knowing Jesus.

DO GOOD

God enjoys people who do what he created them to do. In fact, God wired people with the desire and ability to do what is good. That means, in a world that has rejected God, and as a result is struggling with so much bad, people who do what God created them to do become world changers. People who do what God wants them to do are people who change the world with God's authority and God's ability.

Look around. What problems do you see? What did Jesus do about them? Now ask Jesus to look at you. What potential does he see in you, his follower? What does he want you to do? God rejoices when his people participate in his restorative work for this world. Practice the patterns that God initiated to rescue people from the devastation that is all around them.

"Learn to do good.
Seek justice.
Help the oppressed.
Defend the cause of orphans.
Fight for the rights of widows."
ISAIAH 1:17

Jesus, I have a lot of opportunity to do what you'd like for me to do.
Thank you for inviting me into your line of work. Amen.

DIFFERENCE MAKER

Of the five lines of Isaiah 1:17, which one can you do something about today? What can you do toward that cause? Take immediate action: write it down or tell someone to hold you accountable to do it.

TAKE HEART

If you decide to live for Jesus today, then take heart. It is not easy to decide to go against the flow of the culture, to stand for truth, to rally around those who are outcast, to speak up for those who cannot defend themselves, and to do it with humility and integrity. Following Jesus means not following the patterns in society that are self-serving or peer pressured or garbage grabbing. Following Jesus means making a difference in a world that needs a difference to be made.

And that is not easy. But, then again, Jesus didn't say it would be easy. He said he would give us peace and strength and that he would fight on our behalf. He said he would empower and embolden us and that he would be with us as we stand for the truth. He said he would enable us to love the unlovable and to fight the good fight of faith.

Jesus wants to change this world. And he wants you to change it with him.

"I have told you all this so that you may have peace in me.
Here on earth you will have many trials and sorrows. But
take heart, because I have overcome the world."

JOHN 16:33

Lord Jesus, I'm all in. I will take heart because you are changing this world,
and you are doing it through me. Amen.

DIFFERENCE MAKER

Stand up for Jesus with an emboldened heart today,
trusting him for the outcome.

SEE CLEARLY

In a way that would impress any good redneck, Jesus spit. He hocked a loogie. That wasn't even the gross part of it. His spit was directed straight into a man's eyes. Yes, that's right—Jesus spit into a man's eyes. But the man didn't get mad. In fact, he let Jesus do it. He trusted Jesus. He let Jesus form and create and spit on him. He let Jesus ask him questions and put his hands on his eyes. He didn't rub out the spit, because he knew that Jesus cared for him. Jesus might not always do things for you in the way that makes you feel comfortable. Now and then he enjoys doing things that are a little messy in order to focus your eyes and bring about healing within you.

> Then Jesus placed his hands on the man's eyes again, and
> his eyes were opened. His sight was completely restored,
> and he could see everything clearly.
>
> MARK 8:25

Dear Jesus, someone needs to do the dirty work in my life. Heal me so that I can see everything clearly. Amen.

DIFFERENCE MAKER

Be ready to get messy today. Even if it means doing something that is uncomfortable, don't miss an opportunity to help someone see life clearly.

PLANKINEYETIS

Plankineyetis is a debilitating condition that distorts the way people see reality. It diminishes their ability to see themselves with clarity. Plankineyetis attacks the soul through the eyes, and it evidences itself when a person sees a splinter in someone else's eye and announces with pride that he or she will help clean it out. This is a monstrous proclamation, because what they fail to realize, but what everybody else can easily see, is that the person's judgment is affected by the fact that there is an entire log jammed into their own eye socket.

Chaos ensues as the diseased patient moves around. People have to duck out of the way. Family and friends begin to avoid eye contact with the one who has contracted plankineyetis. It ruins relationships, leads to blindness of heart, and needs to be cured. Luckily, Jesus tells us the cure.

> "And why worry about a speck in your friend's eye when you have a log in your own? How can you think of saying to your friend, 'Let me help you get rid of that speck in your eye,' when you can't see past the log in your own eye? Hypocrite! First get rid of the log in your own eye; then you will see well enough to deal with the speck in your friend's eye."
>
> MATTHEW 7:3–5

Lord Jesus, forgive my judgmental attitude. Heal my condition. Help me see clearly again. Amen.

DIFFERENCE MAKER

Try to catch yourself every time you have a judgmental thought about someone today. When you do have a judgmental thought, cover one eye for one minute.

JESUS…

Jesus seeks after the lost and searches for runaways.
Jesus finds the hidden and heals the broken.
Jesus gives footing to the lame.
Jesus opens the ears of the deaf.
Jesus restores sight to the blind.
Jesus frees the prisoner.
Jesus has coffee with the prostitute.
Jesus loves the sinner and forgives the repentant.
Jesus strengthens the weak.
Jesus fills the empty and dwells with the lonely.
Jesus weeps with the sad, the hurting, and the grieved.
Jesus comforts the mourner.
Jesus breathes into the lifeless.
Jesus lifts up the trampled and gathers the displaced.
Jesus feeds the hungry and quenches the thirsty.
Jesus puts the last at the front.
Jesus eats with the unsanitary and dines with the despised.
Jesus carries the world's sins and burdens.
Jesus dies for his enemies and bleeds for his friends.
Jesus stretches out his arms to welcome you home.

Jesus also did many other things. If they were all written
down, I suppose the whole world could not contain the
books that would be written.

JOHN 21:25

Dear Jesus, you have done so much. Thank you! Amen.

DIFFERENCE MAKER

Jesus asks you to do a lot. What is one thing that he has done that you
should put into action today?

SERVE

As he was preparing for the day ahead, Jesus said something startling. "Normally," he said, "the master sits at the table and is served by his servants. But not here! I am your servant." Jesus could have demanded their allegiance. He could have instructed them to bring him some sandals and iced tea (with a lemon slice and one of those little paper umbrellas). He could have called down his angels and waylaid everyone in his path, especially Judas—the guy who was about to betray him. But instead, he attended to their needs, he washed their feet, and he served them food and drink. Jesus turned the tables upside down.

> "But among you it will be different. Those who are the greatest among you should take the lowest rank, and the leader should be like a servant."
>
> LUKE 22:26

Dear Jesus, I don't deserve to have you serve me. I am humbled to be loved by you so much. Let me be changed by this truth in everything I do today. Amen.

DIFFERENCE MAKER

Serve someone today. Wash the dishes, pay for gas in their car, buy them lunch, leave them a note, or find some other creative way to do something that shows how much you value them.

GAWKING

Crowds gathered at the scene of the horror. They just stood there, entranced at the violence and injustice, hypnotized by the spectacle of it all. When Jesus went to the cross, people just watched—afraid and captivated by the awfulness of the moment. People were ignorant and angry at Jesus. Some were shouting at him while others were silently condemning him to die. Everyone was unable to avert their eyes, and yet they were unwilling to truly see what was going on. The cross of Jesus was hideous—so horrific that people couldn't help but stare.

Jesus, in that very moment, as he hung crucified, was looking back at the crowd. He had eyes on the very people that were watching him die. But instead of a look of revenge, Jesus had compassion in his sight. He wanted those gawkers to make eye contact with him so that he could peer into their souls and overcome their judgment and fear with his forgiveness and hope.

The crowd watched and the leaders scoffed. "He saved others," they said, "let him save himself if he is really God's Messiah, the Chosen One."

LUKE 23:35

Jesus, thank you for dying on the cross for me. Let me look to the cross and look you in the eyes, allowing your gaze to brighten my frightened soul. Amen.

DIFFERENCE MAKER

Draw a cross on something that you will see again and again throughout the day. Let it remind you to look Jesus in the eyes.

THE GARDEN

After Judas had betrayed Jesus, and just before soldiers came to arrest him, Jesus and his disciples went to the Mount of Olives, to the garden of Gethsemane. He warned his disciples to avoid temptation and sin, but in their emotionally exhausted condition they chose instead to sleep. But Jesus walked "about a stone's throw away," knelt down, and prayed. It was in a garden that humans first tasted sin; it was in a garden that Jesus wrestled with it.

His time of prayer was intense. Sin was not going to die easily. Jesus prayed so fervently, with such agony of spirit, that his sweat became mixed with great drops of blood. This condition is known as hematidrosis, which occurs when someone is experiencing extreme stress. While the disciples slept through it, Jesus took it upon himself to do the very thing the disciples were unwilling or unable to do.

Father, if you are willing, please take this cup of suffering
away from me. Yet I want your will to be done, not mine.

LUKE 22:42

Dear Jesus, what can I say? You wrestled against what I have so easily been beaten by. Thank you for what you have done. Amen.

DIFFERENCE MAKER

After he prayed, Jesus told the disciples to get up and pray so that temptation didn't overpower them. Why not take his words to heart? If possible, find a garden to walk through and pray about overcoming sin through Jesus.

QUAKE

The tomb that held Jesus didn't know what hit it! It was a new tomb, a respectful burial spot offered by a wealthy man near a garden. A peaceful place. Then the earthquake hit. The entrance to the tomb, a huge stone chiseled round, was rolled aside. The new tomb, which had been used, was once again available for rent. Jesus had risen from the dead.

The first people on the scene were guards who had been stationed there to keep things from getting shook up. But the tremor, not to mention the angel of the Lord who seemed to be casually sitting on the stone, made the guards quake in their boots. The second group of people on the scene were women who were close followers of Jesus. They actually spoke to the angel, who informed them that Jesus had been raised from the dead just as he said would happen. Instead of fainting like the guards, they turned their fear into great joy and ran to tell others the good news that Jesus had risen.

> Suddenly there was a great earthquake! For an angel of the
> Lord came down from heaven, rolled aside the stone, and
> sat on it.
>
> MATTHEW 28:2

Lord Jesus, not even death could stop you from walking on this earth. Thank you for conquering everything that stood in the way of life. Amen.

DIFFERENCE MAKER

In terms of your awareness of Jesus, do you, or the people around you, need a quake to shake you up a bit? Use this question as a filter throughout your day.

FLASHLIGHT

You know that moment when you've been in a dark room for a while and somebody suddenly flicks on the light switch? Your eyes recoil, your face winces and squints, and you inevitably shield your head from the glare of the bright beams. But even with your eyes closed, somehow behind those eyelids of yours, you can see the image of the light burned into your retinas. Jesus is like that light. And when he shines into the darkness of someone's actions, or the gloom of someone's soul, the glare can be painfully intense. But the light of Jesus is so very good too. It was his light that illuminated the earth at creation. It was his light that led God's people to freedom from slavery. It was his light that represented the greatness and love of God throughout the entire Bible. Jesus created you to walk in his light.

Adjust your eyes to the light of Jesus today. You were made to see his glory, the beauty of his creation, and the worth he gave to every person. Don't recoil back into a shadow of who you were made to be.

"All who do evil hate the light and refuse to go near it for fear their sins will be exposed. But those who do what is right come to the light so others can see that they are doing what God wants."

JOHN 3:20–21

Dear Jesus, help me to stop groping around in the darkness. Call me to walk in your light. Amen.

DIFFERENCE MAKER

Grab a small flashlight and carry it around with you all day. If you find yourself shrinking back into darkness, shine that light in your eyes.

STUPID THINGS

People need Jesus because they make so many frustratingly foolish choices. It's almost like humans can't stop acting out their inner idiocy. Like dogs that return to their own vomit, some people knowingly hurt themselves by pursuing pleasures that interest them in the moment but revolt them in the long run. Like vultures that hunt their prey, some even knowingly hurt others by taking advantage of weaknesses for their own selfish gain. Like sheep that wander, some people simply make wrong choices that end up hurting everyone in their circle of influence.

God did not create people to do stupid things. And yet people continually stray from God's patterns, either intentionally or unintentionally. People constantly find themselves humiliated and trapped by the lure of sin's idiocy. But Jesus overcame humanity's corrupt absurdity by pursuing the cross, where all the stupidity of sin is collected and destroyed. There, the life-giving wisdom and heart-empowering joy of Jesus is offered in exchange. And in this way, the cross of Christ dumbfounds foolish pursuits.

Those who belong to Christ Jesus have nailed the passions
and desires of their sinful nature to his cross and crucified
them there.

GALATIANS 5:24

Dear Jesus, don't let me do stupid things today. Get them out of my life.
Let them hang on the cross. And let me follow you. Amen.

DIFFERENCE MAKER

Don't do something today that you will regret doing. Choose to do
something else instead.

TURNED BACKS

If you had been in the crowd that day, what would you have done? Would you have yelled at him? Would you have denied the miracles your own eyes had seen him do? Would you have looked at the open slices across his back, and would you have patronized him or felt a ping of pity? When somebody spit on him, would you have laughed or would you have watched it unfold? When he collapsed under the weight of the cross, would you have stepped out of the crowd to help him lift it back up? Or perhaps you wouldn't have participated in any of it at all. Maybe you would have fled town, overcome with fear and grief. Afraid or unwilling to honestly confront the rejection absorbed by the Savior, people still turn their backs on Jesus to this day. But, ironically, that's why he carried the cross through the crowd.

He was despised and rejected—
a man of sorrows, acquainted with deepest grief.
We turned our backs on him and looked the other way.
He was despised, and we did not care.

ISAIAH 53:3

Lord Jesus, how did you put up with this? How did you forgive? You took the brunt of all hatred and agony and rejection. Your love overwhelms me. Amen.

DIFFERENCE MAKER

Jesus carried your sorrow. What sorrow can you carry for someone today?

MISJUDGED

Susan Boyle walked out on the stage in front of a theater full of people ready to dismiss her. The judges and the crowd struggled to imagine what she could be doing there. The moment they saw her meek appearance, most concluded that she would be just another *Britain's Got Talent* contestant laughed off the stage. And then she sang. And before she could finish her first phrase to the song, people were overwhelmed, standing on their feet in amazement.

When people looked at Jesus, they dismissed him too. He wasn't what they expected. They thought he was just another Messiah contestant who would be booed off the stage of history. Even worse, they looked at him and thought he deserved the ridicule and punishment he received. Humans don't have a great track record of judging, do they?

Yet it was our weaknesses he carried;
it was our sorrows that weighed him down.
And we thought his troubles were a punishment from God,
a punishment for his own sins!

ISAIAH 53:4

Dear Jesus, you took my sins upon yourself while I pointed and laughed. And then you sang your song of sorrow, and I became dumbfounded and ashamed. Forgive me. Amen.

DIFFERENCE MAKER

Go to YouTube and watch Susan Boyle's first appearance on *Britain's Got Talent*. As you watch, realize that Jesus never dismissed you. Don't dismiss others today.

BEAUTY MARKS

The wounds of Jesus are beauty marks. After his resurrection, Jesus presented himself to one of his followers, a man named Thomas, a man who doubted whether or not the resurrection had actually happened. To prove who he was, though, Jesus showed him the nail scars in his hands and feet, and the spear wound in his side. Not pretty. Certainly terrible. But definitely beautiful.

Even in his resurrected state, Jesus chose to keep his scars. They mean everything to him. His wounds show his story, a story that is woven with more love and intentionality than the world had ever understood before. The Creator of the Universe, the one who had been rejected, was crushed to bring life. His scars are evidence of this good news.

> But he was pierced for our rebellion,
> crushed for our sins.
> He was beaten so we could be whole.
> He was whipped so we could be healed.
>
> ISAIAH 53:5

Lord Jesus, forgive my sin and heal my wounds. Turn the scars of life into beauty marks that will tell the story of what you have done in my life. Amen.

DIFFERENCE MAKER

What wounds do you carry today? What healing do you need from Jesus? How can Jesus use your story to reveal the good news of what he can do?

SHEEP

When people chart their own path, they crisscross and crush one another and create a chaotic, cacophonous confusion to life. God made life so much more simple than that. "Follow me," he said. "Here's how: Listen to my voice. Stay close. If you do that, I'll feed you and take care of you. I'll defend you and give you a home." But nope. People just feel a magnetic pull to *baaaah* their way around boulders and into thickets and wander into the jaws of lions. Thankfully Jesus is the Good Shepherd who knows that his sheep are prone to wander and who is willing to lay down his own life to save them.

All of us, like sheep, have strayed away.
We have left God's paths to follow our own.
Yet the LORD laid on him
the sins of us all.

ISAIAH 53:6

*Dear Jesus, thank you for bearing my wandering soul on your shoulders.
Lead me in your path today. Amen.*

DIFFERENCE MAKER

Simplify your life. Get rid of things that complicate your direction or distract you from following Jesus.

April

Jesus,
Let me be a part of an unflinching movement
of world changers.
Amen.

QUIET POSTURE

Jesus could have talked back, but he didn't. He didn't retaliate when he was accused of blasphemy and evil. He just took it when he was whipped and beaten, and when he was mockingly forced to wear a robe and crown (which was crudely made out of thorns and pressed down on his head). He even carried the cross down the road on the way to his own execution.

Why didn't he defend himself? He knew where their anger and hatred was leading. He knew it meant his torture and eventual death. He knew they were about to make him a spectacle of shame. His accusers even mocked him for his quiet posture. "Who hit you?" they screamed. "Why don't you call down your angels to save you?"

Had Jesus reacted in revenge against their rejection, the world would not have been saved. No false accuser would withstand the unrestrained power of Almighty God. So Jesus, in order to defend and rescue humanity, chose a quiet posture and said nothing.

He was oppressed and treated harshly,
yet he never said a word.
He was led like a lamb to the slaughter.
And as a sheep is silent before the shearers,
he did not open his mouth.

ISAIAH 53:7

Lord Jesus, thank you for not retaliating. My rescue depended on it. Amen.

DIFFERENCE MAKER

Who will you see in the next twenty-four hours who could be helped by your quiet restraint?

UNCOMPROMISED

Just because you do what is right doesn't mean you will be treated fairly. In fact, some of the best people in history were mistreated *because* they were doing what was right. So how committed are you to doing right? If the right road gets tough, will you keep on going?

In the future, when people talk about you, will they be inspired by your example? Will your story encourage them to live with integrity in the face of opposition? It takes tremendous courage to continue to do what is right in the face of adversity. But the world needs uncompromised people who stand for what is right, no matter what.

Jesus pursued the right path and paid a severe price. But the world is forever grateful he didn't join the wrong march, but chose to walk to the cross. Imagine how pessimistic this devotional book would be if he had compromised himself and not gone to the cross!

> He had done no wrong
> and had never deceived anyone.
> But he was buried like a criminal;
> he was put in a rich man's grave.
> ISAIAH 53:9

Jesus, I don't know if I have the courage to live and die like you did. In the face of adversity, give me the strength to do no wrong. Amen.

DIFFERENCE MAKER

Anticipate what difficult situations you might be in today. Pray that Jesus will give you the integrity to do what is right.

GOOD PLAN

One of the most startling lines in the Bible is found in Isaiah 53:10. It says that everything that happened to God's "Suffering Servant"—all the crushing and grieving, the accusations and execution, the carrying of humanity's sin and disdain—was all a part of the Lord's "good plan" for his Son. How is someone—someone innocent, I might add—being betrayed, arrested, falsely accused, tortured, and executed a "good plan"? That certainly sounds like a very bad idea, right?

The "good" in the plan, however, is the key. God created everything "good," but because death was brought to creation through sin, Jesus took it all upon himself through the cross so that he could offer forgiveness and new life. In other words, God's rescue blueprint called for the terrible things that happened to Jesus in order to restore "good" to this earth. As a result of what Jesus did, the day of crucifixion became known as "Good Friday," and the day of resurrection would prove victory over death.

> But it was the LORD's good plan to crush him
> and cause him grief.
> Yet when his life is made an offering for sin,
> he will have many descendants.
> He will enjoy a long life,
> and the LORD's good plan will prosper in his hands.
>
> ISAIAH 53:10

Jesus, your idea of "good" is so much better than mine.
Thank you for being so good. Amen.

DIFFERENCE MAKER

On a piece of paper, brainstorm all that is "good" that Jesus offers through the cross. Which of these things would be life changing for someone you know?

SPEAK OUT

Talk about someone who made a difference—the world was changed by Martin Luther King Jr. He painted grand scenes of unity with words like freedom, justice, and hope. He provided a vision for the future through creative patience, resolve, and forgiveness. People loved him for his voice, and callous people hated him for his impact.

He spoke about the example of Jesus, who gave voice to the voiceless and ushered people to the seat of God's justice. King was especially impacted by the way Jesus offered mercy instead of retribution, even as the forces of hatred closed in around him. When given a chance to fight back or run away, Jesus demanded of his closest follower, "Put away your sword."

Martin Luther King Jr., a champion of the dignity for every person, was assassinated by a narrow-minded bullet on April 4, 1968. It was a very bleak day. But the world's attention had already been caught and the climate had already been changed. Even death cannot hold back the powerful ring of freedom.

Speak up for those who cannot speak for themselves;
ensure justice for those being crushed.

PROVERBS 31:8

Jesus, give me the inner motivation to speak with your voice for those who need an advocate. Amen.

DIFFERENCE MAKER

Read about Martin Luther King Jr.'s story. Who could use your voice today?

SPEND ENERGY

Have you ever felt like you wasted your energy on something before? Have you been frustrated about something you were working on and asked with disgust, "What's the use?" Perhaps the commute is driving you crazy. Maybe the last seven hours of your Netflix binge didn't really improve your life after all. Maybe the effort you put into grocery shopping didn't produce the sort of fruit you had hoped. (Get it? Grocery? Produce? Fruit? Just roll with it.)

Jesus doesn't want you to waste your energy. He doesn't want you to regret how you spent even one minute of your life. What gives purpose and meaning to all that you do, he says, is himself. Pursuit of him, and the life he gives, is worth every effort. You will know you are spending your energy wisely when you are seeking after Jesus and filtering all you do through him. Everything in your life will begin to fall into its proper place as you find your priority in Jesus.

> "But don't be so concerned about perishable things like food. Spend your energy seeking the eternal life that the Son of Man can give you. For God the Father has given me the seal of his approval."
>
> JOHN 6:27

Dear Jesus, help me match my priorities with yours. Amen.

DIFFERENCE MAKER

This devotional time was a great start. How else could you spend your energy searching for the life Jesus offers today?

BELIEVE IN JESUS

It would be wrong, in a book all about making a difference in this world, to give the impression that somehow your good works are what God ultimately wants from you. God actually wants only one thing from you; he has only one requirement. At the end of your life, as you look back over the years, it would be nice to remember the good things you accomplished or ways you were kind. But whether or not you believed in Jesus will be what God ultimately cares about the most. After all, if you believe in Jesus, the good works will come—they will follow. Good deeds are simply a natural overflow of Jesus being alive within you. There is nothing in life that makes more of a difference than this one thing: Believe in the Lord Jesus Christ.

Jesus told them, "This is the only work God wants from you:
Believe in the one he has sent."

JOHN 6:29

Jesus, I believe in you. I believe you died for me and you want me to follow you. I believe you want to use me to impact this world with your good news. Jesus, I place my life in your hands. I believe in you. Amen.

DIFFERENCE MAKER

What would belief in Jesus look like practically today?
What would need to change? What would stay the same?
How would belief in Jesus impact the way you treat others,
approach a tough situation, or prepare you for a meeting?

NOWHERE ELSE

Many people leave the church simply because they can, feeling like they have a choice in the matter. They don't feel compelled to stay. For whatever reason, many just slip away through the crowd.

There was a time when many people left the crowd that was following Jesus too. They deserted him because they couldn't stomach Jesus' calling on their lives. What Jesus was asking them to do was too radical. And once a few people started wandering away, many others took the easy route too.

As a result of this, Jesus turned to his closest followers and asked, "Are you going to leave too?" That's when Peter, the roller-coaster adrenaline disciple, declared that he couldn't imagine anywhere else they would rather be. Jesus was too startlingly compelling, too earth-shatteringly true, too eternally good.

> Simon Peter replied, "Lord, to whom would we go? You have the words that give eternal life."
>
> JOHN 6:68

Dear Jesus, grab ahold of my heart and squeeze tight. Grab ahold of those around me too. Let me be a part of an unflinching movement of world changers. Amen.

DIFFERENCE MAKER

Think of someone you know who has given up on God. Don't let that person walk away from Jesus. How can you invite them to join you in making Jesus the center, not an addition, to life?

NO-ZOMBIE ZONE

Resurrection means to "raise from the dead." To be undead is all the rage nowadays. It could get you your own TV or movie series. But it wasn't always cool to be undead. Two thousand years ago a man named Lazarus had gotten sick and died. A funeral full of wailing was well underway—that is, until Jesus decided to try out this undead thing on his recently deceased friend. He yelled into the tomb, "Lazarus, I want to hang out, bro!" (or something to that effect). So, as anybody would do when Jesus speaks life, Lazarus came out of the tomb walking, much to the astonishment of everyone (except for Jesus, who played it all very cool).

A little later, after of course people unwrapped Lazarus' burial cloths, they ate dinner together—for Jesus, this was just another day of work. Raising people to life is what he does for a living. People didn't know what to think about this situation. They had never seen an undead person before. And even though he was no zombie, Lazarus scared them. And this of course made them scared of Jesus too. The people were challenged to either accept the life-giving power of Jesus or to run away.

Jesus told her, "I am the resurrection and the life. Anyone
who believes in me will live, even after dying."

JOHN 11:25

Jesus, let me hear your voice calling me to life today. Amen.

DIFFERENCE MAKER

Imagine the conversation people had with Lazarus and Jesus at dinner that evening. Why don't you invite some friends out for dinner and bring this story up? See where the conversation takes you.

SEEK

Finding Big Foot has become an obsession for some people. They'll go to great lengths to find the creature, even spending thousands of dollars on camo gear, tracking devices, and all-night surveillance equipment. Some will travel around the continent pursuing alleged sightings.

Tracking Big Foot certainly isn't a lifestyle that's right for everyone, but pursuing God certainly is. What if we had that much passion in our pursuit of God? God has established a kingdom that offers hope, guidance, restoration, and freedom for anyone who wants to be a part of it. What might we find if we spent our energy seeking God's kingdom? What if we kept a vigilant eye open for God's reign throughout each day? What if we began to expect to find him rummaging in our life? And what if we anticipated spotting him in the community around us?

Perhaps we often miss what God is doing because we are often not looking. What people seek defines their lives. It's time to ask ourselves what we seek today.

> "Seek the Kingdom of God above all else, and live
> righteously, and he will give you everything you need."
>
> MATTHEW 6:33

Lord Jesus, keep me watchful for your kingdom today. Help me find you at work in circumstances I hadn't considered before. Amen.

DIFFERENCE MAKER

Seek God's kingdom throughout your day today. Saturate your thoughts with a search for God's reign in creation, in timing, and in interactions.

LEAN

How do you handle a choice that will dramatically shape your future? Do you get stuck with worry that you might make the wrong decision? When you are at an important juncture in your life, how do you select which way to go? What leads you or guides you in that place?

The Bible encourages you to make a decision based upon what God wants for your life. If you get into the habit of walking with God, then the choices become much clearer. Following God naturally improves your confidence in the direction of your life. Your goal in any decision should be to align yourself with God's will. You should not trust yourself more than God for the future of your life. If you seek God's input, then God will give you the ability and the freedom to make good choices that have a positive impact on your future.

Trust in the LORD with all your heart;
do not depend on your own understanding.
Seek his will in all you do,
and he will show you which path to take.

PROVERBS 3:5-6

Jesus, guide me in the choices I make today. Let the steps I take be in step with you. Help me see clearly what I need to do and where I need to go. Amen.

DIFFERENCE MAKER

Lean on something, like a stool or a wall or a desk. As you trust this object to support you, lean on God in prayer for a few minutes. Ask him for his wisdom in any decision you need to make.

THINK THANKS

If you could be with anyone you are not currently with, who would that person be? What is it about that person that makes you long to see them again?

When Paul wrote his letter to some friends in a city called Philippi, he couldn't help but to gush all over the papyrus. He absolutely loved these people. If he could have hopped on a jet and had dinner with them that evening, he would have spent any amount of money to get there. He felt at home, he felt like he could be himself, and he felt like life was more enjoyable when he was with them. Whenever he thought of his Philippian friends, Paul gave thanks to God. He also prayed for them. He was so grateful for these life-giving partners who were also making a difference for Jesus.

Every time I think of you, I give thanks to my God. Whenever I pray, I make my requests for all of you with joy, for you have been my partners in spreading the Good News about Christ from the time you first heard it until now.

PHILIPPIANS 1:3–5

Lord Jesus, thank you for the people in my life who inspire and encourage me. Help me be that way for them as well. Amen.

DIFFERENCE MAKER

Make a connection with someone far away that fills you with joy. Before, after, or during your chat, give thanks to God for that person, and stop to pray for them.

OPEN DOOR

Have you ever walked into a sliding glass door? You thought it was open but it actually wasn't. *Bam!* It took you a moment to figure out that there was a door there, and that the door was closed. And the worst part was probably that all your friends or family were laughing at you. You just had to roll with it. So you smiled and maybe chuckled a bit. But *ouch*, your face hurt!

To find the open door, you must use all the resources God has given to you—sight, hearing, and senses. You must search for it. Ask God to lead you. Listen for his Spirit's guidance and ask for wisdom. Stay close to Jesus so that you aren't led the wrong way. He wouldn't lead you the wrong way. Jesus wouldn't trick you and laugh at you when you smash into a closed door.

The apostle Paul wrote about a wide-open door God had opened for him as well. He didn't assume everything would be easy or perfect because the door was open, but he knew God was giving him an opportunity to make a big impact in the world in which he lived.

There is a wide-open door for a great work here, although many oppose me.

1 CORINTHIANS 16:9

Dear Jesus, lead me to the right opportunities, the ones you want me to go through. Amen.

DIFFERENCE MAKER

Every time you walk through a door today, remember to look for opportunities God is giving you to serve him and others.

BOAST

What would happen today if you boasted about Jesus? What if, instead of bragging about your own accomplishments or calling attention to your own problems, you spoke boldly and favorably about what Jesus did on the cross? What would you even say if you chose to do this? Why would you even do that? People don't want to hear you talk about that, do they?

Well, many of your friends or family are glad to hear you talk about what's important to you, right? What if forgiveness from Jesus through his death on the cross were important to you? Proud parents put their kid's picture on the fridge because they celebrate their child. A good husband buys flowers because he is honored to be married to his wife. A caring teacher displays a student's artwork because she loves what was created. None of these people are worried about what others might think. They just feel the need to share and rejoice.

> As for me, may I never boast about anything except the cross of our Lord Jesus Christ. Because of that cross, my interest in this world has been crucified, and the world's interest in me has also died.
>
> GALATIANS 6:14

Lord Jesus, thank you for dying on the cross to save me from sin. Let your forgiveness sink to the very core of who I am. Let it overwhelm me today. And let me brag about you a bit. Amen.

DIFFERENCE MAKER

In some way today, boast about Jesus.

IN BETWEEN

On a scale from 1 to 10, how antsy do you get when you have to wait? How good are you at waiting? And I don't mean waiting for a couple of minutes, but I mean really waiting—like days, weeks, or even months? When is your patience most easily worn out?

If you want to make a difference in your life or in this world, you might discover that sometimes you'll need to be patient. Everything impactful is not immediate. Some changes take long investment, persistent attention, consistent behavior, and dedicated evidence of your faithfulness. Perhaps you'd like to only do one action, as if you only had to make one motion of your magic wand in order to make everything around you appear better. However, circumventing true process can produce undesirable side effects.

Some things just take time. Making a difference is an everyday endeavor. Your daily commitment to cultivate your heart will harvest huge rewards as time goes on.

Wait patiently for the LORD.
Be brave and courageous.
Yes, wait patiently for the LORD.
PSALM 27:14

Lord Jesus, give me the resilience to work with confident patience today. Let me trust you for the long-term impact of my actions. Amen.

DIFFERENCE MAKER

As an illustration of God's long-term work, and even though you won't see the impact for quite a while, put some money in your savings account today. (Or put some money in someone else's savings!)

RESURRECTION

The cross and empty tomb go together—it is a double event. The cross demonstrated God's verdict against sin, a punishment that Jesus took in our place, while the empty tomb proclaimed hope after judgment, the power of death rolled away by the life and authority of Jesus. We need both. We need the cross because on it Jesus takes our sin to its grave, but we need the empty tomb because from it Jesus offers us life after death.

This is the central truth of Christianity. Without it, everything churchy is just good (or bad) religion that actually offers false hope. All of the Bible points to the crux of history in Jesus. He came to bring God's wrath against humanity for its sin and to also offer forgiveness. Jesus came as a human, took the wrath upon himself, and offered new life that gracefully dances upon the ashes of judgment.

> He was buried, and he was raised from the dead on the third day, just as the Scriptures said.
>
> 1 CORINTHIANS 15:4

Lord Jesus, the most life-changing truth I can ever hold is this: Though I did nothing to deserve it, you died for my sin and offered me new life. Amen.

DIFFERENCE MAKER

How can you live practically in the double event of the cross and the empty tomb? How will forgiveness and new life in Jesus impact the way you interact with others today?

ASK GOD ABOUT HIS DAY

Have you ever had a one-sided relationship with someone who talked all of the time? It's difficult and exhausting. But you love the person so you put up with him or her, just hoping for the day when the friendship becomes a bit more reciprocal, mutual, or friend-like. The truth is that God wants to chat with you. But like everyone else, you can be preoccupied to actually have a conversation with him, too loud to commune. Oh, you probably "pray," but you can be tempted to do all of the talking, using God like a paid psychologist or a call-in radio talk show host.

If you feel like prayer has been too much of a one-sided conversation, try paying attention to God. Ask him what's going on with him. Ask God how he's doing. Silence your life long enough and open your soul wide enough to hear what's on God's heart at that particular moment. In other words, be a friend to God. He's been one to you. It's not that he needs your friendship; rather, it's that he wants it. Perhaps he has something he'd like to say to his friend.

> "My sheep listen to my voice; I know them,
> and they follow me. "
>
> JOHN 10:27

Lord Jesus, what's going on? What would you like to do with me today?

DIFFERENCE MAKER

Stop everything, be still, and listen for God today.

HELPLESS

We often can't help ourselves. We see something tempting and we can't resist it. We hunger for something and we must consume it. Our diagnosis is this: The more we gain, the less we feel like we actually have. This sickness only fuels our thirst for even more. It is a perpetually spiraling cycle: craving and conquest and loss, craving and conquest and loss, craving and conquest and loss. When we live loopy like this, our emptiness is emphasized.

The pursuit of our own happiness leaves us disappointed in our own futility. "No matter how much we see, we are never satisfied," Solomon reminds us (Ecclesiastes 1:8). The fleeting pleasures we have sought cannot satisfy our deep thirst for wholeness. But Jesus can help us. He is able to give us what we cannot grasp by our own power and strength. Christ alone can give us the fulfillment we were created to have.

When we were utterly helpless, Christ came at just the right time and died for us sinners.

ROMANS 5:6

Jesus, why do I keep trying in vain to grab things I don't ultimately need? What I need is you. Only you can help me overcome the looping repetitions of my life. Amen.

DIFFERENCE MAKER

Instead of buying something new today, get rid of something you already have. Simplify your attachments so that you can be more ready to receive satisfaction in Jesus alone.

GARBAGE COMPACTOR

R2-D2 was the only one who could save them. Luke, Leia, and Han Solo were all trapped in the Death Star's garbage compactor. (Yes, this is a geeky but awesome illustration!) The walls started compacting, ready to squish everyone inside. It looked like all was lost—that is, until R2-D2 disabled the detention cell's garbage compactors and the heroes were able to escape.

Sometimes life feels a lot like this. Pressures close in on us like a trash compactor on the Death Star. No matter what creative options we devise to wrangle free, no amount of personal effort could offer rescue forever. But Jesus is freedom. He didn't need to use a cool digital arm with decoding software or a bunch of beeps and boops. Instead, he used the resource at his disposal: his abundant life. Even in overwhelming circumstances, Jesus enables people to escape from being crushed so they can keep on fighting. Stand confidently today by finding freedom in Jesus' everlasting ability to rescue.

We are pressed on every side by troubles, but we are not crushed. We are perplexed, but not driven to despair.

2 CORINTHIANS 4:8

Dear Jesus, in those moments where I become overwhelmed today, give me the hope of your life. Amen.

DIFFERENCE MAKER

Throughout the day, press your fingers together hard for thirty seconds and then release them. Each time you do this, be mindful of the pressing struggles people have, and that Jesus offers rescue.

HYPOCRITE PROOF

Be real today. If you say you are a follower of Jesus, then follow him. Don't be all show. Be substance. Have integrity. Act on your words. If you are a follower Jesus, then do what Jesus is doing.

Faith involves actually putting yourself in action. Faith is risky because it takes proactive effort. You put one foot ahead of the next, trusting that each step is leading you where you should go next. Faith is not lazy. It does not sit around bored, just hoping something good might happen. It is not worried. Faith does not panic at what might occur. Faith is doing what you believe is true. If your faith is in Jesus today, then you will naturally act upon what Jesus is leading you to do.

> What good is it, dear brothers and sisters, if you say you have faith but don't show it by your actions? Can that kind of faith save anyone?
>
> JAMES 2:14

Dear Jesus, let my words and actions match yours. Amen.

DIFFERENCE MAKER

Pick one of these actions to follow through with today (and if you are asked, be ready to share the reason why you are doing it): Tell the truth, help someone, work hard, choose purity, defend someone, listen to a friend, and be calm in a stressful situation.

TEACH KIDS

One of the greatest differences you could make is to help the next generation to follow Jesus. God wants us to be intentional about sharing faith with kids in every circumstance of our lives. Whether you have kids of your own, you have a niece or a nephew, or you are just around kids at church, the call to share faith with children is given to everyone.

Following Jesus is not just a Sunday-morning activity. We follow him and demonstrate our faith to younger people when we are hanging out at home, commuting to work, praying before bedtime, or eating breakfast in the morning. Everything we do and everywhere we are is an opportunity to grow in Jesus and inspire younger people to do the same.

And you must commit yourselves wholeheartedly to these commands that I am giving you today. Repeat them again and again to your children. Talk about them when you are at home and when you are on the road, when you are going to bed and when you are getting up. Tie them to your hands and wear them on your forehead as reminders. Write them on the doorposts of your house and on your gates.

DEUTERONOMY 6:6–9

Dear Jesus, help me figure out how I could share with some kids what it means to follow you. Connect me with a local ministry that teaches children about you. Amen.

DIFFERENCE MAKER

Tie a string around your wrist (loosely, of course—don't cut off your circulation!) to remind yourself to help kids (maybe in a local church ministry?) learn about Jesus.

GIFTED ON PURPOSE

You are uniquely gifted by God on purpose. He gave you specific talents, experiences, and passions so that you can make a difference in the world in which you live. Your unique set of gifts can help others live according to their God-given giftedness too. God has planned to use you to do good things in this world.

Remember that God has gifted other people on purpose as well. You aren't the only one who has been uniquely gifted by the Lord. He also exceptionally wired others so that they could encourage and equip people like you to do what you have been called to do. God has put everyone on the same playing field. Each person is a recipient of this radical generosity so that each person can serve the Lord with his or her whole heart.

Search your own talents and desires today, considering how God might want you to use them for the good of others. At the same time, seek out others who will build you up and help you develop the gifts God has given you.

> However, he has given each one of us a special gift through the generosity of Christ.
>
> EPHESIANS 4:7

Lord Jesus, thank you for gifting me to make a difference in this world. Help me to commit to using my gifts to serve you. Amen.

DIFFERENCE MAKER

Pick a talent God has given to you, and then combine it together with some passion God has given you. Practice putting your gift and passion in action today.

WORK FOR EVERYONE

People have assumed it is the pastor's job to visit a sick person in the hospital, to pray before a meal, or to do the Bible teaching for Wednesday Bible study. After all, it's what he was hired for, right? It is what we pay him to do. This is true to a degree, but just to a degree. Ultimately, the pastor's job is to shepherd people (*pastor* means "shepherd") to a closer relationship with Jesus so that Jesus can empower them to do good work. In other words, the pastor is not the only person who is supposed to be doing ministry. He is simply supposed to equip people to work for Jesus.

The truth is that it is everyone's calling to do work. There is no shortage of good things to do in this earth, so God has called you to use your gifts to do work that builds others up. Walk in your gifting today, knowing you are making a difference in this world.

> Now these are the gifts Christ gave to the church: the apostles, the prophets, the evangelists, and the pastors and teachers. Their responsibility is to equip God's people to do his work and build up the church, the body of Christ.
>
> EPHESIANS 4:11–12

Lord Jesus, help me work for you. Don't allow me to let others do my work for me. Amen.

DIFFERENCE MAKER

Pick one of these ministry "jobs" to accomplish today: Visit someone who is sick, pray out loud before dinner, do a house project for an older person, or volunteer for a ministry role in church this weekend.

WORK TOGETHER

Your ability to work with others to make a difference is much like the hand and the mouth working together. When the hand and mouth refuse to bless one another as a team, eating dinner is really dysfunctional! But when the hand uses its gift to grab onto that Chipotle carnitas burrito, and when the mouth uses its giftedness to open up wide and take a gargantuan bite, the whole of the body benefits and praises the Lord.

The church is an amazing team of great people who are uniquely gifted and uniquely flawed, and who are ready to work together to bring good to this world through faith in Jesus. Practically, this means your life should be lived within a network of others who are striving to follow Jesus and impact this world too. While you use your gifts to bless others, others use their gifts to bless you. No one has a monopoly on God's calling.

The one who plants and the one who waters work together with the same purpose. And both will be rewarded for their own hard work.

1 CORINTHIANS 3:8

Lord Jesus, surround me with others who want to impact this world so that I can be encouraged to become even more effective for you. Amen.

DIFFERENCE MAKER

If you are not involved already in a vibrant church or ministry group, start taking the risk to do so. If you already are involved, then invite others in your group so that they could be built up too.

EAGLE EGGS

There is a scene in the movie *Nacho Libre* where Nacho (a wrestler played by Jack Black) was extremely frustrated with his friend for telling him that drinking the yoke from eagle eggs would give him special fighting skills. After climbing a cliff, finding a nest, cracking open an egg, and guzzling, he went on to embarrassingly lose his next wrestling match. Later, he rebuked his friend, saying, "Those eggs were a lie, Steven! A lie! They give me no eagle powers. They give me no nutrients!"

Lies, even ridiculous ones, mislead and set people up for heartache. Lies sell a twisted lotion that applies to itchy ears, but in reality only serves to make the problems worse. Lies erode trust, cause confusion, and get people into all kinds of convoluted messes. But in Jesus there is transparency and truth. He is refreshing to a world that is oversaturated with untruths. What Jesus says is what is. He isn't selling anything or trying to gain from manipulation. Jesus is genuine, authentic, and confident with his words.

Don't lie to each other, for you have stripped off your old
sinful nature and all its wicked deeds. Put on your new
nature, and be renewed as you learn to know your Creator
and become like him.

COLOSSIANS 3:9–10

Lord Jesus, shape me into an honest person. If I start a lie today, stop me from completing it. Help me speak the truth. Amen.

DIFFERENCE MAKER

Speak honestly today. No tricks. No cover-ups. Only tell the truth.

FINISH

Jesus is so committed to you that he will not give up with you. In fact, he is going to finish what he began in you. As an artist, he might choose to add more texture and lighting. As a sculptor, he might just chisel away some rough edges. And as a gardener, he might decide to prune some dead branches. And then there's his carpentry skills, in which case he might measure and cut and hammer and sand for a while—sometimes a long while. Whatever he needs to do, he is going to continue creating in you until he is finished with his work.

Creating a masterpiece is one of his favorite things to do. You, together with everyone else he is working on, have captured his vision. He wants to pour his heart into his most treasured work. He would never let himself get distracted from his attention to your every detail. And he won't give up until he can step back and look at all he has made and say, "Very good!"

And I am certain that God, who began the good work within you, will continue his work until it is finally finished on the day when Christ Jesus returns.

PHILIPPIANS 1:6

Jesus, don't stop working on me. Form me into who you want me to be. Amen.

DIFFERENCE MAKER

Think of a project that has been hanging over your head.
Finish it today. Get it done. And as you do,
remember God's determination to work on your behalf.

BE YOURSELF

If we truly believed in Jesus, then we wouldn't struggle so much with our identity as individuals. If we trusted him fully, we would embrace our unique self-makeup and triumph in the way we have been wired together.

Imagine waking up in the morning knowing that God loves you and believes in you—that he is there for you and has some pretty great ideas for your day. Imagine living in such a way that you seek to please him rather than seeking to please others. Imagine finding the firmest footing for your feet in the midst of tempting whirls all around you because you are rooted in the firmest foundation (Jesus). Imagine being able to speak the truth in love because you aren't tempted to fold to the ears of others. Imagine having the courage to face your shortcomings because God empowers you. Imagine having the guts to spill your guts because Jesus wants to restore his authority and blessing in you. Imagine being so secure in God that you are able to love your family, your friends, and your coworkers with a love beyond yourself. And imagine finding your identity in God so that no matter what turmoil happens you will not be able to lose yourself.

This means that anyone who belongs to Christ has become
a new person. The old life is gone; a new life has begun!

2 CORINTHIANS 5:17

Dear Jesus, let me find my identity in you so that I can be who you want me to be for others. Amen.

DIFFERENCE MAKER

Because you know that God has a purpose for you, do something bold today that you would not otherwise have done.

CLOTHE YOURSELF

Look at yourself in front of a mirror. What are you wearing? Did you have trouble deciding what to put on this morning? How do you feel about how you look? Are you happy with the fashion option you chose? Isn't it hard to stand in front of the mirror day after day and think that what you are wearing is perfect? Some people change multiple times before heading out of their room. To avoid the wear and tear of deciding what to wear, Steve Jobs, the founder of Apple, famously decided to use only one style of clothing.

In this culture, what you wear reflects who you are in many ways. So that wrinkle in the shirt or that out-of-style fashion pattern can feel annoying. But there is one set of clothes that never fades, never looks bad, and never makes you feel below average. When you put on Jesus you feel like a million bucks—or more. Jesus may not always be "in style," but he always looks great on you.

Instead, clothe yourself with the presence of the Lord Jesus Christ. And don't let yourself think about ways to indulge your evil desires.

ROMANS 13:14

Lord Jesus, when people see me, let them notice your characteristics. Amen.

DIFFERENCE MAKER

If you were to wear Jesus, what sort of "clothing" would you put on? How can you motivate yourself to put him on and keep him on all day long?

PEACE RULES

Does anxiety get the best of you at moments throughout your day? Remember that you are called to let peace get the better of you. For who, by worrying, can solve the unresolvable? No one thinks, "Maybe if I worry enough everything will get better." No, if you let it, worry will play a mad king over your heart.

Peace, not worry, is to reign in your heart. But how? You've learned you cannot attain peace on your own. If you try to grab it without help from anyone, you'll simply snag more stress. It is important to recognize that peace comes from Jesus. And he loves to give it to people who once were separated from him. You see, peace is the restoration of relationship. Peace does not look like you, by yourself, trying to hold it all together. Rather, it looks like you and others learning to entrust your lives together in Jesus.

And let the peace that comes from Christ rule in your hearts.
For as members of one body you are called to live in peace.
And always be thankful.

COLOSSIANS 3:15

Jesus, let your peace have ownership of my heart. Let me be thankful for all that you have done and are going to do. Amen.

DIFFERENCE MAKER

Connect with someone you know who is anxious.
Creatively and personally share Christ's peace with them.

MESSAGE SPILL

If you received a memo straight from heaven, what do you think would be written on it? Perhaps, *We need to talk. Or, Will you be mine?* Or, *Dinner tonight. RSVP. Bring guests.* No matter what that memo would have on it, the message would certainly be good. It might not be an easy message; it could even be convicting or alarming. But it would be grace filled and trustworthy. I'm almost certain the memo would include an invitation to a significant celebration. It would be what you needed to know just at that very moment.

Jesus, the Word of God, wants to communicate with you on a regular basis. His message is this: He has come to fill you with overflowing life. He loves you and wants you to know it in the depths of your being.

Let the message about Christ, in all its richness, fill your lives.
Teach and counsel each other with all the wisdom he gives.
Sing psalms and hymns and spiritual songs to God with
thankful hearts.

COLOSSIANS 3:16

Dear Jesus, overwhelm me with your message of hope today. Catch me off guard with your wisdom and let me spill over with joy. Amen.

DIFFERENCE MAKER

Sing praise to the Lord! It doesn't matter where—the shower, the car, the bus, the sidewalk, the hallway, the elevator, the bike, the dinner table, or the church group. Just sing songs of praise somewhere today.

REPRESENT

Look back on your last twenty-four hours. Would you say that your words reflected Jesus? Did your conversations suggest someone who is letting Jesus make a difference? Don't worry, everyone is guilty of messing up with our mouths. People often have a shoe-shaped hole in the bottom of their face because they keep putting their foot where their mouth is. Everyone allows wrong things past their lips more than they'd like to admit: coarse language, poisonous jabs, vengeful attacks, perverted jokes, abusive yelling, God's name in vain, insults, lies, excuses, and gossip. The mouth can spit venom.

This world needs you to set a different pattern with the words that come out of your mouth. One simple way to make a dramatic difference would be to use your words to express gratitude. "Thank you" is one of those phrases that the world does not hear nearly enough. It is a freeing phrase. In fact, those two words help people feel good about themselves.

And whatever you do or say, do it as a representative of the
Lord Jesus, giving thanks through him to God the Father.

COLOSSIANS 3:17

Jesus, thank you for doing all you have done for me. Help me speak as if I actually realize it. Amen.

DIFFERENCE MAKER

Speak well today. Say thank you more than you ever have before. Watch the change that happens in your heart and in the people around you.

May

Jesus,

Let me learn you.

And let me invite others to learn alongside me.

Amen.

PACED

A busy life is often a stressed life. A life paced around prayer, however, is often filled with thankfulness and peace. On one hand, when people are hurried, they are worried about what might happen or what they might miss. When people are paced by prayer, on the other hand, they develop a growing sense of gratitude because they become increasingly aware of all Jesus is doing in them and around them.

People are often tempted to think they don't have time for prayer. There is just too much going on, too many things to get done. But prayer forms an alert mind and cultivates a thankful heart. It provides wisdom for decisions, reassurance for apprehension, strength for trials, and unity with God's plans.

This is one of the reasons Jesus prayed so much. He surprised people by how often he would withdraw from busy moments to spend time with the Father. At the height of his popularity, he would withdraw from the crowds and spend time in prayer. In the midst of his darkest moments, he would pray. When alone and tempted, he would pray. Before gathering with others, he would pray. His life was paced by prayer, not hectic activity.

Devote yourselves to prayer with an alert mind and a
thankful heart.

COLOSSIANS 4:2

*Dear Jesus, thank you for wanting to spend time with me. Cultivate a more
prayerful mind and heart within me. Amen.*

DIFFERENCE MAKER

At least twice today, set aside several minutes to pray.

MAKE DISCIPLES

The word *disciple* means "learner," so a disciple of Jesus is a learner of Jesus. No matter how young or old someone is, being a learner of Jesus is the goal of that person's life. A Christian is never be a know-it-all; rather, a follower of Jesus is in a continual process of absorbing and practicing the teachings of Rabbi Jesus.

One of the most important things a disciple of Jesus learns is this: Disciples make disciples. Learners of Jesus produce more learners of Jesus. This calling, to make other disciples, has come to be known as the Great Commission. It is the greatest difference-making, history-changing, boundary-breaking strategy this world has ever known. People at all stages of learning have discovered that knowing Jesus is the best thing anyone could possibly do. So from generation to generation and geography to geography, people have come to learn Jesus.

"Therefore, go and make disciples of all the nations,
baptizing them in the name of the Father and the Son and
the Holy Spirit. Teach these new disciples to obey all the
commands I have given you. And be sure of this: I am with
you always, even to the end of the age."

MATTHEW 28:19–20

Jesus, let me learn you. And let me invite others to learn alongside me. Amen.

DIFFERENCE MAKER

Be bold. As a learner of Jesus, whom should you influence
toward Jesus today?

YOU WILL BE

A witness of a crime possesses valuable information to an investigation. A witness of an accident provides important testimony for an insurance company. A witness to a marriage signs a document declaring that the union truly occurred. It is easy to see from these examples that a witness is someone who has seen something and confirms that they actually saw it take place, giving accurate details for those who are interested.

The early followers of Jesus saw him perform miracles, teach crowds, die on a cross, and rise again to life. Then they confirmed what they had seen by telling people about it everywhere they went. Today, followers of Jesus do the same thing. The way that Jesus works in our lives becomes the foundation for what we share with others everywhere we go. Our testimonies speak of what Jesus has done and what he is still doing in our lives. We are witnesses of Jesus Christ.

But you will receive power when the Holy Spirit comes upon you. And you will be my witnesses, telling people about me everywhere—in Jerusalem, throughout Judea, in Samaria, and to the ends of the earth."

ACTS 1:8

Lord Jesus, let it be this simple: Let me share what I have seen you do in my own life. Amen.

DIFFERENCE MAKER

Sit down in a coffee shop or restaurant today. Grab a napkin and a pen. At the top write, *What I have seen Jesus do*, jot down what you have seen Jesus do in your life, and then give your napkin to someone else before you leave.

NEVER LEAVE

If you follow Jesus, then you won't have only the Son of God defending your back, you'll also have God the Father and the Holy Spirit too. You're covered. In a world where abandonment is such a big problem, this is indeed good news. But there is a key concept embedded here that should not be missed. It is true that God won't ditch you, but he also longs for you to not give up on him either. He asks you to love him and, in your love, to obey what he has asked you to do.

To *obey* simply means to "listen." Jesus states the obvious: If you love him then you'll listen to him. And if you listen to him, then you might just hear him asking the Father to give you his Spirit, who will come to your aid, comfort you, empower you, and stand up for you in every circumstance at any given moment.

> "If you love me, obey my commandments. And I will ask the Father, and he will give you another Advocate, who will never leave you."
>
> JOHN 14:15–16

Jesus, just as you promise to be with me, I want to be with you too. Thank you for your attention and care. I love you and will be listening to you today. Amen.

DIFFERENCE MAKER

Name something you should do in obedience to Jesus today. As you follow through with this, listen for the Spirit's presence in your life.

PENTECOST

It would be wrong to say that the first followers of Jesus—you know, the ones who changed the entire course of human history—had a great plan. They didn't sit around large conference-room tables with the best minds in the industry or the most brilliant political strategists checking popular opinion polls every few minutes.

The truth is that they really didn't know what to do. Jesus had given them instructions after his resurrection to wait for him to send the Holy Spirit, who would empower them to be his witnesses to the ends of the earth. So they waited according to his word. They spent time praying. And they spent time going about their daily routines. They would gather together often and eat and talk about all they had seen Jesus do and all they had heard him say. And they waited. And then God showed up.

On the day of Pentecost all the believers were meeting together in one place. Suddenly, there was a sound from heaven like the roaring of a mighty windstorm, and it filled the house where they were sitting.

ACTS 2:1–2

Dear Jesus, show up in my life today. Let your Spirit move me. Let your Spirit move among my friends. Impact our lives deeply today. Amen.

DIFFERENCE MAKER

Gather some other followers of Jesus to wait with you for God to move. Pray and expect him to do something in your lives.

ADDED TO THE CHURCH

We live in an era when people are walking away from church in droves. Some feel church isn't relevant or cool, while others feel church isn't trustworthy. And others just don't see the point of it all. But ultimately people leave church because they can. They don't feel compelled to stay. They simply aren't finding in church what they need to find. When "church" began 2,000 years ago, the feeling was just the opposite. People left behind everything else in their lives because they had to be a part of the church. The reason for this is simple: They needed Jesus, and church was were they could find him.

Church means "gathering" or "assembly." The church is a gathering of people who are compelled to find Jesus and be forever changed by him. Church changes the world because Jesus changes those in the church. It is a light and shelter and rock for communities, in any moment, for all seasons. It is a gathering where individuals discover they are a part of something greater together. Church is where people find Jesus and learn to live with him and for him.

Those who believed what Peter said were baptized and
added to the church that day—about 3,000 in all.

ACTS 2:41

Dear Jesus, don't let me leave church. Help me find you in a gathering of people.
Amen.

DIFFERENCE MAKER

Change the trends. If you are not already a part of a good church or ministry group, find one. And grab some others to join you.

DEVOTED

One of the great losses of our current society is the gathering around the table to share a meal. Mealtimes used to be regular daily moments where people would set aside their busy schedules and spend time together. Now, for many people, meals can often be on the go, last minute, and eaten alone.

But a new generation of Jesus followers seems to be discovering the blessing of having meals together. The lost art of the meal is being revived once again. We are relearning that there is a sacredness to eating with others. It's called "fellowship," that moment in the practice of everyday life when people who intentionally follow Jesus gather together to share life. In fellowship there is a great reminder that we have been drawn together by Jesus. It can be, if we remember, a worshipful experience.

All the believers devoted themselves to the apostles'
teaching, and to fellowship, and to sharing in meals
(including the Lord's Supper), and to prayer.

ACTS 2:42

Lord Jesus, let me be devoted to you, to your followers, and to prayer. Amen.

DIFFERENCE MAKER

Invite some people close to you to share a meal today. During the meal, make sure to give thanks, to break bread, and to drink the cup in remembrance of what Jesus did on the cross for each of you. Try to make this a tradition whenever you gather with other followers of Jesus.

SHARE

"That's mine!" Did you ever yell these words to some kid in your preschool? (Hopefully this only happened when you were five, and not when you were volunteering last week!) Those words, and more so the attitude those words reveal, are a sorry revelation of how even the most pure-hearted among us struggles with humanity's tendency toward selfishness. With all those kids fighting for their preferred toy, preschool play time can look like the Cornucopia in *The Hunger Games*. Life is much more fun for preschoolers when an attitude of sharing prevails. "Here, would you like to play?" sounds so much more freeing than "You can't have that!" or "Get your own!"

The early church was amazing at playtime. They shared. And then they shared some more. There was so much sharing going on that everyone had everything they needed. Jesus had gotten such a hold of their lives that they felt they didn't need to hold onto anything else. The presence of God's grace in our hearts causes us to be a people who share what has so freely been given to us.

> And all the believers met together in one place and
> shared everything they had. They sold their property and
> possessions and shared the money with those in need.
>
> ACTS 2:44–45

*Lord Jesus, make me more generous today. Help me fight the urge to possess
and then to possess more. Amen.*

DIFFERENCE MAKER

Take your extra clothes to a thrift store or homeless shelter today.

SEVEN DAYS A WEEK

The Christian faith was never supposed to be limited to Sunday mornings. Neither was it considered to be just singing and sermons. Those are good, but they are just part of following Jesus. Christianity, in its truest form, involves followers of Jesus gathering to worship God every day of the week, gathering in homes to share meals and communion, and living respectfully and supportively in society.

This sort of lifestyle, saturated in the very way people live, naturally encourages others to want to be a part of church. The difference maker in this pattern of faith is not the weekly service or the seasonal outreach event. The difference maker in this pattern is the everyday practice of following Jesus. It simply works in the ordinary routines of life.

> They worshiped together at the Temple each day, met in homes for the Lord's Supper, and shared their meals with great joy and generosity—all the while praising God and enjoying the goodwill of all the people. And each day the Lord added to their fellowship those who were being saved.
>
> ACTS 2:46–47

Lord Jesus, be alive in me today and every day this next week. Amen.

DIFFERENCE MAKER

On a scale of 1 to 7, how many days a week are you a follower of Jesus? Which of the characteristics mentioned above can you put into action today?

SLOW AND RICH

The world is still here, isn't it? God is a patient, loving God. He initiates and reinitiates love again and again and again. Even though people have repeatedly turned against him, God still desires that no one would perish apart from him. He longs to restore relationship with those he has made. He loves the world so much that he died for every single person. He did that even while they were doing the very things that rejected him. What causes a normal person to react in anger and retaliation causes God to respond with another outburst of grace. If anyone else offered us this much latitude, this much time, this much empathy and support, we would have no excuse but to accept their kindness. How could any of us say no to such an amazing friend?

The LORD is merciful and compassionate,
slow to get angry and filled with unfailing love.
The LORD is good to everyone.
He showers compassion on all his creation.

PSALM 145:8–9

Dear Jesus, thank you for your patient forgiveness. You keep helping me along.
Thank you for never giving up on me. Amen.

DIFFERENCE MAKER

Who can benefit from you being gracious and compassionate today? How can you express a slowness in anger and a richness in love toward them?

LET IT SHINE

The one who created the light when there was nothing but darkness is shining his light into your heart today. If the vast darkness before time could be dissipated by his brilliance, imagine how brightly Jesus could shine in you. Against the glare of his light, icy exteriors melt, dark shadows flee, and murky thoughts clear up. God's light reveals his truth in the midst of confusion and gives knowledge of his glory in the midst of fog.

Jesus is called the Light of the World. The Bible teaches that darkness just doesn't understand the light—it misunderstands it, to be more precise. Darkness thinks it knows how Jesus works but is totally blindsided by his brilliance again and again. Darkness tries to hide but quickly discovers it can't. So let there be light in your heart today, and allow Jesus to reflect his light through you.

For God, who said, "Let there be light in the darkness," has made this light shine in our hearts so we could know the glory of God that is seen in the face of Jesus Christ.

2 CORINTHIANS 4:6

Dear Jesus, shine brightly in me and through me today. Amen.

DIFFERENCE MAKER

Find the sun today. If it's cloudy, find a bright and warm lamp. Go sit under it. Close your eyes. Run this verse through your heart until it sinks in.

HIDE IT UNDER A BUSHEL

The old kids' song went like this: "This little light of mine, I'm gonna to let it shine… / Hide it under a bushel? No! / I'm gonna let it shine / Let it shine, let it shine, let it shine." What is a bushel? A bushel is a form of measurement equal to eight gallons of dry goods. Sometimes the basket, holding a bushel of grain, for instance, was also called a bushel. The idea of the song is simply that no one can hide a candle under a bushel basket. *Why would anyone do that?* you may be thinking. It might as well not be lit. Jesus, the Light of the World, wants to brighten the world through you. Don't hide today.

"You are the light of the world—like a city on a hilltop that cannot be hidden. No one lights a lamp and then puts it under a basket. Instead, a lamp is placed on a stand, where it gives light to everyone in the house. In the same way, let your good deeds shine out for all to see, so that everyone will praise your heavenly Father."

MATTHEW 5:14–16

Lord Jesus, let the same light that you have flooded into my soul overflow into others. Amen.

DIFFERENCE MAKER

Light a candle (maybe a scented one to make your room smell better), then put a bowl over it (not a flammable bowl!). Notice how ridiculous that is. Then relight the candle and let it shine as a reminder of what you were created to do.

LIFE PRESERVER

Out of his loving-kindness the Lord saved us. We had fallen off the boat into the raging sea because we didn't listen to his commands to stay off the deck during the storm. We thought that was unfair. After yelling at him for being too constrictive, we pounded up the stairs to play outside on the poop deck. It wasn't long before we slipped off. But God, always keeping a loving eye on us, called out our name, jumped in the torrent with a life preserver, put it around us, and pulled us back into the cabin of the boat. It was his kindness that saved us, not because of what we have done, but only because of his great mercy.

When God our Savior revealed his kindness and love, he
saved us, not because of the righteous things we had done,
but because of his mercy.

TITUS 3:4–5

Lord Jesus, how could I ever tire of saying thank you? Even when the trouble was my fault, you saved me anyways. Thank you. Your kindness rescues me. Your love warms me. Your mercy simply saves me. Thank you. Amen.

DIFFERENCE MAKER

Do you know anyone who's in the middle of a storm and needs their name called and a life preserver thrown out to them?
Reach out to that person today.

CALLED NEAR

No matter who you are or where you are or what you are with or without today, the Lord is near to you. Whoever you are, call on him today. If you're cool or awkward, just say, "Jesus, I need you." If you're rich or wrecked, just lift up his name and say, "Jesus." Wherever you are, call on him today. If you're lost or found, just reach out and say, "Jesus, will you stand with me?" If you're at home or far away, just speak his name. "Jesus." And whatever you have, call on him. If you have plenty or little, just ask, "Jesus, could you give what I truly need?" If you have a broken heart or a full one, just whisper, "Jesus." In each circumstance, he will hear you and he will do what needs to be done for you. Just be honest about who you are, where you are, and what you have. Don't try to impress, don't try to trick. Just be yourself and call his name.

The Lord is close to all who call on him,
yes, to all who call on him in truth.

PSALM 145:18

Lord Jesus, I call on your name. Be near to me now in the reality of my life.
Amen.

DIFFERENCE MAKER

Take a moment to pray about who you are, where you are, and what you have. Ask Jesus to be close to you in each of these areas of your life.

IN STEP

Have you ever tried to get to the store without actually going there? Or tried to brush your teeth without using a toothbrush—or toothpaste for that matter? Or have you ever tried to make baked ziti without turning on the oven, or using ziti? Any of those would be just plain stupid.

So why try to live today without using the Spirit for your every step and breath? If you want an abundant life, why not walk with the one who gives abundant life? If you need direction for major decisions in your life today, why not walk with the one who provides all wisdom and truth? If you need hope in a time of despair, why not take the effort to walk with the one who gives comfort and counsel?

It can be tempting to complicate something so simple. But if you want to truly live, then walk in step with the Spirit. You were created to walk with God. Do what you were created to do, and see how everything else works out from there.

Since we are living by the Spirit, let us follow the Spirit's
leading in every part of our lives.

GALATIANS 5:25

Lord Jesus, don't let my feet trip. Don't let me wander off. Instead, let me walk in step with you today. Amen.

DIFFERENCE MAKER

Go for a walk with someone. Allow your strides to fall into rhythm together, then talk about how we are to walk with God just like that.

WORK FOR JESUS

Even as our bodies and minds grow tired, and as our emotions need a rest from stress causers (like people and jobs), we should not let up on our responsibilities to the Lord. We are to serve him enduringly, forever, with fervor.

It would be so much easier to play another thirty minutes on Clash of Clans. It would be so much more relaxing to binge watch for the rest of the afternoon. "Me time" is very alluring, especially when responsibilities hang over the head, stresses keep beckoning, and needy people wait out in the real world ready to suck the life out of us.

Do you have something you should do today? Do you have something you could do for someone today? Do you have something someone asked you to do? What if you just did it? Like, right now? And what if, when you did it, you did it really well? And what if you kept in your mind that you were doing it for Jesus?

Never be lazy, but work hard and serve the Lord enthusiastically.

ROMANS 12:11

Lord Jesus, help get me off my butt today. Motivate me to do hard work that helps someone in some way. Mostly, inspire me to focus my heart's work on serving you. Amen.

DIFFERENCE MAKER

Write Romans 12:11 on a piece of paper and tape it where it will serve as a reminder throughout the day.

PROUD OF THE TANK ENGINE

Little kids try to hide bad things from their parents because they feel embarrassed. But no little kid has ever tried to hide something good from his or her parents. When kids have something that is joyful and fulfilling, they run to their parents and tell them loud and fast all about it. If a little boy sees on a video that Thomas the Tank Engine fell off his railroad tracks into the water, he might worry. But if he then saw Thomas' friend James come along and pull him out and get him "back on track" (so to speak), that little boy just might run around with excitement and tell everyone about the good news. If he didn't share, he'd burst.

For some reason, though, the world tricks us into thinking we cannot, or should not, feel the same way about Jesus. If we see God doing something great, it's as if we're conditioned to suppress our wonder or make our faith a private matter. But this is ridiculous. Jesus dying on the cross for our sins to give us abundant life, and get us back on track (so to speak), is better than anything. Let it be known today what God has done in and through you.

> For I am not ashamed of this Good News about Christ. It is the power of God at work, saving everyone who believes.
>
> ROMANS 1:16

Dear Jesus, don't let me feel embarrassed because I know you. There is nothing greater in my life than to follow you with my whole heart. Why should I be ashamed? Amen.

DIFFERENCE MAKER

When the opportunity arises today, be proud that you know Jesus.

BEAUTIFUL

We see a glimpse of it often. The brilliance of millions of stars. The intricate dance of leaves in the wind. The sparkle of wonder in someone's eye. The deep pausing breath of a treasured moment. The hopeful spring of a child's step. This is how the world was created to be. Beautiful. But often we also see the exact opposite. Stars obscured. Creation spoiled. The snarled brow of anger. The mourning of loss. The shattering of innocence. This is how many people perceive the world. Contaminated. What we need today is Jesus because he is the one who created this world to be beautiful. Even though it got messed up, he is ready to re-create it again. And he wants to begin his re-creative work in us.

Instead, let the Spirit renew your thoughts and attitudes.
Put on your new nature, created to be like God—truly
righteous and holy.
EPHESIANS 4:23–24

Jesus, don't stop working on me until I am entirely yours. Continue your re-creative work in my life. Spur others I know to be renewed by your Spirit too.
Amen.

DIFFERENCE MAKER

Invite some people to look at the world with fresh eyes today. Take a moment together to notice the beauty that is inherent in creation. Then imagine what the world would be like if people fully followed God's patterns. Take time to pray, asking God to re-create hearts in this world.

UNICORNS AND GRACE

Wishful thinking. That's how we treat grace. Almost like we treat unicorns. Unicorns are magical and pretty. They can fly and roast marshmallows from their horns. They seem so nice. Did you know that a group of unicorns is even called a "blessing"? But for real, if someone said to you, "Blessings on you," would that be a good thing? What if a stampeding herd of unicorns descended down upon you as these words left their mouth? They could trample you, hee-haw with terror, skewer you, and leave you covered in burnt sparkly marshmallows or something like that.

Thankfully, the difference between unicorns and grace is that grace is real. Don't ever treat grace as wishful thinking, like it is a pretend thing that would be nice to have but is elusive and mythical. No, grace has the power to change lives for real. So accept the power of grace through Jesus in your life. Be graceful and give a dramatic blessing of grace to others.

Each time he said, "My grace is all you need.
My power works best in weakness." So now
I am glad to boast about my weaknesses,
so that the power of Christ can work through me.

2 CORINTHIANS 12:9

Dear Jesus, your grace is all I need. Help me believe and live in that truth today.
Amen.

DIFFERENCE MAKER

Remind someone who feels weak of the reality of God's grace through an act of extreme kindness.

EXTRAVAGANT GRACE

We don't think we can handle this. People in droves rejected Jesus because he was different, or maybe, more accurately, he was more than what they had imagined. They probably tried to go back to their regular patterns, numbing themselves to apathy. *We need grace*, they must have admitted, *but Jesus is too good; he's too much. He would change our lives.*

The only way to truly live according to grace is to be changed by Jesus. But that means giving up control of our lives. Grace doesn't give us the power to do what we want. Rather, grace empowers us to do what Jesus does.

When we receive God's grace, we let ourselves be overwhelmed and we let Jesus use us to make a difference in others—not just in times of catastrophe, but in everything. When we accept Jesus, we start to stand and to overflow with grace toward others. Grace isn't what we deserve; it's what we need. And it's even more than what we need. That might be overwhelming to think about. But this is what followers of Jesus do—they receive and offer extravagant grace.

> Stephen, a man full of God's grace and power, performed amazing miracles and signs among the people.
>
> ACTS 6:8

Jesus, help me to walk gracefully today. Amen.

DIFFERENCE MAKER

The next time you pay for a meal, leave an extravagant tip.

BAPTISM

Baptism is a lot like taking a bath. It is a symbol of cleansing. As we go under the water, it's as if our sin is washed away and Jesus presents us spotless before God. Baptism is also a lot like dying. It is a visual declaration that we have committed our sins and selfish pursuits to Jesus. It's as if we are being buried and agreeing with Jesus to leave our sin in the grave.

Baptism is also a lot like resurrection. It is a picture of receiving new life in Jesus. As we are lifted from the depths of the water, it's as if our old life is gone and a new life has come. It is also like a big step, but it's also a simple one. It gives everyone who wants to follow Jesus a visual opportunity to show faith in Jesus in front of friends, family, and fellow followers of Jesus.

Peter replied, "Each of you must repent of your sins and turn to God, and be baptized in the name of Jesus Christ for the forgiveness of your sins. Then you will receive the gift of the Holy Spirit."

ACTS 2:38

Lord Jesus, thank you for washing me clean of my sins. Let me live a baptized life today. Amen.

DIFFERENCE MAKER

Encourage people you know to take the step of baptism. If you have not been baptized, go and talk to your pastor or ministry leader about it.

CONTINUE

Jesus is the greatest difference maker of all time. The fact that you are reading this book shows that you understand this truth in one way or another. That's great! Keep challenging yourself to be changed by him every day for the rest of your life. Don't ever stop this pursuit.

At some point in your life, you recognized your need for him and received him as your Lord and Savior. You've probably had some ups and downs in your walk with Jesus since then, but today you know he needs to be the primary focus of your life. Just as you received him already, keep receiving him. Treat every day as a new opportunity to give your life to Jesus afresh. Continue to bring the things of your life to him. Continue to discover who he is and what he wants for you. Continue to learn about what he has done and what he is doing for you. And continue to look for him and call out to him and follow him.

And now, just as you accepted Christ Jesus as your Lord, you
must continue to follow him.

COLOSSIANS 2:6

Lord Jesus, thank you for making such a difference in my life.
Keep doing that today. Amen.

DIFFERENCE MAKER

Think for a moment. Because of your commitment to Jesus, what will you
do differently today?

ROOTED

You've been told you're supposed to be an adult. What a ridiculous pressure that is. Society is already too full of grown-ups. Many of them, who rushed to become adults without grounding themselves in Jesus, are more childish than the most tantrum-crazed kids. "Mine!" or "I need this!" or "I deserve this!" are common mantras for today's adults.

People who keep adding other things to their lives in pursuit of fulfillment are never satisfied. That's why the Bible suggests a different way to grow: down in Jesus. People don't need to pursue anything more, unless it is more of him. So instead of growing up and standing on your own, try growing down into Jesus. Root yourself in him. Build your life in him. Draw from him all the nourishment you'll need for each day. Overflow with gratitude for his abundance within you.

> Let your roots grow down into him, and let your lives be
> built on him. Then your faith will grow strong in the truth
> you were taught, and you will overflow with thankfulness.
>
> COLOSSIANS 2:7

Lord Jesus, today I place all of who I am in you. Amen.

DIFFERENCE MAKER

What have you added to your life that doesn't fit with a life rooted in Jesus?

UNLIMITED

If you could do anything to influence this world, what would it be? What is it you would like to see changed? When you look out at the world, what causes you the most angst? If you could, would you change it? "I understand what you're doing here," you might say. "You're trying to make me think about being heroic or something. But really, who am I to do anything about it?"

Who are you? I'm glad you asked. You are child of the King of Heaven. You are an heir of the kingdom of God. You have a seat at the table with the Creator of the World. The King is inviting you to the chance to make a difference in the world he has placed you. He only wants you to know where your heart is in line with his own.

I pray that from his glorious, unlimited resources he will empower you with inner strength through his Spirit.

EPHESIANS 3:16

Lord Jesus, you created this world, and you want to empower me to do extraordinary things in it. Let me take that seriously today. Amen.

DIFFERENCE MAKER

Take your answers to the questions above and offer them to the King. Ask him to empower you to do something about it.

ROOTED DEEP

Jesus just showed up with his moving truck. He motions for you to come help him unload. "Today's the day!" he says. "Thanks for welcoming me in. This is going to be good." You panic when you realize you haven't gotten things ready. You do a quick scan of your heart and realize that there is moldy pasta in the fridge, toenail clippings on the carpet, and chips in the cracks of the couch. And (gross) you haven't cleaned the toilette.

Yes, Jesus is moving in. Will he feel at home right away, or will he have some cleaning to do and some furniture to rearrange? Think quick: What would Jesus need to do to make your heart his home? Having Jesus make himself comfortable in your life might not be such a comforting thought. But it is the best possible scenario. It might mean some disruption for your old habits and routines, but those didn't bring you confidence or peace anyways. The new daily routines with Jesus are going to be so much more fulfilling than what you have been doing.

> Then Christ will make his home in your hearts as you trust
> in him. Your roots will grow down into God's love and keep
> you strong.
>
> EPHESIANS 3:17

Lord Jesus, I'm so glad you are here. Please, make yourself at home within me.
Amen.

DIFFERENCE MAKER

What is one thing you can do to show Jesus he is welcome
in your heart today?

LOVE IS

Have you ever jumped into a pool and allowed yourself to float under the surface in the expanse of the water? In any direction that you waved your arms, there was only water. If you extended right or left, in front of you or behind you, there was only water. If you reached down, water. If you stretched upward, water. Your whole self was immersed in this new understanding.

Now imagine being submerged in an endless pool—no, not one of those pools that spills over the sides and overlooks a valley (though that sounds really nice)—more like a pool with no edges at all. You could swim in any direction (down, up, left, right, forward, back) and still not be any closer to edge than you were before. Overwhelming? Frightening? This is what it is like to be immersed in the love of Jesus.

> And may you have the power to understand, as all God's people should, how wide, how long, how high, and how deep his love is.
>
> EPHESIANS 3:18

Lord Jesus, I'm not sure if I want to be completely overwhelmed by your love. It might be too much for me. But I pray that you will give me the power to understand how much your love covers me. Amen.

DIFFERENCE MAKER

If God's love covers you so much, then shouldn't you live a life surrounded with love? In what ways can you show God's great love to those you will see today?

EXPERIENCE

Do you remember the first time you gave a speech? Did your knees shake and your voice quiver? Did your words get jumbled up? The truth is that you probably are better at giving speeches now than when you were nine years old, though you could still improve with more experience. When you practice something over and over again, you get more comfortable and learn subtleties and rhythms. The more you rehearse something, the more it embeds into who you are.

Growing in your love of Jesus is similar. Gaining experience helps you improve as a person and to know God better. At first, his love was exhilarating, and maybe even nerve racking. But over time, and with daily practice, you began to understand the expectations and rhythms of what it means to know God's love. Keep experiencing Jesus today. Don't ever give up. Pick up his love every day and learn the nuances and empowerment that only comes from experience with him.

May you experience the love of Christ, though it is too great
to understand fully. Then you will be made complete with
all the fullness of life and power that comes from God.

EPHESIANS 3:19

Lord Jesus, I look forward to experiencing you more today. Amen.

DIFFERENCE MAKER

Practice the love of Jesus. Take a chance experiencing his love in a new way that might make you nervous or stretch you a bit. What could you do?

INFINITY

Infinity is impossible to measure. We know infinity is huge, but its never-ending limits are beyond our scope. It leaves us in awe. We can capture enough of the concept to comprehend the idea of "boundless," but never enough to fully grasp it. The greatest imaginations of our mind could never control infinity.

This is how the apostle Paul describes how much God can accomplish when he works through us. Take the greatest thoughts, the greatest dreams, the most inventive requests that any of us could conjure up, lift them up to God, and even that wouldn't scratch the depths of what God is able to do. This reveals God's glory. The beauty, wonder, and power of his action is absolutely boundless. It is why creatures like us fall to his feet in awe. So why would we not expand our understanding of what is possible with God?

Now all glory to God, who is able, through his mighty power
at work within us, to accomplish infinitely more than we
might ask or think.

EPHESIANS 3:20

Lord Jesus, may your glory be seen through your work in my life today. Amen.

DIFFERENCE MAKER

Think your greatest thought and lift up your greatest question to God. Be inventive in the ways that God works in you. Expand your idea of what God is able to do through you today.

ROOTED STRONG

Take a moment and look outside at a tree. The reason you can see that tree right now is because it is seriously grounded below the surface. The root system of that tree, which you can't see (unless some of the stronger roots are breaking through the ground), are equipping that tree to stand tall and flourish. The effort and focus of a tree's growth is downward. The roots supply the nutrition and resources that it needs to thrive.

Likewise, a life rooted into Jesus focuses not on the outward appearance, on what people can see with their eyes, but on the inward growth in Jesus. As a result, though, what people end up seeing is a person standing tall through the winds and trends of culture, a person overflowing with abundant life.

> But they delight in the law of the Lord,
> meditating on it day and night.
> They are like trees planted along the riverbank,
> bearing fruit each season.
> Their leaves never wither,
> and they prosper in all they do.
>
> PSALM 1:2–3

Lord Jesus, I choose to delight in you today. Let my actions be fruit providing for others. Let me prosper in all I do today because I put you first. Amen.

DIFFERENCE MAKER

Find a big tree, sit underneath it, and contemplate the roots beneath you, the trunk standing by you, and the branches and leaves (or springing buds!) above you. How could this visual make a difference in your Christian life?

THRIVE

Even though it is small in size, the olive tree has made a tremendous impact throughout history. It is an evergreen tree that can flower and bear fruit for centuries to come. Its leafy branches are a symbol of abundance and peace, often extended after a violent war between enemies. Olive oil is a useful cooking resource, and it is used symbolically as a sign of blessing in many religious ceremonies and rites of passage around the world.

The olive tree is a metaphor for those who follow God's ways and live daily in his love. Though the world may look upon them as insignificant at first, their lasting impact cannot be disputed. They give shade and refuge in every season of life. The difference they make can be evidenced for generations to come. They supply this world with a source of abundant life and offer the stability of peace. They provide regular daily care for people and also blessing for the major events of life. In other words, followers of Jesus make an incredible difference in this world.

> But I am like an olive tree, thriving in the house of God.
> I will always trust in God's unfailing love.
>
> PSALM 52:8

Lord Jesus, let me thrive in life by trusting in your love every day. Amen.

DIFFERENCE MAKER

Which aspect of the olive tree illustration can you put into action for the people around you today?

FLOURISH

Palm trees in Israel are known as date palms, flourishing for at least 5,000 years. They are a symbol of refuge for travelers and an abundant economic resource for fruit, syrups, grains, fibers, and timber. Their leaves were used to celebrate victory, such as when Jesus entered Jerusalem on what has come to be known as Palm Sunday.

Cedar trees were once abundant in Lebanon. They were tall (sometimes a 120 feet) and strongly rooted. Their wood was world renowned for its beautiful red color, for its lightweight yet resilient strength, and for being resistant to decay and repellant to insects. When people choose to root themselves in the patterns of God, they flourish and bless the world like these two types of trees.

> But the godly will flourish like palm trees
> and grow strong like the cedars of Lebanon.
> For they are transplanted to the LORD's own house.
> They flourish in the courts of our God.
> Even in old age they will still produce fruit;
> they will remain vital and green.
>
> PSALM 92:12–14

Lord Jesus, let me live a life rooted deeply into you so that I may be used to bless others. Amen.

DIFFERENCE MAKER

Do one of the following today: Sit under a palm tree and enjoy life with God (if you are too far north, look at a picture and drool), or make something with cedar wood, remembering the richness of God at work in your life.

June

Jesus,

Don't let me treat you like an add-on to my life.

You are the center of my life.

Amen.

LISTEN QUICKLY

One of the best quotes from the classic 1980s movie *Ghostbusters* occurs when Dan Akroyd's nervous character poses the following question: "Listen! Do you smell something?" We are a very distracted people. We struggle to listen without being flooded by all kinds of other stimulation that stirs all of our other senses. Our challenge today is to be radically different than the preoccupied culture around us.

Listen carefully. Don't speak quickly. Listen quickly. Don't get angry quickly. This is wise advice in a world that can be just the opposite: flare up the temper, vomit the verbal output, and, sorry, what were you saying? While hotheaded and loose-mouthed reactions can be signs of uncaring attitudes, the skill of listening to others shows a heart that cares for people. Listening to someone shows a person they are valued, important, and worth the time. This could simply be life changing.

> Understand this, my dear brothers and sisters: You must all
> be quick to listen, slow to speak, and slow to get angry.
>
> JAMES 1:19

Lord Jesus, let my words be few and my ears be wide open. Amen.

DIFFERENCE MAKER

Go a whole day without talking about yourself (unless you absolutely must, like if you get pulled over for speeding and the officer asks you questions). As much as possible, ask friends and family open-ended questions. (And by the way, if this challenge makes you angry, then you need to read this devotional entry one more time.)

PURE RELIGION

When Christianity is at its best, it is undeniably beneficial for the world. The irony, however, is that Christianity is as its best is when it is countercultural. Spending yourself on behalf of people who cannot pay you back goes against the give-and-receive culture in which we live. If you give money, you get something in return. If you invest your time or energy, you deserve some kind of return on your investment. The world operates this way on a daily basis.

But imagine if you did not have much to give or were unable to invest. Imagine if you lived at the mercy of others, in a mode of complete dependency. Imagine if your parents died while you were a child. And imagine if your spouse passed away while you were elderly and poor. Your opportunity to survive according to the world's standards would be diminished. It is into this reality that the followers of Jesus enter, radically uplifting those society belittles as "the least of these."

> Pure and genuine religion in the sight of God the Father
> means caring for orphans and widows in their distress and
> refusing to let the world corrupt you.
>
> JAMES 1:27

Lord Jesus, make me undeniably radical. Amen.

DIFFERENCE MAKER

Contact a nursing home or an orphanage today. Tell them you would like to invest in caring for those in need, asking them if you can visit to see what opportunities they have.

DISCRIMINATION

In 1955, Rosa Parks was told to give up her seat in the "colored" section of the bus to a white person, even though it would mean she would no longer have a place to sit herself. When she refused, she was arrested. Her bold action drew national attention to the blatant discrimination that prevailed in the (dys)functional order of the country. The society around her favored one type of person over another, the privileged over the oppressed, the rich in status over the poor.

The human heart is full of so much potential. It was made to reflect the love that God has for every person, and yet in its corruption are the ingredients for all kinds of hatred and cruelty. The person who discriminates against people incriminates against himself in twisted, self-regarding ambitions. Each person, no matter their life circumstance, is valuable in the eyes of God. Jesus is calling you to restore the way people are treated to a godly pattern.

If you give special attention and a good seat to the rich person, but you say to the poor one, "You can stand over there, or else sit on the floor"—well, doesn't this discrimination show that your judgments are guided by evil motives?

JAMES 2:3-4

Lord Jesus, let me see everyone through your eyes. Amen.

DIFFERENCE MAKER

To remind yourself of these verses, whenever you have the opportunity, give dignity ("the seat of honor") to someone society doesn't readily recognize as being worthy.

FAVORITISM

Let's pretend for a moment and say you were a sheep. And then let's say that for some reason the shepherd empowered you with the task of inviting any sheep you see into the safety and fellowship of the sheep pen. And then let's say that you saw two sheep outside the sheep pen. One of the sheep was a famous celebrity ewe with a golden fleece, while the other was some chump of a lamb with a crusty flannel wool shirt. Which of these two sheep would you choose to invite into the sheep pen?

Hold on, you didn't say neither, did you? Good. Just checking. Maybe you said the golden sheep because your popularity would go up among the other lambs? Or maybe, out of the pity of your heart, you even said the crusty sheep because you knew that was the right answer. But in humility, for the shepherd's offering, did you say "both"?

Yes indeed, it is good when you obey the royal law as found
in the Scriptures: "Love your neighbor as yourself." But if you
favor some people over others, you are committing a sin.
You are guilty of breaking the law.

JAMES 2:8–9

Lord Jesus, your heart desires that all people would know your favor. Help me to act justly, to love mercy, and to walk humbly with you, my Shepherd. Amen.

DIFFERENCE MAKER

Challenge yourself to equally open doors, be polite, say thank you, give your time, make eye contact, or smile whenever you encounter someone today.

SUPPOSE YOU SEE

We've all seen them. Men and women huddled up on benches with a piece of cardboard or some newspaper. Asleep. Or drunk. Or sick. Or stoned. Whatever. But there is a lot we haven't been willing to see. We haven't seen the families sleeping in cars. We haven't seen the malnourished boy skip gym class because he can't afford running shoes. We haven't seen the runaway daughter trapped in an industry that wants to sell her to the highest bidder. We haven't seen the despair and death in the alley. Oh, we've seen some problems. We know they're there. But we haven't seen the people. And that means we haven't noticed Jesus with them.

Suppose you see a brother or sister who has no food or clothing, and you say, "Good-bye and have a good day; stay warm and eat well"—but then you don't give that person any food or clothing. What good does that do?

JAMES 2:15–16

Lord Jesus, what a miserable wretch I can be. I know you love the "least of these." Quicken the link between my eyes and my soul so that I will care for a neighbor in need. Amen.

DIFFERENCE MAKER

Contact a homeless shelter or food pantry. Ask them when they could use some help and how many people they could use. Then organize a team of people to go and serve.

SATURATE

Summer adventures are just around the corner. How do you plan to spend your days? Earning as much money as possible through work? Bike rides? Sunburns? Iced coffees? Picnics and bonfires? Baseball games? How about a mission project? Or helping at a camp? Or a Vacation Bible School? Mentoring younger students? Summer prayer group? Volunteering at a local youth drop-in center? Food-packing events?

Did you know you have permission to put your faith into action this summer? True adventure happens when all of your activities become saturated with Jesus. Your bike rides become more exhilarating because every aspect of creation you see produces praise from your heart. Your summer employment becomes more rewarding because you practice faithfulness and integrity while saving for your future expenses. Your intentional ministry projects become more fulfilling because they become regular features to your weekly routines.

Don't segregate your faith from your practical life this summer. Faith doesn't live that way and life doesn't truly work that way either. Saturate faith and life with one another, for then you'll see your life reflecting Jesus in this world.

So you see, faith by itself isn't enough. Unless it produces good deeds, it is dead and useless.

JAMES 2:17

Lord Jesus, don't let me treat you like an add-on to my life.
You are the center of my life. Amen.

DIFFERENCE MAKER

Do something adventurous today that is influenced by James 2:17.

WALKING DEAD

Lifeless. No pulse. DOA (dead on arrival). That's how the Bible describes faith that fails to evidence any vital signs. It's a dramatic statement, but the point is valid. Faith inhales and then exhales the very breath of God. So a faith with no indication of dynamic activity is no faith at all. Don't let the coroner be called out to comment on your faith: "Well, what we have here is a depletion of oxygen." No, be alive with Jesus. Let him kick-start your heart and motivate your hands to action in this world. Let others see a living faith, pulsating with the life of the Creator of the Universe.

At the same time, don't let others confuse good works with faith. No one earns a way to salvation or gets badges on their heavenly robes for doing good things. Good "works" are simply the natural outflow of a living and vital faith. Because Jesus loves you, you can't help but share his love with others. Because Jesus forgives, you forgive. Because Jesus gives you security, you offer peace and confidence to your community. You overflow with the life he has given you. Don't be another person counted among the walking dead. Be alive today!

> Just as the body is dead without breath, so also faith is dead without good works.
>
> JAMES 2:26

Lord Jesus, make me alive in all that I do today. Amen.

DIFFERENCE MAKER

As a reminder throughout the day, notice your breathing. Each time you inhale and exhale, think about what a living, breathing relationship with Jesus would look like in that moment.

TAME

We have figured out how to train elephants to stand on buckets—we somehow thought that would be a good idea, so we did it. Also, for some reason, we have persuaded lions to let us stick our heads between their open jaws. We have figured out how to make seals clap, dolphins wave, and killer whales belly flop, all on command. We have even convinced snakes to dance to music, tigers to jump through hoops, and bears to wear tutus and tiaras. And yet none of us has yet to figure out how to control that little muscle in our mouths. Our tongues praise God and then scorch the earth. Our tongues are unbridled beasts that pretend to be housebroken but stain the carpet when the master lets down his or her guard.

People can tame all kinds of animals, birds, reptiles, and fish, but no one can tame the tongue. It is restless and evil, full of deadly poison. Sometimes it praises our Lord and Father, and sometimes it curses those who have been made in the image of God.

JAMES 3:7–9

Lord Jesus, let my tongue offer you praise and speak your truth today. Amen.

DIFFERENCE MAKER

Draw a small smiley face (on your hand or arm) and write James 3 next to it. Keep looking at this as a reminder to speak well all day long.

HUMILITY WORKS

To truly make a difference during your lifetime, it might mean that you don't get the glory for much of what you actually accomplish in your life. Humanity does not need any more egomaniacs drawing attention to themselves. But it does need more people who are willing to do things for the benefit of others.

A rudder on a ship makes what seems like a small impact at first. Of all the impressive parts that make up a great ship, the rudder is small and doesn't get the attention it deserves. But over time, the constant influence of that rudder changes the entire course of direction for that massive ship. Though people don't normally think about the rudder, they do notice where the massive ship goes—the direction it takes.

Those who live a consistent life of integrity, who make wise choices and follow God's patterns, can make an impact that lasts for several lifetimes. But such a way of living takes humility—a terribly selfless word that puts God and others in the position of priority in one's heart.

If you are wise and understand God's ways, prove it by living an honorable life, doing good works with the humility that comes from wisdom.

JAMES 3:13

Lord Jesus, let the good things I do bring you more praise than they bring me. Amen.

DIFFERENCE MAKER

Do something really good for someone today, but don't let them find out it was you.

CLOUDY WITH A CHANCE OF FRUIT

In the movie *Cloudy with a Chance of Meatballs*, an inventor named Flint Lockwood creates a machine that turns clouds into food. Any kind of food. *Zap*. It's done quicker than in the microwave and falls from the sky above. This machine is a blessing, as long as they don't allow selfish ambition to abuse the abundance of food it provides.

God wants to produce an abundance of good works through you. This "fruit from above," so to speak, comes from the inventiveness of your heart and mind as you learn how to walk with Jesus. When you live appropriately in his patterns, God uses your actions to provide precisely what others need at just the right times. His abundance can rain down on anyone, regardless of circumstances in life. Jesus delights in delighting others through you.

> But the wisdom from above is first of all pure. It is also peace loving, gentle at all times, and willing to yield to others. It is full of mercy and the fruit of good deeds. It shows no favoritism and is always sincere.
>
> JAMES 3:17

Lord Jesus, help me follow your patterns so that you can bless others through me. Amen.

DIFFERENCE MAKER

In the wisdom God is growing within you, choose someone you could bless by doing something unexpectedly encouraging today.

PLANT PEACE

Clashes create chaos. One side pitted against the other. Flagrant fouls fueling frustrations. Places where people argue and fight around the world inevitably become riddled with landmines and disturbed by displacement. This is true for wars between nations and even disputes within a family.

There is too much quarrel in our world today. When people who say they are followers of God throw grenades into the mix, the world stumbles even further into battle. No one needs Christians to add to the agitation that already exists. Retribution and followers of Jesus do not make a redeeming recipe for the world. What is needed are individuals, armed with kernels from Jesus, who will patiently but confidently sow peace among those in conflict. Become a person who seeds peace today. Resolve to be a refreshing presence in the midst of the strife.

And those who are peacemakers will plant seeds of peace
and reap a harvest of righteousness.

JAMES 3:18

Lord Jesus, let your peace reign in my heart so that I can bring calming assurance to others. Amen.

DIFFERENCE MAKER

Have you offended or hurt anyone recently? Think of a way to humbly approach them, ask for forgiveness, and make peace with them today.

HUMBLED

Humility is such an elusive, ironic beauty. The moment we think we have it, haven't we lost it? Could anyone ever accurately say, "I am humble"? Yes. Someone could. Jesus could. But he's the only one who was qualified to do so. Jesus is the ultimate King and he is the ultimate Servant. Although he is greater than the greatest greatness that could ever be, he humbled himself to the point of dying on a cross for our sake. He voluntarily gave up all of his glory so that we could live. No one can ever be as truly great as Jesus or as truly humble as Jesus. And that fact should humble us even further.

Humble yourselves before the Lord,
and he will lift you up in honor.

JAMES 4:10

Lord Jesus, thank you. Thank you. Thank you. I can do nothing else but bow before you. I am not worthy to be called yours, and yet that is exactly what you call me. Let me respond to you with the honor you deserve from me today. Amen.

DIFFERENCE MAKER

Today, don't ask God to honor your plans or to do something for you. Instead, consider how you might honor the Lord through your words and actions today.

POUNCING PROSECUTORS

What if lawyers could make the judgment in a case? Instead of pleading or prosecuting, what if they just jumped to their own conclusions of freedom or condemnation? Or what if the witnesses in the case could declare innocence or guilt based not on what they had seen but on their one-sided perceptions? In either of these scenarios, the justice system would absolutely crumble. There is only one person who is ultimately allowed to make the final judgment, and that is the judge. The judge might use a jury occasionally, but even the jury relents to the rules established by the judge.

So when people are judgmental against or in favor of someone, justice is skewed. Pouncing prosecutors and drooling defenders are unreliable in their accusations and discernment. Ultimately, judgmental attitudes themselves will be tried and sentenced. Every person will appear before the Judge one day, and those who took the Lord's responsibility upon themselves will have some pretty tricky explaining to do.

> God alone, who gave the law, is the Judge. He alone has the power to save or to destroy. So what right do you have to judge your neighbor?
>
> JAMES 4:12

Lord Jesus, make me slow to judge others and quick to place myself before the mercy of your court. Amen.

DIFFERENCE MAKER

Prosecute yourself. Make a case against your sin. Then read Romans 5:8 a few times. Consider how the generosity of the Judge should be reflected in your treatment of others today.

OMISSION

It's wrong to hit your little brother when your mom isn't looking, right? We know it's a sin to do bad things. Bad behavior leads to bad consequences. It's a transaction that we have learned does in fact take place. But if sin was just about not doing bad things, then someone could conceivably lock themselves up and never do anything bad to anyone. This, of course, would be ridiculous, but at least that person wouldn't sin against others. Or would they?

Well, what if sin also involved *not* doing good things? If your little brother got his hand stuck in the refrigerator ice-making machine and started crying for your help, it would be wrong to just walk away and do nothing for him. You didn't put his hand in the ice maker—check. You didn't hit him while his hand was stuck in the ice maker—check (how kind of you!). But you didn't help him either. There is a lot going on in this world where people are stuck. Don't just walk away.

> Remember, it is sin to know what you ought to do
> and then not do it.
> JAMES 4:17

Lord Jesus, don't let me be like the jerks who walked by the man stuck on the side of the road. Let me be like the Samaritan, doing what is good in your eyes. Amen.

DIFFERENCE MAKER

Today be on the lookout for people who could use your help, in a big or small way. Then actually help.

GRUMBLE

There is a lot to complain about, isn't there? Maybe your day has been disrupted by a friend's grumpiness. Maybe your to-do list is getting longer because your boss keeps giving you more and more to do. Maybe someone cut you off while driving to work this morning. Maybe somebody let you down. Maybe you didn't get something you thought you should have gotten from your friend. Or maybe you got something you didn't think you should get from someone.

Complaining about someone else is our bratty way of venting our frustrations with others. Being frustrated with friends or family or bosses is not necessarily a bad feeling to have; in fact, it is quite normal to be frustrated with others. But turning that frustration into a kind of venting gossip or passive-aggressive attack displays a sour heart.

There is a better way of handling your angst with others. Pray about it. Take a deep breath. Realize that someone else's rudeness reflects upon them, so don't let it echo off of you. A heart that grumbles is a heart that is empty. Fill your heart with Jesus instead.

Don't grumble about each other, brothers and sisters, or you
will be judged. For look—the Judge is standing at the door!

JAMES 5:9

Lord Jesus, change my grumbling heart into a fulfilled one. Amen.

DIFFERENCE MAKER

Stop at a bank and get a pile of one-dollar bills. Every time you catch yourself complaining today, put one-dollar in a jar. Then donate that money to your church.

ACCOUNTABILITY

When you mess up, simply admit it. Don't let the mess fester. Free yourself from the self-imposed shackles of your sin. Let if off your heart. Share it with someone you can trust and who will help you take the next steps toward freedom. This is especially true if you have a recurring mess that you keep stepping into.

It would be good to find someone to hold you accountable—a friend who will follow up with you and encourage you and watch where you step, a friend who will pray for your healing and change. The goal isn't to find someone who will haunt you every time you sin. You don't need more guilt heaped on you. You don't need more oppression. You've already given yourself enough constriction as it is. What you need is freedom. The goal, ultimately, is to walk toward faithfulness with Jesus. Fidelity, not accountability, is what you truly need. But accountability might just help get you there.

Confess your sins to each other and pray for each other so that you may be healed. The earnest prayer of a righteous person has great power and produces wonderful results.

JAMES 5:16

Lord Jesus, forgive me for my sin. Let me trust my steps to another person so that I can find the support I need to be faithful to you. Amen.

DIFFERENCE MAKER

If you haven't already done so, ask someone you trust to be an accountability partner for you.

REACH OUT

One of the most gut-wrenching things in life is a friend who wanders away from relationship with God and with you. This can be especially difficult when the person has sung with you during worship or served alongside you in helping others. It is much harder when he has laughed with you during times of joy, or she has supported you through your struggles.

Don't give up on your friend. Reach out. Extend a loving invitation back into relationship. Organize people in your church community to show love and acceptance, forgiveness and joy. Don't try to push or trick your friend. Simply and vigilantly, just as the father ran to embrace his lost son (Luke 15:11–32), keep watch for the moment of restoration.

My dear brothers and sisters, if someone among you wanders away from the truth and is brought back, you can be sure that whoever brings the sinner back from wandering will save that person from death and bring about the forgiveness of many sins.

JAMES 5:19–20

Lord Jesus, use me to help restore others to relationship with you and with your church. Amen.

DIFFERENCE MAKER

Think of a friend you have not seen for a while who has slowly wandered away. Contact them. Let them know you are thinking of them. Invite them to grab a coffee or to hang out sometime.

B = S + C

Be strong and courageous. Notice the command here. Don't just be strong and don't just be courageous. But be strong *and* courageous. This is what the Lord told Joshua as he was about to take a huge leadership role. The responsibility must have been overwhelming. Moses, Mister Miracle Man, who had effectively led Israel for forty years, had passed the baton on to Joshua. Everyone must have wondered, *Are we going to be okay? Will Joshua be able to lead us like Moses did?*

The Lord can enable anyone he wants, to do anything he wants them to do. Joshua had proven himself to be a consistent, dedicated person who put God's interests above his own. So when the grand moment came, the Lord was ready to empower him and use him. "Don't listen to everyone's fears. Don't be led astray by your own anxiety. Trust me."

God is calling you to make a difference in the world. Trust him to work through you today. He is with you when you are following his lead in your life.

> "So be strong and courageous! Do not be afraid and do not panic before them. For the LORD your God will personally go ahead of you. He will neither fail you nor abandon you."
>
> DEUTERONOMY 31:6

Lord Jesus, empower me to do what you want me to do today. Amen.

DIFFERENCE MAKER

What do you believe God has called you to do, but you have struggled to take the initiative to get started? Apply this verse to your life today.

SELAH

Stop whatever else is in your mind right now except for this very moment with God. Halt any distraction. Press pause. This moment right now is an interlude in your life. Let the activities prior to this moment be still. Let the activities that will come after this moment wait. You'll get to them soon enough. They don't need you for the next few minutes. Stop. Quiet your soul. And listen.

Selah is a Hebrew word used dozens of times throughout the Psalms. Scholars think it means something like "interval" or "quiet break." It seems to be a moment in the activity of a song where everything pauses. In the vacuum of words and sound, people are encouraged to give reflection to God's mighty work. So take all of your to-do lists and hanging-over-the-head worries and put them aside for a moment. Reflect on this passage from Psalm 46 and then *selah* for a moment.

God is our refuge and strength,
always ready to help in times of trouble.
So we will not fear when earthquakes come
and the mountains crumble into the sea.
Let the oceans roar and foam.
Let the mountains tremble as the waters surge!
Interlude [Selah]

PSALM 46:1–3

Lord Jesus, let me pause my life in you for this moment. Amen.

DIFFERENCE MAKER

Make a quiet break with God a regular pattern in the hectic activity
of your life today.

SPIRIT OF POWER

Look ahead a few years into your life. For this moment right now, as you envision the potential God has for you, don't let yourself worry about things that are out of your control. Instead, think about the type of person Jesus wants you to be. Consider the sorts of things he is preparing you to do. As the picture takes shape in your mind, ask yourself: Between now and then, what would Jesus want me to do today to get ready for tomorrow?

Contemplating your future can be both overwhelming and exciting. God's long-term goals for you can seem too far away or even too blurry. Yet, at the very same time, as Jesus brings clarity to your steps, they could send your heart racing in anticipation for what is ahead. Just like an expectant mom who is waiting to hold her child in her arms, treat each day with the confidence, love, and self-discipline that you need to bring about God's plans in your life.

> For God has not given us a spirit of fear and timidity, but of power, love, and self-discipline.
>
> 2 TIMOTHY 1:7

Lord Jesus, overcome my hesitations to do what you want me to do. Give me a new boldness of heart and hands today. Amen.

DIFFERENCE MAKER

What is the next step you can take today toward what God has called you to do?

TO GOD

Imagine your heart and mind being squashed by a bus. Or two buses! How about three? And the buses that are squeezing you are rusty yellow hulks of metal belching out smoke and overflowing with sugar-crazed middle school kids screaming for your attention! The driver just keeps turning the radio up louder and louder in a futile attempt to drown out the cacophony of noise, and the station just keeps playing the same annoying pop song that always gets stuck in your head on repeat. Repeat. Repeat. Repeat. Aaahhh!

Life can feel like this sometimes. Pressing. Heavy. Anxious and crushing. Loads of concern piled on hectic demands shrieking for your immediate attention. Your burdens need to be lifted off of you somehow, or else your heart will struggle to beat. The cares need to be taken off of you sometime, or your mind will struggle to think. But who is able to lift your burdens for you? Peter gives us a pretty good hint.

Give all your worries and cares to God, for he cares about you.

1 PETER 5:7

Dear Jesus, I lift up my concerns to you now. Take them. They're yours. Amen.

DIFFERENCE MAKER

Write down your concerns on a piece of paper. Once your list is complete, on the top of the paper write, Jesus can have these now. Pray. Then crumple up the paper and throw it in the trash.

YOUR PLANS

If you wanted to rob a bank, and you committed this plan to the Lord, would you succeed? Of course not! The whole robbing-the-bank part wouldn't work out because God wouldn't support it. He'd probably hand you back your blueprints and tell you to get a life.

To commit your plans to God means to hand them over, let him look them over, and work them over until they match his will. He'd be glad to work with you on any necessary changes (instead of "robbing" he might suggest "investing"). If you accept God's revised plans and act on them, then you have shown that your plans are committed to the Lord. Once this is true, your plans will succeed. In other words, do what God wants you to do today. Make your plan of action in line with God's plan of action and all will go according to plan.

> Commit your actions to the LORD,
> and your plans will succeed.
>
> PROVERBS 16:3

Lord Jesus, I have big things in the seasons ahead. Please guide the goals that I have and the steps I take. Amen.

DIFFERENCE MAKER

Work on your résumé (or scholarship applications for the fall), and practice interviewing for the opportunities God has for you in the future. As you do, ask yourself this question: Do God's plans for me match my plans for me?

BUT...

During their last meal together, tensions were high. Jesus spoke about being killed, and Judas got up and left after being marked as the betrayer. Jesus had washed their feet, served bread and wine as symbols of his death, and spoke about going away for a little while. Jesus told his disciples, "Love each other." But his disciples thought of everything else but love.

Their heads were spinning and their hearts were flooded with worry. Instead of loving, they stressed, "What's happening here?" Peter blurted out, "Lord, where are you going?" Thomas anxiously cried, "Lord, we have no idea where you are going." They grew exhausted from apprehension and began to drift apart. By the end of the night, overwhelmed by their fear, most of them denied Jesus and ran away from each other.

"Love each other." But Lord, I have a big test. But Lord, I have so much going on in my life right now. Lord, I am really tired today. Lord, that guy drives me crazy. "Love each other." Lord, I don't like the style of music they play. Lord, he literally stinks. Lord, I'm busy. Lord, I'm worried. Lord, I don't feel in control of things. "Love each other."

> "So now I am giving you a new commandment: Love each other. Just as I have loved you, you should love each other."
>
> JOHN 13:34

Lord Jesus, with everything happening right now, help me to love my friends and family. Amen.

DIFFERENCE MAKER

Think of the three closest people you have in your life. Find a practical way today to show each of them that you love them.

OOPS

"Oops. Didn't know I was supposed to do that." Picture saying that to your boss after missing an important deadline. Then imagine hearing yourself say, "Uh, yeah, it's not really my fault because I didn't even know about it. So…no big deal." Yeah, right. That project was assigned to you and was supposed to get done. Sorry, but you're going to be looking for a new job pretty soon.

At the end of your life, imagine feeling pretty fine about all the good stuff that you did, but then Jesus informs you that you missed several significant projects. There were some people you passed by whom you could have helped. There were times when you didn't defend someone who was being hurt. There were kind words you could have said, doors you could have held open, and patience you could have given. Oh, and then there was all the time you could have spent praying for people, but you played Candy Crush instead.

> And he will answer, "I tell you the truth, when you refused
> to help the least of these my brothers and sisters, you were
> refusing to help me."
>
> MATTHEW 25:45

Jesus, I have missed so many things that I should have done. Poke my heart today when I begin to miss the work you have for me. Amen.

DIFFERENCE MAKER

Be attentive to what you can do for others today.

GENERATION →?

Why are we so easily drawn away from God and toward things that hurt us? Why are we so attracted to detrimental people or activities? And why do we secretly adore things that leave us empty, unfulfilled, and worse off? Why do we look for empty pleasures? And why do we like immediacy more than we like patience? Why do we think that selfishness is justified?

Those questions are the sad story of the book of Judges. A people who once experienced God in spectacular, personal ways became a people far from God, not knowing his presence, not following his patterns. Generation after generation grew more disgusting, more degrading, and more depraved than the one before it. People grew more and more removed from God, less and less aware of right and wrong, more confused and less secure, and more shallow and less happy.

One of the most significant things we can do today is to pray for our generation to have the courage to turn from darkness and to walk toward the light of Jesus.

After that generation died, another generation grew up who did not acknowledge the LORD or remember the mighty things he had done for Israel.

JUDGES 2:10

Lord Jesus, my heart breaks for my generation. Don't let us walk away from you. Restore us to relationship with you. Amen.

DIFFERENCE MAKER

Grab some friends and set aside time to pray for your generation today.

IMPOSSIBLE INSTRUCTIONS?

Two thousand years ago, the apostle Paul encouraged a church to "always rejoice" and to "pray without ceasing." He also told them to "give thanks always," no matter what they were going through. This, Paul said, was God's will for their very lives.

But are these instructions practical? Is it realistic to think that anyone could truly "always rejoice"? Is it actually possible to "pray without ceasing"? Or what if life absolutely stinks (absolutely, repulsively, horribly stinks)—is it thinkable to "give thanks always" in those situations? Are these instructions from Paul just pleasant "Christianese" phrases similar to "keep your chin up" or "it'll all be okay"? Or can people actually live these commands out?

These must be more than just empty commands. Perhaps in our fallen human strength these are mission impossible, but perhaps in the power of Jesus there is potential to actually live these out. Perhaps in Jesus people can be captured by joy, be caught up in conversation with God, and be overwhelmed to overflowing with his grace.

> Always be joyful. Never stop praying. Be thankful in all circumstances, for this is God's will for you who belong to Christ Jesus.
>
> 1 THESSALONIANS 5:16–18

Lord Jesus, I don't know how, but give me the mind and heart to live these verses out today. Amen.

DIFFERENCE MAKER

Pick one of the three instructions and write it on your hand to remind yourself throughout the day what Jesus wants do within you.

SKY

Look at the sky. What do you see? How far can you see? What is up there? How does what you see change throughout the day? During the day, watch the clouds form and pass by in the atmosphere. If it is rainy, marvel at the science involved. If it is stormy, be humbled by the power of the winds and weather fronts. If it is sunny, feel the warmth of the sun on your skin. Enjoy the light it gives to reveal God's creation. At night, look at the stars. How many are there? Where are they all? Examine the detail of the moon. Think of the importance of its pull on the earth. Look at the sky. What do you learn about God and about what he created you to do?

The heavens proclaim the glory of God.
The skies display his craftsmanship.
Day after day they continue to speak;
night after night they make him known.
They speak without a sound or word;
their voice is never heard.
Yet their message has gone throughout the earth,
and their words to all the world.

PSALM 19:1–4

Jesus, your love can be seen in the what you have made. Today, let me look up often and be amazed by you. Amen.

DIFFERENCE MAKER

Get outside and enjoy what God has made. Let the expanse of the sky cause you to wonder about how great he is and about your role on this earth.

STRUGGLE

Many people don't *struggle* with bitterness, they just let it waltz into their lives without a fight. Bitterness seems like a natural fit to hurting hearts. If they have been wronged, the company of resentment is often welcomed. If they have been disappointed, many people invite anger to take up residence in their lives. Once bitterness has taken root, however, it's not much of a stretch to invite retaliation to the party also. No one needs to get special training to become skilled in revenge. With resentment driving the heart, retaliation flows like lava. It wells up without much effort when bitterness kicks in its tectonic push. It's all too easy.

Many people, however, do struggle with forgiveness. To offer forgiveness seems almost like a heavenly pummel on top of bruises. It is a radical countercultural response to wrong. Extending reconciliation strains people when they have been wronged, because mercy demands that pride be put down and grace be picked up.

> Make allowance for each other's faults, and forgive anyone
> who offends you. Remember, the Lord forgave you, so you
> must forgive others.
>
> COLOSSIANS 3:13

Lord Jesus, I see your example of mercy and forgiveness and I am in awe.
Help me to live with the same heart. Amen.

DIFFERENCE MAKER

If you face the easy fall into resentment today, write this phrase on the first piece of paper you can find: *Jesus, help me to forgive.*

IF GOD WANTS

If God wanted to, of course, he could crash into our party and force us to listen. But he would rather get our attention through a gentle whisper. It's God's way of being gentle on our fragile hearts and ears. God's voice of wrath could tear the skin from our bones; his word could completely destroy us. Or God's voice of grace could create us. His breath could mend our tissue back together and his word could give us new life—if he wants.

But do *we* want it? Are we willing to listen to his gentle whisper? If yes, then God will call out gently. If no, then God might eventually need to clap his hands and thunder his voice in our direction.

"Go out and stand before me on the mountain," the LORD told him. And as Elijah stood there, the LORD passed by, and a mighty windstorm hit the mountain. It was such a terrible blast that the rocks were torn loose, but the LORD was not in the wind. After the wind there was an earthquake, but the LORD was not in the earthquake. And after the earthquake there was a fire, but the LORD was not in the fire. And after the fire there was the sound of a gentle whisper.

1 KINGS 19:11–13

Jesus, open my ears to hear you speak. Amen.

DIFFERENCE MAKER

Set aside uncrowded time today to listen for God's voice.

STUPID

Have you ever given a speech that you thought was incredible, only to have the teacher find some things wrong with it? You didn't realize that you had said um twelve times, but the teacher noticed. You thought your opening illustration about the space monkey and the alien was hilarious, but the teacher thought it would have been better if you could have tied it in to your main point somehow. You thought you showed enthusiasm, but your teacher thought you talked too fast.

Being corrected can feel really annoying if you're not looking for it. You might even be tempted to get angry with the one who corrects your mistakes. Maybe you're one of those people who always got a ribbon as a kid, even if you were in last place. Get over it. Learn from someone's discipline. And do even better next time as a result.

To learn, you must love discipline;
it is stupid to hate correction.
PROVERBS 12:1

Dear Jesus, let me find my confidence in you, and be willing to bear the weight of correction in my life. Amen.

DIFFERENCE MAKER

Find someone you trust and whose advice you would like to have in your life, and arrange a time for them to give you some constructive feedback on the plans you have for your life.

July

Jesus,

help me realize all that I could be,

and all that I could do,

with you shepherding my steps.

Amen.

-DOM

A suffix at the end of a lot of words is –dom, which refers to domain or rank. For example, a kingdom is the realm of the king, stardom is the realm of a popular person (a "star"), and boredom is hopefully not the realm you have just entered because of this silly grammatical study.

Freedom is the realm where a person can act or speak without prevention. When someone is free, they can do what they'd like and know that it is good. Freedom is not hedonism, where people choose to ignore the consequences and do whatever *feels* good (only to be forced to deal with their bad decisions later). Rather, freedom is so much better than a temporary suspension of morality. It is being able to walk where you need to go, say what you need to say, laugh when you need to laugh, and cry when you need to cry. Freedom is being able to wander with friends, dine with family, and enjoy what God has made. To enter the domain of freedom, people must follow the Spirit of the Lord. Life lived against the Spirit restricts people's ability to find true fulfillment.

For the Lord is the Spirit, and wherever the Spirit of the Lord is, there is freedom.

2 CORINTHIANS 3:17

Lord Jesus, let me turn to you so that I can walk in freedom with you today. Amen.

DIFFERENCE MAKER

Connect with a friend who is weighed down by his or her bad decisions. Invite them to turn to the Lord and walk in freedom today.

SET FREE

In *The Lord of the Rings*, when Gandalf is stuck and when he is truly in distress, he summons the eagles to come and help him. These aren't ordinary eagles, however. These are massive birds of prey with a forty-foot wingspan that are able to destroy orc armies and carry the heroes off to safety.

The Bible is full of times when God's people summon the Lord for rescue in the midst of distress. For whatever reason, they have found themselves in trouble. Sometimes it was stupid and sinful decisions that got them stuck right where they are, and at other times circumstances beyond their control overwhelm them. Repeatedly, as these individuals cry out to the Lord, they make this note: *And the Lord answered me and set me free.*

We don't always know the details of the distress, nor do we always know the details of the rescue either. The trouble and the escape certainly don't always look like the people expected. But we do know this: God rescues those who call out to him in their time of need.

In my distress I prayed to the LORD,
and the LORD answered me and set me free.

PSALM 118:5

Lord Jesus, I pray to you, and I ask you to please come to my aid when I find myself in trouble. Amen.

DIFFERENCE MAKER

If you get yourself stuck today, instead of trying to dig yourself out, start by praying to the Lord for rescue. Then, while placing yourself in his guidance, look for his path of rescue.

MESSIAH

Hundreds of years before Jesus was born, Isaiah gave a message to the people of Israel. Israel was suffering under the weight of bad decisions and oppressive nations. However, God had good news for them. He would send a Messiah, his Servant, who would restore people to freedom. This messianic Servant-King would focus his rule on healing, forgiveness, and rebuilding a nation that was released from the chains of oppression.

God's idea of a reigning king has always been radically countercultural to the human idea of a king who reigns. God's idea is that a king sacrificially walks in godliness, serves the people, frees them from any form of tyranny, and lifts them up to a status above himself. Ultimately, this was fulfilled in the reign of Jesus Christ, but it is also fulfilled in the way that we serve others through the good news of his kingdom.

> "The Spirit of the Sovereign Lord is upon me,
> for the Lord has anointed me
> to bring good news to the poor.
> He has sent me to comfort the brokenhearted
> and to proclaim that captives will be released
> and prisoners will be freed."
>
> ISAIAH 61:1

Lord Jesus, your concern is that I would share your good news with those who need to know you. Show me how and when to do this today. Amen.

DIFFERENCE MAKER

Ask yourself: Does my daily activity reflect God's good news kingdom mind-set?

FREEDOM

You may notice that the verse in today's entry looks exactly like yesterday's. That is because these words occur in two places in the Bible. The first was taken from Isaiah 61, when Isaiah introduces what the coming Messiah's ministry will be like. The second—today's verse—is taken from Luke 4, when Jesus read the very words from Isaiah 61 in his first sermon.

Jesus read these words in a synagogue gathering. He opened the scroll, read the messianic passage, sat down, and then said, "What you've just heard has been fulfilled this very day." Jesus was making a statement, thereby proclaiming, "This is who I am and this is what I am going to do." As Christians, we follow Jesus, whose purpose was to share refreshingly good news and to proclaim unexpected release, renewal of sight, and the dignity of freedom.

> "The Spirit of the Lord is upon me,
> for he has anointed me to bring Good News to the poor.
> He has sent me to proclaim that captives will be released,
> that the blind will see,
> that the oppressed will be set free."
>
> LUKE 4:18

Jesus, because of your death on the cross, I am unshackled. Thank you for the good news of your freedom. Amen.

DIFFERENCE MAKER

Let off fireworks tonight in celebration of the freedom that comes from the sacrifice of life so that you can be truly free.

SHEPHERD

If you know that Jesus supports your cause, then you can be confident to tackle it full on. With Jesus standing behind you, ready to defend you and poised to refresh you, what have you got to lose? He has already laid down his life for you. He made it clear that he wasn't going to let anything snatch you away from his grip. He has absolutely given his whole self for you. So don't hold back anything from him or from the calling he has broadcast.

Jesus isn't urging you to go forward just because he wants you to follow his example (though he certainly does want you to do that). Jesus wants you to learn to be bold for him. There is no need to stand with trepidation; no need to let fear or timidity slow you down. There is no need to be a "Minnesota Nice" passive-aggressive believer. Jesus is absolutely good! And Jesus is your Shepherd—he is your Good Shepherd. And because he is the one who guides you and protects you, feeds you and grows you, challenges you and restores you, the calling he has given you is yours to pursue.

> "I am the good shepherd. The good shepherd sacrifices his
> life for the sheep."
>
> JOHN 10:11

Jesus, help me realize all that I could be and all that I could do with you shepherding my steps. Amen.

DIFFERENCE MAKER

Do something remarkably good for others today, something that you otherwise wouldn't have done, all because Jesus supports you with his life.

SHEEP

No offense, but you are a sheep. Just a dumb little lamb. Have you ever had a motivational devotional entry tell you that before? You are a wandering, stinky mess of an animal. A simple-minded, ego-headed, fragile-hearted, bleating lamb.

The Lord, though, the Lord…he is your Shepherd. You are so significant that the Lord has chosen to shepherd your flock. Not some two-bit sheep, not some random hired hand, not a nomadic wanderer. The Lord alone shepherds you because he thinks you are worth his very life.

Just listen to what your Shepherd does for you. You don't need anyone or anything other than him. The Lord carries you, cleans you up, feeds you full, protects you, frees you, guides you, leads you, shears you, serves you, nudges you, pokes you, comes beside you, hears you, speaks with you, walks with you, calms you, excites you, instructs you, finds you, gathers you, waters you, mends you, quenches you, rests you, exalts you, lifts you, enjoys you, anoints you, tends to you, offers his life for you, and dwells with you—and he does this for all of your life. The Lord is your Shepherd. And he is so, so good.

> The LORD is my shepherd;
> I have all that I need.
>
> PSALM 23:1

Jesus, help me to live in the truth of this verse today. Amen.

DIFFERENCE MAKER

Avoid the temptation to fill your life with extra stuff today. Every time you are tempted to "need" something else, turn your attention to Jesus instead.

REST

Where is the most restful place you have ever been? A sandy beach, with the lapping waves and warm sun? A recliner chair with an ice-cold glass of lemonade after a busy day? If you were a sheep, your answer would be a green meadow, a gentle warm breeze, and a nearby source of fresh water. A good shepherd would navigate his sheep toward a place like this. The frantic environment of exhaust-spewing vehicles and noise-making appliances and retina-displaying screens and time-rushing schedules is not the proper ecosystem for sheep. Sheep fare better when their rhythm includes intervals of rest.

If a lamb wanders off to create a restful experience without the guidance of the shepherd, however, off-track bets are that the lamb will soon find itself in a precarious predicament. Rest is the one thing that was not created when God made the world. It was simply embedded in the Lord's shepherding rhythm.

He lets me rest in green meadows;
he leads me beside peaceful streams.

PSALM 23:2

Lord Jesus, don't let me lead myself toward my own pursuits today. I want you to lead me toward those things that you desire for me. Let me rest in the knowledge that you are guiding me today. Amen.

DIFFERENCE MAKER

Set aside time in a comfortable place, with a comforting snack, and open up your Bible to Psalm 23 and let it sink into the rhythm of your soul.

GPS

In the old days, people used to unfold road maps over their steering wheels and on their dashboards. Then, in order to figure out where they were going, they would look up at the road, down at the map, up at street signs, down again at the map, up at visual markers, and down at the map again—eventually, hopefully safely, getting to where they needed to go.

Today, of course, things are quite different. Instead of a paper map, we have Siri. On your iPhone you can tell Siri to find the location you need to go and route you there. You merely follow her navigation (or his if you have changed its voice), including instructions to change lanes or to avoid construction. Many times you don't even know for sure that you are being led in the right direction, but you consent to follow Siri because you trust she/he knows where you are going.

Where do you need to go in your life? Siri can only get you so far. But Jesus can get you where you were created to be. Are you willing to let him tell you when to turn or when to take an exit? Do you trust yourself to his guidance, even if you don't always know all the steps to take? If you do, you will be strengthened by his Spirit to pursue your calling.

He renews my strength.
He guides me along right paths,
bringing honor to his name.
PSALM 23:3

Dear Jesus, I trust your steps of guidance for my life today. Help me listen to you.
Amen.

DIFFERENCE MAKER

The next time you use your navigation app, consider how it is a metaphor for how you should follow Jesus' direction for your life.

EVEN THOUGH

If you realize that Jesus is there for you, then you can be there for others who find themselves in need today. Once you recognize the comforting presence of your Savior next to you, it is the natural next step to reach out to someone else with the good news about the Good Shepherd.

Jesus has a deep desire to walk with anyone through even the most difficult of circumstances. He knows how raw real life can be. He knows there is not one person who doesn't walk through dark times. Jesus knows this because he came to walk with, to guide, and to shepherd his people. Once you realize his presence in the hardest of circumstances, you notice that his stride carries strength and his care provides protection. And when your fear dissipates, you want to let others know just how good the Good Shepherd happens to be.

Even when I walk
through the darkest valley,
I will not be afraid,
for you are close beside me.
Your rod and your staff
protect and comfort me.

PSALM 23:4

Jesus, thank you for being with me even though I go through difficult times. Empower me to reveal your presence to others too. Amen.

DIFFERENCE MAKER

Reach out to someone who is struggling today. Find a creative way to let them know that Jesus is ready to walk close beside them, and that so are you.

FEAST

Giordano deep-dish pizza. Lobster saturated in garlic butter. Turkey with thick gravy, potatoes on the side, and delicious stuffing. Slow-cooked barbeque pulled pork. Chipotle steak and queso burrito with corn, cheese, sour cream, and extra guacamole. The freshest Caesar salad you've ever had. Rich marble lava cake drizzled with strawberry cream. An unending chocolate fondue fountain with freshly cut fruit and those cool little wooden skewers. Iced tea and lemonade and cappuccinos. Serving after serving after serving placed in front of you. All of this doesn't even come close to the sort of attention that your Good Shepherd intends to lavish upon you.

You are worth it to Jesus. He wants you to be overwhelmed by his extravagant love today. Let his abundance disturb your comfort zone, shatter your walled-up insecurities, and cover your brokenness. All that has intended harm against you must cease, because your Savior has prepared a meal in your honor.

> You prepare a feast for me
> in the presence of my enemies.
> You honor me by anointing my head with oil.
> My cup overflows with blessings.
>
> PSALM 23:5

Jesus, I don't know what to say, but thank you. Amen.

DIFFERENCE MAKER

Gather the people who are closest to you and share a vibrant feast together. Go overboard with your preparations and planning. Celebrate the life God has given you. And speak about this meal together as a metaphor for the communion Jesus offers all of you.

SURELY

In the old days, when a man fell in love, he courted the woman he wanted to marry—he "pursued" her. This didn't happen in some Neanderthal sort of way, nor in a creepy stalker sort of way. No, no, no, no, no. When a man fell in love, he tried to win the heart of the woman through gentleness, politeness, good intentions, and through proven stability and strength of character. He would have sent her flowers and written her notes (using his actual hand and a pen). He would have sacrificed his own well-being in order to lift up her life and treasure her.

This is the way Jesus pursues us. His goodness and unfailing love go everywhere we go. He tries to catch our attention with his kindness and his grace. He opens doors and prepares opportunities for us to get to know each other better. Because he follows after us in love, we learn to follow after him in love as well.

Surely your goodness and unfailing love will pursue me
all the days of my life,
and I will live in the house of the Lord forever.

PSALM 23:6

Lord Jesus, thank you for pursuing me, a wandering soul.
You have captured my heart. Amen.

DIFFERENCE MAKER

Everywhere you go today, imagine that Jesus is following you, trying to get your attention. Every now and then be sure to pause your activities to allow Jesus to share his life with you.

DOUBT

Is it okay to doubt God? That's a question many people often wonder about. We struggle as humans to completely trust anyone, including God. At times we're not sure God is really watching out for us, or we don't feel God cares about us. Or maybe we wonder why God allows tragedy to happen in our lives or even in the world at large. We are disappointed that God doesn't seem more real. Doubt is normal. But is it okay?

The Bible is filled with doubt. "Heroes" of faith appear to have serious trust issues. Gideon, for one, is a pessimist when it comes to God in his life. The Psalms echo with cries of bewilderment and despair. Martha was agonized that Jesus didn't arrive when she wanted him to. Peter and the disciples fail miserably on more than a few occasions. But is that okay?

Doubt can be a sign that we are trying to work out our faith in real life. For instance, we believe God is there, so we wonder why we don't feel him; we know God is good, so we struggle with all the bad in the world. When our doubt is lifted to God, it reveals our faith. And God honors the heart that trusts its deepest doubts to him.

The father instantly cried out, "I do believe, but help me overcome my unbelief!"

MARK 9:24

Lord Jesus, my faith is not always full, but whatever I have I lift to you. Amen.

DIFFERENCE MAKER

Entrust whatever doubt you have to the Lord in prayer today.

GRIEVE

Too often we are looking for the quick out. When we see someone grieve, we try to make them immediately feel better. Rare is the person who is willing to wait in pain with someone who is actively in pain. It is much too tempting to throw pleasantries and consolations of religion as if they were placebo drugs: "God has a plan for you," "Everything happens for a reason," "It will all be okay," and "Just trust God." Sometimes, one of the worst things we can do is encourage someone to stop grieving. After all, Jesus wept. He wept for Lazarus and his friends. Jesus wept for Jerusalem. He wept sweat from his pores in Gethsemane. Jesus grieved.

Love is the willingness to embrace pain. Yes, it is patient, kind, never failing, and it is not easily angered. Each of those attributes requires an intentional willingness to hurt for someone else. Endurance, perseverance, forgiveness, trust…each takes a purposeful step of entering into pain. Blessed are those who mourn. Love is not weakness; it is strength. We have a strong God who loves us, even in the midst of our pain.

Then Jesus wept. The people who were standing nearby
said, "See how much he loved him!"

JOHN 11:35–36

Lord Jesus, give me the strength to love enough to grieve. Amen.

DIFFERENCE MAKER

Remember a friend who is hurting today. Do something for them to show
that you are by their side in their time of grieving.

HASTY MISTAKES

Have you ever stopped at your local coffee shop for a vanilla skinny latte with extra whip cream, a bit weary eyed from too little sleep the night before, and in line just in front of you was someone you thought you knew? This person had the same hairstyle and the same coat and height as your friend Haley. From a quick glance, it was definitely her. So you said what you would normally say when you see your friend Haley—you said, "Hey, Haley!" But your friend didn't turn around. So then you did what any determined extroverted encourager would do in that situation—you took out your gloves and playfully smacked her in the back. You know, just to say hello. Well, this someone you thought was Haley turned around and looked at you with gaped astonishment. The only thing you could think of saying in the moment was, "Oops. You're not Haley." Real life reveals your deficiencies.

Enthusiasm without knowledge is no good;
haste makes mistakes.

PROVERBS 19:2

Jesus, thank you for loving me through my everyday mistakes. Help me roll with them today, slow myself down, and be more aware of what I'm doing. Amen.

DIFFERENCE MAKER

Take extra effort to take care of yourself today in order to limit your mistakes. Get good rest, eat healthy, don't rush your attitude, and breathe deeply.

WAKE UP

Have you ever wondered how Jesus woke up? Did he startle awake? Did he slowly yawn and stretch out his arms? Did he rub his eyes, grumble his voice, and gruff his shoulders? Do you think he smiled a sly smile, as if he knew something amazing was going to happen? Or do you think he wished he could hit his snooze button a few times?

One time Jesus woke up because he was awakened frantically by his disciples. They were in a boat, and the boat was in the middle of the sea, and the sea was in the middle of a storm. Jesus wasn't worried, however; he was obviously able to get comfortable enough to rest. Maybe he enjoyed the sensation of danger out there on the sea. The Creator of the Universe had the opportunity to ride in his own storm (which would be kind of like the creator of a roller coaster strapping himself in for the thrills). Jesus wasn't shocked by what was going on when he awoke. The chaos didn't overwhelm him. That day, just like any other day, was completely in his control.

> When Jesus woke up, he rebuked the wind and said to the waves, "Silence! Be still!" Suddenly the wind stopped, and there was a great calm. Then he asked them, "Why are you afraid? Do you still have no faith?"
>
> MARK 4:39-40

Jesus, give me even a small dose of your confidence for today. Amen.

DIFFERENCE MAKER

The next time you wake up, trust the circumstances of your day to Jesus.

NO LOBOTOMY

Here's some good news for you: Jesus doesn't want you to have a lobotomy. He's not asking for a turn-your-mind-off kind of commitment. He doesn't want numb faith. He wants you to thoughtfully give him your afraid-ness. If you find yourself in the middle of trouble, he doesn't want you to freak out. Rather, he wants you to think about who he is and where he is and what he is all about.

Even in the midst of the storm, Jesus is with you. He is not afraid, and neither should you be. He is in control, even if you feel like you're the only one trying to bail you out, or even if you feel alone in your struggle against the current. Jesus more often than not will reveal his posture of peace. That's right, in the middle of what is causing you your greatest panic, Jesus is holding himself together. He is amazing. In the end, he may either calm the storm or he may calm you, so in the middle of it you must remember to trust.

> "Don't let your hearts be troubled. Trust in God,
> and trust also in me."
> JOHN 14:1

Lord Jesus, you are the only person who could have genuinely made that statement. I trust myself to you in the middle of my circumstances today. Amen.

DIFFERENCE MAKER

When your stress level starts to rise, remember that Jesus is not panicking. So take a deep breath and walk confidently through it.

STAND IN HISTORY

At important moments of history, when rivers collided and torrents swelled, this world has needed people to take a stand for Jesus. If the opportunity was missed, if people failed to plant their feet, spectators were caught up in the rushing current and swept away. But when the opportunity was seized, when people stood up for what was right, the course of history was stabilized and Jesus brought healing to the scattered.

We are perhaps now at one of those moments. We need people bold enough to position their feet as a rock in the rapids, undeterred and unmoved. Then, with loving arms stretched out wide, we need those bold people to catch others before the pressure sweeps them away. For as soon as people are caught, they are enabled to catch their breath, steady their stance, and join in the rescue effort.

At one of these pivotal moments in history, Jesus asked Peter, "Who do you say I am?" Peter, against the current, stood boldly and unashamedly, and declared, "You are the Messiah, the Son of the living God."

"Now I say to you that you are Peter (which means 'rock'), and upon this rock I will build my church, and all the powers of hell will not conquer it."

MATTHEW 16:18

Jesus, give me the strength to boldly stand for you in this important moment of history. Amen.

DIFFERENCE MAKER

What would it practically look like to stand against the current and for Jesus today?

ETERNITY

If you knew you had the rest of eternity to pursue your goals in life, would it change the sort of goals you would pursue? Think about the long-term goals you have your life. If you had all the time in the universe, would those goals be big enough? If you had every day for thousands and thousands of years, what would usher its way to the top of your long-term priority list?

In the movie *Groundhog Day*, Bill Murray's character, a weatherman named Phil Connors, woke up on the same day over and over again. It has been estimated that Phil repeated the day 12,395 times. At first, Phil lived for himself, setting goals of manipulation and self-service. But then he discovered each time that these goals ultimately left him feeling empty. So, as eternity seemed to set in, he changed his priorities and began to deepen his character and strengthen his ability to help others. When we trust our lives to Jesus, we begin to live our days in light of eternity. And, as a result, our priorities and goals become grand endeavors that truly can change this world.

> For you have been born again, but not to a life that will
> quickly end. Your new life will last forever because it comes
> from the eternal, living word of God.
>
> 1 PETER 1:23

Lord Jesus, make the goals I set in life reflect the eternal life you have given me.
Amen.

DIFFERENCE MAKER

How would you answer the questions in the first paragraph of this devotion? Sit down with a friend today. Bring a pen along. Get out a napkin and begin dreaming big about what sorts of things Jesus might be calling you to do.

HOW YOU LIVE

People don't learn about Jesus just from going to church. In fact, most people learn most about Jesus through everyday, regular-life encounters with his followers. This means that if people regularly go to the grocery store, then they will repeatedly run into followers of Jesus who also naturally go to the grocery store. If people regularly sit down for meals, or spend hours at work, or hang out at community events, or watch a baseball game, it is very likely that followers of Jesus will be there too.

While good behavior at church is noteworthy, it could be argued that it is significantly more important how followers of Jesus live the other six days of the week in the regular routines of everyday life. It makes a difference what kind of words followers of Jesus use on Monday. It matters how they speak about others on Tuesday, how they stand in a checkout line on Wednesday, whether or not they are trustworthy at work on Thursday, how they spend their money on Friday, and if they are reliable as neighbors on Saturday. How we live seven days a week is important.

> Be careful to live properly among your unbelieving neighbors. Then even if they accuse you of doing wrong, they will see your honorable behavior, and they will give honor to God when he judges the world.
>
> 1 PETER 2:12

Dear Jesus, change me every day of the week so that I can draw my neighbors to you. Amen.

DIFFERENCE MAKER

Next time you are not at church but still find that you are with people, consider how important it is to follow Jesus right in that moment.

LIVE DIFFERENTLY

Bashing the reputation of Christians can be a bit too popular in our culture today. They are an easy target. Christians are supposed to exhibit a different standard in society—not in terms of strict rules, but in terms of values and priorities and actions and lifestyle. They are supposed to be different. Almost everyone knows this. Because Jesus was so radically countercultural, so amazingly revolutionary in his bold love and humble authority, it is natural to expect that his followers are to be radical too. So when Christians pretend to be radical like Jesus, but turn out to be hypocritical messes, society rightly gets a bit critical.

The way to avoid the justifiable critique, however, is to actually live differently—not in a way that is removed from and judgmental of society, but in a way that is life breathing in every ordinary and dramatic circumstance of each day. Those who follow Jesus can dismiss public accusations simply by being consistently decent to neighbors, beneficial to their communities, and trustworthy in their words.

It is God's will that your honorable lives should silence those ignorant people who make foolish accusations against you.

1 PETER 2:15

Dear Jesus, let my talk and my walk be so saturated in you today that others will see you in me. Amen.

DIFFERENCE MAKER

Help a neighbor with something today without expecting anything in return.

BEAUTY WITHIN

Try filtering everything you do today through this earth-shattering concept: Who you are on the inside is much more important than who you make yourself to be on the outside.

The modern Western culture spends more money on outward beauty than half the world spends on food. This pursuit of unattainable beauty standards is worthless. Skin will wrinkle, muscle will weaken, and hair will gray. And while it is right and healthy to take care of your body, it is even more valuable to invest in those things that can mature and strengthen over time, such as wisdom and skills, character and reliability, loving relationships and faith in Jesus.

Peter, the brash disciple who lived everything outwardly, eventually grew inwardly mature enough to give some great insight. His words were directed to wives who, because of the culture's wrong standards, tried to impress their husbands in all the wrong ways. Peter's words could apply to most everyone in our society today.

> Don't be concerned about the outward beauty of fancy hairstyles, expensive jewelry, or beautiful clothes. You should clothe yourselves instead with the beauty that comes from within, the unfading beauty of a gentle and quiet spirit, which is so precious to God.
>
> 1 PETER 3:3–4

Dear Jesus, beginning in my heart, transform my life to reflect your beauty. Amen.

DIFFERENCE MAKER

Go a full day without looking in the mirror. Notice how the strong the temptation is to be self-conscious, and how conformed to the addiction of "looks" our society has become.

KEEP CALM AND...

"She gossiped about me! I have every right to spread rumors about her!"

"He cheated on me, so I should be able to get back at him!"

"What did that guy call me? Well, he's just a big $%##^^!"

Just because people do awful things to you doesn't mean you can do awful things in return. Keep calm and respond with gentleness. But in your response be shrewdly aware of the creative way that Jesus would like to work through you. Instead of repaying with retribution, try reimbursing someone's nasty deposit with a blessing. Surprise them in your dignity and graciousness. Don't let their stupidity destroy your dignity. Instead, as you recognize their idiocy, have pity and lift their distorted soul to the Lord. Take the posture of Jesus' blessing from the cross and leave any retribution to the Lord's good judgment.

Don't repay evil for evil. Don't retaliate with insults when people insult you. Instead, pay them back with a blessing. That is what God has called you to do, and he will grant you his blessing.

1 PETER 3:9

Dear Jesus, this is a radical challenge to respond to evil in this world with the power of your goodness. Help me to live in the audacity of your authority today. Amen.

DIFFERENCE MAKER

When you feel anger and retribution welling up within you today, take a breath and pray for the person who has upset you.

ANSWER FOR HOPE

Is hope something you can actually hold? Is it tangible? Would you say that you can grasp enough hope that someone might notice that you have it? Or is hope something that you can't really hold, like a wish-upon-a-star-but-probably-isn't-likely sort of dream? The Bible says Jesus gives actual, relevant, and real hope when you intentionally become more and more defined by him in the everyday raw realities of life.

A real relationship with Jesus actually changes you. People notice that. If someone asked you about your hope, how would you answer? Would you shy away from the question, trying to avoid mentioning Jesus altogether? Would Jesus even come to your mind, or would your "hope" be based on your circumstances? In other words, is hope placed in Jesus or in your longing for things to work out for good (as in, "I have hope because of Jesus" versus "Boy, I really hope I have a good day")? What would you say if you asked these questions?

> Instead, you must worship Christ as Lord of your life. And if someone asks about your hope as a believer, always be ready to explain it.
>
> 1 PETER 3:15

Dear Jesus, increase your hope in me so that I may give it to those who ask me about it. Amen.

DIFFERENCE MAKER

If someone were to ask you, "Where do you get your hope?" what kind of answer would you like to hear yourself say?

GIVE UP BAD STUFF

Even though it might hurt, it is better to give up something harmful than to continue doing it. For instance, cigarettes cause premature aging, constriction of your blood vessels, trachea damage, cost an arm and a leg and a lung or two as well, and they lead to a little thing called cancer. It would be better to go through the misery of giving up smoking than to suffer for the addictive habit. The short-term frustration caused by doing the right thing can be intense, but, in a long-term view, the temporary suffering is well worth the pain.

Following Jesus might cause you some suffering in your life. It may even mean that people will treat you unfairly or speak against you at times. But as a result of your good decision to wholeheartedly follow Jesus, your life will thrive long term in Jesus Christ.

Remember, it is better to suffer for doing good, if that is
what God wants, than to suffer for doing wrong!

1 PETER 3:17

Dear Jesus, let me serve you no matter what it costs; let me stay true no matter what temptations arise. Let others see the hope you give in the everyday realities of life. Amen.

DIFFERENCE MAKER

What bad habit do you keep falling into? Resist that urge today. Instead, as tough as it may be, keep your conscience clear by following Jesus.

THE RIGHT STUFF

One of the greatest things about following Jesus is the difference he makes in your life. And one of the most difficult things about following Jesus is the difference he makes in your life. Jesus gives freedom and he urges restraint. Jesus gives fulfillment and he asks you to give up everything. Jesus gives you a high calling and he asks you to serve others.

This tugging in two opposite directions can be extreme at times, especially for those whose lives were dramatically transformed by Jesus. Some old friends or family might have difficulty understanding why you won't join them in some of your self-serving past activities. Your task, in the face of frustrated friends, is simply to listen to Jesus. He will help restore your spirit. Your calm focus and confident assurance in Jesus will keep you from flinching.

Of course, your former friends are surprised when you no longer plunge into the flood of wild and destructive things they do. So they slander you. But remember that they will have to face God, who stands ready to judge everyone, both the living and the dead.

1 PETER 4:4–5

Dear Jesus, I am tugged in multiple directions. Help me drown out the disruptive noise and stay true to you today. Amen.

DIFFERENCE MAKER

Take time to sit down with either an old friend or a new one and talk about how your life is different now because of Jesus Christ.

YOUR HOME

In his first letter, Peter offers great advice, challenging advice, and some downright oh-man-that-is-really-going-to-change-my-life advice. It was just the sort of advice that enabled the first followers of Jesus to transform the course of history. One piece of advice urged the early Christians to continually offer their homes to others. But, Peter said, don't open up your houses and beds and dinner tables begrudgingly. Don't do it as a "sacrifice" that burdens you. No, share all that you have with joy. Be happy about it. You get the chance to give what you have to someone else. How blessed you are to be able to bless someone else!

The example of early churches changed people. No one had ever seen such an unselfish, unencumbered community before. No one knew that humanity had such an incredible capacity to care for others. As this reality set in, neighborhoods, cities, and nations were turned upside down.

Cheerfully share your home with those who need a meal or
a place to stay.

1 PETER 4:9

Dear Jesus, let the generosity of your heart overflow in me. Amen.

DIFFERENCE MAKER

Do you know anyone who needs a clean bed or a warm meal, new clothes or house supplies, a used vehicle or payment of loans? Think of someone in need today, then share what you can spare.

YOUR GIFTS

If every year every person got every gift, this earth would become a miserably boring and overstuffed planet. Imagine all the Rock 'Em Sock 'Em Robots, Teddy Ruxpins, Bratz Dolls, and Xbox consoles piled up in every spoiled person's closet. If everybody got the same thing, then no one would get anything exceptional.

God blesses people abundantly with uniqueness—each person is gifted differently by God's design. He has the resources to give whatever he wants in whatever quantity and quality he desires. But he selects each gift precisely for each person.

The gifts God has given to you are intentional. He wants you to use your specific gifts so that you can bless others in extraordinary ways. You don't have everything, so you can't boast in arrogance, but you do have something that no one else has. Your mix of talent, passion, experience, context, and timing is unlike the gift mix given to anyone else. And, as a result, God has some very important work he wants you to do.

> God has given each of you a gift from his great variety of
> spiritual gifts. Use them well to serve one another.
>
> 1 PETER 4:10

Dear Jesus, teach me to serve others through my unique gifting. Amen.

DIFFERENCE MAKER

Do something encouraging for others today according to the unique way God has wired you.

YOUR COMMUNITY

Stop. Look at your surroundings for a moment. What do you see? Describe the place where you are. Describe the street you are on, the activity level all around you, and the city where you reside. What kind of environment is it? What are the people there like? Think about all the nuances and noises and neighbors around you right now.

You know, where you are is where you represent Jesus. What a privilege that is. You. *You* get to represent Jesus. And you get to do this by caring for all that is around you. You have the opportunity to cherish God's creation, to treasure the rhythms and culture of families and communities, to uplift your city and celebrate its people. You have the incredible honor of praying for everyone around you. You can pray for blessing, for reconciliation, for restoration and prosperity and peace and joy and freedom and truth and whatever else your loving heart can think to pray. And, as you fill yourself with the practice of loving your neighbors, the Lord Jesus will honor you.

And work for the peace and prosperity of the city where I sent you into exile. Pray to the LORD for it, for its welfare will determine your welfare.

JEREMIAH 29:7

Dear Jesus, I praise you for the people and places of my community. I ask you to care for all of us today. Amen.

DIFFERENCE MAKER

Before you do anything else, stop and pray for God to deeply bless your community.

THE NAME

God's name is too often tossed about like a dirty rag in a garage. If we slam our thumb in the door or if we get some frustrating news, we launch his name into the air like a ballistic missile fueled by our irritation. If someone cuts us off in traffic, we grab the Lord's name and throw it back in reaction. Or if we get a juicy morsel of gossip or some unexpected news, we erupt in a barrage of flippant repetitions of his name. And, sadly, we use various mutations of the name of Jesus—frequently laced with the vulgar power of profanity.

This needs to stop. We wouldn't want our own name discarded in the mud, cast carelessly about, and coupled with cursing. How can we dare do that with God's name then? Importantly, out of the Ten Commandments, God placed the honor of his name as number three. We must not misuse God's name, but rather seek to honor it in all that we do.

You must not misuse the name of the Lord your God.
The Lord will not let you go unpunished if you
misuse his name.

DEUTERONOMY 5:11

Lord Jesus, let me honor your name and, from this day forward,
never take it for granted. Amen.

DIFFERENCE MAKER

Put Deuteronomy 5:11 into action today. Check yourself and gently remind others. As much as you are able, in your presence today, make a difference in how Jesus is talked about.

RESTORATION

You know that day when you had hoped to rest, but instead had to catch up on all the work you neglected to do during the week? You know that test you had to cram for because you procrastinated on studying? By wasting time, you placed yourself in the stressful position of needing to stuff all of your needed work into the final moments of what should have been a rest-filled day. But instead of a day set aside for recuperation, you spoiled it into a day of preoccupation.

The idea of Sabbath, which is taken from the Bible, is that every seventh day people would pause their hectic lives in order to rest and remember what God has done in their lives. But it required that they do a couple things. First, they actually had to live and work for God during the week and, second, they actually had to rest with God on the seventh day. The goal was to set a rhythm in life that would help keep God's people healthy in every area of life. Sabbath was to be a day to *restore* all that was out of whack with the world—a day to rest in relationship with God and to remember all that God had done for them.

Observe the Sabbath day by keeping it holy, as
the LORD your God has commanded you.
DEUTERONOMY 5:12

*Jesus, teach me to live in rhythm with you so that I can find the restoration
I truly crave . Amen.*

DIFFERENCE MAKER

Within the next week, set aside an entire day to restore yourself with God and with others.

MOM AND DAD

Let the following question stir deep feelings within you: What kind of relationship do you have with your mom or your dad? For some people, this is a question that erupts tears of reassurance because they have been loved by their parents and they have deep love and respect for their parents. However, others who hear this question want to hurl and harbor hurt and hatred. This can be such a visceral question because it evokes the deepest victories and vacuums of a person's identity.

God established parents as the key to transfer the hope and love of the Lord to a future generation. Parents who don't follow this call find themselves in a precarious position, not just with their kids but primarily with God. But God also established kids to set an example to their parents. As children grow to know the Lord, one dramatic way they are expected to display God's love is by showing respect and encouragement to their parents. This command isn't so much about whether the parents have raised their children well as much as it is about whether the children will follow God's instructions. This posture of honor for parents ultimately honors God, and, as a result, will have long-term benefits for the child.

Honor your father and mother, as the Lord your God
commanded you. Then you will live a long, full life in the
land the Lord your God is giving you.

DEUTERONOMY 5:16

Dear Jesus, let me learn how to love my parents with your love. Amen.

DIFFERENCE MAKER

Reach out to your mom or dad (or another significant mentor figure in your life) in a way that would meaningfully show them respect, gratitude, and love.

August

Jesus,
Let me dance your steps,
sing your songs,
and see your vision.

Amen.

LAUNDRY

Are your clothes getting stinky this summer? A little bit of BO? Are you the reason that "sweat" pants got their name? For the sake of everyone around you, please keep your laundry fresh. Each day try to wear what is clean, not what is old and crusty. Your socks should not be able to stand on their own. And change that pair of underwear.

In much the same way, the Bible encourages you to keep your attitude and actions fresh. Don't put on lazy heart clothes, with stained grudges, a nasty chip on your shoulder, and frayed emotions on your sleeves. Strip off any of your stinky old perspiring perspectives and instead put on a fresh outlook, washed in Jesus Christ. When you wake up in the morning, the first thing you should do is spray yourself with the eye-awakening fabric softener of Jesus. Then, piece by piece, put on the character and love of your Savior. Those around you will thank you.

Since God chose you to be the holy people he loves, you
must clothe yourselves with tenderhearted mercy, kindness,
humility, gentleness, and patience.

COLOSSIANS 3:12

Dear Jesus, if I could look half as good as you, everyone around me would be changed. Clothe me in who you are today. Amen.

DIFFERENCE MAKER

Want to make a difference in those around you? Do your laundry.
Take a shower. Brush your teeth. Put on fresh clothes.
And when someone asks you why you smell so good,
tell them it's because of Jesus—then see what happens.

TEXTING

Older generations can be confused by things like lol, rofl, or idc. If you add a ;) or >:(to the message, some older brains might not be able to handle the strain.

The early Christians probably would have loved texting. Just imagine all the networking they could have done. People like Paul, Peter, and John wanted to share with others what Jesus was doing in their lives. You can feel their sense of urgency in the New Testament letters. If they could do what you can do, they would have utilized texting and Twitter feeds and Instagram and a whole host of other social media platforms to get their message out to their friends.

Writing letters the old-fashioned way was the closest thing the early church had to texting. They had to use ink and paper (well, papyrus). But they did their best and were very prolific. When God put something passionate and important on their hearts, they couldn't wait to write to their friends about what Jesus was doing in their lives.

We proclaim to you what we ourselves have actually seen and heard so that you may have fellowship with us. And our fellowship is with the Father and with his Son, Jesus Christ. We are writing these things so that you may fully share our joy.

1 JOHN 1:3-4

Jesus, let me use the opportunities I have to share with my friends what you are doing in my life. Amen.

DIFFERENCE MAKER

Using whatever method of communication you want, share with some of your friends what Jesus is doing in your life.

KEEP YOUR WORD

Do you marinate your explanations with all kinds of filler words and excuses? A lot of people soak their answers in mazes of confusion and alibis because they are either too afraid to be honest, too afraid to hurt someone's feelings, or just too afraid to make up their mind. From politicians to puppets, confidence and clarity are rare traits of character these days.

Simply let your yes stand for itself and your no be well defined. Gain your assurance of integrity from your walk with Jesus. Let your words stand firmly in him. Don't compromise your character by pandering to what seems politically correct or presently popular. Don't avoid honesty just to get out of an uncomfortable situation. Make your responses with clarity, your promises with conviction, and your comments with constructive truth and caring fairness. In the long run people will trust you and will seek your wisdom.

"Just say a simple, 'Yes, I will,' or 'No, I won't.'
Anything beyond this is from the evil one."

MATTHEW 5:37

*Lord Jesus, give me clarity to clearly articulate what you want me to say,
and then conviction to back it up. Amen.*

DIFFERENCE MAKER

If someone asks you a direct question today, try answering succinctly and clearly. Give thought and honesty to your words. Don't meander around speaking the truth.

BE GENEROUS

There is a dreaded moment when your buddy asks you, "Can you help me move my things?" You would much rather be lazy—after all, it's a beautiful day for a nap. You've had a somewhat busy week and you were hoping to chill. And if you help, you're just going to get sweaty. And now that you think about it, your back feels a little bit stiff. Your knees suddenly begin to throb. And your pocketbook started crying because your friend probably isn't even going to pay you anything. This is a favor for a friend.

It is too easy to want to say no to someone who could use your help. But think about this for a moment—it usually isn't strangers asking you to come to their rescue; it's those who are close to you. If you truly cannot help, that's one thing, but if you can help and choose not to help, then what does that say about your friendship? Make a simple but remarkable difference in the lives of those around you. If they take the initiative to reach out to you, take the initiative to reach back to them.

> "Give to those who ask, and don't turn away
> from those who want to borrow."
> MATTHEW 5:42

Dear Jesus, help me get off my behind and help others today. Amen.

DIFFERENCE MAKER

As long as it is within your means, practice saying yes
to requests for help today.

BE ANONYMOUS

It's nice when people give to a church or a charity, or when they come to the aid of someone who is in need. But what if they brag about it? How does that make you feel about what they've done? What does that say about their motivation for giving in the first place? What does that reveal about their character?

Because God has allowed someone to have an abundance of possessions, that person should never boast about giving some of them away. Every good gift comes from God. Donations and offerings should be given in humility of heart and with a grace-filled gratitude. Someone who brags about their good deeds demeans those to whom their gifts were given. To puff up one's own grandeur at the expense of another person's dignity ultimately contributes to a continually oppressive cycle. Gifts should be given with a selfless burden to benefit the one who receives. The irony, of course, is that God will know and give honor to the anonymous giver.

But when you give to someone in need, don't let your left
hand know what your right hand is doing. Give your gifts in
private, and your Father, who sees everything, will reward you.
MATTHEW 6:3–4

Jesus, let me trust you for my fulfillment and not seek glory
in my service to others. Amen.

DIFFERENCE MAKER

Make a donation to a ministry without letting anyone else know. Ever.

PRAY LIKE THIS

When Jesus taught his disciples to pray, he gave them an example, almost like a template to follow. When you pray, Jesus modeled, start with your focus on God the Father. Remember who God is and don't take for granted that he holds the universe that holds you. Give honor and respect to his name, a name that is incomparable to all others.

Next, Jesus said, desire what God desires. Filter all of your own thoughts and requests through his will and kingdom. Consider what God wants to have happen in your life and in the world in which you live. Think about what God already is doing and get on board with that. Whatever God desires for his kingdom, desire that for your world, your community, your home, and your life. On earth as it is in heaven.

> "Pray like this:
> Our Father in heaven,
> may your name be kept holy.
> May your Kingdom come soon.
> May your will be done on earth,
> as it is in heaven."
>
> MATTHEW 6:9–10

Dear Jesus, in prayer, let my knee always be bowed to you and my heart always be changed by you. Amen.

DIFFERENCE MAKER

Take time to pray. But this time, focus your prayer simply on God's greatness and God's great desire for the world. After a while, ask him how he wants you to respond.

PRAY GOD'S WAY

If we want something, we should simply ask for it. That's what Jesus told us to do. "How should we pray?" his disciples asked him one day. Jesus said that we are to start our focus on who God is ("Our Father…") and what God wants ("Your will be done"), and then ask away for what we need. When we remember how great God is and how great God's desire for this world is, then we are able to ask for those things that fit with his heart.

God provides for his people, so it is sensible to ask for what is needed today. Dependency on God is a beautiful characteristic. Independence and isolation from God, however, fending for ourselves, only creates a mess. God is gracious, so it is good to ask God to forgive us, even of our most terrible sin. As his heart saturates ours, we can't help but extend that same grace to others. And God is shepherding, so it is perfectly right to honestly put our fears and temptations at his feet and ask for his sheltering strength.

> "Give us today the food we need,
>   and forgive us our sins,
>   as we have forgiven those who sin against us.
> And don't let us yield to temptation,
>   but rescue us from the evil one."
>
> MATTHEW 6:11–13

Dear Jesus, I place myself before you today. Feed me, forgive me, free me. Amen.

DIFFERENCE MAKER

Which aspect of the Lord's Prayer do you most need today?
Pick at least one of these and take time to pray through that request.

DO TO

Do you remember when you felt left out? Or laughed at? Or mistreated? How did this impact your perspective on life? On the other hand, do you remember when you felt invited and welcomed? Or encouraged? Or treated like royalty? How did this impact your perspective on life? The truth is that the way a person is treated can change his or her entire stance in life. If treated harshly, a person is understandably much more likely to develop a negative or despairing outlook. But if treated with dignity, a person is certainly more likely to flourish in their God-given purpose.

The way you treat someone says a lot about you. What erupts out of you reveals what is within you. If you harbor things like apathy or hatred in your soul, then you'll probably act uncaringly toward others. But if you have a love for God and a love for others embedded in your heart, then that is what will overflow in your daily practice, even when times get tough.

"Do to others whatever you would like them to do to you. This is the essence of all that is taught in the law and the prophets."

MATTHEW 7:12

Dear Jesus, fill my heart with your love so that my hands will act with your love. Amen.

DIFFERENCE MAKER

Out of God's love, do something profoundly kind today. For instance, when you get to the drive-through window to pay for your meal, pay for the person behind you as well.

WITH

One of the greatest words in the Bible is the word *with*. Again and again we learn in both the Old Testament and the New that God is *with* his people. Yahweh, the great I AM, is also Immanuel, who is God *with* us. He tells us over and over again throughout the Bible, "I am with you."

This concept of the Lord being so intimate and so near is especially important to the prophet Isaiah. The people of Israel, who at the time had become a scattered and scared nation, needed to know that God was not distant from them. In fact, God spoke, God heard, God loved, God moved, and God dwelt closely. "Everyone!" Isaiah shouted, "listen to what the Lord says! We are not alone! He is with us! So hold fast!" Knowing that God is near makes everything much more bearable.

> "Don't be afraid, for I am with you.
> Don't be discouraged, for I am your God.
> I will strengthen you and help you.
> I will hold you up with my victorious right hand."
>
> ISAIAH 41:10

Dear Jesus, I can be bold today because you are with me. No matter what circumstances I find myself in today, let me dance your steps, sing your songs, and see your vision. Amen.

DIFFERENCE MAKER

Think of a bold action, something that God has been wanting for you or for others but that you have been reluctant to tackle. Knowing that God is with you, take a step in the right direction today.

OVERFLOW

Could God ever be depleted of his resources? How many times can we keep asking for more? If we keep pulling up to God's station to fill up our tanks, will God eventually run out of energy? Will he finally say, "Enough! I can't take the pressure! Please ask somebody else"?

Come on. If God wanted to fill you, don't you think he could? The fact is that he does want to fill you, and he is totally able to do so. In fact, he's got more than you can ever bear. When he fills you up, it's not one of those leave-some-room-in-the-top-so-I-won't-spill sort of fills. No, God fills to overflowing. All of his unending hope, unlimited joy, and unrelenting peace is available in abundance for you. Perhaps the true question is this: Do you want him to fill you?

> I pray that God, the source of hope, will fill you completely
> with joy and peace because you trust in him. Then you will
> overflow with confident hope through the power
> of the Holy Spirit.
>
> ROMANS 15:13

Dear Jesus, I don't want to be empty, and I don't want to be filled with things that will leave me empty. Lord, I want you to fill me with your Spirit. Amen.

DIFFERENCE MAKER

It's summer (unless you are south of the equator!). Go outside and enjoy what God has made. Jesus, who fills the entire creation with his presence, is the same one who fills you with his vast love.

WORDS AND THOUGHTS

What if everything you ever said and everything you ever thought was pleasing to the Lord? Just think for a moment how radically different, for example, yesterday would have been. If every word that coursed through your brain and crossed over your lips was ordained by God's beauty, how would that have changed the direction of your conversations? How would that have impacted what you put your mind to?

Jesus is your rock, but he is also your redeemer. If you are like many people, in the traps of your words and thoughts, it is so easy to forget that he is there for you. Perhaps if your conversations and quiet times were to be saturated in God's patterns, in those things that please his heart, then today will bring a new level of recognition of the Lord's firm presence in your life.

May the words of my mouth
and the meditation of my heart
be pleasing to you,
O LORD, my rock and my redeemer.

PSALM 19:14

*Dear Jesus, throughout this day, may my words and my thoughts
be pleasing to you. Amen.*

DIFFERENCE MAKER

This might feel really annoying at first, but choose one hour today where before you say a word you write the words down. Use this process as a filter for your mouth and your mind, so that everything you say and everything you think will become pleasing to the Lord.

SO MUCH

God wants to be with you so much that he would leave the comforts of heaven to walk with you on earth if he could. Oh wait. He can. And he did! There may not be a greater desire on his heart than to be with you. He wants to talk about news and sports and weather on your way to work. He wants to help you make a sit-down dinner and then throw soapsuds at you when you clean the dishes. He wants to throw a ball in the park and sing you a lullaby at night.

In the Bible, a guy named Zephaniah (Zephy to his mom, maybe), spoke about how God's joy hit its peak when he was with his people. Much like a parent enamored by their first grader in the Christmas concert, or a husband staring into the eyes of his bride on their wedding day, or a soldier who would give his life to save yours, the Lord loves you with an everlasting love.

> For the Lord your God is living among you.
> He is a mighty savior.
> He will take delight in you with gladness.
> With his love, he will calm all your fears.
> He will rejoice over you with joyful songs.
> ZEPHANIAH 3:17

Dear Jesus, thank you for delighting in me. Amen.

DIFFERENCE MAKER

Listen to praise music. Join others in singing. Go for a walk and enjoy what God has made. Whatever way you choose to worship, be sure to celebrate God's heart as he celebrates being with you.

SLOW WORK

The farmer knows how to work hard. Day in. Day through. Day out. Before the sun. During the sun. After the sun. Cold. Hot. Rain. Storm. Winter. Spring. Summer. Fall. It doesn't matter. The farmer works. Many people shy away from this kind of raw, real effort. They'd much rather just spontaneously drive through and buy food: "Ah, yes, I'll have a fast something now. Extra fast. Hold the slow. Oh, and I'll have an apple crisp too."

Throughout the Bible, our life of faith is compared to the slow, intentional process of planting, cultivating, and harvesting. A quick drive-through fix of faith, however, is how many of us tend to treat our walk with God: *Ah, yes, just fix this now, Jesus. Bless me fast. I don't really have time for this to take very long. Oh, and I'll have an apple crisp too.* God is invested in us over the long haul, not for the short term.

So let's not get tired of doing what is good. At just the right time we will reap a harvest of blessing if we don't give up.

GALATIANS 6:9

Dear Jesus, give me a depth of character committed to the long, slow work of faith. Amen.

DIFFERENCE MAKER

Today, as you may have done before, take time to prepare a meal. With each measurement and minute, consider what will result from your labor. Invite people to join you in the harvest of your work. And have a discussion about what it means to follow God day in and day out.

HAPPY

In his hit song "Happy," the pop poet Pharrell Williams sings, "Here come bad news talking this and that. Yeah, give me all you got, don't hold back, because I'm happy." How could he challenge hardship to not hold back? And how could he say he was happy even as bad news talked smack to his face? Is it possible for humanity to glimpse joy even in the midst of frustration and suffering?

Pharrell Williams, whether he intended to or not, touched on an old idea, one that the first followers of Jesus knew well. No matter what circumstances people find themselves in, whether dire or dry or dreaded, Jesus emboldens them to stand strongly with a remarkable joy. People who had been enfolded in the deepest darkness find in Jesus an infusion of light that lifts the heart. God truly does make us joyful despite our circumstances.

Always be full of joy in the Lord. I say it again—rejoice!

PHILIPPIANS 4:4

Dear Jesus, let your joy pierce the shroud around me. I need your light and life. Let my heart smile wider and wider and wider today. Amen.

DIFFERENCE MAKER

Smile. All day. Try it. Smile on your own. Smile with others. Exercise the muscles around the mouth all day long. And every time you do, remember that Jesus is dwelling in you, giving you strength and hope and lighthearted joy. Your cheeks will hurt tomorrow, but it will be worth it.

LET THEM SEE

When a person does what is good, they walk an interesting line. Sometimes the Bible says that good deeds should be done anonymously. After all, the world doesn't need anymore big egos. But at other times, the Bible says that good deeds should be put on display for others to see. This is not to be done in a boasting sort of way, but certainly in a publicly evident way, where attention is drawn to the good action.

What gives? Which is it? Good deeds, yes. But private or public? Well, it seems that sometimes good deeds can be contagious. If someone who respects you, who knows your heart, and who knows your motives, sees you serving others, what might they be likely to do as a result? And when you help people, that can spark something within them to respond in a similar way. Your unselfish actions encourage others to serve unselfishly as well.

Let everyone see that you are considerate in all you do.
Remember, the Lord is coming soon.

PHILIPPIANS 4:5

Dear Jesus, check my heart and kick me into gear. Let your good work in me spur me to serve others. Amen.

DIFFERENCE MAKER

Think of three people in your life and then find three simple ways you can surprise them with encouragement today.

FIX YOUR THOUGHTS

Are your thoughts broken? Do they work? Or do they sputter and smoke? Do they make that turning-the-key-but-the-engine-won't-start-because-the-battery-is-dead sort of grinding noise? Or do your thoughts make that muffler-busting blast that sends people to the ground for cover?

One of the benefits of knowing Jesus is that he is a great mechanic. He doesn't cut corners or swindle you into doing more than you actually need done. If your thoughts haven't been in for a tune-up for quite a while, or if they have gotten bent out of shape, Jesus is your guy. He is honest and tells you clearly what's wrong. Then—and this is the really good part—he can take your broken thoughts and fix them, and he can fix them on what is good.

> And now, dear brothers and sisters, one final thing. Fix your thoughts on what is true, and honorable, and right, and pure, and lovely, and admirable. Think about things that are excellent and worthy of praise.
>
> PHILIPPIANS 4:8

Dear Jesus, don't let my mind keep clogging and seizing up. Free me to focus on what I've been created to consider. Amen.

DIFFERENCE MAKER

Stretch your mind for a moment. What are those things that you should fix your mind upon? Write down at least five things you believe Jesus would like you to be thinking about today.

STRETCH ARMSTRONG

Stretch Armstrong was an elastic plastic wrestling toy whose arms could be pulled and stretched for several feet. And Stretch was supposed to be superstrong. But the sad thing was that Stretch couldn't really do anything. He couldn't actually lift any big object, or stop some bad guy. His stretchy strength was only imaginary. It wasn't real.

Is Jesus like Stretch Armstrong? Some people treat him in the same way. They think he's a great idea, and maybe if he were in a comic book fighting zombies that would make him even cooler. But he doesn't really do anything real, does he? He's a nice thought, yes, but is his strength actually real?

The apostle Paul was certainly convinced his strength was real. After Jesus knocked him to the ground with his mere words, blinded him with his very presence, and then healed him through another person's faith, Paul was forever convinced that Jesus had real power (Acts 9). Later, in a letter about the strength of Jesus, Paul wrote these very words:

> For I can do everything through Christ,
> who gives me strength.
> PHILIPPIANS 4:13

Dear Jesus, because you are truly strong, I can be strengthened to do what you want me to do. Amen.

DIFFERENCE MAKER

Put away your social media and roll up the sleeves of your soul for at least one hour today. Be prayerful and ask, *Jesus, what can I do in your power today?*

SUPPLY

What are you lacking today? Don't think about material things for a moment. What is it that you are missing inside your soul that you so desperately need? Don't think of something that just fills the void for a moment. No overstuffed and stocked-up warehouse could ultimately supply you with everything you actually need. Expand the search within yourself. Dig deeper. What do you lack, and that if you found it, your life wouldn't just be full, your life would be fulfilled?

The most famous psalm of David, Psalm 23, begins with these words: "The LORD is my shepherd, I have all that I need." Jesus famously told the woman at the well in John 4: "Those who drink the water I give will never be thirsty again. It becomes a fresh, bubbling spring within them, giving them eternal life." And having discovered that Jesus was true to his words no matter what circumstances he faced, the apostle Paul later wrote:

> And this same God who takes care of me will supply all your needs from his glorious riches, which have been given to us in Christ Jesus.
>
> PHILIPPIANS 4:19

Dear Jesus, whatever I face today, whether hardships or joys or busyness or rest, I invite you into my life because I really don't need anything else. Amen.

DIFFERENCE MAKER

Write the word *supply* on a piece of paper, then fold it up and put it in your pocket. For the rest of the day, think about what you truly need versus what you would like to have.

GIVE AWAY YOUR FAITH

Faith is not yours; rather, faith is yours to give away. God did not give you your faith so that you could keep it private, never to show it, or shut people out of it. Faith is not something that people have as an individual property right. Yes, faith is personal, but it is relationally personal, not isolationally personal. It is shared. It's not stolen or hidden; it is lived out and given away.

You have been entrusted with the good news of Jesus Christ. He has saved you and he has loved you, he is challenging you and he is calling you to make a difference in this world. He has given you faith in him so that you can give faith to others as well. Inspire people by the way you live out your faith today. Giving away your faith is one of the most important things you can do today.

> You didn't choose me. I chose you. I appointed you to go
> and produce lasting fruit, so that the Father will give you
> whatever you ask for, using my name.
>
> JOHN 15:16

Dear Jesus, thank you for giving me something so wonderful to give to others. Don't let me keep it to myself today. Amen.

DIFFERENCE MAKER

Try sharing your faith with someone else today. Ask Jesus to open the opportunity. Trust him to lead you. And be ready to impact someone with the abundant life produced in you by Jesus.

GET CONNECTED

It's way too easy to be passive about relationships sometimes. It's nice to be noticed and to be loved. It's great when others ask you questions about yourself or celebrate things about you. But if you were to live every day wishing people would do these things for you, life would become a miserable monotony of isolating stress. It doesn't make healthy sense to spend your time getting anxious about others becoming your Facebook friend, or clicking Like on a post, or watching your Vine loops, or retweeting you.

What if you took the initiative to show love toward your friends? What if you were proactive about connecting with others rather than being passive? What if you took the step to ask your friends questions, to celebrate their unique qualities? Over and over again in the Bible, people are encouraged to become risk-takers for the benefit of others. Paul told the Romans, for instance, to use their unique gifts to sincerely connect and serve one another. Followers of Jesus are to set the pace in developing healthy, real relationships.

> Love each other with genuine affection, and take delight in honoring each other.
>
> ROMANS 12:10

Dear Jesus, motivate me to become someone who truly connects with others. Let me take the initiative to be a good friend. Amen.

DIFFERENCE MAKER

Look up ministry groups to get involved in this fall. Do some research and make some plans to get connected.

BE REAL

One of the most impressive things about the Bible is its raw honesty. Even the "heroes" of faith, like Moses, David, and Paul, are real people with real issues and real problems. In fact, their problems are absolutely astonishing at times. Each of these guys was a murderer, each of them had blatant public sins, and each of them had to make dramatic U-turns in life. They all needed Jesus to change them and heal them.

Perhaps you can relate to these guys? Each of them had a "past" that was filled with wrong decisions and regrets. But remarkably, even with all of their baggage, Moses, David, and Paul learned how to follow God. How can this be? God got ahold of Moses and helped him walk with a fire in his heart every night. God relentlessly worked to help David remember the pure-hearted faith of his youth. And God knocked Paul to the ground and used his once-blinded heart to change many people. In the process, each of them learned to be raw and real before God and others. As Paul told some dear Philippian friends of his, no fake celebrities here:

> We are in this struggle together. You have seen my struggle in the past, and you know that I am still in the midst of it.
>
> PHILIPPIANS 1:30

Dear Jesus, knock down the walls I have put up, and let me become a vulnerably honest person. Amen.

DIFFERENCE MAKER

Examine your social media accounts. Do they represent a glamorized version of yourself, or do they reveal the true you?

IMPOVERISHED

This guy had it all together. He was wealthy. He had influence. He was good. He followed God's patterns. Surely he was handsome too. Hollywood producers would have tried to snag him to star in the next season of *The Bachelor*. He was as good a man as there is out there. But he felt like he was lacking something.

When the young man heard Jesus was in town, he went to ask him a question, which was a strange thing to do. Jesus, after all, was not wealthy. He wasn't a businessman. He didn't even own a pillow. And he probably wasn't that great looking. Their conversation went something like this:

"It looks like you've got life and faith all figured out," Jesus told the young man.

"Yes, I know it looks that way, but I'm still missing something. What is it?" the rich man asked.

"Well, you lack what you don't have," Jesus answered. "Nothing. You've got everything, but you're possessed by your possessions. To be truly rich, free your heart to follow me."

Jesus told him, "If you want to be perfect, go and sell all your possessions and give the money to the poor, and you will have treasure in heaven. Then come, follow me."

MATTHEW 19:21

Dear Jesus, let me fill my life with nothing unless it is you. Amen.

DIFFERENCE MAKER

Gather any extra stuff that you've accumulated over the years and drop it off at a local thrift store.

BEING AND SEEING

You are in a privileged role. You get to represent Jesus today. You! In your unique circumstances, with your unique character and gift mix, you can "be" Jesus to others through acts of service. Jesus said that when you follow him, you become part of his body, which is the church. In effect, with the Holy Spirit working through your actions, you become the hands and feet of the Savior.

And not only do you have this great responsibility to "be" Jesus to the world, but you also have the calling to see him in others. Jesus wants you to see where he is, what he is doing, and who he is with. He says over and over again that he is with those who desperately need him. So when you serve people, you are serving Jesus himself. In fact, Jesus identifies himself with the humble and he empowers you to be humble with him. Look for him today. Be with him. And take action with his love.

> "For I was hungry, and you fed me. I was thirsty, and you gave me a drink. I was a stranger, and you invited me into your home. I was naked, and you gave me clothing. I was sick, and you cared for me. I was in prison, and you visited me."
>
> MATTHEW 25:35–36

Dear Jesus, don't let me miss chances to love others today. Amen.

DIFFERENCE MAKER

Think of someone you know who has one of the needs Jesus mentions in Matthew 25:35–36. Figure out a way to serve that person today.

MIRROR

This is a mind-boggling thought: Jesus considers you better than himself. Now certainly you understand, and Jesus understands, that Jesus is greater than you—he will always be greater than you. After all, we know that he created everything that we can see, and even those things we can't see. He is the I AM. He is the Prince of Peace, Almighty God. He holds everything together by the word of his power. In him is life in abundance.

And yet, in his mind, in his sight, he considers you. In his vision, as he moves and acts in this world, is you. Given the choice between saving his own life or saving yours, he would save yours. In fact, that's exactly what he has already done. So how could you, or anyone, keep returning to selfishness? How could anyone still try to impress others as if they think they need to their approval? You already are being lifted up in the loving gaze of the Savior.

Don't be selfish; don't try to impress others. Be humble, thinking of others as better than yourselves. Don't look out only for your own interests, but take an interest in others, too.

PHILIPPIANS 2:3–4

Dear Jesus, forgive me for filling so much of my life with myself. Help me to put others first today. Amen.

DIFFERENCE MAKER

For fifteen minutes, walk around using only a handheld mirror for sight. While doing it, think about how difficult it becomes to navigate through life when you're only looking at yourself.

CITIZENSHIP

In which country does a follower of Jesus most belong? The United States? Canada? Britain? Perhaps Brazil or Argentina? Maybe even China, because there are millions of Christians there. Or how about India? The Philippines? Israel? Egypt? Russia or Ukraine? Perhaps Italy or France or Mexico? Singapore? Hong Kong? Japan? Where should followers of Jesus call home?

How about heaven? What if we were actually strangers in the land, making our home here for a lifetime as landed immigrants? What if we were to invest our time and heart and energy into our local communities and schools and neighborhoods because Jesus wanted us to be his ambassadors representing our true home with him? And what if we began to long for our true home? What if we kept our heart connected to our Savior-King while we carried out the instructions of our current assignment? I think this world would be much different.

But we are citizens of heaven, where the Lord Jesus Christ lives. And we are eagerly waiting for him to return as our Savior.

PHILIPPIANS 3:20

Dear Jesus, don't let me forget that you have adopted me into your kingdom. Remind me to live as a part of your family wherever I happen to be. Amen.

DIFFERENCE MAKER

Write at least two of your local government representatives, thanking them for their service and letting them know that you are praying they will be blessed and they will follow God's character and patterns in their decisions.

ALWAYS PRAY

Some people don't think it makes much of a difference to pray. It would be better, they assume, to actually get something done rather than pray. Prayer, after all, doesn't make much sense in an achievement-based society because it can be difficult to see the immediate outcome of time invested in prayer. It would make more sense, to some people, to be get hands dirty in real "work."

But, lest we're mistaken, prayer *is* hard labor. Prayer gets knees dirty in passionate commitment to God and others. It also gets hearts dirty through love, worries, desires, fears, and joys—through trusting life to God. And prayer also gets movements started. Through prayer God strengthens commitments and raises awareness; he also invites people to join his passion and action already at work in the world.

No one could ever question the action-based mind-set of the apostle Paul. And yet he prayed perhaps more than he did anything else because he wanted so much to participate with what God and his friends were doing in the world. We are to always pray, giving thanks to God—it is worth the time.

We always pray for you, and we give thanks to God, the
Father of our Lord Jesus Christ.

COLOSSIANS 1:3

Dear Jesus, right now I pray for my friends and family, both near and far. Thank you for their investment in my life. Please draw them closer to you and bless them today. Amen.

DIFFERENCE MAKER

Use social media to your advantage today. Scroll through your contacts and stop to pray with thankfulness for people as God gets ahold of your heart.

DON'T STOP PRAYING

There isn't anything magical about prayer. You can't say any special formula that will twist God's arm or trick him into doing what you want him to do. God will never say, "Oh, you got me there. You said the secret password." Prayer is much more simple than that. It's about matching what is on your heart with what's on God's heart. No tricks. Just a relationship.

One of the things that is always on God's heart is his care for people. He's already thinking about others, so he loves it when you lift people up to him in prayer. When you pray for others, you match the very rhythm of God. The apostle Paul was amazing at this. He begins many of his letters with this sort of heartbeat:

> So we have not stopped praying for you since we first heard about you. We ask God to give you complete knowledge of his will and to give you spiritual wisdom and understanding.
>
> COLOSSIANS 1:9

Dear Jesus, I pause everything else right now and ask you to bring to my mind those you would like me to be praying for. Amen.

DIFFERENCE MAKER

In a continued posture of prayer, listen for God's lead as he brings names of people in your life to your mind. Take several minutes to pray for those people right now.

DREAM

On August 28, 1963, over 250,000 people gathered around the reflecting pool by the steps of the Lincoln Memorial. A young preacher named Martin Luther King Jr. stood up and gave what has been considered the greatest speech of the twentieth century.

At one point, with most of his prepared speech completed, Martin Luther King Jr. was beginning to wrap it up. Near him on the stage was an internationally famous gospel singer named Mahalia Jackson. As he was about to finish, she yelled over to him, "Tell them about the dream, Martin! Tell them about the dream!"

Martin, without hesitating, pushed his notes to the side of the podium, stared out to the river of people before him, and with words from Isaiah and prayers from his heart, he began to paint a picture that changed the nation: "I have a dream that one day…"

> Then the glory of the LORD will be revealed,
> and all people will see it together.
> The LORD has spoken!
>
> ISAIAH 40:5

Dear Jesus, may your justice roll through our land, bringing a righteousness that changes my heart toward you. Amen.

DIFFERENCE MAKER

Get online today and watch Martin Luther King's "I Have a Dream" speech. Don't skip a word of it. Let it soak in. (And, if possible, plan a trip to Washington, DC to stand on the very place where this speech was delivered.)

TELL OTHERS

In the first chapter of Colossians, the apostle Paul gives a heartfelt greeting to his friends in Colossae (a town in what is now southwest Turkey), writing about how much he prays for them. He also gives thanks for them because they are a part of the spread of the good news about Jesus "all over the world." And that's a great thing, Paul writes, because Jesus has rescued people from sin. The world needs to know that even though we were once enemies of God, Jesus, the "visible image of the invisible God," "in all of his fullness," made peace through his death on the cross. It's a lot to pack in the first chapter of a small letter! But his point is simple: Because the Colossians were a part of a growing movement that was sharing Jesus with others, many people were developing a life-saving relationship with Jesus.

> So we tell others about Christ, warning everyone and teaching everyone with all the wisdom God has given us. We want to present them to God, perfect in their relationship to Christ.
>
> COLOSSIANS 1:28

Dear Jesus, motivate me to be a part of the vast movement of people, spanning history and geography, who have told the world about you. Thank you for those who shared your life with me. Help me to do the same with others. Amen.

DIFFERENCE MAKER

Tell someone about Jesus today.

TREMBLE?

What are you afraid of? Why do you hesitate? What stops you from doing what you are called by God to do? Is the obstacle confusion, apathy, or perhaps a lack of conviction? Maybe you are tired, or hungry, or upset at someone? Or perhaps you are struggling with a nagging sin? Do you feel alone in pursuing God's call? Are you worried about how people might respond to you?

What are you afraid of? The Lord is flawlessly focused. God is passionate. He restores your verve for life. He fills your soul. The Lord heals your hurt and forgives your sin. He gives you strength to overcome your weaknesses. He offers companionship and invites you to join others in his mission. The Lord reassures you that he will respond to you with joy and blessing, even if others don't. So what are you afraid of? In the Lord's power, live for Jesus today.

> The LORD is my light and my salvation—
> so why should I be afraid?
> The LORD is my fortress, protecting me from danger,
> so why should I tremble?
>
> PSALM 27:1

Dear Jesus, I choose to stand for you today. Amen.

DIFFERENCE MAKER

What are you facing today that causes you concern? What could you do differently knowing that the presence of Jesus is with you?

EYES

You can usually tell when people are afraid or lying or unconfident because their eyes dart all around when speaking to them. It's as if they think they're being followed, or that they're feeling too insecure or too intimidated to look someone in the eyes. Such a lack of focused vision causes people to make mistakes, either intentionally or unintentionally, out of chaos or anxiety.

But those who perseveringly follow Jesus keep steady eyes. A steady gaze on Jesus allows people to notice and absorb his already focused gaze upon them. Their concentration on their Savior teaches them to walk securely in situations that seem impossible to eye rovers. This is the way of Jesus. Eyes secure. Sight enabled. Vision clear. Steps assured.

> Look straight ahead,
> and fix your eyes on what lies before you.
> Mark out a straight path for your feet;
> stay on the safe path.
> Don't get sidetracked;
> keep your feet from following evil.
>
> PROVERBS 4:25–27

Dear Jesus, halt my wandering eyes today. Enable me to steady my gaze on you and in the direction you want me to go. Amen.

DIFFERENCE MAKER

What do you need to do to take the next intentional step in your life to focus on Jesus? Write it down and post it where your eyes will see it throughout the day.

September

Jesus,

I refuse to get lost in the fleeting

experiences of this world.

Amen.

GET TOGETHER

Finding a small group of people to study the Bible with is one of the most important habits you can develop during your lifetime. By meeting with people regularly to focus on Jesus, you'll be encouraged to grow deeper in your faith and make healthy decisions in your life. You'll find people who will support you, care for you, laugh with you, and pray for you. Such a group can become one of those deep gatherings where every word is cherished and treasured, where the surface serves not as a barrier but as an invitation to know what's underneath.

As you head into this fall, be sure to intentionally find such a group. It is too easy to fall into hectic schedules or slip into mundane routines of life that usurp an active relationship with God. Don't let that happen to you. Gather others around you to keep you present in relationship with Jesus Christ.

For where two or three gather together as my followers,
I am there among them.

MATTHEW 18:20

Jesus, thank you for promising to be present with me if I am present with others who follow you too. Let me be an encouragement to a small group of people this fall. Amen.

DIFFERENCE MAKER

Be proactive. Contact local ministries or churches, ask friends who are already plugged in somewhere, or gather some people you trust and ask them to start a small group with you.

GET CONNECTED

The book of Romans is a soaring theological argument. For fifteen chapters, the apostle Paul explains humanity's history with God. He summarizes profound truths with memorable phrases and simple language. He writes things like "we all fall short of God's glorious standard," "for the wages of sin is death, but the free gift of God is eternal life through Christ Jesus our Lord," "nothing can separate us from God's love," and "don't copy the customs of this world, but let God transform you."

With all of this amazing clarity, many people overlook the last chapter. After all, instead of eloquent rhetoric, there is just a bunch of people Paul writes to and about. Dozens by name and hundreds, perhaps thousands, of people by reference. Some were famous (like the apostles), while others were obscure (like Junia, or Nereus and his sister, or Rufus' dear mom). Romans 16 should not be overlooked, however, because in this real-life network of people is the real-life theological truth of Romans. What Paul talks about actually works in the everyday fabric of people's lives. Jesus unites people in a growing network that changes everything in this world.

Greet each other with a sacred kiss. All the churches of
Christ send you their greetings.

ROMANS 16:16

*Jesus, give me the jump start I need to network with others who are
living for Jesus. Amen.*

DIFFERENCE MAKER

Contact a local ministry group so that you get plugged in this fall.

NICKNAME

His real name was Joseph, but the leaders of the early church gave him the nickname Barnabas, which means "Son of Encouragement" (Acts 4:36). This guy, Joseph…*er*, I mean Barnabas, was a Jewish man from the tribe of Levi, and had come to Israel from the island of Cyprus. The book of Acts describes how he had owned a field, had sold it, and had given all of the money to the leaders of the church so it could be distributed to those in need.

Barnabas repeatedly came alongside people who needed support and lavished them with encouragement. Just read the book of Acts and you'll see what I'm referring to. He believed in Paul when no one else did. He raised money for the poor, he advocated for the outcast, and he stood by John Mark. Anybody who knew him could say, "Oh, Joseph? Yeah, he totally gives me courage!" If people who know you gave you a nickname that reflected the way you live, what would that nickname be?

Barnabas was a good man, full of the Holy Spirit and strong in faith. And many people were brought to the Lord.

ACTS 11:24

Dear Jesus, let the way I live today represent what you have gifted me to do. Amen.

DIFFERENCE MAKER

Be proactive about equipping people today. Focus on identifying and affirming their God-given qualities.

KICKOFF

People all around the country are preparing for several months of frenzied worship on Sundays. They're going to fill their coolers, grill their burgers, turn on their TV sets, plop down on couches, froth and scream as their favorite football teams kick off inflated pigskins in packed-out stadiums.

Other people all around the country (some who are also deeply embedded in the category above!) are preparing to launch several months of activities and events designed to bring people closer to God. They're going to fill their kitchens, pray for needs, get their hands dirty, lean on each other, welcome new guests, study the Bible, sing and serve and enjoy the proactive fellowship that comes from people who have been changed by Jesus. This is an answer to the prayer of Jesus that he prayed just before he was arrested and crucified. He wanted his followers to get involved, to get connected, and to change the world through their fellowship.

I am in them and you are in me. May they experience such
perfect unity that the world will know that you sent me and
that you love them as much as you love me.

JOHN 17:23

*Jesus, kick me in gear to get involved in a ministry group this fall. Help me to
follow through with connecting deeply with others who follow you. Amen.*

DIFFERENCE MAKER

Take another step today toward a deeper commitment to a
local ministry group.

SPEAK UP

"What? Did you say something?"

Justice is the process of restoring people to their created relationship with God. Justice fights against whatever it is that unjustly shackles. It gives dignity to those who are being crushed, and it fights for life for those whose lives are being cut off. It lifts up downtrodden souls, forgives the debts of those who have fallen short, and advocates for those who are trapped in unbreakable cycles. Justice gives more hope to those who hope less. It gives voice to shut mouths. It speaks up and lifts up and rises up on behalf of those who are caught in the despair and oppression of this broken world.

But if you act in justice, it will cost you something. In fact, it must cost you something. Justice impoverishes your resources and it disturbs your comfort. Justice takes your effort, your compassion, and your determination. It doesn't take your revenge, your pity, or your charity. Justice takes you. In other words, justice isn't fair—it is love.

Yes, speak up for the poor and helpless,
and see that they get justice.

PROVERBS 31:9

Jesus, let me love. Not for my own sake, but for the sake of others. Amen.

DIFFERENCE MAKER

Whom do you know that needs an advocate today?
Creatively think of a way you could speak up on their behalf.

PRUNE

A prune is a fruit. Or, it was a fruit. Actually, it is (or was?) a plum—a plum which is preserved by being dried and becoming all dark and wrinkly. But to prune is also an act of cutting off parts of a plant that are dead, that aren't producing fruit, or even healthy aspects that the gardener believes will be better for the life of the plant in the long run. A gardener decides to remove a branch or bud so that the plant can flourish in times to come. Pruning something like a grapevine requires specialized attention so that it can become more abundantly fruitful.

Jesus promises that those who want to follow God will go through the pruning process too. God wants his people to become fully what he intends. You can try to be a prune and fight against getting pruned or you can let Jesus prune away in your life so that you can produce more prunes. Or something like that. Jesus said it so much better when he was talking to his disciples.

> "I am the true grapevine, and my Father is the gardener. He cuts off every branch of mine that doesn't produce fruit, and he prunes the branches that do bear fruit so they will produce even more."
>
> JOHN 15:1–2

Jesus, remove those things from my life that keep me from becoming all you created me to be, and from doing all you created me to do. Amen.

DIFFERENCE MAKER

Buy a bonsai tree, learn how to care for it and prune it, and keep it in your room all fall and winter as a reminder of the difference God makes in your life.

REMAIN

Imagine that your relationship with Jesus is fastened together with duct tape—you hold his hand and you both strap that magical silvery gluey adhesive around your wrists. As long as you are fastened to Jesus, whatever you do begins to produce abundance in your life. Your ugly habits begin to disappear because you are securely connected to Jesus who sanctifies you, and your beautiful habits begin to flourish because you are being grafted into Jesus who nourishes you.

Imagine, however, what would happen if you decided to loosen the tape just enough to slip out of relationship with Jesus—just for a moment here and another moment there. Not for good, of course. At least, not at first. It's just that those ugly old habits are so alluring at times. *Just a minute, Jesus. I'll be back soon.*

Remain in me, and I will remain in you. For a branch cannot
produce fruit if it is severed from the vine, and you cannot
be fruitful unless you remain in me.

JOHN 15:4

Jesus, don't let me slip away. Tighten our relationship today. Amen.

DIFFERENCE MAKER

Wrap a piece of duct tape around your wrist or finger (not too tightly!).
Wear it as a reminder today to be in close relationship with Jesus.

FRUIT

Fruit maker—that's what you are. You are a producer of fruit. Fresh fruit; the kind of fruit that people love and pick up at the grocery store, examine, and bring home; the kind of fruit that people crave, like a beautiful strawberry or a delicious orange. You are a producer of the kind of fruit, you know, where one a day keeps the doctor away; the kind of fruit that restores a quenched soul, like a watermelon on a warm summer day. You produce the kind of fruit that, when planted, seeds a harvest of fruit into others.

The way you produce fruit, of course, is through abiding in Jesus. He delights in giving you everything you need to make a refreshing impact on others. So reach deeply toward Jesus today. Rely upon him for your nourishment, your resources, your rest, your stretching, and your productivity. Trust him today with your interactions, schedules, and dreams, and he will yield magnificent results through you.

> When you produce much fruit, you are my true disciples.
> This brings great glory to my Father.
>
> JOHN 15:8

Jesus, I am yours. Produce in me the abundant fruit of a deep relationship in you. Amen.

DIFFERENCE MAKER

Buy some fruit from the store and offer it to friends today. Use this simple offering as a reminder to stay close to Jesus and to let him produce life change in you and through you.

JESUS HAD YOU IN MIND

Jesus had you in mind. Right before he was arrested and crucified, Jesus had a strategic time of prayer. He and his disciples had finished their Last Supper and walked to the garden of Gethsemane. Jesus spent his time in the garden praying. He prayed for his disciples, who were about to get scared and scattered. And he also prayed for you.

In his prayer, Jesus looked forward to the day when you would be tested as his follower. Would you run and fall, like the disciples would later that night? Would you be restored and empowered to spread his good news, just as the disciples soon would? Jesus prayed in the garden for you—he had you in mind. He prayed that you would stand close to him so that the world would be changed through you.

> "I am praying not only for these disciples but also for all who will ever believe in me through their message. I pray that they will all be one, just as you and I are one—as you are in me, Father, and I am in you. And may they be in us so that the world will believe you sent me."
>
> JOHN 17:20–21

Jesus, thank you for praying for me. May your prayer be true today. Amen.

DIFFERENCE MAKER

Be intimate with Jesus through a dedicated time of prayer and reading the Bible, and then share his message with someone today.

SO MUCH MORE

We haven't begun to understand all that Jesus has done or all that he will yet do. The Bible only begins to reveal the great works he performed, the great love he shared, and the great hope he restored. Healings and miracles, signs and wonders. He fed, he healed, and he walked on water. Oh, and he created everything. Jesus is a pretty big deal.

So much more—that's what Jesus did. So much more. He did more than could be written about. He did more than his followers would ever be able to explain or share. So much more. That's what Jesus will do for you and for me. So much more. Our greatest desires for change in this world are but a scratch of what Jesus has envisioned. John, his closest follower, who wrote down so much that we know about Jesus, said it so simply toward the end of his book.

The disciples saw Jesus do many other miraculous signs in addition to the ones recorded in this book.

JOHN 20:30

Jesus, there is so much more to you than I know. Let my eyes be full of wonder. Let me see more of your miraculous works in action today. Amen.

DIFFERENCE MAKER

Pray and look. Pray for the miraculous work of Jesus in the lives of others. Remember all that he has already done and look expectantly for what he will do today.

9/11

It is the beauty of that day that adds shock. The eternally brilliant blue sky was broken by the sudden strike of horror. How can a day so beautifully clear be clouded with such darkness? The mechanics of death, moving across the highest reaches of the sky, drew hell to earth.

God's presence stands in stark contrast to the visceral hate-filled nature of evil. God runs to the disarray, concerned for his earth, fighting through the smoke, embracing the hurting, carrying the fallen, paying honor and restoring dignity to those stripped of life; he is weeping with those in fear, mourning with those in loss, emboldening people with courage, and thus making our hearts alive in the valley of the shadow of death.

> O LORD, I give my life to you.
> I trust in you, my God!
> Do not let me be disgraced,
> or let my enemies rejoice in my defeat.
> No one who trusts in you will ever be disgraced,
> but disgrace comes to those who try to deceive others.
>
> PSALM 25:1–3

Jesus, I remember those lost in the debris caused by evil. I remember those who responded with your courage and love, offering their own lives for the sake of others. I hate evil, Lord. May your brilliance overcome it. Amen.

DIFFERENCE MAKER

Ask some people where they were on this day in 2001. Listen to their stories. And then pray together for Jesus to restore peace to this world.

TRUST, DO, AND THEN...

Trust in the Lord. This was the Lord's number one message to his people. He repeated it over and over again. Trust in the Lord, lean not on your own understanding, rely upon your God. Let him restore you, empower you, and sustain you.

Do good. This was the Lord's second message to his people. Trusting in the Lord led to an overflow of care for others. Doing good in life is a command, but it is actually more of a response too. When people trust God, they are so dramatically changed by his love that they learn to live in God's patterns.

Then, as people trust the Lord and do good, the Lord gives blessing. Communities and nations that learn to do these things become safe and productively fruitful places. Trust in the Lord, do good, and then watch God bless all that is around you.

Trust in the Lord and do good.
Then you will live safely in the land and prosper.

PSALM 37:3

Jesus, help me to do these two things today. Help me trust you with whatever is ahead, with whatever is pressing on my mind and heart. And help me to put others first in all that I do. Amen.

DIFFERENCE MAKER

Practice serving people all day long through acts of politeness and kindness. Trust that the Lord will bless you and others as you serve.

TRAINING

Usain Bolt is the fastest person on the planet. He holds world sprinting records and gold medals. But he didn't become that way overnight. He grew into it. He disciplined himself and the gift he was given. In fact, he has dedicated his entire life to a dramatic training regimen. His workouts are plyometric, meaning he engages in rapid exercises that maximize power in explosive succession. Sounds tiring? Or exhilarating? Both?

Following Jesus asks for a similar type of dedication. Part of the reason for *Make a Difference* is that we need a daily push to practice our faith. We are called to run through this world, spreading the good news and sharing its blessings. We need the determination of Rocky Balboa, mingled with the coaching of Knute Rockne, and the unflinching focus of Jesse Owens. Even as competitors try to defeat us or even take us out, we grow strong in the life of Jesus.

All athletes are disciplined in their training. They do it to win
a prize that will fade away, but we do it for an eternal prize.

1 CORINTHIANS 9:25

Jesus, discipline my routines and my focus so that I can exercise my faith today.
Amen.

DIFFERENCE MAKER

What aspect of your faith feels ill prepared? Whom could you ask to coach
you and strengthen you daily in this area of your life?

ENDURE

Every day you will have opportunity to flail and fall and flop. There will always be chances for you to be sidetracked or sideswiped or blindsided. You can give in yourself or be lured into the snare. Every day. And you are not alone.

You also have the opportunity to stand every day. There will always be chances for you to remain strong in the face of fear, or to resist the trap of temptation. In the throws of an alluring struggle you have the authority to choose freedom. You do not have to relent. You can endure. And you are not alone.

God wants to walk with you and empower you to do what is right. He does not expect it will be easy for you, but he does expect you, just as he expects everyone else, to follow him through every struggle, every day. You can endure with his help and his empowerment.

The temptations in your life are no different from what others experience. And God is faithful. He will not allow the temptation to be more than you can stand. When you are tempted, he will show you a way out so that you can endure.

1 CORINTHIANS 10:13

Jesus, fight by my side today. Show me the way through each trap. Amen.

DIFFERENCE MAKER

You know yourself. What traps are waiting for you today? Identify them by name. Don't let them catch you off guard. How might God be leading you to avoid them or overcome them?

CONSTRUCTIVE

Have you seen those talent shows where the contestant argues with the judges? Even though the person may have just sung completely off key or stumbled through their dance, still they stand there and refuse to accept any avenue for critique.

When someone tells you that you're wrong, and it's clear they're right, how do you handle it? If a teacher corrects your error, do you make excuses? If a friend points out one of your annoying traits, do you point out two of theirs right back? If an expert shows you a better way, or an older person gives you instructions, or a coach tells you to work harder, are you patient and thankful and willing?

Accepting feedback is evidence of godly character. Resisting feedback and reacting negatively to feedback, however, evidences a lack of understanding and maturity. We need to be people who accept feedback in whatever form it comes so we can live looking more and more like Christ.

> If you listen to constructive criticism,
> you will be at home among the wise.
> If you reject discipline, you only harm yourself;
> but if you listen to correction, you grow in understanding.
>
> PROVERBS 15:31–32

Dear Jesus, search me and point out those things in me that need correction or realignment with your will. Amen.

DIFFERENCE MAKER

Take some deep breaths and ask a trusted friend to offer you constructive feedback on a recent project, on an assignment, or perhaps on your leadership skills.

WORK

You've heard the stories, right? Some lucky guy strikes it rich in the state lottery, only to squander it all away carelessly. All of his money didn't stand a chance against all of his spending. What once seemed like an endless supply of resources one day leaked away to nothing.

It's great to have dreams and have passions. It's wonderful to want to travel and play. It's even okay to pray for an unexpected windfall. But, ordinarily, to truly obtain the sort of stable life that puts food on the plate and clothes on the back takes healthy planning and hard work. Food doesn't magically appear on the plate and savings don't miraculously appear in the account. Ask any aging pop-culture child superstar or any one-hit musical wonder. The combination of fantastical consumption mixed with a lazy attitude depletes the reservoirs of life.

A hard worker has plenty of food,
but a person who chases fantasies ends up in poverty.

PROVERBS 28:19

Jesus, kick my butt into gear. Let me become known as a hard worker and a person of character. Amen.

DIFFERENCE MAKER

No procrastination on any projects today. Finish your to-do list before allowing yourself to play.

ALIGN

Do know what happens when the tires on your car get out of alignment? They start to wear unevenly, balding on one side. Then picture a man who went bald on the left side of his scalp but still had full treads on the right side—and then he tried to do that comb-over thing. Not a fabulous look. Okay, mixed metaphors here. Maybe they are not helpful. Back to the tires. When the tires of your car lose their hair on the left side, the car wants to veer you out of your lane even if you try to steer straight.

This wonderful mash-up of metaphors is just like your life with Jesus. If you let yourself get out of alignment with him, two things happen: first, you begin to work harder to keep yourself from veering off the road, and second, even though you try to hold it together, people eventually begin to notice the inconsistency in your life. It's called hypocrisy. And trust me, it's not a fabulous look on anyone.

So we are lying if we say we have fellowship with God but go on living in spiritual darkness; we are not practicing the truth.

1 JOHN 1:6

Jesus, let me be true to you. Align me with your Spirit. Amen.

DIFFERENCE MAKER

Where is your lifestyle out of alignment with your faith? Take one deliberate step to practice integrity in your life today.

DE-JUICE

Did you ever see *Willy Wonka and the Chocolate Factory*? Remember the kid who turns into a blueberry? Her name was Violet Beauregard. Violet was addicted to chewing gum. Oh, dear.

When Mr. Wonka reveals a new type of gum in his inventing room, Violet can't contain herself. The gum serves as a full meal, complete with different courses of meat and dessert. Mr. Wonka instructs that the gum isn't ready for humans yet, but Violet snatches the gum and plops it in her mouth. Once she begins to taste the blueberry pie, her skin turns indigo and she begins to swell into an enormous blueberry. To save her, Violet needs to be de-juiced.

Well, in a way, Jesus offers to de-juice us. We've snatched what never belonged to us, we are paying the horrendous price of that sin, and we need to be rescued before we explode.

But if we confess our sins to him, he is faithful and just to forgive us our sins and to cleanse us from all wickedness.

1 JOHN 1:9

Jesus, I've become swollen with pride and arrogance and harmful habits. Forgive me and restore me to what you created me to be. Amen.

DIFFERENCE MAKER

Whatever sin you have been holding onto, let it go today. Confess your sin to Jesus and accept his forgiveness in its place.

NO COVER

When you were a kid and did something wrong, it is likely that at some point you ran to your room and buried yourself under the covers. Your deprived and depraved thinking process was that if you couldn't see out, perhaps your parents couldn't see in. You were covered. Or so you thought.

There is an old adage: "Everyone eventually gets caught." Sin, in whatever form, eventually undermines your life. It sneaks up and snatches control of you. It can slowly erode your willpower to do what is right, and, if you try to hide, it can twist your perception of truth. No amount of covering actually conceals your sin.

The irony of covering up wrongs, of course, is that the crime committer always knows—and God always knows too. It is never a secret to everyone. The best way to deal with sin is to expose it. Be honest with God, yourself, and others. Fess up. Change your heart. And let God uncover you in a shower of mercy.

People who conceal their sins will not prosper,
but if they confess and turn from them, they will receive mercy.
PROVERBS 28:13

Jesus, no more hiding. I am right here. And I admit you can see me. Amen.

DIFFERENCE MAKER

Confession is not easy. But if there is any concealed sin in your life, turn it over to God right now and take steps to gain freedom from it today.

THE WORLD OFFERS...

Take a look at all your stuff. Then take a look at your schedule. Then take a look at your goals and then take a look at your wish list. What have you added to your heart that complicates your simple walk with God or with others? What have you tied yourself to? What anchors have you purchased?

Today might be the day when you choose to let go, quit stressing, quit filling, and quit consuming. The options will still be there. The tractor beam of the next great item or opportunity will still pull on you and try to suck you into its vortex. The question is whether you will let yourself be induced into those things rather than motivating yourself to pursue Jesus. Don't let the fragmented shards of society trick you. They are but a broken image of what is good. Gaining more fragments gives you less room to thirst for God.

Do not love this world nor the things it offers you,
for when you love the world, you do not have the love
of the Father in you.

1 JOHN 2:15

Jesus, give me discernment to choose what is good from your perspective.
Help me to stop pursuing all the offerings of the world, and instead
to pursue you alone. Amen.

DIFFERENCE MAKER

Ask someone to sit down with you and help you prioritize your
commitments, contents, and calling.

...TOO MANY CHOICES

You've consumed too much and now you're are hovering over the bowl to belch, burp, and barf. You say, "But there was so much to take in! So many desirable things!" *Belch.* "There were just so many options!" *Burp.* "How could I say no to things that make me feel so good?" *Barf.*

Um, have you seen yourself lately? You don't look like you actually feel so good. You had a craving for pleasure, but you tried to fill it the wrong way. No wonder you turned green with envy and putrid with excess. Gluttony has gotten you nothing but sick. Your stuffed-up life hasn't fulfilled you. You look more like a dog that returns to its vomit even though it can't gratify its true needs (Proverbs 26:11). And, sadly, in the broken crevices of our world, there is a seemingly endless cafeteria of vomit.

For the world offers only a craving for physical pleasure, a craving for everything we see, and pride in our achievements and possessions. These are not from the Father, but are from this world.

1 JOHN 2:16

Jesus, I need you. Why do I keep pursuing other things? I need only you today. Amen.

DIFFERENCE MAKER

Whatever empty thing to which you would normally return to today, resist it. Instead, do something more proactive to bring lasting life to your soul.

GOD OFFERS...

What a day this is. It was made just for you. God created this day as a taste of what you could have forever. He offers you another chance to spend your day living in step with him. He is already knocking on the door of your heart, asking to be vibrantly linked with you in all of your journeys today. Since the day you were born he has had in his mind this day, and every day for the rest of eternity, to spend with you.

Of course, sin would love to derail that everlasting experience. It has tried. Sometimes it even seems like it is withering everything. But you won't let it win out, right? Why would you? Of course you won't. No way. You'll follow hard after Jesus. You'll seek his will for you today. You'll pursue what he has created you to embrace: life forever with him.

And this world is fading away, along with everything
that people crave. But anyone who does what pleases God
will live forever.

1 JOHN 2:17

Jesus, I refuse to get lost in the fleeting experiences of this world. Instead, I choose to be found in everything that is marked by your good, pleasing, and perfect will. Amen.

DIFFERENCE MAKER

Think through your plans and desires for today. Filter out what won't matter in the long run and pursue what will matter.

YOU AND THE HOLY SPIRIT

There is a lot of talk in our culture today about people leaving churches. This isn't true everywhere in the world, but it does seem to be a common theme in our society. You probably know many people who once were a part of a church but who just don't seem to be interested anymore.

The apostle John, as an older man, wrote to followers of Jesus in the first century about the same concerns. He discussed how many people had been leaving churches because they were unwilling to commit to the truth of Jesus. But he counseled those who stayed: "You must remain faithful to what you've been taught." But John wasn't worried because he knew God wasn't worried. God would continue to spread his message and grow his movement around the world. John could see this and he wanted people to know it too. Jesus, after all, had sent his Spirit to encourage, embolden, and employ his people in his mission.

> But you are not like that, for the Holy One has given you his Spirit, and all of you know the truth.
>
> 1 JOHN 2:20

Jesus, fill me with your Spirit so that I may stay true to you. Amen.

DIFFERENCE MAKER

Reconnect with some people you know who were once connected to church with you, but who have, for whatever reason, walked away.

DISCERNMENT

Have you noticed how some older and wiser people don't waste their words? It's as if they have learned to measure what they say in order to have maximum impact with their message.

When the apostle John chose to write a letter to the early Christians, he didn't want to waste words either. As an older person, he wanted his "children" to live freely in the eternal truth of Jesus and not get caught up in the trends of culture that ebb and flow throughout history. He wasn't going to throw away words and ink and papyrus on people who weren't going to listen. He knew that these early followers of Jesus would be strengthened by his message.

How do you receive advice and encouragement from older people in your life? Are there some experienced people in your life who have wisdom to share with you? How are you going to make time to listen to them today?

So I am writing to you not because you don't know the truth
but because you know the difference between truth and lies.

1 JOHN 2:21

Lord Jesus, thank you for the wisdom and guidance of those who have led the way for me in faith. Amen.

DIFFERENCE MAKER

Connect with an older person who know you has some wisdom to pass on to you. Consider asking him or her to become a mentor to you in life and in faith.

VIGILANT

Are you vigilant? Like a dog sniffing the air and scanning the horizon, are you on the lookout? Some people keep falling into the same traps over and over again. They repeatedly walk into the same pitfalls and perils, each time just as surprised as the last. *How did this happen?* or *Why do I keep doing this?* become common mantras. For some reason they just haven't learned to notice the signals, to scout the land, and ready the defenses.

Are you like that? Do you get caught unaware, even though you knew trouble was brewing, or you knew the temptation was coming, or you knew someone would try to undermine your purity, your message, your good work, or your success? You're shrewder than that, right? This world needs you to be. Don't give in to apathy only to be jolted upright by failure. Don't give in to a reactionary life, surprised by the perils that find their way to you. Be ready. Be strong. Be close to Jesus.

I am writing these things to warn you about those who
want to lead you astray.

1 JOHN 2:26

Dear Jesus, help me to outwit any trouble ahead today. Let me be sensitive to your guidance and strength. Amen.

DIFFERENCE MAKER

Scan the day ahead. What potential obstacles might you face? Develop a plan to remain resolute in the things God would have you do today.

BE STRONG AND COURAGEOUS

"Remember that time when Jesus healed the demoniac? I was so scared by that guy. And that time when he told the authorities they were hypocrites? They wanted to kill us, which might have been even scarier," one disciple said.

"Which time was that? He did that almost every day," some of them replied.

Another disciple said, "I was even more afraid when he fed the thousands of people with virtually nothing. Every time I passed the basket I trembled under the weight of all the food. Then there was that storm. He just stood up and told it to shut up. I was thinking, 'Who is this guy?'"

"Heyguys,howaboutwhenIwalkedonwater?Ha!Ibetyouwetyourtunics," Peter teased.

"We did! We soaked them. But so did you, Peter, when you got scared and sank."

"Yes, that's true. But he saved me, didn't he? I guess I've learned to fear him much more than anything else in this world."

> This is my command—be strong and courageous! Do not be afraid or discouraged. For the LORD your God is with you wherever you go.
>
> JOSHUA 1:9

Jesus, you are more powerful and more present and more amazing than anything or anyone. Let me walk courageously today. Amen.

DIFFERENCE MAKER

Name an action God has put on your heart that you know will be a blessing to others. Knowing that Jesus is with you, pursue it today.

NO LONGER I

We know, in the hindsight of the resurrection, that the crucifixion of Jesus is beautiful terror…or terrible beauty. It wasn't just the beatings—as wretched as they were. Nor the insults—as hideous as they were. And it wasn't even the nails—as horribly awful as they were. It was also the asphyxiation. The very breath that Jesus gave to us at the creation of the world, stolen from him. He couldn't keep leveraging his legs to push himself up enough to catch air in his lungs. And still he mustered enough strength, swallowed more pride than all of humanity combined, and spoke out those resoundingly refreshing words, "Father, forgive them."

> My old self has been crucified with Christ. It is no longer I who live, but Christ lives in me. So I live in this earthly body by trusting in the Son of God, who loved me and gave himself for me.
>
> GALATIANS 2:20

Jesus, just as you gave your life for me, I give my life for you. As I am stretched out and lifted up, may people be drawn to you, and may they find forgiveness and peace, salvation and hope. I trust you to lovingly lead others to life through me today. Amen.

DIFFERENCE MAKER

Speak to some people today about the hope of the cross. As you risk your pride and comfort, invite them into deeper relationship with God through the loving work of Jesus.

THE PLANS

What a special day this is. A day uniquely set aside for you to follow the Lord. A day when your steps can be placed on his path. A day when you won't need to fear what will be. This day, and all the days to come, are in God's hands. He knows what will happen and he knows what won't happen.

You are incredibly precious to the Lord. He sees his own reflection in your eyes. He hears his own rhythm in your heart. He made you to be with him for the rest of eternity. He has done and will do everything necessary to be with you. While you may not comprehend all that he does, embrace the good that the Lord has for you. Cherish the challenge to trust yourself completely to him today.

> "For I know the plans I have for you," says the LORD.
> "They are plans for good and not for disaster,
> to give you a future and a hope."
>
> JEREMIAH 29:11

Lord Jesus, thank you. I trust myself to your plans today. Amen.

DIFFERENCE MAKER

This verse was written to the scattered people of Israel during their exile under King Nebuchadnezzar. In their circumstance, they struggled to see how the Lord was planning good for them. Where do you struggle to see God's good plan in your own life? How can you reconcile this with the Lord's promise?

ACCIDENTAL WORDS

It happens in slow motion. You can sense your lips separating, feel your muscles forming, and hear the sounds emerge from your vocal cords, and still you can't stop the words from screeching out of your mouth, through the red light, and into the intersection. The accident caused by your words ruins relationships, opportunities, cooperation, and even hope. The debris of your words can shatter people and can be a mess that others need to clean up.

One of the best impacts you could have on this world is to learn when to speak and what to say when you actually do speak. Those who speak with right words and right timing speak life. But those who speak with harmful words and harmful timing speak only ruin.

Jesus was a master with his words. He is even called the Word by the apostle John. Jesus spoke everything into existence, and he speaks truth even now into your heart and mine. He responded wisely in tricky circumstances, gently in heated moments, and truthfully in the face of sin. He knew just what to say and how to say it so that people would be able to discover God.

Those who control their tongue will have a long life;
opening your mouth can ruin everything.

PROVERBS 13:3

Jesus, give me your words and prompt me when to use them. Don't let my mouth get in the way. Amen.

DIFFERENCE MAKER

Challenge yourself to not speak unless necessary today. Practice going through the day only saying those things you believe Jesus would want you to say.

HOTHEAD

Hothead. Jesus was never called this, but Peter was. Certainly. He was ready to retaliate, to take a swipe at someone if necessary. But Jesus told everyone to put away their swords. Chill out, Peter. Calm down, Andrew. James, that's enough. Take it easy now.

Jesus had passion. Buckets of it. But somehow he was able to harness this passion into effective action rather than ineffective anger. Even as the rulers plotted against him, as the mobs rejected him, as the disciples slept while he wept, Jesus never lost his cool.

His holiness was at his fingertips. His wrath at his disposal. His creative and destructive capability within the sound of his summons. But he kept them sheathed. He would only use it when needed against those who would dare try to stop his eternal plan. He would only let it simmer when people were oppressed from finding him. His anger was only and ever righteous. And it was under his control.

People with understanding control their anger;
a hot temper shows great foolishness.
PROVERBS 14:29

Lord Jesus, make me like you. My temper has done more to destroy relationships than to create them. Forgive me and help me wisely control my anger today. Amen.

DIFFERENCE MAKER

Try taking ten long, slow, deep breaths anytime you get fired up today. As you breathe, pray for God's control in your life.

October

Jesus,

Every good thing comes from you.

Produce good things in me so that I can be an

encouragement to others.

Amen.

AUTUMN HOPE

October 1 is another one of those wrong-side-of-history days for the Chicago Cubs. In game three of the 1932 World Series, the Yankees had come to Wrigley Field. Babe Ruth was being ridiculed by some Cubs players, so he famously (or infamously?) pointed to the bleachers, took his stance, waited for the pitch from Chicago's Charlie Root, swung, and hit the ball to deep center. Home run. The Cubs, who hadn't won a World Series since 1908, had lost once again. For Cubs fans, though, there is always a chance. Once more the autumn games will come, and once more the Cubs will win. Eventually. Right?

The Psalms tell us to look ahead to the future, to what God will do. Don't get lost in the calamities that have happened, because God will restore all things. He proves it each year by the seasons. Just as the leaves change colors, just as the weather brings rich moisture, so he will bring blessing to his people. And maybe, just maybe, the Cubs will win a World Series again.

Rejoice, you people of Jerusalem!
Rejoice in the LORD your God!
For the rain he sends demonstrates his faithfulness.
Once more the autumn rains will come,
as well as the rains of spring.

JOEL 2:23

Jesus, let me trust your promises to your people. Amen.

DIFFERENCE MAKER

Root, root, root for the Cubbies. Or gather some friends and make plans in a few weeks to rake leaves for people who could use some hope.

HOW TO BE A FOOL

Here is a time-tested way to guarantee foolishness: Don't ever learn anything. Just refuse to do it. If someone corrects you, reject their input. If a teacher marks an answer as wrong, just get mad and blame him. If a police officer tells you to use your blinker, just go ahead and swear up a blinkin' storm and tell her you're no longer going to pay taxes. If a friend offers you some constructive feedback, tell him to shove it.

In John 21, when Jesus corrected Peter, it wasn't a comfortable scenario by any means. But Peter had begun to learn. His foolhardy tendencies were (mostly) behind him. He was ready to discipline his life according to the patterns of Jesus. In other words, he was ready to be a learner of Jesus, for a disciple is a learner (they are the same word in the New Testament).

People who accept discipline are on the pathway to life,
but those who ignore correction will go astray.
PROVERBS 10:17

Dear Jesus, let me learn you today. Let me absorb your training in my life. Let me not be closed to instruction, but be an approachable, teachable person. Amen.

DIFFERENCE MAKER

Pick an area of your life where you need more discipline. Ask someone to hold you accountable, to correct you when you are wrong, and to help you learn.

SEASONS

The leaves beginning to change color, and summer is gone. The warm days are behind us. Winter is just around the bend. Colder weather is ahead. Fall is the transition.

The Autumn Blaze Maple tree grows to be about fifty feet tall and forty feet wide. It is a beautiful fast-growing, leafy green tree in the summer, providing deep shade. It is strongly resistant to pollution and its robust health helps purify air all around it. It also flourishes in various environments. But in the fall its leaves turn a vibrant orange-red that transforms the landscape.

Many of us try to live our lives without seasons. We'd like to have predictability and safety all year long. But change in us, especially when generated by Jesus, produces brilliant opportunities to change the world in which we live.

For everything there is a season,
a time for every activity under heaven.
A time to be born and a time to die.
A time to plant and a time to harvest.
ECCLESIASTES 3:1–2

Lord Jesus, change me through the seasons of my life so that I might bless others. Amen.

DIFFERENCE MAKER

Gather some friends and spend a day together at a corn maze or a pumpkin farm. Enjoy this month. And let Jesus' work in you give vibrancy to others.

THE GOOD FIGHT

Were you ever told not to fight as a child? Did you know that whoever told you that was wrong? You are supposed to fight at times. You aren't supposed to just let yourself fall apart, and you aren't supposed to just let the world crumble around you. You are supposed to stand up for what is right and repel what harms the people of this planet. You are supposed to join in the struggle, the resistance movement, the revolution that refuses to allow evil to have its way. You are supposed to pick up the weapons of Jesus' powerful grace and mercy and wield his enduring love. You may, at first, find that others are afraid to stand with you or afraid to understand why you take risks to represent Jesus. But hold tight to this calling and don't hesitate to call others to unite with you.

But you, Timothy, are a man of God; so run from all these evil things. Pursue righteousness and a godly life, along with faith, love, perseverance, and gentleness. Fight the good fight for the true faith. Hold tightly to the eternal life to which God has called you, which you have declared so well before many witnesses.

1 TIMOTHY 6:11–12

Jesus, in this world's struggle against good, you fought with an unyielding love. Thank you for inviting me to join you. Amen.

DIFFERENCE MAKER

Find other followers of Jesus and start a weekly prayer meeting for the revival of your community.

MORTALS

So there is water on Mars, eh? It's cool that we found that out. But this is no surprise to God. It's ironic how we can be so proud to discover things that God already knows. It's not truly a discovery, except to us.

It's no different than Columbus "discovering" by accident a "new" land. "North America" and "South America" were already there in 1492. They didn't suddenly appear when Christopher Columbus accidently ran into them. There were already trees and rivers and mountains and animals, and, wait for it, families who made the land their home with farms and livestock and livelihood.

In some ways our "discoveries" reveal more about our limitations than our achievements. The more we find the more we realize the feebleness of our advancement. This is ironic, because it is precisely our desire to steal knowledge that led us to disavow the Creator in the first place. We failed to acknowledge God; will we continue to miss knowing him as well?

When I look at the night sky and see the work of your fingers—
the moon and the stars you set in place—
what are mere mortals that you should think about them,
human beings that you should care for them?

PSALM 8:3–4

Dear Jesus, I fall to my knees as I consider the works of your hands. Amen.

DIFFERENCE MAKER

Go to NASA's website and explore the universe with a posture of humble awe toward our Creator.

FACE TO FACE

It wasn't easy for the early church to connect. Not only were they missing out on Facebook, but they also had little issues of communication to deal with, like, say, an authoritarian Roman Empire threatening to arrest and execute them.

One guy who knew this reality very well was one of Jesus' closest disciples, a man named John. For decades, John himself was displaced as a result of the persecution and scattering of Christians. Yet, even in transition, John was determined to carry on friendships with those he had shared so much of his life with.

In his third letter, he wrote specifically to a friend named Gaius, a name both familiar and strategic in the New Testament. Gaius was a key figure in the spread of the good news about Jesus. And John, somehow now separated from him and distressed by conflict, missed the encouragement of his friend and was determined to see him soon. He wanted to be face to face with him once again.

I have much more to say to you, but I don't want to write it
with pen and ink. For I hope to see you soon, and then we
will talk face to face.

3 JOHN 13–14

Dear Jesus, thank you for the encouraging friends you have placed in my life.
Amen.

DIFFERENCE MAKER

Sit down face-to-face with a friend today, then share the peace of Jesus as you remember old times and old stories together.

SAVIOR

In the middle of the Bible is an important question. At least it's a critical question to those who understand what it means to be in trouble. "I look up to the mountains," the psalmist writes, "where does my help come from?" (Psalm 121:1).

The concept of "salvation" can be difficult to understand for someone who has never felt in need of rescue. People who have lived fairly comfortably postpone discomfort and, as a result, can struggle to comprehend the desperation caused by trouble. It's one reason Jesus said that it's harder for the rich to get into heaven than for a camel to fit through the eye of a needle (Matthew 19:24).

Eventually, though, everyone's constipated comfort gives way to the need to be rescued. Something inevitably breaks through the coziness: sin, evil, sickness, death, or separation from God. Something eventually urges everyone to cry out for Jesus. Those who choose to look up and ask for his help will be saved and shout with joy.

> And they were shouting with a great roar, "Salvation comes from our God who sits on the throne and from the Lamb!"
>
> REVELATION 7:10

Jesus, you are my Savior. Amen.

DIFFERENCE MAKER

If you have never stopped to accept salvation from Jesus, recognize your need and look to him now and ask for it. Then encourage someone else today to look to Jesus for salvation too.

SANCTIFIER

Fruit is best when it is ripe and washed, but fruit that is forced is bitter. Fruit that is infected is sickening and fruit that goes wasted is rotten. I'm sure glad that Jesus produces ripe, clean fruit in you. As you root deeply into him, he prepares his characteristics to emerge from you and have tremendous impact, both in your life and in the lives of those around you. In this way, Jesus changes you and he changes everything every day through you.

Jesus is hard at work in your life. He doesn't just check in with you when you are afraid and call out to him. He checks in with you constantly. He is connected to you. You have infiltrated his heart and he is flowing through you. Allow him to separate you from sin and dedicate you to a new life in him. Allow him to conform you to his Spirit, to be made like him in the way you think and in what you imagine is possible.

And I will give you a new heart, and I will put a new spirit in you. I will take out your stony, stubborn heart and give you a tender, responsive heart. And I will put my Spirit in you so that you will follow my decrees and be careful to obey my regulations.

EZEKIEL 36:26–27

Jesus, as you are producing your good within me and through me, let me be a blessing to others. Amen.

DIFFERENCE MAKER

In trials and temptations, choose not to rely upon yourself. Instead, draw near to God and give the test to him.

HEALER

Jesus came to heal. Our self-dependent culture can overlook that fact sometimes. Jesus came to heal. In just one chapter in Matthew, for instance, he heals a man with leprosy, he heals the paralyzed servant of a centurion, he heals Peter's mother-in-law of her fever (which must have won her son-in-law some brownie points!), he heals many demon-possessed people with a simple command, and he healed many others who were sick. Oh, and, by the way, he calmed a storm.

That's an impressive chapter indeed. And these sorts of miracles weren't out of the ordinary for Jesus. Matthew wanted us to know that this is what Jesus does. "This fulfilled the word of the Lord through the prophet Isaiah," Matthew wrote, "who said, 'He took our sicknesses and removed our diseases'" (Matthew 8:17).

> Then Jesus said to the Roman officer, "Go back home. Because you believed, it has happened." And the young servant was healed that same hour.
>
> MATTHEW 8:13

Jesus, I trust you to restore people to relationship with God. I ask that you would bring healing to my life and use me to bring your healing to others too. Amen.

DIFFERENCE MAKER

Pray to the Lord for healing, either for yourself or for someone you love. Don't be afraid to ask the Lord for what is honestly on your heart. And don't be afraid to gather others to pray with you.

THE COMING KING

J. R. R. Tolkien's third volume in The Lord of the Rings series is called *The Return of the King*. In the story, the prophesied rescuer, Aragorn, returns to the land of Gondor, fights victoriously against evil forces, and is joyously crowned king. As a result, the land is restored, creatures return home, and refreshing peace reigns over the land.

Tolkien's story had Jesus in mind. The prophecies spoke about Jesus' coming to launch his rescue mission, but they also promised he would return to fight an apocalyptic battle to destroy evil and complete his restorative work.

Jesus is called the Alpha and the Omega—the beginning and the end (Revelation 1:8). What he started he will finish. He has promised to return to gather us—all of us—to him once again (John 14:1–3). Having once carried our sin, he has promised to return to save us absolutely and finally from it (Hebrews 9:28). He wants us to watch for him (Matthew 24:44) because he has promised to fight for those who look for him (John 6:39–40).

> Look! He comes with the clouds of heaven.
> And everyone will see him—
> even those who pierced him.
> And all the nations of the world
> will mourn for him.
> Yes! Amen!
>
> REVELATION 1:7

Jesus, when you return, let me not be caught looking for something other than you. Amen.

DIFFERENCE MAKER

Look for Jesus today. Look for glimpses of his coming and anticipate the stirring of his Spirit. Be aware of his work. Don't miss him.

GENEROUS WAYS

Jesus changes lives. It's actually what he's good at doing. And those who are changed by Jesus change lives too. From one person to the next, there is a passing on of Jesus' generosity, life overflowing with life because Jesus has given himself in abundance. Here are just some of the generous ways someone who has been changed by Jesus can live today:

- Leave a 25 percent tip at a restaurant.
- Give a larger than normal offering to a church or nonprofit organization.
- Listen to a friend longer and less distractedly.
- Give assistance to someone who is overwhelmed with a project.
- Tutor a younger person in a subject you can handle pretty well.
- Buy a second meal and give it to someone who is hungry.
- Visit someone who is going through a rough time.
- Spend time encouraging patients in a children's hospital.
- Be the first one to set up and to clean up.
- Look someone in the eyes during a conversation.
- Smile. A lot. Naturally. Let the muscles form and let it happen.
- Volunteer your time on a mission trip, either locally and internationally.
- Mentor teenagers in a local youth group.

The generous will prosper;
those who refresh others will themselves be refreshed.

PROVERBS 11:25

Jesus, you are changing me. Help me to live that way today, letting you work through me to change others. Amen.

DIFFERENCE MAKER

Choose at least one of the generous ways listed above to put into practice.

PLANT IT FORWARD

Those who do good things encourage others to do good things too. It really is a simple formula. One person doing something good leads to another person doing something good, and so on. Before long, good deeds pile upon themselves into an expanding difference-making movement.

Good deed x good deed x good deed = world change.

This really is the regular love-your-neighbor calling of everyone on this planet. A true follower of God is someone who follows the LAW (love, action, walk) of God. It is not about a list of commands, not about a rulebook to be followed, and not about a set of bylaws to implement. Following God involves personally living out God's heart of love, God's patterns of action, and God's walk on this earth alongside others. When people live according to God's good heart and God's good acts, the world is transformed by God one small footstep at a time.

The seeds of good deeds become a tree of life;
a wise person wins friends.

PROVERBS 11:30

Jesus, every good thing comes from you. Produce good things in me so that I can be an encouragement to others. Amen.

DIFFERENCE MAKER

Spend the day doing good things for people. Everywhere you go, intentionally and spontaneously sow kindness into the lives of others so that they can flourish.

CAN YOU SEE?

Stop and hear this. The Lord cares deeply for those who have lost the most basic of human abilities. It surprises many people to hear that the Old Testament was ahead of its time in terms of promoting access and respect for those who were physically disadvantaged. The Lord elevates those with physical disabilities to a high status in society, and he calls others to serve them with honor.

Stop and see this. The Lord himself came to the aid of those with physical limitations. If someone who is deaf is mocked, the Lord takes it personally—very personally. If someone who is blind is ridiculed, God says we are messing with him directly. Jesus himself says that the way we treat people who are in disadvantaged situations is how we treat him (Matthew 25:31–46). He will not stand by idly as we mock, neglect, or create difficulties for those who are less fortunate physically.

> Do not insult the deaf or cause the blind to stumble.
> You must fear your God; I am the LORD.
> LEVITICUS 19:14

Lord Jesus, you came to heal eyes and ears. Help me to honor you by honoring those you deeply care about. Amen.

DIFFERENCE MAKER

Sign up for an introductory course that teaches sign language or braille so that you can better empathize with someone who is deaf or blind.

PLAYING FAVORITES?

Can you see beyond labels? Can you see people for who they truly are? Are you willing to make decisions based on the truth of their heart and their actions? Or will you bend to peer pressure and make decisions based on the winds of culture?

At times the court of opinion favors the wealthy, because there is benefit to the judge and politicians, or to the community, or to the news outlets, or to _____ to have leniency on those with the power of influence. At other times, the court of opinion favors the impoverished, because there is benefit to the judge and politicians, or to the community, or to the news outlets, or to _____ to have leniency on those with the power of critical mass. Jesus doesn't care about whom the court of opinion favors. Jesus judges people according to what they have done and according to how they respond to him.

> Do not twist justice in legal matters by favoring the poor or being partial to the rich and powerful. Always judge people fairly.
>
> LEVITICUS 19:15

Lord Jesus, thank you for dying on the cross for each person, no matter their status in society. Amen.

DIFFERENCE MAKER

Make a plan to attend a public session at the local courthouse. With a prayerful attitude, survey the aspects that seem fair and those that seem biased.

RESPECT AGE

God loves old people. Do you?

He loves their long stories and deeply grained smiles. He loves their rascally outlook and feisty concern for the world. He loves their wrinkles and wisdom and wit. He loves people who have aged like good wine, without whining, of course. He loves those young-hearted warriors who have lived through generations, through wars, through terrors, through economies, through leaders, and they still stay simple and focused on what is right and true.

God seems to believe that someone who has lived a long life has earned the right to be respected. The years haven't always been easy on them. For every ring of the tree they have borne the weight of joys and sorrows, jubilation and loss. Their memories are both sweet and bitter. And the Lord knows every fiber of their being and he loves them with every fiber of his being.

Stand up in the presence of the elderly, and show respect
for the aged. Fear your God. I am the Lord.
LEVITICUS 19:32

Dear Jesus, how can I expect to be respected if I fail to respect those who have come before me. Help me to honor you by honoring those older than me. Amen.

DIFFERENCE MAKER

Do something that shows respect for an older person, such as sending a thank-you note, extending an invitation to lunch, offering to do yard work, going fishing, or simply sitting down for a long conversation.

LEGACY

When Israel's leader Joshua died, a remarkable comment was made. It was said that during his lifetime that the people of Israel "served the Lord." The way that Joshua lived his life encouraged people long after he died to continue following hard after God. He left a remarkably good legacy for the generations to come.

If you could look ahead many years into the future, what kind of legacy would you like to have left on this earth? One way of thinking about this is to consider what kind of words you would like spoken about you at your funeral, or what phrase you'd like written on your epitaph (the message that is etched onto your tombstone). This isn't a morbid thought about death. Rather, it is a proactive thought about your life.

How will you have lived? What stories do you want told? Do you want others to follow in your footsteps? What difference do you want to have made in this world? Living in the light of our legacy should cause us to live for eternity rather than the fleeting pleasures of this world.

> The people of Israel served the LORD throughout the lifetime of Joshua and of the elders who outlived him—those who had personally experienced all that the LORD had done for Israel.
>
> JOSHUA 24:31

Jesus, let my choices today leave a positive impact on others for years to come. Amen.

DIFFERENCE MAKER

Write an epitaph for yourself that you would be proud to have etched on your tombstone.

MIDNIGHT

Paul and Silas healed a slave girl. They healed her! And her masters got upset because they made a lot of money off of her affliction. And because she was now healed, they had lost their ability to profit from her. So the masters grabbed Paul and Silas and incited the authorities against them in the city's marketplace. Because they had disrupted the unjust economic system, a mob formed against them. Paul and Silas were severely beaten and then thrown into prison, where they were chained by their feet to the walls. Then Paul and Silas sang praises to God.

Around midnight Paul and Silas were praying and singing hymns to God, and the other prisoners were listening.

ACTS 16:25

Dear Jesus, I'm not sure that would have been my response in this situation. How were they able to bring themselves to sing praise after being treated so harshly? How were they able to continue praising you publicly? The jailer heard them, the other prisoners heard them, and you heard them. Lord, give me the heart to praise you today. Amen.

DIFFERENCE MAKER

At midnight tonight, gather some people together, read through Acts 16:16–36, and have someone lead in singing praises to the Lord.

CAUSING TROUBLE

Paul and Silas kept traveling and sharing about Jesus. From town to town. The more they shared, the more they seemed to disrupt the economies and political structures of the regions. When they came to a city called Thessalonica, several people, including a lot of prominent women, gave their lives to Jesus. This upset the local marketplace, which relied upon the corrupt worship system in the local temples. So a mob started a riot. They were so angry they attacked the home of a man named Jason, where Paul and Silas had been staying. They dragged Jason to the city council, along with some other Christians, and threatened them with treason against the government. How would you respond in this situation? Would you stand tall in faith and love them, even in the midst of their threats?

> Not finding them there, they dragged out Jason and some of the other believers instead and took them before the city council. "Paul and Silas have caused trouble all over the world," they shouted, "and now they are here disturbing our city, too."
>
> ACTS 17:6

Dear Jesus, I understand that there will be people who reject the good news because it disrupts their habits and desires. This might mean they'll reject me too. Give me courage to stand tall in faith and love, even in the midst of threats. Your gospel turns the world upside down. Use me to make a difference in this world for you. Amen.

DIFFERENCE MAKER

Pray for those who follow Jesus to be loving and bold within their communities.

THEOLOGICAL EYES

Through what lens do you see your culture? Do you notice that the good news of Jesus is embedded in the popular stories of your society? Look with theological eyes for a moment. That great story about human survival is so riveting because God created us to live life eternally. That great song about the heartache of a broken relationship is so true because God created us to live in communion with him and with others.

At one point in his life, the apostle Paul walked around the city of Athens. He could have seen everything wrong with the false system of worship there, but instead, as he observed that culture, he found connection points to share Jesus. We must learn to view our world through the theological eyes of the Lord.

So Paul, standing before the council, addressed them as follows: "Men of Athens, I notice that you are very religious in every way, for as I was walking along I saw your many shrines. And one of your altars had this inscription on it: 'To an Unknown God.' This God, whom you worship without knowing, is the one I'm telling you about."

ACTS 17:22–23

Lord Jesus, thank you for making your message evident throughout the world. Give me eyes to see where your story breaks into the story of others. Amen.

DIFFERENCE MAKER

The next time you watch a popular movie or listen to a popular song, try to find the theological connection points or the gospel story embedded within.

AN EXAMPLE

Mother Teresa didn't call attention to herself. She was just determined to work hard for Jesus on behalf of the poor. As she continued steadily in her humble tasks of caring for those with afflictions, her hard work won her an incredible following. Her example of helping those in need in Calcutta inspired others to launch life-changing efforts to help those in need around the world.

One reason why Christianity spread so rapidly was because the first followers of Jesus led by example in caring for the poor. They worked tirelessly on behalf of widows and orphans. They started movements to support those suffering from famine and they constantly addressed the needs of the afflicted. Through these efforts the world could tell that there was something remarkably genuine and refreshing about those who followed Jesus.

And I have been a constant example of how you can help those
in need by working hard. You should remember the words of the
Lord Jesus: "It is more blessed to give than to receive."

ACTS 20:35

Jesus, you are the ultimate example of how to help those in need. Help me to
follow your lead. Amen.

DIFFERENCE MAKER

Be an example of how to help those in need. Work hard to organize food and clothing drives, after-school youth drop-in programs, or a trip to a local rescue mission or food provider. Set the example so that others will join in.

KNELT DOWN AND PRAYED

Praying with others, especially praying out loud, can be an intimidating experience for many of us. As a result, many of us leave the praying up to someone else, or we just avoid prayer times completely. We might be afraid to say the wrong thing, or say something that sounds stupid, or simply be afraid to say anything at all.

Prayer is indeed a solemn activity, but it is also supposed to be a relational activity as well. Prayer is simply talking with God. And when several people pray together, it is really a group conversation.

When the apostle Paul was preparing for his final big endeavor in life, he shared with some close friends what he thought his plans were going to be. Afterward, through tears and friendship, they got down on their knees and prayed for one another. They didn't worry about what they sounded like or who was better, they simply had a conversation with God together.

When he had finished speaking,
he knelt and prayed with them.

ACTS 20:36

Lord Jesus, give me the courage to pray with people. Amen.

DIFFERENCE MAKER

At certain points today, as you feel led by the Holy Spirit, ask people if you could pray for them and the situations they are facing. If it helps, use the ABCs of praying with others—keep it audible, brief, and Christ centered.

NACHO LIBRE

Many of us struggle with God's calling on our life. We are tempted to think that if God wants something from us, then he'll make the path clear for us. But when we hit fog and gravel, we can grow uncertain about the path God has. Nacho Libre, the Luchadore, found himself wondering about the same thing. (Yes, this is from a movie, and it is a bit cheesy, but be patient with me here.)

At one point, after losing another match in the ring, Nacho grew quite concerned about his calling to wrestle. So first he prayed: "Precious Father, why have you given me this desire to wrestle and then made me such a stinky warrior?" Secondly, he didn't let go of the yearning. No matter what testing he faced, he wouldn't let go of his holy angst to do something for God. This determination, along with the support of his closest friends, refined Nacho's heart. He came to comprehend that God wanted him to serve his calling rather than be served by his calling.

Therefore I, a prisoner for serving the Lord, beg you to lead a
life worthy of your calling, for you have been called by God.

EPHESIANS 4:1

Jesus, let me never give up my pursuit of how you want to use me in this world.
Amen.

DIFFERENCE MAKER

Pray. Then serve your calling from God. What can you do today to pursue
his will in your life?

BETTER THAN A SNOOZE BUTTON

When that alarm goes off, say at 6:15 in the morning, do you hit the snooze button with a bad attitude? Do you ask God to help get your mind in the right frame for the next nine minutes? When the alarm goes off again at 6:24, do you feel any more refreshed than when it went off nine minutes earlier? Did those minutes rid you of your grumpiness? Or do those problems in the world, including your own flaws and festering worries, continue to mock you and make you want to go back to bed?

When that alarm goes off, you may not feel like you are ready for what's ahead, but God believes you can do good work today. All he asks is that you give him your attention. He gave you his Word to help you prepare for your day. Nine minutes in the Bible can be much more effective than hitting the snooze button and getting nine more minutes of sleep.

All Scripture is inspired by God and is useful to teach us what is true and to make us realize what is wrong in our lives. It corrects us when we are wrong and teaches us to do what is right. God uses it to prepare and equip his people to do every good work.

2 TIMOTHY 3:16–17

Jesus, use me to help others by changing me through your Word. Amen.

DIFFERENCE MAKER

Instead of hitting the snooze button tomorrow morning, use those extra nine minutes to read 2 Timothy.

FUTURE GENERATIONS

Psalm 22 is a messianic lament that is intermingled with hope. Even though the writer, David, is going through terror, his song offers a prayer of blessing for future generations. He envisions a time when his generation's unselfish faith and sacrifice will produce abundance among the generations who are yet to come.

The unborn take a place of importance in David's vision. They are, perhaps, the most important generation to be considered in the foundation being established. David foresees that those alive today should consider the practice of faith of those yet to be born. One generation is to equip the faith of the next, who in turn equips the faith of the next, who in turn equips the faith of the next, and so on, for generations to come. David believed that how people respond to their circumstances today impacts how generations not yet born will respond in the future.

Our children will also serve him.
Future generations will hear about the wonders of the Lord.
His righteous acts will be told to those not yet born.
They will hear about everything he has done.

PSALM 22:30–31

Jesus, right before you gave your life on the cross, you had the same attitude when you prayed in the garden for future generations. Amen.

DIFFERENCE MAKER

When you face your next frustrations, consider how your reactions could impact the faith of future generations.

MIGHTY MOWER OF THE YARD

Our world is full of monstrous men who fear nothing other than peace. And to be honest, on the world scene, most of us worry about that. But what if we were to truly trust the words of the Bible? How would our engagement with the world change? Would our actions be driven by faith and hope and love rather than fear? Would we be empowered that in the end God would not allow evil to triumph?

There is nothing in the Bible to interpret as soft or mindless. There is no avoidance of conflict. In fact, conflict and strife are inherent in the raw reality of the words of the Bible. There is, after all, historically and cosmically, a fight launched by principalities who would wreak destruction against the everlasting hand of God. In God's power, we are called to stand against the world's adversaries without buckling our knees.

After all, why should we be afraid? Whose arm of might and justice will prevail? We choose to join sides with the Mighty Mower of the Yard, the Almighty Trimmer of the Flowers.

> Don't worry about the wicked
> or envy those who do wrong.
> For like grass, they soon fade away.
> Like spring flowers, they soon wither.
>
> PSALM 37:1–2

Jesus, give me the courage to trust you today. Amen.

DIFFERENCE MAKER

Take some time to attend to the news today without fear. Instead, pray and give courage to your community through the confidence of God.

TAKE DELIGHT

Take delight in the Lord. Let God be your definer. Let your will be saturated by his. Let what you want be shaped wholly by what God wants. For as you delight in the Lord, the desire of your heart becomes what he wants for your life. When you learn to align your will with his, your desires merge with what God wants to give you. Your hearts delights in what God desires, and God delights in giving you what your heart desires.

Does that mean if you live perfectly in his will that you won't suffer loss or pain today? No, this verse doesn't say that. It doesn't say that if you are good, you will get a big house and live a trouble-free life and be healthy and wealthy. No one should read that into this verse. But if you follow after the Lord, if you do his will and delight in him, then you will receive the desire of your heart: God himself.

Take delight in the LORD,
and he will give you your heart's desires.

PSALM 37:4

Dear Jesus, teach me to want what you want. Amen.

DIFFERENCE MAKER

Stop right now to ask God what he desires for you. And then ask him to make that your desire too.

COMMIT TRUST

Today may not make much sense; in fact, it may be a struggle. We may feel blind to the way God is working and wonder what in the world is going on. Partially because it's so important, and partially because our struggles are so real, the Bible reinforces the instruction to trust in God. As difficult as it may be to maintain that focus, it is what we must do. Our daily actions are to be subjected to the eternal scope of the Lord, not to our short-sighted understandings.

God sees our daily toil. He is aware that division and deviousness in this world detracts from our ability to live fully. He is aware that the sin and destruction of others hinders our own pursuits. God is fully cognizant that things don't always work out the way we want them to work out. So we trust everything we do to him because he is going to use our work to make a difference in the world in which we live.

Commit everything you do to the LORD.
Trust him, and he will help you.
He will make your innocence radiate like the dawn,
and the justice of your cause will shine like the noonday sun.

PSALM 37:5–6

Jesus, every action of mine today is yours to use. Amen.

DIFFERENCE MAKER

Use this question as a filter today: What difference would it make to commit this action to the Lord?

WAIT

Is there anything more difficult than waiting quietly? Probably. But by the way many of us act when we are supposed to be calm and watch time pass by, you would think we we were having a root canal done on our funny bone! (Not really sure what that means, but it sounds really uncomfortable!)

The phrase "good things come to those who wait" is not in the Bible. But it seems like it should be. It is a proverb, probably, that has been used by Heinz ketchup. You can't rush a good thing. Don't count your chickens before they hatch. What did you expect, it's McDonald's? The early bird gets the worm and then gets eaten by the eagle.

We want God's salvation now, our worries to go away now, evil people to be gone now, our families to be blissful now, our health to be perfect now, and money to fall into our lap now. Perhaps we need to chill out right now, in this instant. We cannot afford to wait any longer. But it is good to wait on the Lord.

The LORD is good to those who depend on him,
to those who search for him.
So it is good to wait quietly
for salvation from the LORD.

LAMENTATIONS 3:25–26

Lord Jesus, I struggle to be willing to wait for you to act. Help me to trust you.
Amen.

DIFFERENCE MAKER

Practice waiting today without taking out your phone. Fill the void instead with an active pursuit of God.

TRAIN WRECK

A train wreck disrupts the rhythm of creation at the end of Psalm 104. The psalm is an awe-inspiring ride through the skillful wonder of the earth and sky and oceans. The waters are stretched out like a garment and bursting through the ravines, the mountains erupting, the seas teeming with life, the whales playing games, the lions depending on God, the birds nestled in the trees along the streams, the night active with life, and the day provided for the gathering of food.

And then the train wreck. It's as if the gentle song of creation suddenly hits a dissonant crash. The psalmist is jarred from considering God's wondrous work when the shocking vision of the work of humanity enters into his mind. The writer's mind is suddenly flooded and defiled by the thought. The murders, the wars, the adultery, the profanity, the abuse, the destruction, the lying, the betrayal, the envy, the arrogance—all of this insurrection in stark contrast to the beautiful dance of the planet. The point of the psalm is to refuse to step into the fall of creation, but to instead be reconciled to a waltz with God on the dance floor that he has made.

> May all my thoughts be pleasing to him,
> for I rejoice in the Lord.
> Let all sinners vanish from the face of the earth;
> let the wicked disappear forever.
> Let all that I am praise the Lord.
> Praise the Lord!
>
> PSALM 104:34–35

Jesus, let my steps be in rhythm with yours today. Amen.

DIFFERENCE MAKER

Dance in wonder of what God has made. Hike or drive or just sit marveling at the wonder of creation. And pray for humanity to be restored to God.

PRODUCES GOOD

You can be confident that God will use you to make a difference in this world because he is at work right now making a difference in you. Every time he chisels a sin out of your life, every time he prunes away a fear, every time he molds your faith into shape, the Lord is preparing you. He asks a lot from you because he knows he can empower you. God trusts himself to generate good work through you. God accepts the fact that he is pretty masterful at producing the right results in your life. He is removing anything false in you so that his truth will be brilliantly evident through all you say and do.

For once you were full of darkness, but now you have light from the Lord. So live as people of light! For this light within you produces only what is good and right and true.

EPHESIANS 5:8–9

Jesus, I am yours. Make me as you intend. Amen.

DIFFERENCE MAKER

Buy some Play-Doh and make things out of it all day long. Carry it around and use it as a stress reliever if necessary. And as you shape the dough, consider how the Lord is shaping you into the person he wants you to be so that you can do what he wants you to do.

WHAT TO DO TONIGHT

Some followers of Jesus think we should avoid Halloween because of its flirtation with evil and the busy occult behaviors taking place every October 31. It would be incredibly foolish, these people would say, to open ourselves up to such demonic activity. Other followers of Jesus think we should participate in Halloween because it is the one night of the year when our neighbors are all outside interacting with one another. It would be ironically wrong, these people say, to be the only dark house on the street on Halloween night.

Wherever we fall in the great Halloween debate, our concern should be twofold. First, we should seek to love the Lord in everything we do, and second, we should seek to be a loving light for our neighbors in a darkened world.

> So be careful how you live. Don't live like fools, but like those who are wise. Make the most of every opportunity in these evil days. Don't act thoughtlessly, but understand what the Lord wants you to do.
>
> EPHESIANS 5:15–17

Dear Jesus, give me creativity and discernment as to how to be a loving witness to my friends and neighbors today. Amen.

DIFFERENCE MAKER

Whatever you do tonight, make the most of your opportunity to keep Jesus and your neighbors as the focus of your heart.

November

Jesus,

Help me to use the gifts

you have given me for your glory.

Amen.

SHARING TRUTHS

Why is it that many of us who have long ago left the realm of childhood can learn more from children's messages than all of the hymns and sermons of "big church"? Perhaps this is because children's messages capture the simplistic beauty of Jesus while also drawing us into a more profound life, and adults have an inherent need to share their faith rather than sit on it. Something spectacular happens to people when they see young people come alive with vibrancy of faith and hope and love through Jesus.

Faith should not be reserved to the realm of adulthood. Faith is not ours; rather, it is ours to give. Someone at some point introduced us to a life-changing relationship with God, and now it is our turn to creatively and passionately pass that faith on.

> O my people, listen to my instructions.
> Open your ears to what I am saying,
> for I will speak to you in a parable.
> I will teach you hidden lessons from our past—
> stories we have heard and known,
> stories our ancestors handed down to us.
> We will not hide these truths from our children;
> we will tell the next generation
> about the glorious deeds of the LORD,
> about his power and his mighty wonders.
>
> PSALM 78:1–4

Jesus, if I ever become an old tightwad who is reluctant to share my faith, loosen me up—a lot! Amen.

DIFFERENCE MAKER

Connect with your local church children's ministry director and ask how you can support them (either with time or resources or encouragement).

GENERATIONAL VISION

Broaden your scope today. As you go about your own business, consider the impact that your actions have, not just immediately but for the long term. Consider not just the impact your actions have on you, or on your immediate family or friends, but on those who will come after you.

The scope of vision in the Bible is incredibly forward thinking. When we make our lives only about the here and now, when we make church or faith about the current benefit, we squander the immensity of impact visualized within Scripture. Our faith was meant to impact generations. Those who came before us passed faith down through the generations, and eventually that faith in Jesus was entrusted to us. Now it is our turn to equip those who follow us with faith, so that they not only embrace faith but are enabled to empower the generations after them to follow Jesus too.

> For he issued his laws to Jacob;
> he gave his instructions to Israel.
> He commanded our ancestors
> to teach them to their children,
> so the next generation might know them—
> even the children not yet born—
> and they in turn will teach their own children.
>
> PSALM 78:5–6

Dear Jesus, let my vision of faith never be navel-gazing. Amen.

DIFFERENCE MAKER

Ask yourself this question: Am I helping to equip people in the next generation in such a way that they will be able to pass faith on to the generations that follow them?

SERIOUSLY, DO I HAVE TO?

"That guy absolutely drives me crazy. Why do I need to be patient with him? Why can't I be caring just toward the people I like? Why do I have to show love to people who suck the life out of me?" Because that's what Jesus would have done. In fact, it's what he did. There were days when he was tired, exhausted, exasperated, fed up, weary, lonely, upset, and he still kept serving. He didn't give up being humble and gentle and patient and forgiving, because of his intense love for people.

Jesus isn't calling you to absolutely step into destruction. When he needed restoration, he would step away for lengths of time to find refreshing with God the Father. He often withdrew to solitary places to rest, pray, and be revitalized. Distinguish yourself as a follower of Jesus in the way that you care for others and rely on Jesus to refresh you as you give of yourself.

Always be humble and gentle. Be patient with each other,
making allowance for each other's faults because of your love.

EPHESIANS 4:2

Lord Jesus, in your love you are humble, gentle, patient, and forgiving of me.
Don't let me forget that as I grow weary of others. Amen.

DIFFERENCE MAKER

Think of somebody you struggle to withstand, and take even the smallest
of steps toward extending them a loving attitude today.

ONE...

People in this world seem to understand that followers of Jesus, if they are true, are a united community rather than divided. There is something terribly wrong when Christians tear each other down, rip each other apart, fight publicly, react vehemently, or judge harshly. Jesus states what people all around the globe affirm: "Your love for one another will prove to the world that you are my disciples" (John 13:35).

Jesus draws people to himself, which means those who gather around him are naturally supposed to draw together. Imagine a scene where people gather around Jesus, but in frustration and jealously, in anger and a heated sense of righteousness, they start spewing venomous vocabulary and pummeling each other. We know there is such a thing as heresy of doctrine, but there is also such a thing as heresy of behavior. The church is called the body of Christ for a reason—it should never be dismembered.

> Make every effort to keep yourselves united in the Spirit, binding yourselves together with peace. For there is one body and one Spirit, just as you have been called to one glorious hope for the future.
>
> EPHESIANS 4:3–4

Lord Jesus, enable me to tirelessly build up others who follow you. Let me be an encouragement to your people so that the world will know you are love. Amen.

DIFFERENCE MAKER

Check yourself. If you have spoken or acted inappropriately against another follower of Jesus, take a step toward forgiveness and reconciliation today.

SEND ME

Awe-inducing angels called seraphim (meaning "fiery") gathered around the Lord, who was sitting on a throne. The angels sang, "Holy, holy, holy is the Lord Almighty. The whole earth is filled with his glory!" Their resounding praise shook the foundations of the temple and filled the sanctuary with smoke.

As Isaiah had this vision, he became certain that his destruction was sealed. How could any human stand in the presence of Almighty God? He was overwhelmed. But one of the seraphim flew over to Isaiah and touched his lips with a burning coal, telling him, "Your guilt has been removed. Your sins are forgiven." Then the Lord wanted to know who would share the message.

> Then I heard the Lord asking, "Whom should I send as a
> messenger to this people? Who will go for us?" I said,
> "Here I am. Send me."
>
> ISAIAH 6:8

Lord Jesus, let me have the heart of Isaiah. Overwhelm me with your presence and clean my lips so that I can share your words with others. Amen.

DIFFERENCE MAKER

Spend some time with the Lord, asking him to prepare you and to send you to share the good news of Jesus with those you will see today.

YET

Of the entirety of his creation, God's greatest joy is reserved for his chosen people. For regardless of how much God possesses, and regardless of how broken people become, his most esteemed treasure is humanity.

To Nicodemus, Jesus said, "For this is how God loved the world: He gave his one and only Son, so that everyone who believes in him will not perish but have eternal life" (John 3:16). In other words, people were in a state of perishing, yet because of his deep love for his people God chose to initiate the process by which his people could be reclaimed.

In the whole of the Bible, it is clear that God is holy, yet he has chosen to offer forgiveness to people (Romans 3:23–24). The Psalms resound with wonder as they recognize that creation is so marvelous, yet God gives humankind his utmost affection (Psalm 8:5). Isaiah reveals that humanity has gone astray, yet the Suffering Servant of God will carry humanity's weakness, sorrow, and punishment (Isaiah 53:4–6). The *yet* of God is a wonderful gift indeed.

Look, the highest heavens and the earth and everything in it all belong to the Lord your God. Yet the Lord chose your ancestors as the objects of his love. And he chose you, their descendants, above all other nations, as is evident today.

DEUTERONOMY 10:14–15

Jesus, I am a sinner and yet you love me. Thank you! Amen.

DIFFERENCE MAKER

Take a few moments and allow yourself to be overcome by the yet of God. Give thanks for his amazing love that is found in Christ Jesus.

(IN)FORMATION

Information gives us control. We access information, we search for it, and that information gives us power. Because we live in an information-driven world, we tend to open the Bible for information, like some archaic magical Google. We look for information about God, about life, about faith, about a decision, about parenting, about work, about _____.

The Bible wasn't written to fill our heads with information, however. It's true that within its pages the Bible contains some interesting and helpful material. But even more than solid information, the Word of God is focused on our formation as God's people. The Bible exists so that we can be shaped and transformed and empowered by God.

> Have you never heard?
> Have you never understood?
> The LORD is the everlasting God,
> the Creator of all the earth.
> He never grows weak or weary.
> No one can measure the depths of his understanding.
> He gives power to the weak and strength to the powerless.
> Even youths will become weak and tired,
> and young men will fall in exhaustion.
> But those who trust in the LORD will find new strength.
> They will soar high on wings like eagles.
> They will run and not grow weary.
> They will walk and not faint.

ISAIAH 40:28–31

Jesus, change me through your Word. Amen.

DIFFERENCE MAKER

Read prayerfully through these verses from Isaiah a few times.
As you do so, ask God how he would like to form you today.

PRAY FOR YOUR LEADERS

This is the time of year when politicians seek your vote. As you sift your way through the myriad of sound bites for streams of truth, you are considering electing leaders who will make a significant impact in the lives of millions of people. That's a big deal. So your vote makes a tremendous difference. Elections have consequences.

It is essential, no matter how you feel about a leader, to pray before voting for him or her. Pray for the nation and pray for its leaders. The push to pray for healthy and safe governance has always been a prevailing perspective for followers of Jesus.

I urge you, first of all, to pray for all people. Ask God to help them; intercede on their behalf, and give thanks for them. Pray this way for kings and all who are in authority so that we can live peaceful and quiet lives marked by godliness and dignity. This is good and pleases God our Savior, who wants everyone to be saved and to understand the truth.

1 TIMOTHY 2:1–4

Jesus, encourage me to use the energy that I put into complaining about elected leaders toward praying for my leaders. Amen.

DIFFERENCE MAKER

If this is a voting year, be sure to vote. Be sure to support and pray for candidates who will champion your ability to peacefully follow God's patterns.

LIVING ROOM

Your soul is a living room. It is not a storage closet or a garage. It's not a garbage bin or an attic. Your soul is where you invite God to make himself at home.

Imagine if Jesus walked in and sat down among all the clutter, in the midst of stains, crumbs, filth, dust, and the garbage you'd been putting into your soul. And before you could protest, Jesus gets the vacuum out, the carpet cleaner, the dust rag, and the window cleaner, and he repairs the rip in the couch and throws away the trash and puts his Word out on the coffee table. And then he sits down on the sofa and puts his feet up with a smile. *Ah.*

That's when you ask your guest, "Um, can I do anything for you, God? What have you been up to lately?" And that's when Jesus tells you all about his life, what he does for fun, his relationships around the world. And Jesus asks you about your life, and you share a laugh together, you invite others to come in genuinely, you revel in songs of joy, and you play vintage Super Nintendo because it was the best video game console ever. Your soul is the living room where Jesus wants to take up residence.

> Jesus replied, "All who love me will do what I say. My Father will love them, and we will come and make our home with each of them."
>
> JOHN 14:23

Jesus, please come in and make your home in my soul. Amen.

DIFFERENCE MAKER

Clean up your physical residence today. As you do, think about Jesus making himself at home in you.

WALK OF DISCOVERY

Jesus wants to walk with us and talk with us so that we can discover who he is. There is no greater way to change everything in our lives than to spend time in personal conversation with him.

On the Sunday of the resurrection, two of Jesus' followers were walking about seven miles outside of Jerusalem. He suddenly caught up to them, but he kept them from realizing who he was at first. "You seem to be having a deep conversation," he said to them.

"You must be the only person who hasn't heard what happened the last few days!" they replied. And they went on to describe to Jesus how they thought he was the Messiah but the rulers had executed him. Then they shared how his body was no longer in the tomb, and how angels declared that Jesus was alive.

Jesus responded in disbelief at their confusion. "This shouldn't surprise you!" he said. "Wasn't it clearly predicted that the Messiah would have to suffer all these things before he entered his glory?"

> Then Jesus took them through the writings of Moses and all
> the prophets, explaining from all the Scriptures the things
> concerning himself.
>
> LUKE 24:27

Lord Jesus, would you give me just a taste of that conversation? Walk with me intimately today, unveiling my eyes to see you and my ears to hear you. Amen.

DIFFERENCE MAKER

Get together with some other followers of Jesus and investigate what Jesus might have said on this walk.

LOOK AT WHAT
GOD LOOKS AT

We love looking at good-looking people. We elevate the glamorous, we celebrate the stylish, we exalt the pretty face, and we spend a lot of time and energy and money on cosmetics. As Billy Crystal's old character, Frenando, used to say, "Yooouuuu look marvelous! And it's better to look good than to feel good, you know what I'm saying to you, darling?"

The world has bought into this ideology for a long time. Three thousand years ago, Israel was searching for a king. The Lord told the prophet Samuel to anoint a king from the family of Jesse, a shepherd from Bethlehem. As Jesse's oldest son, Eliab, was presented to Samuel, the prophet was convinced he had the "looks" of the next king. But the Lord gave Samuel a bit of a rebuke. For God sees things differently than we are initially inclined to see. The Lord is concerned about something other than good looks—he cares about our hearts.

> But the Lord said to Samuel, "Don't judge by his appearance
> or height, for I have rejected him. The Lord doesn't see
> things the way you see them. People judge by outward
> appearance, but the Lord looks at the heart."
>
> 1 SAMUEL 16:7

Lord Jesus, help me care more about my relationship with you and my heart for others than a shallow approach to life. Amen.

DIFFERENCE MAKER

Don't take a selfie for the entire next week. Instead, take pictures that highlight others doing good things (would that be called an "otherie"?).

YOU CAN DO MORE THAN YOU THINK

It was remarkable for David, a teenager, to slay Goliath. It wasn't just how he did it, with a slingshot and a rock, but also *that* he did it. The fate of an entire nation was in his arm. But this wasn't the first time David had done the remarkable. He had already killed lions and bears that had tried to attack his sheep. He had already been anointed as the next king, and he had the guts to stand up to the current one face-to-face.

David, as a young man, also managed the family business. When he was instructed by his dad to bring supplies to his brothers at the battle lines, David had the authority to put another employee in charge while he was away. Perhaps our society doesn't champion young people enough? Perhaps we don't challenge ourselves enough either? We can do more than we think we can do, especially if God is with us.

So David left the sheep with another shepherd and set out early the next morning with the gifts, as Jesse had directed him. He arrived at the camp just as the Israelite army was leaving for the battlefield with shouts and battle cries.

1 SAMUEL 17:20

Jesus, challenge me to step up my level of responsibility and action. Don't let me listen to the lies that young people are not ready to do great things. Amen.

DIFFERENCE MAKER

Tackle a higher-level responsibility today that you had not yet felt encouraged to do.

STEALING COMPLIMENTS

It is a sad reality of our culture that those who consistently do the best work often don't get the recognition they deserve. It's like a fun little game called "stealing compliments." You should try it sometime. If someone says, "Oh my, that is a beautiful sunset!" you simply say, "Thank you!" If someone says, "I love the paint color in this restaurant," then you say, "Thanks for noticing." And if someone says, "The Bugatti is the coolest sports car ever," you say, "Thank you. I'm glad you think so."

This is a ridiculous game, of course, because someone else is responsible for the work behind each of those items. Someone else designed that car, painted that restaurant, and someone else created that sky. But it is also ridiculous that our culture takes for granted, or even steals praise from, the effective influence of a person of creative integrity and productive talent. It's as if the fruits of their work are stolen from them. Many of our best and brightest people could use more resources, more acknowledgement, and more encouragement than they are given.

Do not withhold good from those who deserve it
when it's in your power to help them.
PROVERBS 3:27

Jesus, I have often been blind to those around me who deserve my praise. Help me to recognize their work, to invest in their future, and to enthuse their hearts. Amen.

DIFFERENCE MAKER

Celebrate someone who has done good work without much fanfare (like a teacher or a grandparent or a volunteer). Think of a way to honor their trustworthy contributions and to champion their future success.

USE YOUR GIFT

When a basketball player releases a jump shot from the three-point line, giving the ball a perfect arc on the release, and thousands of fans watch the ball swish straight through the hoop, nothing but net, it's one of those moments when everything seems to slow down, harmony and precision combine to form in wonder, and life just seems to make sense. But unless we are mistaken, those moments only come from a player's dedicated commitment to improving their skill over a period of years. Investment. Hard work. Study. And joy.

In his grace, God has given us different gifts for doing certain things well. So if God has given you the ability to prophesy, speak out with as much faith as God has given you. If your gift is serving others, serve them well. If you are a teacher, teach well. If your gift is to encourage others, be encouraging. If it is giving, give generously. If God has given you leadership ability, take the responsibility seriously. And if you have a gift for showing kindness to others, do it gladly.

ROMANS 12:6–8

Jesus, thank you for investing in me. I pray that you will motivate me to invest in improving my skills so that I can use them to make a positive difference in others. Amen.

DIFFERENCE MAKER

What skill set has God gifted you with to use for the benefit of others? What do you need to do, both today and also in the long term, to become even better at it?

YOU NEVER KNOW HOW

Four young men had been displaced by war. They were removed from their homes and relocated to the enemy's capital. They were forced to give up their families, to change their diets, to change their names, and to lose much of their heritage. But they never waivered in what mattered most to them, which was their faithful commitment to the Lord.

Not one of us knows exactly how God will end up using us to impact the world. But he will use us. These four men had every reason (in the world's standards) to let down their guard and let go of their pursuit of God. Instead, they dedicated themselves to a life of integrity and character and excellence in the ways that God called them to live.

When the moment came to use their gifts to impact the world around them, they were ready. The enemy king took notice of the outstanding character and skills of these young men. And before long, God used them to change an empire.

God gave these four young men an unusual aptitude for understanding every aspect of literature and wisdom. And God gave Daniel the special ability to interpret the meanings of visions and dreams.

DANIEL 1:17

Jesus, no matter how you choose to do so, prepare me to serve you today. Amen.

DIFFERENCE MAKER

If you were to lose everything else, what would be the one thing that would keep you pursuing the Lord?

EXCEL

Jesus sees your unique role. You are a part of his body, working to bring good change to this world. You have a unique, significant, and strategic role to play in God's mission on this earth. He loves seeing you use the gifts he has given you to make a difference around you for his glory.

The Lord has always gifted people differently so that each person can love him completely and serve others fully according to their unique abilities. When each person draws upon the excellence of the Lord to use their distinctive gifts to serve one another, then the world is built anew.

The Lord has filled Bezalel with the Spirit of God, giving him great wisdom, ability, and expertise in all kinds of crafts. He is a master craftsman, expert in working with gold, silver, and bronze. He is skilled in engraving and mounting gemstones and in carving wood. He is a master at every craft. And the Lord has given both him and Oholiab son of Ahisamach, of the tribe of Dan, the ability to teach their skills to others. The Lord has given them special skills as engravers, designers, embroiderers in blue, purple, and scarlet thread on fine linen cloth, and weavers. They excel as craftsmen and as designers.

EXODUS 35:31–35

Jesus, help me to use the gifts you have given me for your glory. Amen.

DIFFERENCE MAKER

Grab three friends. Together, identify and affirm three unique things that each one of you loves to do really well. Then dream up a mission project you could do together using your gifts.

FIRST

Humility is one of those personal characteristics that is nearly impossible to admit you have. Right? Once you admit it, do you still have it? This is the intentionally tricky logic of Jesus. He is shrewd. He knows that we humans love to be recognized for being great, which really makes us not so great. So he ensnares his followers with a little teaser about humility. "So," he said, "you'd like to be recognized for being great, eh?" (Yes, Jesus can speak Canadian English.) "Well, then just make sure you treat everyone else as if they are greater than you."

The disciples, learning the secret formula to God's great sauce, must have been excited at first. "Aha! Now we'll be greatest in the kingdom of heaven!" Little did they know that by continuing to serve others, by continuing to make themselves "last," the disciples would be transformed. In the persistence of their good service, they would be changed more and more into the likeness of Jesus.

> He sat down, called the twelve disciples over to him, and said, "Whoever wants to be first must take last place and be the servant of everyone else."
>
> MARK 9:35

Jesus, thanks for tricking me into being transformed by you. Amen.

DIFFERENCE MAKER

Serve people today. Open doors. Wash dishes. Clean up messes. Vacuum. Carry things. Sit down and listen. Make eye contact. Don't interrupt. Let others go first in line. Speak up in defense of someone. Give extra help when needed. Serve people today.

GIVE

No one goes to heaven because he or she puts money in the offering plate at church. Giving to church was never about being a "rule" or a price of membership; rather, giving to the assembly of God's people has always been about the attitude of the heart. The Bible talks about tithing, where a person gives back to the Lord a tenth of what the Lord has blessed them with. The Bible also talks about laying down one's whole life for God and for others as a result of all that Jesus has done on our behalf.

At Israel's major annual festivals, the people of God were encouraged to remember the ways that God had blessed them throughout the year. As a sign of gratitude for all of God's blessing, people were to offer a "gift" to the Lord. The gift was to be personal and related to the blessings the Lord had given them. To appear before God without a heart of thanksgiving showed a lack of forethought and respect. We give because he first has given to us.

All must give as they are able, according to the blessings
given to them by the Lord your God.

DEUTERONOMY 16:17

Lord Jesus, help me to pause long enough today to recognize all you have done for me this year. Amen.

DIFFERENCE MAKER

Out of the response of your heart for all Jesus has done, give 10 percent of this month's income to your local church.

GREET WELL

Whassup! How we greet each other says a lot about how we think about each other. The way that the writers of the New Testament greet people reveals an incredible attitude of blessing. Focusing on how to greet well is a good way to enter these winter months when some people tend to retreat and hibernate. Greeting people well prioritizes our hearts, gets us out of our shells, and prayerfully encourages others.

Paul begins all of his letters with some form of this greeting: "May God our Father and the Lord Jesus Christ give you grace and peace." Peter launches his letters with these words: "May God give you more and more grace and peace." John starts his third letter with a remarkable greeting to his friend Gaius: "To Gaius, my dear friend, whom I love in the truth." And Jude begins his letter this way:

> This letter is from Jude, a slave of Jesus Christ and a brother
> of James. I am writing to all who have been called by God
> the Father, who loves you and keeps you safe in the care
> of Jesus Christ. May God give you more and more mercy,
> peace, and love.
>
> JUDE 1–2

Jesus, remind me to intentionally greet others with a blessing. Amen.

DIFFERENCE MAKER

Say something more profound than hello today. Put thought into a simple prayer of blessing when you greet people.

FOR EVERYTHING

Give—Ah, come on! That one hurts. Whatever I have, I need to give it?

Thanks—Oh, okay. So I just need to give the gratitude I have. Okay, I can do that. Give thanks. Cool. I've got some things I could give thanks for, I guess.

For everything—Huh? What was that? You don't mean *every thing*, do you? Like, the opposite of nothing? That's what I'm supposed to give thanks for? You mean the most anti-no-thing there is? Everything. Really?

To God the Father—Well, okay. I've got no problem with giving God thanks, but I'm still stuck on *everything*. Could we compromise on this a bit? Meet halfway perhaps?

In the name of our Lord Jesus Christ—Oh, um…so I have to mean it too? I can't just say thanks, like, according to the way I feel in the moment? I shouldn't just say thanks for the things I like? You mean I should put myself in the perspective of Jesus? Ah man, I thought you might say that.

And give thanks for everything to God the Father in the
name of our Lord Jesus Christ.

EPHESIANS 5:20

Jesus, help me be saturated in who you are today so that I can learn to be truly thankful. Amen.

DIFFERENCE MAKER

Contact a local homeless shelter and make a plan to serve a meal during the Thanksgiving week.

FOR HE IS GOOD

There is so much bad in this world. We are sick and tired of how sick and tired this world is. And yet we keep asking for it. We are glued to our news sources looking for more and more bad news. If there is a disaster, the ratings go up and news providers and advertisers make more money. Even the coverage of bad news is bad.

God is so different—he is so good. Why don't we gravitate toward the Lord instead of getting sucked into another terrible vortex day after day? Why does "bad" entice us more than "good"? What's wrong with us that we keep giving "bad" undue attention while ignoring all the good things that are going on around us? Why do we let the one bad tree withdraw our attention from God in the garden? We sensationalize what is bad, when what is good is right before us. This Thanksgiving, don't give in to bad. Give thanks to the Lord, for he is good.

Give thanks to the LORD, for he is good!
His faithful love endures forever.

PSALM 107:1

Jesus, let my eyes attend to you and you alone. You are so good! Thank you!
Amen.

DIFFERENCE MAKER

Write the words of this verse on a sticky note and paste it to something you will see throughout your day.

FOR WHAT HE HAS DONE

Stop. In the margins of this page, or on a napkin, or a blank piece of paper, brainstorm all of the things God has done for you. Just start listing whatever comes to your mind. Think of things both large and small, grand and intricate, massive in scale and microscopic to the eye, beautiful and strange, wonderful and surprising, overwhelmingly powerful and perplexingly gentle. Think of things he has promised and things he has fulfilled. Think of things he has said. Think of songs he has written and dances he has led. Think of meals he has prepared and sacrifices he has made. Think of the authority he has used and the hope he has shown. How could you begin to give thanks for all of these wonderful blessings? How could you begin to tell the world about what God has done?

Give thanks to the LORD and proclaim his greatness.
Let the whole world know what he has done.

1 CHRONICLES 16:8

Dear Jesus, you are so great and have done so much to reach this world, to rescue and redeem this world. Thank you! You've changed me forever. Teach me how you'd like me to tell people about you so that they will be changed too. Amen.

DIFFERENCE MAKER

Using the list you have made and the creative talent you've been given, create a work of art, a poem, or a song that proclaims the greatness of God.

FOR HIS MIGHTY POWER

Anarchy isn't all it's cracked up to be. Or is it? Whatever anarchy is, it is certainly a mess that cannot control itself. Controlled anarchy would be the opposite of anarchy, after all. Anarchy is a void of power and the absence of control. The flames of it spread through terror and false agreements, fear and disasters. What people initially think of as "freedom from authority" quickly devolves into a civil war between power mongers.

Isaiah was concerned about this very thing 2,700 years ago. And yet, he had a vision. He saw the Servant of the Lord, the Messiah, rising out of the destruction of a nation, with the Spirit of the Lord resting on him, defending the poor and the exploited, ruling against the wicked and destroying them with the commissioning of his breath, and overwhelming them with fairness and truth (Isaiah 11–12). Isaiah's fear of the disintegration of society was overcome by the coming King. Aren't you glad someone is actually in control?

In that wonderful day you will sing:
"Thank the LORD! Praise his name!
Tell the nations what he has done.
Let them know how mighty he is!"

ISAIAH 12:4

Jesus, you are the hope of the nations.
Commission me to tell the world about you. Amen.

DIFFERENCE MAKER

Take some time to pray for the spots of chaos in our world. Pray for people to discover the peace of Jesus in the midst of turmoil.

WORDS FROM THANKSGIVING

If you take the letters of *thanksgiving* and scramble them up, you can create some great vocabulary omelets. Words like giving and thanks are obvious, but think of all the others: think, hang, tang, gnat, king, gang, sing, singing, hanging, skiing, than, thin, snag, thing, nag, kin, stinking, thanking, thinking, hank, gain, gin, sang, it, at, is, as, gist, gas, its, ant, tan, shin, gash, kit, hat, saint, skit, angst, taking, van, skin, hint, sting, hint, asking, tasking, ah, sin, in, an, gig, inn, gag, tag, tank, stag, staging, aging, gist, ski.

The Bible speaks often about other words that derive from a heart of thanksgiving. An attitude of gratitude causes people to erupt in thankful expressions. For instance, in 1 Chronicles 16:8–36, David overflows with thanksgiving, which creates in him a litany of other words too: sing, praise, tell, miracle, generations, glory, acts, wonderful, name, known, nations, good, joy, rejoice, remember, seek, face, Lord, strength, dwelling, declare, ascribe, resound, splendor, holiness, tremble, heavens, salvation, everlasting, people, say, amen.

Give thanks to the Lord, for he is good!
His faithful love endures forever.

1 CHRONICLES 16:34

Jesus, giving thanks to you produces wonderful things in me.
Keep creating a thankful heart within me. Amen.

DIFFERENCE MAKER

This may seem like the cheesiest devotional entry you have ever read before. But imagine doing this with people over the Thanksgiving holidays. What other words overflow from a heart of thanksgiving?

WITH ALL OF MY HEART

What does "all" of your heart look like? When the Bible encourages you to praise the Lord with "all" of your heart, what does it have in mind...*er*, I mean heart—what does it mean? Can you praise God with just three out of four chambers? What if you put all of your ventricles into it but let your atria rest? How about the arteries? The inferior vena cava and pulmonic valve too?

Put your hand over your heart for a moment. Do you feel it pumping? Your heart, your whole heart, right now, is pumping deoxygenated blood from the body in the right atria and the right ventricle, and your heart is pumping oxygenated blood from the lungs through the left atria and the left ventricle. The blood that comes into the heart must be pumped out, otherwise the heart would seize up in an attack.

When you receive life from the Lord, you must pump out praise. When someone helps you see what Jesus has done for you, you can't contain that joy and wonder, and you must push it on. The truth of God that fills your heart must come out or you will seize up.

I will praise you, LORD, with all my heart;
I will tell of all the marvelous things you have done.
PSALM 9:1

Lord Jesus, keep my heart beating for you! Amen.

DIFFERENCE MAKER

Take time to write a heartfelt thank-you note to someone who has made a difference in your life by telling you about Jesus. Include Psalm 9:1 in the note to show your gratefulness for the way God used them to impact you.

WITH THE RIGHT WORDS

Consider all the effort we spend on profanity. Much of the most popular music, media, and Internet outlets are riddled with it. Our culture has become saturated in obscenity, which, of course, makes it seem less obscene with each passing day. This is a difficult path to walk for those who want to follow Jesus. The prevailing winds of culture that blow against us on the path shape so much of what we think and speak on a daily basis, often without us stopping to realize it.

Paul, a man who was certainly not afraid to use provocative language when necessary (for the right reasons), encouraged people to substitute words of thanksgiving for words of vulgarity. What if, he thought, instead of spending our energy on poisonous words, we spoke gratefulness? How would we be changed? And how would our example have a slow, steady impact on those around us?

Obscene stories, foolish talk, and coarse jokes—these are not for you. Instead, let there be thankfulness to God.

EPHESIANS 5:4

Jesus, make me aware today of the words I say. I pray that my heart would overflow with thankfulness today. Amen.

DIFFERENCE MAKER

To retrain your mind and mouth, try to say thank you at least a hundred different times throughout the next twenty-four hours. (Keep track with simple tally marks.)

WITH GLADNESS

Do you know that church isn't supposed to be boring? Did you know that? Some people have been engrained to think that church is always supposed to be solemn and respectful and ordered and hallowed (which sounds especially seriously religious if you pronounce it Old English-style: "Hal-low-ed"). But this just isn't a full picture of church.

Can you see Jesus being satisfied to fall asleep as a speaker drones on and on? Can you imagine Jesus looking blank faced as choruses are repeated and a pew bench cramps his lower back? Can you picture Jesus trying to draw something on the bulletin with that little tiny golf pencil found next to the old red hymnal?

Or do see Jesus engaging in discussion about the Bible? Do you imagine him smiling as people make discoveries about the greatness of God? Do you picture him preparing a meal over a fire and giving thanks for the food and for time with his friends? He loved being with the gathering of his followers! When he entered Jerusalem, as people rallied to him, he declared, "Even the stones will burst into cheers!"

Shout with joy to the LORD, all the earth!
Worship the LORD with gladness.
Come before him, singing with joy.

PSALM 100:1–2

Jesus, let my heart come alive with joy before you today. Amen.

DIFFERENCE MAKER

Pick up some musical instruments or get a karaoke machine. Then gather some friends, put on smiles and laughter, and spend some time loudly singing praise songs.

WE ARE HIS

If a congressional special committee were to examine every aspect of your day—all your e-mails and Internet traffic, how you spend your money, what you say, what you think about—would it be clear that the Lord is your God? Would your actions from an hour ago, or an hour from now, be in line with someone who follows after Jesus?

The irony here is that whether we act like it or not, the Lord already is God. What we think about him or the way that we treat him has nothing to do with whether or not he is God. Our opinion doesn't change who the Lord is at his very core. What is changeable, what is subject to our opinion and actions, is whether or not we will acknowledge that the Lord is our God, that we are his people, and that he is our Shepherd.

Go ahead and let that special committee examine you. As they find all the warts and all the flaws, publicly confess this one thing: "Yes, I am a sinner. But the Lord is God, and I choose to belong to him."

> Acknowledge that the LORD is God!
> He made us, and we are his.
> We are his people, the sheep of his pasture.
>
> PSALM 100:3

Jesus, I really am just a dumb sheep sometimes. Thank you for being my Shepherd. Guide me today in my every step I take. Amen.

DIFFERENCE MAKER

Think ahead one hour from now. What could you do that would evidence that the Lord is your God?

WITH THANKSGIVING

We are coming to the end of November. As you look back at the last eleven months, how would you describe God's work in your life and in the lives of those around you? Are you able to see his faithfulness, even in the difficulties? Are you able to recognize his hands through the ebbs and flows of daily routines? Do you notice those moments where he tried to get your attention? Did you feel him tugging at your heart to respond to others, to care, to love, to do the right thing in the hard moments? Can you feel him drawing you gently into his presence right now? The Lord loves you. From generation to generation, from season to season, from month to month, and even on this very day, he is faithful to give you his unfailing love.

Enter his gates with thanksgiving;
go into his courts with praise.
Give thanks to him and praise his name.
For the LORD is good.
His unfailing love continues forever,
and his faithfulness continues to each generation.

PSALM 100:4–5

Lord Jesus, I come to you with praise and thanksgiving today. Thank you for loving me. Amen.

DIFFERENCE MAKER

Go to the homes of friends and neighbors collecting cans of food for a local food pantry. When someone gives you a can, hand them a thank-you note with Psalm 100:4–5 written on it.

NEW MERCIES

His mercies are new every morning. Repeat that phrase. His mercies are new every morning. It doesn't matter what yesterday was like—his mercies are new every morning. It doesn't matter how you feel about how how you did, for his mercies are new every morning. Even if you feel like you blew it, his mercies are new every morning. Whether you feel like you'll never get another chance or whether you'll never recover, his mercies are new every morning.

The truth is this: Jesus loves to redeem and he loves to restore. And he loves a fresh new day because he gets to lift you up again and walk with you. His mercies are new every morning. So don't try to take a twisted advantage of God's mercy, where you sin a little bit while anticipating that he'll forgive you again tomorrow. Instead, take full advantage of his mercy! Live in it! Let it refresh you and change you into a new person who lives in his faithfulness each and every day.

> The faithful love of the LORD never ends!
> His mercies never cease.
> Great is his faithfulness;
> his mercies begin afresh each morning.
> LAMENTATIONS 3:22–23

Jesus, thank you. Thank you that I can wake up tomorrow and embrace your mercy deeper and fuller than today. Overwhelm me. Amen.

DIFFERENCE MAKER

Be merciful to others today, just as God has offered you mercy.

December

Jesus,

You came to earth because you were

willing to be real with me.

Now I pray that I will be real with you.

Amen.

HIDE

Some people hide things so they won't be found, while others hide things so that they'll be discovered. Which type of hider are you? It is important to bury God's Word deeply in your heart so that it can be discovered there. Don't wallow in the shallow end of your heart because life is meant to be lived deeply. Seed the Word of the Lord into you heart. This way, when a relationship calls for deep commitment, you'll find sacrificial love there. When a challenging moment probes the depths of your character, you'll find integrity. When people need a stable leader, you'll find a treasure of endurance. And when justice demands an advocate, you'll find God's voice speaking out from within you.

> I have hidden your word in my heart,
> that I might not sin against you.
>
> PSALM 119:11

Jesus, find your way to the deepest parts of my life so that when called upon, I will reflect your heart and respond in action just like you. Amen.

DIFFERENCE MAKER

To help you embed truth in your heart, write this verse out on ten small sticky notes. Then hide the notes in places where you might need the reminder in the coming week.

SEEING

It is often said that leaders who make the most significant difference in our world are people who have "vision." They see what is and they envision what could be. They don't waste the focus of their sight on despair, they don't allow their sight to be distracted by sin or selfishness, and they don't develop blurriness or nearsightedness from binge-watching the wrong things.

Leaders who make a significant difference in our world have keen insight into the immediate landscape and also crisp foresight on the horizon. They choose to see the God-created potential in humanity and they help others to see it too. A. W. Tozer (why do all the cool writers get initials for first names?) once wrote, "Faith is the gaze of a soul upon a saving God." In other words, looking and believing are the same thing. What we choose to see reveals what we believe should be the focus of our lives.

> Turn my eyes from worthless things,
> and give me life through your word.
>
> PSALM 119:37

Jesus, let me see you and you alone. Repair my sight and fix my eyes upon you.
Amen.

DIFFERENCE MAKER

As you use your eyes today, imagine that Jesus is seeing what you see. How would that change the way you look at people? How would that change what you look at?

PRIORITIES

Would you rather be incredibly wealthy or have instructions from God? Think about that for a moment. Would you rather receive millions upon millions of dollars deposited right into your bank account for you to use in whatever manner you deem fit, or would you like to have God give you instructions on how to live?

Which of those options would be more valuable to you? Which would last longer? Which would change your life more? And which would be better for the people around you? You probably know the right Sunday school answer, but is that the right answer practically for your life?

The writer of the longest chapter in the Bible played the Would You Rather game and felt passionately about his answer. In prayer, he turned to the Lord and made his turn-the-world-upside-down decision.

Your instructions are more valuable to me
than millions in gold and silver.

PSALM 119:72

Jesus, where are my priorities today? Would I rather follow you or follow my own desires? Please walk with me and shape my thinking. Amen.

DIFFERENCE MAKER

Prayerfully filter your goals in life against this verse. Where do your priorities match up and where do they clash? What could you do today to reinforce your connection to God's purpose for your life?

PERFECTIONISM MERSCHMECTIONISM

No wonder perfectionists are always dissatisfied! Perfect is never good enough. Even if everything were completed to its most excellent potential, it still would fall short. The problem is that perfection sets a bar—a very high bar—that has a limit. Once it is reached, if it ever truly is, it leaves a person feeling incomplete because it is limited. The enjoyment of perfectionism is limited, the scope of perfectionism is limited, and the lasting effect of perfectionism is also limited.

But God's patterns have no limit. They are boundless. Perfectionists are always dissatisfied because they are chasing the wrong pursuit! God's commands blow right past the limited gratification of perfectionism and open the door to abundant, overflowing life—life that is more fulfilling than any limited human goal could ever dream to be.

Even perfection has its limits,
but your commands have no limit.

PSALM 119:96

Jesus, don't let me stress ever again about being perfect. Let me strive to hear your voice and pursue your commands for my life. Amen.

DIFFERENCE MAKER

Make a to-do list. Draw a line across the middle of the paper, then on the bottom side list everything important you think you really need to accomplish, and on the top side write Pursue Jesus. As you work to complete the important bottom items, seek your satisfaction in the one item on the top.

LIGHT FOR MY FEET

LEGOs are the most spectacular toy ever invented. You can create anything your ingenious mind allows—vehicles, spaceships, buildings, abstract works of art, and on and on and on. But there is also a dark side to LEGOs. Inevitably in the voracious generative process a few pieces get scattered and go missing. Somehow, those pieces find their way to the middle of your bedroom floor in the middle of the night. Angry from being neglected, they plot out their revenge and lie in wait for your nightly ritual to the bathroom, at which point they will position themselves under your footstep so that excruciating pain will scream up to your brain. All it would have taken to avoid the agony of a misplaced step was a simple light for your feet.

> Your word is a lamp to guide my feet
> and a light for my path.
>
> PSALM 119:105

Jesus, let my eyes see where you are leading and let my childlike feet find their traction in your footprints. May your Word guide the direction of my life today. Amen.

DIFFERENCE MAKER

In the dark hours of the morning or evening, go for a walk in a well-lit, safe place (or use a flashlight in your room!). Use the light to guide your steps while you pray about where God wants your life to go.

PURPOSE AND INFRASTRUCTURE

Every building, every society, every product, every family, and every person has some sort of purpose and some sort of infrastructure that supports it or them. Whether those things or those people have success is directly relational to whether the infrastructure serves the purpose. If a building was meant to be fifty stories high and house hundreds of high-tech office spaces, it would be a farce if the infrastructure were made out of wood and a few dial-up modems.

It has been said that the "chief end" of humanity is to glorify God. But humans have often created a dilapidated infrastructure around themselves that has hindered their pursuit of their purpose. The good news is that through Jesus, God has given humanity the foundation and the resources it we need to love the Lord and to love our neighbor as ourselves.

Let me live so I can praise you,
and may your regulations help me.
I have wandered away like a lost sheep;
come and find me,
for I have not forgotten your commands.
PSALM 119:175–176

Jesus, forgive me for those times I have used the wrong materials to build my life. May I always follow your blueprint so that I can bring glory to you. Amen.

DIFFERENCE MAKER

What long-lasting materials do you need to invest your life into today? Choose at least one of the following to build yourself up: God's Word, serving others without calling attention to yourself, time spent in prayer, or mentoring a younger person in their walk with God.

DAY OF INFAMY

The attack on Pearl Harbor startled the nation. Three hundred and fifty-three Japanese planes crippled the United States Pacific Fleet and nearly 200 aircraft. Worse than that, however, over 2,400 people were killed that day. The next day, the United States declared war on Japan—a war that would involve the death of hundreds of thousands of soldiers and civilians over the next few years.

The horror of war reminds us that life and peace on this earth are fragile. Fear strikes unexpectedly and wreaks long-lasting devastation. Yet the Lord is stronger than the worst war. He will restore this world from its rubble, he will honor those who offer their lives for the good of others, and he will reestablish our steps as we follow him.

Even though the fig trees have no blossoms,
and there are no grapes on the vines;
even though the olive crop fails,
and the fields lie empty and barren;
even though the flocks die in the fields,
and the cattle barns are empty,
yet I will rejoice in the LORD!
I will be joyful in the God of my salvation!
The Sovereign LORD is my strength!
He makes me as surefooted as a deer,
able to tread upon the heights.

HABAKKUK 3:17–19

Jesus, this world needs you! I place my hope in your salvation today. Amen.

DIFFERENCE MAKER

Look through the news of turmoil around the world and pause on each geographic location mentioned and pray for the people in those regions.

RECORD

Jesus makes you free. Did you know that? He loves you so much that he does not keep a record of your sins. Every time you mess up, he is not going to bring out *The Book of Sin* with your name on the cover, open up to page 1,378, and say, "Aha! See! I knew you were no good! You're always failing!" That's just not the way of Jesus. He won't do that.

In fact, when you mess up he might actually pull out another book that we call the Bible. He might open to a myriad of different passages like 1 John 1:9, which says, "But if we confess our sins to him, he is faithful and just to forgive us our sins and to cleanse us from all wickedness," or Isaiah 43:25 where God says he "will blot out your sins and will never think of them again." Jesus might even quote from the "love" chapter of the Bible, 1 Corinthians 13, which says that love "keeps no record of wrongs." This is the way of Jesus, and it makes you free.

> Lord, if you kept a record of our sins,
> who, O Lord, could ever survive?
> But you offer forgiveness,
> that we might learn to fear you.
>
> PSALM 130:3–4

Jesus, a record of my wrongs is not a record I'd like anyone to keep. Thank you for keeping forgiveness in your heart for me. Amen.

DIFFERENCE MAKER

As the Christmas season approaches, string up new lights, bake some gingerbread cookies, listen to carols, and share the good news of Jesus with others.

THE ADVENT OF IMMANUEL

The birth of Jesus Christ is such a powerful event that Isaiah explains it as if it is just around the corner. Good as gold. Seven hundred years before Jesus is born, Isaiah already knows it is about to happen. The child is as good as born. His birth is bigger than past, present, and future itself. It's as if his birth was planned outside of time to impact all of time. His birth is the all-time greatest birth.

Isaiah is seeing it happen. He understands it is a birth yet to come, for back in Isaiah 7:14 he declares it as a future event. This child will be born among us, he will be with us, Isaiah declares. We will know him as "God with us."

All right then, the Lord himself will give you the sign. Look!
The virgin will conceive a child! She will give birth to a son
and will call him Immanuel (which means "God is with us").

ISAIAH 7:14

Lord Jesus, your plan is greater than time itself. Thank you for having us on your mind through all of time. Amen.

DIFFERENCE MAKER

If possible, volunteer to babysit for someone you know who has a baby. Consider how Jesus was once a child just like this.

CHILD

Back in Isaiah's day, the nation of Assyria inflicted intense physical distress and spiritual misery upon Israel. But not to worry, because Isaiah proclaimed that a child would be born. A child. "Hey don't worry, everyone—a baby is coming." Well, this wasn't just your normal, cute little bubble-blowing baby. The power and majesty of this child would be utterly astonishing. Isaiah was not afraid to emphasize this.

Child is the prominent word in Isaiah's prophecy. For upon this child would hinge everything. If you were to take the child out, the entire prophecy falls apart. If this child is not born and does not step into darkness, the entire world collapses. If this child does not make an impact, the world's very soul crumbles. Without this child being born, darkness still reigns, oppression still weighs people down, despair and struggle and restriction still overwhelm. And they always would, if it was not for the amazing capacity of this child to change everything.

> For a child is born to us,
> a son is given to us.
> The government will rest on his shoulders.
> And he will be called:
> Wonderful Counselor, Mighty God,
> Everlasting Father, Prince of Peace.
>
> ISAIAH 9:6

Jesus, how did you come in such fragility and still know you would change the world? I am in awe of you. Amen.

DIFFERENCE MAKER

Give someone a thoughtful, encouraging, early Christmas gift today.

JESUS IN CHARGE

In Isaiah 9:6, the prophet wasn't joking. The Christ child would not be just another boy. His responsibility would be the heaviest burden any person could carry: "The government will be on his shoulders."

Isaiah foresaw that Jesus wouldn't simply rule a local community or write a constitution or enforce laws. This child would rule everything—all of creation. The scope of the responsibility of administration and management and care and livelihood of the entire planet would be upon him. The weight of the world—the consequences of justice and redemption—would rest upon his shoulders. His kingdom would extend beyond borders and jurisdictions (John 18:36). He would have complete authority (Matthew 28:18) and would hold everything together (Colossians 1:15–20), both in heaven and on earth (John 13:3).

The reason Christmas brings so much joy is because a child is born, a child whose shoulders are greater than all nations, greater than all powers, greater than all darkness, and greater than all sin both now and forever. And this child was to be born as a baby and be laid in a manger.

And I will give you the keys of the Kingdom of Heaven.
Whatever you forbid on earth will be forbidden in heaven, and
whatever you permit on earth will be permitted in heaven.

MATTHEW 16:19

Jesus, thank you for carrying me on your shoulders. I trust you to govern my life.
Amen.

DIFFERENCE MAKER

Speaking of government, take time today to write an encouraging Christmas note to one of your city or state leaders, congress members, or senators. Include Isaiah 9:6 in your message.

WONDERFUL COUNSELOR

In Isaiah 9:6 are four sets of word pairs that are used to describe the child who would be born to us. The first is "Wonderful Counselor." By itself in English, this is pretty cool. Imagine putting this title on his birth certificate: "Yes, that's what I said. His name is Wonderful Counselor." But this title is even more impressive in Hebrew, the language Isaiah used. It is a title of awe. The Hebrew is *pele yoetz*.

Pele means "wonder." In the Old Testament this word usually refers to God and his miraculous works. He is astonishing and marvelous and indescribable. *Pele* hints at the deity of this child who is to be born. It is a word that could even stand alone, and Isaiah 9:6 could be translated, "He will be called Wonder."

And not only will he be called Wonder, but he will also be called Counselor. The Hebrew word *yoetz* means "counselor," "adviser," or "advocate." This child will sit on the throne of the world with wisdom and with judgment. He is a counselor who needs no other consultants or analysts around him. This child does not need a cabinet to help him make decisions. He himself is the Counselor to whom everyone else will turn. The child born among us is called Wonderful Counselor.

The Lord says, "I will guide you along
the best pathway for your life.
I will advise you and watch over you."

PSALM 32:8

Jesus, if you find I am not in awe of you, shake me up a bit today. Amen.

DIFFERENCE MAKER

Entrust your concerns, worries, and troubles to Jesus today.

HERO GOD

The second word pair that is used in Isaiah 9:6 to describe the child that will be born to us is "Mighty God." Is that really what Isaiah 9:6 says? How could a child actually be called "Mighty God"—especially in the monotheistic Hebrew worldview? But Isaiah says *El-Gibbor*, which is "Mighty God."

El is the Hebrew word for God. Isaiah never uses it in reference to anyone other than the one true God of Israel. For Isaiah to use this title upon a child is absolutely astonishing. The reason people in the future will rejoice, the reason darkness will be destroyed, the reason light is coming into the world, is because somehow a child who is God himself will overturn all the consequences of sin and despair and distress and misery.

And this God is mighty. *Gibbor* literally means "hero." This child is the hero God. God is going to be the hero of the story. Are you walking in darkness? Don't fear, because God will give you light! Are you oppressed? Hang in there, for God is coming to the rescue. Is your soul imprisoned? God will free you! Are your struggling? God will revive you! He is the hero God who comes to save the world.

> He heals the brokenhearted
> and bandages their wounds.
> He counts the stars
> and calls them all by name.
> How great is our Lord! His power is absolute!
> His understanding is beyond comprehension!
>
> PSALM 147:3–5

Jesus, if I am not blown away by who you are yet, get my attention today. Amen.

DIFFERENCE MAKER

If Jesus is the hero God, what does that mean for you as his follower?
Do something heroic for someone else today.

FOREVER FATHER

The third word pair that is used in Isaiah 9:6 to describe the child who will be born to us is that he is the "Everlasting Father." The Messiah, this child who was to be born, this son upon whom the weight of the entire world would be carried, will be known as "Father." The Hebrew for this title is *Abbi-'ad*. *Abba* means Father, while *'ad* refers to endlessness. That means this child will be a father to his people forever and ever.

When God's children return to God the Father, Isaiah says, they will return to this child. He will stand guard over them, supply their needs, and cascade them with tenderness and protection and love. He will shepherd them, guide them, and lay his life down for them. All of this is not for a brief period of human life; rather, this child will be their Father forever (Isaiah 63:16), a Father who will never abandon his children (Matthew 28:21).

> "I give them eternal life, and they will never perish. No one
> can snatch them away from me, for my Father has given
> them to me, and he is more powerful than anyone else.
> No one can snatch them from the Father's hand.
> The Father and I are one."
>
> JOHN 10:28–30

Lord Jesus, during this Christmas season, help me to not see just a sweet baby in the manger. Help me to see Jesus as the Everlasting Father who is with me forever. Amen.

DIFFERENCE MAKER

How would your regular routines today be different if you were to remember that Jesus will be leading you forever?

PEACE PRINCE

The fourth and last word pair used in Isaiah 9:6 to describe the child who will be born to us is the "Prince of Peace." Prince of Peace. *Sur-Shalom*. Physical distress and spiritual misery will be conquered through the power and authority of this Christmas child. He will establish peace, a peace that is very much more than a temporary ceasefire. His power and rule will launch a new heaven and a new earth. All suffering and frustration and angst and weapons of darkness will be obliterated.

Shalom is the wholeness and fulfillment that only God has. *Shalom* is the purity and the perfection and the knowledge and summary of everything that is right. And it will come from a child, a child who is the ruler of peace. This peace will come from child who has in his hand the power to dispense peace. It will come from a child who will inherit *shalom* from God the Father because he is God's Son, the heir to the throne of all creation. This child is going to be one who rules with the power of eternity, a child who is born among us and for us, a child who is too wondrous to describe with just one name. He will be the child who holds titles unimaginable, a child who saves the world, and a child who inaugurates the *shalom* of God.

> Therefore, since we have been made right in God's sight by faith, we have peace with God because of what Jesus Christ our Lord has done for us.
>
> ROMANS 5:1

Jesus, let your peace fill my anxious soul today. Amen.

DIFFERENCE MAKER

Because Jesus is the Prince of Peace, pray about this: If you are separated from someone because of something you have done, take the necessary steps to make peace with them today.

BLINDING LIGHT

Heavy storms had created a melting mess on the salty, sandy, slushy road. A straight stretch of road was banked on both sides by huge walls of snow. In front was a truck, and behind was another truck. Brownish slop was spraying up onto the windshield, which made driving difficult. The wipers and washer fluid rid the glass of only half its mess.

As the road bent, the sun shattered through the low-lying clouds and smashed down on the stained windshield. As the sun hit the caked slop, the driver became completely blind. He couldn't see anything in front of him except hardened slush and an intense spot trying to penetrate through the grime. Attacked by the sun, blinded panic rushed through the driver's brain and fingers as he clutched the steering wheel that controlled his life. "Go away!" he yelled at the sun. "I want the shadows!"

As the road bent again, away from the direct glare of the light, the driver developed a deep gnawing fear that the sun had found him.

And the judgment is based on this fact: God's light came into the world, but people loved the darkness more than the light, for their actions were evil.

JOHN 3:19

Jesus, don't let me be comfortable with driving blindly through life. As difficult as it is, help me give in to your brilliance. Amen.

DIFFERENCE MAKER

The next time you're driving through winter weather, pray to Jesus.

TRADITIONS

Some people have developed strong Christmas traditions over the years. Some people read the Christmas story in Luke 2, while others put a present for Jesus under the tree. Some ask the younger kids in their families to tell the story of Jesus' birth, and still others go to special church services. Some simply rip open presents and gorge on good food.

Christmas traditions are supposed to do two things, really. They are to draw us to Jesus and draw us toward each other. We celebrate Christmas because Jesus has been born, because he has entered into history. We receive and give gifts because God gave his only Son so that we might have abundant life. By accepting presents together, we are reminded to be humbly thankful for the abundant life and the abundant fellowship we share in Christ Jesus.

Because of your stage in life, this might be an interesting year of change for you. Be sure to follow Mary's example. Even in the midst of visitors and transitions, she paused to treasure the birth of Jesus and made it a regular routine to remember.

They hurried to the village and found Mary and Joseph. And there was the baby, lying in the manger. After seeing him, the shepherds told everyone what had happened and what the angel had said to them about this child. All who heard the shepherds' story were astonished, but Mary kept all these things in her heart and thought about them often.

LUKE 2:16–19

Jesus, let me remember the meaning of this season—which is you. Amen.

DIFFERENCE MAKER

This Christmas season practice a tradition from your childhood and start a new one that will help draw you and your family to Jesus.

CHRISTMAS INFORMATION

Mary and Joseph weren't really into the Christmas spirit. They didn't decorate a Christmas tree. They didn't bake cookies or drink peppermint mochas or put up the mistletoe. Can you believe that they didn't go caroling either? Look, they weren't scrooges; they just had other things on their mind. There was no place for roasting chestnuts over a fire. They couldn't even find a place. Some (generous?) person allowed them to stay with their animals, but that was no place for a teenage girl who was going into labor.

Christmas is just a week away. Have you read—actually read—the account of Jesus' birth this year yet? Rather than just getting your Christmas details from carols or from reruns of old holiday TV programs, what if you were to read a couple pages of the Bible too? You might be surprised to find out that Father Christmas isn't real, Santa isn't in the Bible, and eggnog is not biblical.

Jacob was the father of Joseph, the husband of Mary.
Mary gave birth to Jesus, who is called the Messiah.
MATTHEW 1:16

Jesus, don't let me take you for granted this next week. Amen.

DIFFERENCE MAKER

Get some people together and read the first two chapters of Matthew and the first two chapters of Luke. Even try to pronounce any awkward names out loud. Talk about details you thought you knew that weren't there and other details you discovered but had never realized were there before.

VENITE ADOREMUS

For 2,000 years people have been celebrating the birth of Jesus. Actually, it has been longer than that, because even before Jesus was born people were anticipating his arrival. The prophet Micah had predicted his arrival in Bethlehem, Isaiah had foreseen his powerful ministry, and Simeon had waited his whole life to hold him. Celebrating the birth of the Messiah is one of the greatest traditions of history.

In the 1700s, John Frances Wade published a song known as *Adeste Fideles* in a collection of hymns known as the *Cantus Diversi*. He wanted the world to come and adore the birth of Jesus.

Adeste fideles,
Laeti trimphantes,
Venite, venite in Bethlehem.
Natum videte, Regem angelorum.
Venite adoremus;
Venite adoremus;
Venite adoremus, Dominum.

But you, O Bethlehem Ephrathah,
are only a small village among all the people of Judah.
Yet a ruler of Israel,
whose origins are in the distant past,
will come from you on my behalf.

MICAH 5:2

Jesus, let me, and countless others,
adore you this Christmas. Amen.

DIFFERENCE MAKER

Search the internet to figure out what these lyrics mean.
Then watch a video of Andrea Bocelli singing this song.
How could such grandeur be given to the birth of a baby
in a small, backward town twenty centuries ago?

JESUS COMING TO US

Christmas is about Jesus coming to meet each one of us. The Christmas passages, and the rest of the whole Bible, tell us that Jesus came to the earth so that he could meet us and have an eternal relationship with us. For example, the book of Matthew is jam-packed with this concept of Jesus coming to meet us. In Matthew 3, John the Baptist references Jesus when he says, "Someone is coming soon who is greater than I am." In Matthew 5, Jesus urges people, "Don't misunderstand why I have come." In chapter 9, Jesus says, "I have come to call those who know they are sinners." And in Matthew 20 Jesus sums it all up for us when he says, "The Son of Man came not to be served but to serve others and to give his life as a ransom for many." Christmas is about Jesus coming to meet us so that we can have a relationship with him.

> "For the Son of Man came to seek
> and save those who are lost."
>
> LUKE 19:10

Lord Jesus, thank you for coming to give your life up for me. Amen.

DIFFERENCE MAKER

This Christmas season, where you will notice them frequently, set up both a manger and a cross.

US COMING TO JESUS

Christmas is about each of us coming to meet Jesus. The Christmas passages, and the rest of the whole Bible, share that each of us is to come and meet Jesus so that we can have an eternal relationship with him. For example, the book of Matthew is absolutely full with this concept of each of us coming to meet Jesus. In chapter 4, Jesus calls out to two brothers, "Come, follow me, and I will show you how to fish for people!" In Matthew 11, Jesus invites everyone, "Come to me, all of you who are weary and carry heavy burdens, and I will give you rest." In Matthew 14, when Peter asks if he can walk out to him on the water, Jesus simply responds, "Yes, come." And in chapter 28, after Jesus' resurrection, even the angels get into the action, saying, "Come, see where his body was lying." Jesus has come to meet you. Will you come to meet him today?

Jesus was born in Bethlehem in Judea, during the reign of King Herod. About that time some wise men from eastern lands arrived in Jerusalem, asking, "Where is the newborn king of the Jews? We saw his star as it rose, and we have come to worship him."

MATTHEW 2:1–2

Jesus, I come to you now and give you my whole life. Amen.

DIFFERENCE MAKER

Go meet with Jesus today. Seek him and find him, for he is inviting you to do just that. Set aside some time today just to worship him.

FAIRY-TALE VERSION

There's the fairy-tale version of Christmas: A quiet baby in a warm manger surrounded by a beautiful young mom and an incredibly gentle adoptive father, graced by gentle shepherds and cute little lambs, all the while a star hovers just overhead. Angels sing sweetly o'er the plain while the earth is placid.

Then there's the reality: A screaming baby, messy with an umbilical cord and misshapen skull, held by an unwed teenage mom who fled her family with her boyfriend, visited by terrified shepherds on a strange order from angels. The local king demands the baby's death, so soldiers descend upon the town and murder every young child present. The new family frantically escapes to Egypt, where his ancestors had been enslaved years before. Eventually the baby grows, gifted with authority to heal the sick and raise the dead. Crowds clamor for his kingship, but when he refuses to incite a revolt, the crowds betray him, beat him, and execute him—all while his mother wept at his bloody feet.

No wonder we like the fairy-tale version much better. The sweetness of a carnation is nicer than the shock of the incarnation.

Then Simeon blessed them, and he said to Mary, the baby's mother, "This child is destined to cause many in Israel to fall, but he will be a joy to many others. He has been sent as a sign from God, but many will oppose him. As a result, the deepest thoughts of many hearts will be revealed. And a sword will pierce your very soul."

LUKE 2:34–35

Jesus, you were willing to be real with me. I pray I will be real with you. Amen.

DIFFERENCE MAKER

In the next few days, consider the raw reality of Jesus' birth.

HELLO!

The award for the most awkward hello of all eternity should go to the simply spoken angel Gabriel. Luke tells us that God sent him to Nazareth to speak to Mary, a young virgin who was engaged to a carpenter named Joseph. Gabriel went to her and politely said, "Greetings." He then "delivered" the good news to Mary that the Lord had chosen her to conceive the very Son of God.

But Mary wasn't so sure his hello was a good thing. She was quite afraid of him and greatly troubled at the blunt verbiage of this supreme heavenly warrior. But with his amazing angel abilities, Gabriel must have sensed Mary's discomfort at his little announcement. So he decided he would try to reassure her with words that every unwed teenage girl wants to hear: "Don't be afraid, Mary. You're pregnant!"

I'm sure that calmed her nerves, Gabe.

> Gabriel appeared to her and said, "Greetings, favored woman! The Lord is with you!" Confused and disturbed, Mary tried to think what the angel could mean. "Don't be afraid, Mary," the angel told her, "for you have found favor with God! You will conceive and give birth to a son, and you will name him Jesus."
>
> LUKE 1:28–31

Jesus, don't let me be comfortable with the details of Christmas this year. Let its simplicity profoundly shake me awake. Amen.

DIFFERENCE MAKER

Write an encouraging note to someone who finds the Christmas season saddening or troubling to their heart.

CHRISTMAS EVE

Trying to help the poor…*er*, I mean "favored" girl understand her predicament—*er*, there I go again—I mean "blessing," the angel Gabriel went on to deliver to Mary information about her bundle of joy. He told her she would be with child, give birth to a son, and give him the name Jesus. Then Gabriel said, without shaking his wings, "Oh, and Mary, he will be very great." Uh, yeah.

No one could disagree one bit with Gabriel's assessment of Jesus. Jesus simply, no argument, would be great. Not kind of great. He would be the definition of and the very model of greatness. Masterfully great. Awe-inspiringly, knee-shatteringly, jaw-droppingly, arms-raisedly, angel-dumbfoundedly great. Gabriel couldn't have said it any simpler. Never before or since has one uttered such an eternal understatement.

To his credit, Gabriel did elaborate a bit. Besides the fact that Jesus would be great, Gabe casually reassured Mary, "Your son will be the Son of God and, by the way, his kingdom will never end. So, uh, don't be afraid, Mary."

He will be very great and will be called the Son of the Most High. The Lord God will give him the throne of his ancestor David. And he will reign over Israel forever; his Kingdom will never end!

LUKE 1:32–33

Jesus, you are greater than I realize. Let that sink into my heart tonight and tomorrow. Amen.

DIFFERENCE MAKER

In celebration of Jesus, for every Christmas gift you get, challenge yourself to give two gifts to others.

CHRISTMAS DAY

God used Caesar Augustus like a puppet, and he wasn't concerned about Quirinius complicating things or Herod stopping the show. He had set this plan in motion long before any of those men changed their diapers. A King, the only true King, was going to be born to a humble girl in a lowly corner of the world in the midst of fragility so that the broken people of the world could draw near and embrace their Almighty Savior.

At that time the Roman emperor, Augustus, decreed that a census should be taken throughout the Roman Empire. (This was the first census taken when Quirinius was governor of Syria.) All returned to their own ancestral towns to register for this census. And because Joseph was a descendant of King David, he had to go to Bethlehem in Judea, David's ancient home. He traveled there from the village of Nazareth in Galilee. He took with him Mary, his fiancée, who was now obviously pregnant. And while they were there, the time came for her baby to be born. She gave birth to her first child, a son. She wrapped him snugly in strips of cloth and laid him in a manger, because there was no lodging available for them.

LUKE 2:1–7

Lord Jesus, thank you for coming in a way that draws me to you. Amen.

DIFFERENCE MAKER

Gather together with people whom you love
and read Luke 2:1–20 together.

GIFT

On December 25 of every year, people around the world celebrate God who took on human flesh. On December 26, people return their gifts. And by the New Year they've moved on. Should we leave Jesus, and our faith, in the manger? That isn't where Jesus stayed. He was wrapped in swaddling cloths and laid in a manger, but later he was wrapped in burial cloths and laid in a tomb. His incarnation is an intense story that encompasses his entire life: the Creator took upon himself blood and body and bones and entered humbly into the world of his created ones to sacrifice himself.

We are inclined to opt for a consumerist faith, selfish in its assumption of undeserved grace and shallow in its apprehension of the crude *carne* of Jesus Christ. That the holy God of the universe would take on the fragility of flesh in this violent, sinful world exposes God's determination to go to the most extreme lengths to love his people. How can we leave Jesus, and our faith, in the manger?

> And so, dear brothers and sisters, I plead with you to give
> your bodies to God because of all he has done for you. Let
> them be a living and holy sacrifice—the kind he will find
> acceptable. This is truly the way to worship him.
>
> ROMANS 12:1

Lord Jesus, let me be more and more like you every day of my life. Amen.

DIFFERENCE MAKER

Wrap up some simple but meaningful gifts and make arrangements to give them away in a soup kitchen, homeless shelter, prison ministry, nursing home, hospital, or group home.

POST-CHRISTMAS

When the child was born, angels declared peace on earth to humankind. So here's some good news: You are a kind of human, and you are on earth, so the angels declared peace for you. The post-Christmas peace comes from this: Jesus will destroy sin. He will obliterate distress. He will liquefy misery. And he will do all of this through the weapon he extends in his hands—forgiveness. Nothing can overcome forgiveness. It is the most powerful offense this world could ever embrace. It is futile to fight forgiveness. Everything surrenders or succumbs to Jesus' peaceful, abundant love.

Even though Christmas is past (and because it is it 363 days in the future), be careful not to resist Jesus. Embrace him. Pull him close to your heart. Let him overcome any shadow of death that you pass through. Let his victory break the chains in your life. Let his peace conquer the conflict in your soul. Let his wonder surpass your understanding. Let his counsel restore your heart. Let his might empower your passion. Let his everlasting life awaken you. Let his birth connect you to God.

I am leaving you with a gift—peace of mind and heart. And the peace I give is a gift the world cannot give. So don't be troubled or afraid.

JOHN 14:27

Jesus, Christmas is all about you, and yet you have gifted me. As much as this sinks in, there is still room for me to embrace you more. Thank you! Amen.

DIFFERENCE MAKER

Pray. Go to someone who is in conflict and creatively, effectively, and wisely share the peace of Jesus.

GOD REMEMBERS HIS PROMISES

God's house is full of joy. Do you know why? Because there is not one broken promise to be found anywhere within it. God not only makes promises to those he loves, but he also keeps those promises.

For instance, he told Abraham one of his future children would become a blessing as numerous as the stars. He promised David he would have a future son who would rule on his throne forever. He promised Mary she would have a child who would save the world from its sins. He promised Paul he would use him to bring the good news of Jesus to people who had never yet heard of it. He promised he would bring freedom and healing and joy and abundant life. He promised the Holy Spirit. He promised also to come again to judge evil and restore his creation. He promised to be with us always, even to the very end of the age.

God's house is full of joy because he keeps his promises.

He is the Lord our God.
His justice is seen throughout the land.
He always stands by his covenant—
the commitment he made to a thousand generations.

PSALM 105:7–8

Jesus, thank you for remembering me and for remembering your promises so many generations ago. I praise you today for keeping your Word. Amen.

DIFFERENCE MAKER

Tell people today how God remembers his promises for them.

WHAT A DAY

What an incredible day this is. Smack in-between Christmas and New Year's, this day cannot be overlooked. It's like the perfect blending of those two major holidays. Christmas marks the day we celebrate the birth of our Savior, while New Year's marks the celebration of our opportunity to start anew. It seems that December 29 is the bridge between them both.

At some point, we need to allow the birth of Jesus to change our lives so that we can start again, leave our sin behind, and resolve to pursue all that Jesus has planned for us. This is a day of renewal where we can prepare for works of service that will make a beautiful difference in the year to come.

> "For I am about to do something new.
> See, I have already begun! Do you not see it?
> I will make a pathway through the wilderness.
> I will create rivers in the dry wasteland."
>
> ISAIAH 43:19

Jesus, thank you for coming to give me new life. Guide me in the new directions you have for my life in the year ahead. Amen.

DIFFERENCE MAKER

You'll need a pen and a paper and a place to think. Old-fashioned style now. While praying with Jesus, brainstorm a list of what God intends for you in this upcoming year.

WRAP UP

At the end of the most famous sermon in history, Jesus looked back. He had offered world-changing thoughts through beatitudes, salt and light, teaching on anger and adultery, love for enemies, giving to the needy, the Lord's Prayer, ideas on money, instructions to not worry, to not judge; he encouraged people to seek and find, keep the Golden Rule, pass through the narrow gate, and discover who his true followers are. Some of the most famous sayings in history come from the Sermon on the Mount. History would say it was a pretty good message.

Jesus himself thought it was pretty good too. In fact, before he finished, he looked back on it all and encouraged everyone who heard his words to put them into action. If a person applied his teachings, he said, then they would have a stable foundation for life. So he wrapped up his words with one of the greatest analogies the world had ever heard.

> Anyone who listens to my teaching and follows it is wise,
> like a person who builds a house on solid rock.
>
> MATTHEW 7:24

Jesus, thank you for making a difference in my life. Keep teaching me. Help me be changed even more so that I can change the world around me. Amen.

DIFFERENCE MAKER

Look back through the daily entries of this book that impacted you throughout the year. Highlight some of the Difference Makers that changed you or those around you, and then choose one of those to repeat today.

LAST DAY

The first book of the Bible, Genesis, launches our understanding of God's purpose in creating the world. The last book of the Bible, Revelation, has us calling for God to come back and re-create. We long to be fully restored to the relationship that God intended us to have in the world that God intended for us to live in.

John, the writer of Revelation, can hardly wait for God's promised restoration. As he writes what will become the very last words of the Bible, he is filled with awe and anticipation. He chooses to respond to Jesus with a few wonderful words that capture his heart: "Come, Lord Jesus." John knows of no better way to conclude than this thought for his readers. The greatest blessing he could give to the world would be a prayer for Jesus to come back once again.

He who is the faithful witness to all these things says,
"Yes, I am coming soon!" Amen! Come, Lord Jesus!
May the grace of the Lord Jesus be with God's holy people.

REVELATION 22:20–21

Lord Jesus, in the year ahead, come to restore all things in my life and in this world. Amen.

DIFFERENCE MAKER

Gather some good friends or family and celebrate the last year, and look ahead to the upcoming year. But tonight add a twist. Stop to pray for Jesus' return so that the world will be remade as it was intended to be.

ACKNOWLEDGMENTS

To Kathy: You have made a difference in me and right beside me. You exemplify this book. You are the most consistent, most trustworthy, most sincere difference maker I know. Thank you. I love you.

To my amazing and unique kids, each one chosen by God to know him and do good for him: Each of you will be out from under my wings soon, a freedom you'll enjoy because nests can get exceedingly cramped and stinky if people don't get out of their parents' basement and start to fly. Zachary, may you always remember Jesus and lead people to him. Ben, may you serve God's right hand with grace and power. Elly, may you know God's promises and make them known. I love you all with more life than I knew I had.

TO LEARN
WITH LOVE

A COMPANION
FOR SUZUKI
PARENTS

WILLIAM AND CONSTANCE STARR

Cover Design: William J. Starr, Jr.

SUMMY-BIRCHARD INC.

Library of Congress Cataloging in Publication Data: 83-081442
ISBN: 0-87487-606-0

First Printing March 1984
Second Printing October 1984
Third Printing April 1986
Fourth Printing May 1992

Summy-Birchard Inc.
exclusively distributed by
Warner Bros. Publications Inc.
265 Secaucus Road
Secaucus, New Jersey 07096

The Suzuki name, logo and wheel device are trademarks
of Dr. Shinichi Suzuki used under exclusive license by
Summy-Birchard, Inc.

To our dear children,
Kathleen, Teresa, Greg, Tim,
Judith, Bill, Michael, and David,
With gratitude
For the loving, living, and forgiving
That we have shared.

To the many children, parents, and teachers
Who've enriched our lives
With their love and friendship
Over these last twenty years.

And to Shinichi Suzuki
For the inspiration
That created an environment of learning with love.

"If love is deep, much can be accomplished".

William and Constance Starr

THE AUTHORS

William Starr made his debut as soloist with the Kansas City Philharmonic at the age of seventeen. He acquired two degrees and a Performer's Certificate at the Eastman School of Music and played first violin in the Rochester Philharmonic. While a member of the faculty at the University of Tennessee he was first violinist of the University String Quartet and concertmaster of the Knoxville Symphony, appearing as soloist fourteen times. In 1977-82 he served as Head of the Music Department. He is now an adjunct professor at the University of Colorado. His books, "Scored for Listening", a music appreciation text (Harcourt, Brace), "Music Scores Omnibus", a music anthology (Prentice Hall), and a music theory text, "Perceiving Music", (Harcourt, Brace), have been widely used in colleges since 1959. In 1972-74 Mr. Starr was a member of the Fulbright National Screening Committee for Strings, serving as its chairman in 1975. He began the Suzuki violin program at Tennessee in 1964, visiting Japan in 1967 and 1968-69. His Suzuki students performed at a conference of the World Organization for Human Potential in Philadelphia, the Music Educators' National Conference in Atlanta, the American Symphony Orchestra League national convention in Memphis, and toured Venezuela twice, appearing with the Venezuelan Symphony. His book, "The Suzuki Violinist" has been in demand by parents and teachers since its publication in 1976. A later book, "Twenty-Six Composers Teach the Violinist", is gaining wide use with advanced students. He has taught at all of the International Suzuki Conferences and in Canada, England, Australia, Venezuela, and Switzerland. One of the founders of the Suzuki Association of the Americas, he was its first president from 1972-74, and is chairman of the board of the recently formed International Suzuki Association.

Constance Starr studied piano at the Chicago Musical College and at Interlochen, where she was also principal violist of the orchestra. While earning a degree in piano performance at the Eastman School of Music, she was an active member of the Eastman Concert Bureau, appearing as soloist and assisting artist. She was both violist and pianist with the Knoxville Symphony, appearing five times as piano soloist. While playing viola in the University of Tennessee String Quartet, she also performed piano chamber music and served as part-time piano instructor in the music department. Because of their intense interest in early childhood education, the Starrs were co-founders of the Knoxville Montessori Association of which Ms. Starr served as first president. In 1971 she wrote, in collaboration with William Starr, a widely used text, "Practical Piano Skills", published by Wm. C. Brown and now in its third edition. Ms. Starr is writing a series of books called "The Music Road, A Journey in Music Reading". Volumes 1 and 2 have been enthusiastically received and Volume 3 is scheduled for 1984 release. In 1968-1969 Ms. Starr spent fourteen months in Japan with her husband and eight children, observing in depth the piano teaching of Haruko Kataoka and Shizuko Suzuki and making video tapes of student lessons and performances. She wrote an article in CLAVIER introducing Suzuki piano to the U.S. and gave the first workshops for piano teachers in the U.S. Students from her Suzuki piano program in Knoxville have won contests, appeared as soloists on two tours of Venezuela, on the Suzuki International Tour and at the International Conferences. She has served SAA as chairman of the piano committee and as piano editor of the Journal. A member of the piano faculty at four international conferences, she is actively sought after as clinician and teacher-trainer at institutes and workshops in the U.S. and abroad.

The Starrs have performed frequently on faculty recitals at Suzuki institutes and international conferences.

Preface

For a number of years we have been giving talks to parents at workshops and institutes throughout the country, sharing experiences and insights we have gained from our own family and from the families of students we have taught. At the same time we learned a great deal from the questions that were repeated by parents again and again and by their sharing possible solutions to problems that seem to exist universally! "How I wish there were more time to spend with you!" appreciative members of the audience frequently commented. "Why don't you write a book?" others suggested. And that was the spark that started our project!

We are neither child psychologists nor graduates in child development yet our large family and our introduction to Suzuki led us to read and study hundreds of books related to the child and his world.

Having taught and performed on our respective instruments for many years, having studied and adopted the Suzuki method as teachers and parents for a good number of those years, and having raised eight children—one of them still in the process—we have chalked up a lot of experience. That experience has included many errors, failures, successes and triumphs. It has contained pain and suffering, joy and enthusiasm in abundance. It has made us more knowledgeable human beings. But even more important, hopefully it has molded us into more loving, caring, and forgiving human beings.

Life is made up of many significant facets—like the characters in a play. Each role is an important part of the complex whole. Just as the Suzuki method deals with the whole child, not just his musical life, so "To Learn With Love" is not a book covering only musical pursuits. Each of the subjects covered is one we have considered important in a family's growth.

Suzuki has said "If love is deep much can be accomplished." In Willa Cather's "Death Comes to the Archbishop", the bishop affirms the same belief, "Where there is great love there are always miracles".

Suzuki has opened our minds and hearts to the fact that learning with love can be a great and glorious adventure—and that miracles can happen anywhere when that environment of love is surrounding us.

Notes About the Text

This book is a shared venture. Although we have collaborated on all of the material in this book, we have used italics to indicate the passages written by Connie, and roman type for Bill's writing. Regardless of who is designated as the writer, all of the text is the result of our cooperative efforts.

In regard to the perennial problem of 'he' and 'she', we have decided to mix their use. The student will be 'he' and the teacher 'she' for several chapters, then the pronouns will be reversed. This alteration continues throughout the book.

CONTENTS

The adult's idea that freedom consists in minimizing duties and obligations must be rejected. The foundation of education must be based on the following facts: That the joy of the child is in accomplishing things great for his age; that the real satisfaction of the child is to give maximum effort to the task at hand; that happiness consists in well directed activity of body and mind in the way of excellence; and that true freedom has, as its objective, service to society and to mankind consistent with the progress and happiness of the individual.

Maria Montessori

Learning: A Fascinating Process

The development of musical skills in children is a fascinating subject for study, but those of us teaching and parenting don't have access to much research in this area. Scientific studies of the growth of musical skills in children are almost non-existent. Measurement of success is obviously too complicated. If a child makes seven good serves out of ten in volley ball, we can all see and record the results; however, a student may play all the correct notes insofar as pitch and rhythm are concerned, only to be judged by a musician as deficient in dynamics, balance and phrasing. One can understand why studies are lacking in this area.

Fortunately, many of the principles of learning observed in other areas will help us in our work with children. Both the Suzuki parent and the Suzuki teacher can profit from a knowledge and understanding of the ways in which young children learn both motor and cognitive skills. Psychologists have done extensive research in these areas. Observations drawn from this research do have a bearing on problems we face in working with young children in music.

Although Suzuki says that he gave up reading books by psychologists some time ago, he did arrive at many of the same conclusions after his own extensive study of children. Such statements as "At age three children are unable to . . .", or "A four year old cannot comprehend. . . .", caused him to reject others' opinions and led him to study children directly himself.

Suzuki observed the learning habits of children. These observations and his reflections on them gave birth to his idea to apply the mother-tongue method to the teaching of music to small children. As his success tells us, he found that children have enormous potential for learning and that poor teaching, poor environment, and inadequate adult expectations have been the principal causes of limiting that potential.

Suzuki's Discovery, The Mother-Tongue Method

"All Japanese children speak Japanese!" exclaimed Suzuki to his friends one day. He had suddenly realized the astonishing fact that every normal child old enough to talk had been successfully educated by the mother-tongue method. "Children everywhere learn to speak their own tongues fluently which shows that they have a very high level of ability. The most successful example of the learning process is the mother-tongue method. Not only do normal children all over the world learn the basics of their mother-tongue without text, test, or classroom, but they also learn to speak the dialect with its often subtle nuances, and they are able to build an amazing vocabulary before they ever set foot in a school".

Natural Learning

The characteristics of the mother-tongue method are actually those of the child's natural learning period in every area, the period in which the child's intuitive learning ability is at its peak, and the period in which he is in the driver's seat controlling his advancement. It is only when the child learns to walk, to talk, and to use his hands for holding, grasping, and manipulating that he determines when he is ready to walk, talk, and use his hands. We should reflect on all of the aspects surrounding the development of these skills. What an exciting period of growth to observe!

It is obvious that the environment encourages such learning. Adult interest and praise are usually strong, the desire to imitate the adult and other children is powerful, and there are usually good models for observation. The child develops at his own rate, most often with a staggering number of repetitions.

Suzuki, in his approach, capitalizes on the principal features of the natural learning method. He stresses: 1) A favorable environment, with encouragement, interest, praise, and models of sight and sound to observe (listening to recordings is an important part of that

12

environment); 2) The awakening and growth of a desire to play a musical instrument; 3) Absence of stress, no problem with self-image; 4) A very slow rate of progress at the beginning; 5) Great number of repetitions; 6) Individual rates of progress; 7) Joy of learning; 8) Realization of potential of all.

Slow Rate of Progress. Many Repetitions

"Beginners learn so slowly. Same as mother-tongue. The baby does not say 'Mama' and then immediately speak many different words. No!", Suzuki says emphatically.

Lawther (1968) states that observations and experimental studies show a very slow rate of progress in primary or sensory-motor learning in young children. He calls attention to the youngster's need to automatize each activity before it can be integrated with another for a higher stage of learning. This process requires a great number of experiences.

Suzuki says, "The mother does not say to the child, 'You have said "Mama" enough times. Next word.' No. The child must repeat and repeat if he is to learn. Knowledge is not skill. Knowledge plus 10,000 times is skill."

Many studies of children report that they repeat, rework, and reiterate. When very young, they often repeat or try to repeat the same expression, phrase, or sentence over and over again. As many as seventy repetitions of a word, phrase, or sentence have been made in one period by a child. (Lawther, 1968)

Dr. Helen K. Billings, an innovative educator and the keynote speaker at the International Suzuki Conference in Amherst, Massachusetts in 1981, tells this anecdote in her book, "A Priceless Educational Advantage". "Once I observed a child trying to climb up one step! Thirty-seven times she tried and failed; but the thirty-eighth time she made it! And the look of joy and satisfaction on her face as she turned to survey the world from this hilltop position of one step was something that will always remain with me! I was well rewarded for waiting patiently, exerting great control and letting her do it herself. Such occurrences reveal the capacity of a child to become absorbed in a task and to persist."

LEARNING: A FASCINATING PROCESS

(A recording of Dr. Billings' book, "A Priceless Educational Advantage", read by Dr. Billings herself, is available on audio cassette tape. See Appendix.)

Researchers have found that even older children and adults need many repetitions to accomplish a skill.

Each time that I observed lessons in Haruko Kataoka's studio in Matsumoto, I became more excited by what I heard. On one particular day I sat quietly at the rear of the studio and watched students, parents, and observers come and go. Most of the time there were at least eight or ten people sitting behind the tables at the back of the room.

When we were in Japan five years before, I had been delighted by the playing of a four-year-old girl, Kaori Maruyama. Her performance of the first movement of Beethoven's Sonata, Opus 49, No. 2, was beautiful. Now I was hearing her again at age nine. During her lesson, as she was working on the Italian Concerto by Bach, an office secretary came in to notify Mrs. Kataoka of a phone call that must be answered immediately. Mrs. Kataoka left the room, and Kaori continued to work without interruption on a short, difficult passage that she had been asked to practice. She didn't turn away from the keyboard during Mrs. Kataoka's absence, but continued to practice without a pause. By the time Mrs. Kataoka returned, Kaori had repeated the passage thirty-five times!

Growth Rates. Maturation

It's odd that we parents who accept without question the fact that our children learn to talk and walk at different times forget all about this when our children begin any kind of formal training. Perhaps we accept each child's timetable for talking and walking because we know we can't do anything about it. How ridiculous we would feel trying to force a baby to say a new word!

When our first daughter, Kathleen, was born, we bought one of the first home tape recorders. It was an exciting toy. We were going to record all of our daughter's first words, or so we thought. We now have, in the family tape file, a ridiculously silly thirty-minute tape of Mommy, Daddy, and Grandma saying "Mama — Daddy — dog — me — boy — girl, etc." fifty or sixty times, followed by silence or the

14

sound of Kathleen chewing on the microphone! And her learning to walk! I must admit I was a little impatient when she took several steps holding tightly to one of my fingers, but steadfastly refused to walk by herself. I simply could not disengage my finger from that powerful grip! I tried to trick her. I gave her a stick to hold at one end while I held the other, then attempted to distract her so that I could let go. It never worked. As soon as I released the stick, she sat down immediately.

Later, I thought that I had succeeded in tricking Kathleen into walking. I handed her two baby food jars and told her, "Take these to Daddy." Imagine my surprise when she walked off, taking six confident steps! I know now that I had done nothing clever. She knew that the time was right. She was ready. The baby food jars and my request were merely coincidental!

Yes, during her natural learning period Kathleen was absolutely independent in determining her rate of progress, as were her many and varied younger siblings who all learned at different rates, but at rates that were uniquely their own. Teresa, our second daughter, for instance, was traveling fast and furiously at nine months, climbing everything in sight as well as walking. Tim, our second son, didn't start talking until he was over a year old, but when he started, it came in a torrent! It amazes us when we hear a parent proclaim, "They begin to walk at eleven months." We haven't the slightest idea when they should be expected to begin to walk. All of our children's rates of progress were so different that we became hopelessly confused. If someone asks one of us, "when do children . . . ?", we tell them to ask the parent of a single child!

Unfortunately, it seems that the child loses the unerring timetable guide that he possesses during the period in which he learns basic skills. Does he really know when he is ready to go on to the next step when he is studying math at school or violin at home? Do we teachers and parents really know when he is ready to move on? I call experienced teachers 'educated guessers' in this matter.

Kyoko Kawamoto, a gifted teacher who worked in Japan and in Knoxville for a few years, said, "Sometimes I take a big step with my students. If it works, I am happy. We save a lot of time. If it doesn't, I say, 'Let's go back and prepare you better for that step'. Then I try to determine how many small steps I may need to fill in."

Sensitivity to Each Child's Growth

You should discuss the rate of your child's growth with the teacher. In fact, this should be one of the most important topics of discussion between you. You should know why the teacher is doing what she is doing with your child. If you are concerned that Susie is being allowed to progress more rapidly than your Johnny and the reason for it is not obvious to you, you most certainly should talk to the teacher about this. If you ask that your child be allowed to move more quickly, your teacher may react defensively, perhaps with good reason. She may feel that the qualitative standards you have for your child are too low, and that you seem to be more concerned about keeping up with Susie rather than the good of your child. However, if your child is becoming uptight about his study and you report this, your teacher will most likely lessen the requirements as you request.

We teachers and parents need to keep reminding ourselves that ALL CHILDREN MATURE AT DIFFERENT RATES, and that assignments and expectations should reflect these differences. We must also remember the child's need for adequate repetition to automatize each activity as he progresses.

Growth Rates Change

Growth rates are by no means constant. "Once a slow learner, always a slow learner" is simply not true. We should not put a tag on the slow beginner. Remember the story Suzuki told in "Nurtured by Love" about the parakeet named Peeko Miyazawa? Peeko had to hear 3000 repetitions of the word 'Peeko' before he was able to say it, but only 200 repetitions of his family name, 'Miyazawa'. "Ability breeds ability", Suzuki says.

Suppose the owner had taken Peeko back to the shop after only 2700 repetitions of 'Peeko'. "This is a stupid parakeet. He'll never learn. I want another that learns at a reasonable rate". What would have happened to Peeko's development? What actually did happen was that Peeko, after learning to say his name, began to imitate everything he

16

heard, even after only one hearing! I'm sure people marveled at Mr. Miyazawa's parakeet. Did he tell them that Peeko was an especially slow learner? Did anyone ever ask Winston Churchill when he learned to talk? . . . Or ask Jesse Owens when he learned to walk?

Initial Levels of Proficiency

Psychologists state that initial levels of proficiency are not valid for predicting future achievement levels in a specific endeavor. In Suzuki's speeches he often makes this point, mentioning a fine advanced student who is known to the audience, and recalling that student's slow beginnings. "I was a very slow beginner," said Yukari Tate, the brilliant fourteen-year-old soloist at the first appearance of the Japanese children at the Music Educators National Conference in Philadelphia in 1964.

Singer (1972) quoted research support for the observation that the relationship between initial and final status is quite low on more complex tasks. THIS IS ESPECIALLY TRUE WHERE ENOUGH TIME AND PRACTICE ARE ALLOWED FOR LEARNING TO OCCUR.

Many teachers have encountered parents who have asked, "Is there any test that you can give my child to determine whether or not he has innate musical ability?" Suzuki, confronted with such an inquiry, jokingly asks, "Did your child walk in here with you? Can he talk to you about studying the violin? If he can do both of these things, he has already demonstrated high ability."

In answer to the parental inquiry about a proficiency test, we can quote the observations of Singer (1972). "Ability tests of complex tasks involving both physical and personality variables are not of any practical value."

The Three Phases of Skill Learning

Psychologists mention three phases of skill acquisition (Robb, 1972):

1) In the first phase, the learner understands what he is supposed to do.

17

2) The second phase consists of meaningful practice with appropriate feedback.

3) The third and final phase is automatic execution. (When the movement pattern is largely automatic, the musician can concentrate on interpretation.)

First Phase of Learning

Suzuki's awareness of the first phase of learning is shown clearly in his approach. He is constantly telling his teachers that the mothers, and thus their children, should know exactly what the student is supposed to practice and how to practice it.

Mitsumasa Denda, an outstanding teacher in Nagano, says that mere demonstration and explanation are not enough. "I ask the student to play the passage that he is to work on at home several times at the lesson until I'm sure that he and the parent understand the objective and how to accomplish it."

It is up to you to find out from your teacher precisely what your child is expected to achieve. Never leave the studio without a clear picture of the goals for the week. Don't be afraid to say, "I don't understand . . . please explain again. . . . please show me."

Second Phase of Learning

The second phase of learning, consisting of meaningful practice with appropriate feedback, is often filled with shortcomings that seriously hamper learning. Because of its scope, meaningful practice will be discussed in the chapter entitled Practice.

Knowledge of results, or feedback, is considered by psychologists studying skill learning to be one of the most significant factors in practice. Authorities have long recognized (Oxendine, 1968) that the learner improved much more quickly if he received specific information about the relationship of his performance to his goal. Feedback is described in cybernetic theory (Wiener, 1950) as error information and is one of the most important variables controlling and regulating human behavior.

18

The archer sees his arrow strike the target to the left of the bullseye. The bowler sees his ball roll into the right gutter. The basketball player sees the ball bounce off the front edge of the hoop. The golfer watches his ball careen off the fairway.

Knowledge of results, or feedback, in the above instances is automatic, instantaneous, and easily observed. Faults contributing to the errors mentioned above may not always be easily seen but the errors are perceived immediately.

In the study of a musical instrument, however, many errors can be made without the student being aware of them. To an extent, due to Suzuki's emphasis on listening to recordings, the Suzuki student does have a built-in error recognition system in that he notices when something he plays doesn't sound like the recording. A wrong note should leap out at him if he has listened enough. This, however, is not sufficient feedback. Parents need to provide additional information.

Appropriate Feedback from Parents

How should parents give their children appropriate feedback? To be most effective, the feedback must be meaningful to the child, specific in nature, and must be given immediately after he plays.

We should not, however, remain content with supplying him with feedback, but should endeavor to help him recognize his own feedback. We should assist him in observing his own sensory information from the task.

You might say, "Your bow is moving crookedly toward the fingerboard", and leave it at that. Better awareness training for him would be for you to draw the bow in a straight line, asking, "Can you feel the difference? Close your eyes and draw the bow. Without opening your eyes, tell me whether you think the bow was straight." After his response, you can ask him to open his eyes, and then tell him how the bow did move.

Most children do need help in learning to focus their own awareness on what they are doing as they play. It is possible, and so easy for them, to be a kind of 'middle man' between teacher and parent.

Teacher tells parent what must be done, parent sees that child does it. The child can become a passive non-observer, totally uninvolved! *Asking questions of the students instead of telling them what is wrong or what needs change or improvement makes it necessary for the children to pay close attention or they cannot answer. For that reason I have done a great deal of questioning at lessons. If the tone is weak, I play a passage with a good singing tone, and then with a weak tone asking, "Which one did you like better?" After they have answered— and they do answer 'the first one' ninety-nine percent of the time—I ask, "Which one sounded like your tone?" If they have no idea I ask them to play again and then tell me what they think. We do this again and again if it is necessary until they are confident that they can trust their own feedback.*

Parents can do similar things during practice at home. "After you play this passage, tell me whether it sounded like your recording." "Your teacher asked you to practice finger action. When you play this part tell me whether your fingers were lazy or active." "Does the rhythm in that part sound like your recording? Let's listen and then play it again. Tell me if it sounds the same." This kind of involvement cannot help but improve the climate of practice time and at the same time develop the student's trust in his ability to observe what he does.

I wish it were always easy to supply appropriate feedback. There are so many qualitative judgments to be made. You should work to become a keen observer and help your child to become one, too. Often children practice without any feedback except their own unskilled observations that everything is o.k., so they can get on with it. Of course, practice time is shorter and easier that way.

You should have confidence that you can improve as an observer not only in visual matters but also in aural perception. (Suzuki said that he puts tapes on the violin fingerboard so that the beginner's mother can see if the finger is in the right place and not have to rely on her ear to know whether the note is in tune!)

More on feedback can be found in the chapter on Concentration.

Third Phase of Learning

Automatic execution is found in the third phase of learning. Anyone seeing Suzuki's demonstrations with tour groups knows that his goal is automatic execution, not that performance should be automatic without musical sensitivity, but that the technical problems should be executed automatically. The large musical audience greeting Suzuki in Philadelphia at the Music Educators National Conference in 1964 was made well aware of this goal as he directed the youngsters to play a Vivaldi concerto. While they were playing, he asked them, "What is your name? How old are you? What city is this?" They answered without missing a note of the music.

In fact, Suzuki's whole program of reviewing pieces reinforces the principle of automatic execution. He has always been sensitive to the need for automatized activity, wherein the students gain great confidence in their abilities and are able to refine and develop their performances continually through constant review. Again, "Ability breeds ability."

Concert artists who are constantly performing in front of the public must have complete automatic execution. A good example of this is a story told about Artur Rubinstein, the famous concert pianist. After a performance with the Philadelphia Orchestra of the Concerto in B Flat by Brahms, an exuberant fan came backstage to see him. "Oh, Mr. Rubinstein, that was the most exquisite playing I have ever heard you do!"

Rubinstein smiled and replied gently, "Thank you. Before the performance I received a telephone call telling me of the birth of our son. Actually, I don't remember anything about the performance at all. . . . I wasn't aware of playing any of it!"

This is a case of a seasoned performer who had performed the work many times and whose whole body was programmed to artistic as well as technical excellence.

I remember Isaac Stern rehearsing the Prokofieff D Major Violin Concerto with Leonard Bernstein conducting. Stern was racing through a difficult passage in the last movement and talking to Bernstein at the same time without missing a beat! During intermission the air backstage was filled with difficult excerpts from violin concerti as the orchestral violinists congregated in twos and threes, trying to talk to each other while playing!

Parental Expectations

Wisely held and wisely expressed parental expectations can be extremely helpful to the child's growth. Nancy St. John, in a study done in 1972, found a significant correlation between mothers' and childrens' attitudes toward scholastic success. Maternal estimations and aspirations were found to be more optimistic than those of their children, but were also found to be better predictors of children's attitudes than family socio-economic status.

Unreasonable parental expectations, however, can be a stressful factor limiting a small child's development. Parental expectations must be transmitted in a loving, caring way that conveys to the child our belief in him and our respect for his feelings.

Margie, a bright four-year-old piano student, was elevated on a pedestal by her parents who spoke openly in front of her about her high IQ and her need for 'accelerated' instruction in the classroom . . . in this case, kindergarten! Margie believed that the love and approval she received was conditional, that it was based on her performance in all areas. Naturally she didn't want to jeopardize her position.

She had done very well, learning quickly, until we reached the point of putting hands together in Lightly Row. After two weeks of struggling with little sign of improvement she announced to me at her lesson that she didn't want to put hands together and she wasn't going to practice on it anymore. Realizing that meeting this head-on would probably have negative results, I quickly prayed for guidance! "O.K., Margie," I answered agreeably. "You can practice your left hand part and the melody separately. When you feel you're ready to practice them together, let me know."

About two weeks later she decided to risk it. Her desire to 'get on with it' was stronger than her fear of facing her apparent weakness. This same reluctance occurred whenever there was anything that couldn't be learned immediately after its introduction. Because I understood the terrific responsibility she had to live up to her parents' image of her, I tried to help her as much as I could by not pushing. Parental expecta-

tions that put a heavy burden on a child actually make her want to give up rather than strive for further goals.

When parental expectations are conveyed in the proper way the results can be far different. Alison began the study of violin at age four, the piano at age six. She was a lovely little girl, attentive and interested, with a beautiful spirit. Her mother spent a great deal of time with her, sacrificing time from her own activities without resentment. Indeed her mother showed nothing but pleasure and enthusiasm when she was involved with Alison's musical activities.

Nothing was too difficult for Alison. If somthing did not respond immediately to practice, her mother would say, "We're working on it. We'll get it soon." And Alison would!

Alison excelled academically as well as being a superior performer on both the violin and piano. Upon her graduation from high school, she gave a beautiful recital, playing both instruments. She is now a music major at the Indiana University School of Music, an excellent example of the child who is nurtured by a parent with wisely held and wisely expressed expectations.

In thinking about our children and in talking and working with them, we should always maintain a confident view of their potential. They may take a longer time than others of the same age to accomplish certain goals, but we owe it to them and to ourselves to keep an optimistic and enthusiastic attitude.

Teacher's Expectations

Suzuki says that he finds many examples of inadequate adult expectations limiting children's potential. "Even in Japan I must keep convincing mothers that their children have high abilities. When I started Talent Education I didn't know the extent of the potential of young children with the violin. I was convinced that they had great potential but I had no precise goal in mind. Gradually I began to expect that all children could play the Vivaldi A Minor Concerto very well. Then I raised my expectations to the Bach A Minor Concerto. And now I must raise my expectations again. It depends on how well we teach."

23

LEARNING: A FASCINATING PROCESS

Many experienced teachers who've started working with the Suzuki approach have confessed that their expectations of their students' growth have increased a great deal and have been borne out by the students' consequent development.

Yamamura-sensei, an extremely successful teacher in Nagoya spoke of his change of attitude when he became a Suzuki teacher. "In my earlier days of teaching I was polite to a slow learner, but I know I must have conveyed my limited expectancy to the student. Now if a child doesn't learn well, instead of judging him to be untalented, I ask myself, 'How can I help this child unlock his abilities, abilities I know he must have?' "

In their book, "Pygmalion in the Classroom, Teacher Expectation and Pupils' Intellectual Development," Robert Rosenthal and Lenore Jacobson cite a study made by the Harvard-National Science Foundation. "In a certain elementary school 20% of the children were reported to their teachers as showing unusual potential for intellectual growth. The names of these children had been drawn out of a hat although tests had been administered to lead the teachers to believe the choice was being scientifically made. Eight months later these "magic" children showed significantly greater gains in IQ than the children who had not been singled out. The change in the teacher's expectation had led to an actual change in the intellectual peformance of these randomly selected children."

You may have heard the story about the teacher who was overjoyed when she received the roster of her new class. Next to the children's names were a series of numbers in the 130s and 140s. "They've given me the students with the high IQs!" she exulted. The class did exceedingly well as she expected. It wasn't until months later she found that the numbers were locker numbers!

Goals

Learners must have goals. The fact that the Suzuki repertoire is common to all students propels the youngsters onward as they desire to play the next piece they've heard on the recording and in performance by more advanced students. It is Suzuki's cherished hope that this will be the principal goal motivating students to practice and progress. This desire to play the next piece can get out of hand, however, if the parent allows the child to go ahead of the teacher's assignment. He may learn the piece with serious mistakes that will be very difficult to correct.

Constant dwelling on far-off goals does not provide the healthiest environment for learning a skill. The parent who has only distant goals such as "I hope my daughter will be concertmistress of the school orchestra when she grows up", "I want my son to win the youth talent contest", or "It would be wonderful if my daughter wins a scholarship to Juilliard!", may miss all the fun of watching her children develop day by day.

Mischa Elman, the celebrated Russian violinist, in an interview, urged students not to dwell too much on their aspirations to be concert artists. He compared learning to play the violin with the activity of a mountain climber. "The mountaineer doesn't spend much time and energy gazing at the far-off peak he is trying to ascend but rather devotes most of his attention to the problem of the next rock or crevass that is facing him." Elman assured students that when they did pause for self-appraisal, they would be delighted to see how far they had come, taking one hurdle at a time.

Habits

An adult or child generally approaches a skill-learning situation with a wide variety of habits already available. The swimmer, for instance, already knows how to kick, move his arms, and breathe in and out. These are all examples of what is called relatively well-developed 'serial' behavior.

The child approaching the study of violin, however, usually does not have a relevant repertory of habits. It is doubtful that he has had much experience holding something firmly between his chin and shoulder, looking to the left to watch something closely, holding his left hand up to the side and turned so that the little finger points to the face, grasping any object with the peculiarities of the bow hold, or moving the right arm so as to draw the bow in straight lines.

I feel that the bad habits developed by the beginning violin student are due principally to the fact that the child not only does not have relevant habits already available, as does the swimmer, but does have habits that seem related and so he uses them. He is accustomed to looking at objects closely by holding them down in front of him, so he wants to hold the violin that way. He is accustomed to holding fragile objects securely, or being told to, so he holds the violin neck firmly in his left fist and the bow firmly in his right fist. He generally moves his right arm in an arc, so he moves the bow crookedly. And so on. I think it helps to point this out, perhaps even to a small child. It certainly is helpful to parents to understand that many errors made by beginners are the result of natural inclinations. This is why Suzuki insists that beginners should move so slowly.

Since I play the viola as well as the piano, I can make a comparison. Extension of the pianist's arms and hands over the keyboard does not run counter to any previously acquired habits. He plays upon the keyboard and does not have to support the instrument as he plays. Only the fingers cannot rely upon past habits. It is doubtful that the child has had any experience using firm, independent fingers. He will need to develop this habit but he will not be hindered by a previous related habit.

Acquiring new habits may be difficult but is very valuable training for the child. Psychologists show that CHILDREN LEARN NEW HABITS WITH EASE OR DIFFICULTY DEPENDING UPON THE QUALITY AND QUANTITY OF THEIR PREVIOUS EXPERIENCE IN HABIT FORMATION.

Rate of Improvement

Both parent and child should know that the rate of improvement during practice on a specific complex task is by no means stationary. The rate of improvement is often very fast at the start. The first repetitions contribute a great deal to the mastery of the problem. Children are sometimes quite disturbed by the fact that the following repetitions seem to contribute increasingly less to the total performance.

This is one advantage of the Suzuki review work. In fact, Suzuki doesn't expect the student to have complete mastery of a piece before he goes on to the next one. Hundreds of follow-up repetitions are scattered through the student's practice days as he reviews earlier material.

26

These repetitions, contributing more slowly to the learning process, are not as stressful as they would be if the student were to do all of them immediately after the notes and fingering were learned. The refinement and growth are very gradual, perhaps not perceived by the child, yet very real, contributing significantly to the child's developing skill.

Plateaus

Another characteristic of the rate-of-learning curve that bothers all of us at times is that period of no observable improvement called a plateau. Plateaus are not always predictable, but teachers do witness their appearances at various points in the Suzuki study.

Researchers in motor learning say that plateaus appear when separate response components begin to emerge into continuous, smooth acts. At this time habits are being overlearned. The student is becoming freer and approaching automaticity, a state in which later learning becomes easier. Plateaus seem to be unavoidable, but if their nature is understood, the student will not become so discouraged and frustrated.

Suzuki's choice of literature provides some breathing points. Some pieces require no additional technical skills. The student feels he is learning more easily as he learns a new piece without realizing that it presents no new problems.

Positive and Negative Transfer

Transfer is an interesting aspect of the learning process. We most often think of it in a positive way, rejoicing when we notice that something learned earlier aids us in learning a similar skill. Children are especially delighted when they find that, because of something they have already learned, they are able to play quite easily similar passages in other works. "If you learn this part well," you may encourage your child," you'll not only be able to play it well but will also be able to play easily a part like it in another piece."

Understanding negative transfer is helpful to the student or parent who is wondering why the fingers persist in going down incorrectly. A good example of this is often encountered as the student starts Lightly Row after a long period on Twinkle. He plays open E, then down comes the third finger on the A string even though his ear tells him that this is not the right finger, that it should be the second finger following the open E. How helpful to the child if he knows why this happens! "Just look at the third finger! He's so well trained to come down after he hears the open E string. You'll have to tell him to wait this time, because in Lightly Row it's second finger's turn to play right after open E!"

A similar negative transfer takes place when the piano student has learned to play the left hand of Cuckoo and then proceeds to the left hand of Lightly Row. In Cuckoo the first two notes are fingered 5-3; in Lightly Row 5-1. Invariably when Lightly Row is first being practiced, the fingers come down 5-3. "You'll need to remind number three to wait this time," you can suggest. "His turn comes after the thumb in this piece."

In helping to erase well-established habits like this or even when first learning a fingering in a new piece, I find that asking the child to say the finger numbers aloud requires attentive thinking and results in fewer repetitions needed for accomplishment.

Reminiscence

Most teachers say they have had the following experience. A student plays. "That was fine! Better than the last lesson." Then the child starts laughing, often looking triumphantly at his mother. "But I practiced only one day this week!" Since I have experienced the same phenomenon, I say, "Isn't it wonderful how our bodies keep learning after we've done good practice? If you hadn't practiced well, this nice surprise wouldn't have happened!"

The phenomenon of reminiscence, that is, improvement during a period in which there is no practice, is an interesting one which has long fascinated those studying learning. The most frequent explanation has been that some subconscious mental practice goes on in the student even without his knowledge.

Overlearning

Singer (1972) states that overlearning, or practicing past a criterion, results in better retention of that which has been learned. Over-

learning plays an important role in Suzuki's success. Children are asked to review old material again and again, making it a part of them.

There are always points needing attention and each time a piece is reviewed one of these points can be the focus of attention. Because of this we needn't have "irksome uniformity" or "lack of variety" as the dictionary defines boredom. Repetition should always be a vehicle for growth. If the student has reached a high level of performance, he can be asked to "play with all your heart" as one Japanese mother told her child, or "feel the spirit of Bach and Mozart" if he is more advanced.

If parents will think of the necessary repetitions for overlearning as parallel to building a beautiful structure in which every block is the same but the end result is a magnificent monument, there should be anticipation and excitement instead of boredom or tolerance.

To be fully effective, says Oxendine (1968), overlearning must be practiced as seriously as the initial task and with as much attention. Teachers must plan for overlearning. Too often parents and children get the feeling that once you get the hang of it, you can stop practicing. IT IS THE DRILL THAT MAKES HIGH LEVEL PERFORMANCE AUTOMATIC.

"Don't stop practicing a passage until you can play it well three times in succession," Suzuki advises his students. He knows from experience that a task may be learned well as shown by one fine performance, but if the student stops with this, his later retention of the skill will be less than if he practices an additional series of successful trials.

Overlearning often taxes the ingenuity of us parents. Just because a student may have been successful in performing a certain piece does not always mean that he will want to repeat the same piece. Suzuki always asks for the repetitions to be "better tempo, better tone, more musical, better intonation".

Negative Factors Affecting Achievement

It is good to stress the positive factors affecting achievement but negative factors simply cannot be ignored. Gallwey (1977) calls these 'obstacles to learning'. One of the principal obstacles is a poor self-image which spawns all kinds of fears: fear of making a fool of oneself, fear of not being able to learn, fear of not meeting others' expectations. (See the chapter on Self-Image).

The fears that attack the person with a poor self-image are easy to understand. The person who thinks little of himself spends all of his time thinking about himself - what others thought, are thinking, and will think about him and his abilities. How can he be free to think about the task at hand? His fear of making mistakes takes all of his power of concentration. To eliminate this fear we must repeat, again and again, that NOBODY, SIMPLY NOBODY, EVER LEARNS A SKILL WITHOUT MAKING MISTAKES, that WE LEARN PRE-CISELY FROM OUR MISTAKES. There is no way to grow and learn without mistakes.

Perfectionism

We all know the child or adult who is a perfectionist, constantly frustrated because he or she cannot do things perfectly. A child who approaches his study of a musical instrument with a perfectionist attitude should be prepared by parents and teacher for the realities of learning an instrument or he will experience increasing stress as he strives for perfection.

Teachers often encounter frustration in the bright student who is accustomed to understanding and excelling with little effort, and who easily stays at the top of his class. When this student is confronted with the repetitions necessary for learning to play a musical instrument, he often can't understand why this should be necessary and becomes angry with himself because of his inability to perform perfectly immediately. Fear of making mistakes is common but the perfectionist has an extreme aversion to errors. You must say to this kind of child, "People aren't going to be disappointed in you or dislike you because you can't play a new piece right away. Everybody makes mistakes while they learn."

Children should be taught that all human beings are imperfect and fallible. "We strive to be less fallible," writes Dr. David Burns, "but we don't try or pretend to be perfect." A child can and should enjoy the process of doing something very well, but when his primary goal is perfection, each step can be filled with tension and anxiety.

Fear of Success

A fear that usually does not bother the beginner but may affect a more experienced student is the fear of success. This may sound strange because we think that it is natural for every human being to want to succeed, but it is such a common fear that entire books have been written about it. For some reason a student who has tasted success and has received the reinforcement of remarks like, "He's really got it!", "It's going to be fun to watch how fast she progresses!", may react negatively to all of these encouraging comments. Fear of the added responsibility associated with high achievement seems to be the cause. An ex-performer is occasionally heard to say, "I could have been great if I had practiced."

Gregory, our third child and first son, puzzled us by his reaction to success. When he was ten and had been studying piano for several years, he performed on a recital. Congratulatory comments came from all sides. "You play with such musical feeling and vitality!", "What a delightful performance!", "It's obvious that music is very much a part of you!" I looked on, smiling and enjoying a moment dear to mothers. (Parents are rewarded at these moments for the struggle and heartache that seem to be an inescapable part of parenting.)

Not long afterward Gregory asked if he could study the cello instead of the piano. Since he had been studying piano with me, I thought this might be a good idea. He would be playing an instrument that neither parent could play. This might make him feel more independent.

After a year of successful cello study he participated in an elementary orchestra clinic in our area. The results of the tryouts placed him in the first chair of the cello section.

"Why must everyone in the Starr family play a string instrument or piano?" he questioned a few weeks later. So he dropped the cello and began to study French horn. This continued through his high school years.

After an excellent performance of the Mozart Concerto No. 3 with the orchestra at Suzuki's Institute in Matsumoto, he received encouraging compliments on his fine playing. Later as he prepared to return to Japan to go to college, he told us that he wanted to sell his horn. "If I want to play again later, I'll find another."

I always marveled at the fact that comments we expected to motivate and inspire him turned out to have the opposite effect. Was the challenge missing or was the responsibility too great for a child having two professional musicians as parents?

*   *   *   *   *

Further aspects of the learning process will be discussed in the sections on Practice, Concentration, and Coordination of Mind and Body.

For the things we have to learn before we can do them
We learn by doing them.

Aristotle

Gregor Piatiogorsky, the famous concert cellist, remembered that his always cheerful father played the violin day and night. When Gregor was small his father took him to a symphony concert where he heard a cello for the first time. He had never heard anything so beautiful! He soon had his own make-believe cello—a set of two sticks, a long one for the cello, the short one for the bow—which magically conveyed him into his own world of sound. When he was given a real cello on his seventh birthday, he kept it next to him at meals and beside his bed at night, never letting it out of his sight.

Practice

Parents' Attitude Toward Practice

When we lived in Matsumoto we watched groups of mothers meeting with Suzuki on a regular basis. As we became acquainted with some of the mothers we asked them, "What does Suzuki-sensei talk about in these meetings?"

They laughed. "Always the same things. Answering questions about home practice, giving us suggestions on how to motivate our children, and encouraging us to believe that our children all have high ability."

It was comforting to know that even with Suzuki's thirty-year environment, the problems we all face were of concern to him and the mothers in the Matsumoto program.

In a videotape interview for the Suzuki-Starr tapes, I asked Suzuki, "When you speak of mother-tongue education, you mention the fact that the desire to speak gradually awakens in the baby. Would you please give us some advice on how to motivate the child so that he will practice willingly and eagerly?"

"The mother's attitude is so important", Suzuki replied. "Teachers and mothers should teach with love, and should always try to make learning fun. Mothers should not scold their children. When we wish children to learn something, we must first create a willing attitude and a happy environment."

(A recording of this interview is available on audio cassette tape. See Appendix.)

And so, taking Suzuki's advice as we approach the problem of home practice, we must first look at ourselves and our attitudes. Most of us, if not all, would say that our principal motive was that of enriching the child's life. On the large scale our attitudes can be quite healthy, but on a day-to-day basis, faced with our child's reluctance to practice, we may exhibit far different attitudes.

Shigeki Tanaka, kindergarten director working under Suzuki's guidance, stated, "Since nothing is as important as the beginning, I

34

take plenty of time there. I foster the joy (confidence) and interest (concentration) of doing the simple things everyone can do, more and more skillfully (accurate and fast)."

If we look forward with pleasure to the daily practice sessions with our children, this joy will show in everything we say or do. If we have to learn to feel this way, we should act as though we already do. Didn't William James tell us that an emotion acted out repeatedly becomes our own?

Practice: When, Where, What, How Much

A regular practice schedule is the best for small children. They grow to expect practice every day at the same time. Practice then takes on the quality of inevitability. It becomes part of the routine.

"Where" to practice should be a place that has no aural distractions, and visual distractions should be minimal. If there is likely to be anything distracting outside, the child should not face a window.

Here's an example of "when, where, and what" in our home when Michael was five years old. The time is 7:00 a.m. and the place is the bathroom off our bedroom. I'm shaving and Michael is standing on the commode practicing his newest most difficult passage. He liked to do the hardest part of his practice first. My ears are open and my eyes move his way enough so that he sees that Daddy knows what's going on. Actually, it was my shaving that was on 'automatic' at these times.

I used to delight in his concentration on repetitions of small fragments. I never knew how long each period of concentration would last. It varied every day, but most often Michael did his best work at the very beginning of each morning practice. Judith and Tim took a little longer to warm up but lasted longer.

When Michael seemed to tire, I changed direction, asking him, "Which piece would you like to review first?" I can still picture him, now six feet two, standing on the commode playing Minuet No. 2 with great fervor.

A Japanese mother who was known to be very successful working with her little daughter said, "I left the violin out where Hitomi could reach it. When I heard her pick it up and start to play on it, I appeared quickly and guided her for a few minutes of practice." (I should mention that this was a mother who did not work outside her home and who had only one child.) Hitomi's mother did not regard this as a sacrifice. "I just loved to watch my daughter play. It was a game for me, too." Years later we saw this mother, whose daughter was then a very advanced violinist, watching young beginners with childlike delight.

When I've told this story of Hitomi and her mother, I've had mothers protest, saying, "I've done the same thing, but my son simply wants to scratch on the violin. He doesn't want me to regulate him in any way. When I try to get him to practice the way his teacher asked him to, he won't do it. He just walks away."

My advice was for the mother to say to the child, "I'm glad you want to play the violin. Let's play some games the teacher wants you to do, and then you can play a game of your own", or, "Can you show me the way your teacher asked you to play?"

Length of Practice Periods

Suzuki points out that practice periods should grow along with the span of concentration. "At home two or three minutes of practice may be enough for a beginner. Perhaps this can be done four or five times a day. Gradually each practice period can be longer as the child begins to play the Twinkle Variations. If he can play all the variations of Twinkle, which may take four minutes, his ability to concentrate is also developed to that length of time. As other pieces are added, the period of concentration lengthens naturally".

Psychologists agree that a given amount of practice time distributed over several short sessions, with rest or contrasting activities in between, leads to more learning than the same amount of time spent in continuous practice. Of course, the short sessions have to be long enough to overcome the warm-up period which is generally inefficient. An interesting aspect of separated practice sessions is that errors often disappear during the intervening time but correct responses are retained. Intervening periods also give the child a chance to recover from physical or mental fatigue.

In some instances it has been shown that more skill can be attained from less total practice time if practice time is divided into several short segments. As children become more advanced and are practicing much more, it becomes difficult to find time to create a number of short practice periods. When a long period is unavoidable, it is best if there is contrasting material covered in each session.

Quantity and Quality of Practice

Suzuki often comments on the rapid advancement of the children who practiced well and hard. "A child who practices well shows it in his playing. You can tell immediately. Practicing according to the correct method and practicing as much as possible is the way to acquire ability. If one is faithful to this principle, superior skill develops without fail. If you compare a person who practices five minutes a day with one who practices three hours a day, the difference, even though they both practice daily, is enormous. Those who fail to practice sufficiently fail to acquire ability. Only the effort that is actually expended will bear results. There is no short cut. If a five-minute-a-day person wants to accomplish what the three-hour-a-day person does, it will take him nine years to accomplish what the other does in three months.

"For someone to complain, 'But I studied for five years' means nothing. It all depends on how much he did each day. What a person should have said is, 'I did it for one hundred and fifty hours and I'm still no better.' To put your talent up on the shelf and then say you were born without any is utter nonsense.

"The development of ability is straightforward. People either become experts at doing the right thing, which is seen as a fine talent, or they become experts at doing something that is wrong and unacceptable, which is seen as lack of talent. So it behooves everyone to become expert in the right things, and the more training he receives, the better. Depending upon these two things — the amount and the quality of the practice — superior ability can be produced in anyone."

Most American children don't seem to be spending as much time practicing as their Japanese counterparts. We parents shouldn't lament the fact that our children don't progress as rapidly. We should

PRACTICE

accept the hard facts about quantity and quality of practice, and strive
to help our children practice as much and as well as possible. Our
commitment of time and energy will of course depend upon our family
priorities.

*During the last few years Suzuki has been urging students to prac-
tice a minimum of two hours a day.* I wonder how many families are
following this advice. Fourteen years ago when we spent our year in
Japan we found that many students in the middle and high school years
were thought to be doing well managing one hour a day for practice.
Homework assignments took a great amount of their time. Although
they were in the minority, one always heard more about the students
who were practicing three and four hours a day.

Conditions of Practice

*Practice alone is not sufficient for improvement. According to Sin-
ger (1972) practice is wasted unless it is accompanied by the student's
interest and attention, meaningfulness of the task to the learner, understanding of the goals, intent to learn, readiness to learn, knowledge of
results, and a strong relationship of the practice conditions to the
performance conditions.* Slightly overwhelming, isn't it? If all of these
factors were present at practice times, a parent's life would be easy!

In line with the above statement, perhaps it is not too bold to say
that no practice between lessons might be superior to poor practice.
Mitsumasa Denda said he preferred his beginners not to practice at
all between lessons if the mother and child didn't understand what
was to be done, or if the child were allowed to practice very badly and
get into habits difficult to correct.

"Children learn," Suzuki insists. "They learn either good or bad
habits. It is wrong to say that they haven't learned when they play
badly. They have learned — they have learned to play badly."

Observers note that children who have bad playing habits are
consistent in the application of these habits. They've learned well how
to play badly. Watch a child who is holding the violin incorrectly
while playing. He always holds it incorrectly in the same manner. He
does not shift from one poor playing position to another.

We must realize, however, that students cannot produce perfection as they learn. Current thinking among physiologists (Wilson, 1982) is that we begin to learn to make complicated moves rather laboriously — working out the details step by step, making corrections when we observe our own mistakes, and consciously and deliberately establishing patterns of movements that eventually become less tentative and finally become smooth and sure.

Practice Format and Goals

The child should be given opportunities to express himself about the practice format. This helps foster a responsible attitude toward his practice.

Kyoko used to ask Michael to do certain things ten times a day. In the first practice session I would say, "Let's see, Michael, Kyoko asked you to play this part ten times every day. How many times do you want to do it now?" He often gave a number higher than I expected. If she hadn't requested a specific number of repetitions for a certain passage that we found troublesome, I would ask him how many times he thought it should be played. Again he most often gave a number higher than I had anticipated.

Each practice session should have a goal, even if it seems to the child to be only a number of correct repetitions. Judith, Tim, and Michael all showed expressions of self-satisfaction after completing a number of repetitions, often heaving a sigh of relief for having gone over the hurdle. Children are proud of accomplishments, even small ones.

Most children like to count repetitions. One of the best things Kyoko did for Michael was to ask him to draw the bow straight twenty thousand times. "Twenty thousand!" Michael exlaimed in dismay. "But when you play the last variation of Twinkle once you will have played almost two hundred bowings", Kyoko reassured him. Michael really enjoyed checking off two hundred at a clip. He was delighted to see that five playings gave him one thousand. Twenty thousand didn't seem so far off at all!

PRACTICE

As the children got older, we found that it was more difficult to sell them on counting repetitions as a goal. Many teachers have reported that they've had trouble with certain bright youngsters who, after they understood how a passage should be played and then played it well, couldn't see the necessity for repetitions. "I already know how it should be played," one might say. This is where Suzuki's famous saying comes in, "Knowledge is not skill. Knowledge plus ten thousand times is skill!" In later pages we'll discuss how we can aid in making these repetitions not only palatable but enjoyable for our children.

Repetitions of pieces already learned are much more pleasant for the children since the appearance of variable pitch tape recorders. Since the pitch is adjustable to the piano's tuning, beginning pianists can play their first melodies along with the recorded left hand part, while the more advanced pianist may sometimes do the review pieces along with the complete recording. Violinists can play along with accompaniment tapes or the recording itself. Most children enjoy playing straight through pieces with accompaniments. This is a musical experience that seems far removed from practice. I remember watching a small Japanese girl in her home in Matsumoto playing piece after piece with the recording. She looked as though she were imagining herself on a stage performing before a rapt audience!

Sometimes on those "bad days" it's very difficult to get the children to attempt anything new. I remind parents that one can still benefit a great deal from review practice. If you sense that your child, for whatever reason, is too disoriented to practice new material effectively, why don't you suggest the child play a mini-concert just for you? For each piece that is played you can suggest one point to be observed for improvement.

Specific, Reasonably Hard But Attainable Goals

Teachers have the responsibility of establishing goals for the student's lessons, and the parent, the goals for each practice session, although the student should participate in setting particular practice goals. Goals that are specific, and reasonably hard but attainable, will produce much better performance than too easy goals or a gen-

40

eral goal to do one's best. "Reasonably hard" is difficult to define. Both the teacher and parent will, by trial and error, become more proficient at guessing what "reasonably hard" goals should be for each particular child.

At a workshop for teachers in Knoxville I brought our eight-year-old Michael to take a lesson on the second violin part of the Bach Double Concerto. I wanted to demonstrate to the teachers an example of a 'specific, reasonably hard but attainable' goal for a single practice session. "Michael always likes to work on the hardest passages first", I explained, "and then coast the rest of the session".

Directing him as a parent would, I guided him through six repetitions of a portion of the difficult c minor passage on the second page, a passage that is usually played quite badly out of tune because of improper practice. I asked Michael to play the 'taka' rhythm on each note. "Place your fingers very carefully as Kyoko asked you to do", I requested.

This passage is thirty-one notes in length, but I asked him to play only the first twelve notes, making sure that his hand was in the proper position before he started each repetition. Then I stopped. Michael had been giving total attention to his work and I wanted to stop while we were both ahead.

I turned to the teachers and said, "I think that was a reasonably hard goal, because I was being so specific about the placement of each finger. It was also attainable because Michael knew it would be short. Didn't you think that was enough on that passage, Michael?"

"It sure was! And you didn't yell at me either!"

Perhaps his remark demonstrated that my goals during practice at home were at times unreasonably hard and evoked tension in him and me. At any rate, it exposed my human frailty as father and home teacher and at the same time strengthened my credibility as one who understood parents' problems.

Kyoko Kawamoto told of asking a small Japanese boy to go over a passage again and again. Since he was doing so well, she kept on and on. "Suddenly he put the violin down and started to scream! I hadn't noticed the tension building up in him. I told myself that in the future I would have to be more observant of the student's feelings."

41

PRACTICE

Manual Guidance. Knowledge of Alternatives

When Michael was three, I decided to start him on the violin by guiding his bow arm in the 'taka-taka' rhythm one thousand times! I had seen so many beginners bow crookedly that I intended to program him with correct input only. Since he had never done it incorrectly, I thought he would naturally do it correctly when he began to draw the bow by himself. It seemed inevitable that he would fall into the pattern that I had established. (I learned later that psychologists called this "external manipulation of the passive learner".)

When I finally asked Michael to do it himself, I found out how truly passive he had been! His bow wandered all over the place as though he had never moved the bow before! I didn't realize that training by guidance, particularly of a passive learner, may restrict the information offered to the learner by withholding a knowledge of alternatives. According to Holding (1965), "Knowledge of the correct response is incomplete if there is no opportunity to define it against the alternatives. We cannot be said to understand 'red' if we have never identified other colors."

Samuel Belov, one of my teachers at Eastman, said, "You should be wary if, when practicing a difficult new passage, you play it well from the beginning. You will know it better if you can compare your correct and incorrect renditions". At that time I was astonished to hear what I later found was excellent advice.

Good teachers and parental home teachers often show alternatives to students by drawing their attention to the feel of an appropriate movement contrasted with the feel of inappropriate alternatives. A student playing incorrect alternatives occasionally is not learning those errors as long as he knows which response is the correct one.

I said that Michael was truly a passive learner during that period. A strong indication of this passive role came one day when, in the middle of repetitions of 'taka-taka' in which he was totally uninvolved, he released both bow and violin and walked off to do something of his own choice. I made a violent lunge and managed to catch both before they hit the floor! After I recovered, I walked into the living room.

"You know", I said to Connie, "since we're leaving for Japan in six months, it's really foolish of me not to delay Michael's study until we get there. That way we can observe first-hand how a Japanese teacher works with a beginning student."

"That's a good idea," she replied. Then she added with a grin, "Was that a sigh of relief I heard?"

Mental Practice

Mental practice works well with older students, but there has to be sufficient prior experience before mental practice becomes valuable. Fritz Kreisler, the famous Austrian violinist, was known to be a master of mental practice. It was said that he could study a new piece from the printed page, then perform it in a recital without ever having played it before! Of course, the idiom and the passage-work must have been very familiar to him.

The use of a mental review following a performance may provide feedback that the performer might not have noticed otherwise. Many performers have said that after a concert they are mentally able to play over an entire performance in explicit detail with very keen aural and kinesthetic images. In fact, some have said that they couldn't avoid playing the program over, that it came to them unbidden!

The great violin pedagogue, Ivan Galamian, taught that mental control over physical movements was paramount in importance. In guiding the technical development of his students, he sought to make the sequence of mental command and physical response as quick and precise as possible.

Mental anticipation of motions to be made and mental reflections on motions made are valuable tools for the student. Suzuki's 'stop-and-prepare' method gives the student ample time to make a mental image of what he is doing before he plays the passage. Mental reflection on a motion just made is more difficult for students but it is very helpful if they can retain, even for only a moment, the feel of a certain motion, whether it was right or wrong.

PRACTICE

Aids to Mental Practice

I like to play games like the following with students to develop more sensitivity to mental placement.

"Put your violin up in playing position. Close your eyes. Now move your hand up to third position where the first finger should rest on the note A on the E string. Now before you play the note, can you tell me whether it will be flat, sharp or on target?" If the student is not able to tell me anything at this point, I ask him to play the note and then try to associate the pitch with the distance he moved up the string. I ask him to repeat the process to see if he can improve his judgment of the distance his hand should move.

I use this game for bow placement. "Put your violin in rest position. Close your eyes. Raise your violin into playing position. Now place your bow on the E string at the very middle of the bow. Do you think your bow is straight? Is it in the middle? Is it midway between bridge and fingerboard? Now open your eyes."

If the child has not placed it correctly, I ask him to place it correctly while his eyes are open, then close the eyes and try to be aware of the feel of the hand and arm in the correct position. He should then return the violin to rest position and repeat the whole game.

Even beginners profit by the use of mental preparation before practice or performance. It is an excellent habit to develop.

I use this game for the placement of hands and fingers on the keyboard. "Please put your hands on your thighs in rest position. When I tell you the name of the piece I'd like you to play, find the notes on the keyboard with your eyes only, then tell me the name of the first note in each hand and which finger plays it." I allow enough time here for the student not to feel rushed. "When you are ready, put your fingers on those keys but wait until I say 'ready, play' ". If the child fumbles, we go back to rest position and begin again. The student must be able to place the fingers exactly in position before starting to play.

Another version of the same game may be done with the student's eyes closed. I name the piece, then ask the child to tell me the name of the first note in each hand and the fingers that play those notes. After he does that, I ask him to open his eyes and place his fingers in the correct places.

I use another game for 'listening' mental preparation. "Put your hands in place for 'Go Tell Aunt Rhody'. In your head listen for the beautiful tone you will hear when you play. Think of the tempo that you will play. When you have done this, you are ready to begin."

The New Piece

Some children are so motivated to learn a certain new piece that they will easily agree to practice carefully. These are wonderful times for parents, as are the times when the children review pieces with eagerness. In these cases, motivation is created by the music itself. This is the best, the healthiest kind of motivation.

The desire to play a new piece may not always work out so well. Unfortunately, some children are so impatient to play a new piece that they don't want to take the time to stop and practice it carefully. How wonderful it would be if there were some gadget that prevented the child from making any sound at all if the piece wasn't played well! But again, unfortunately, a child may be able to get through a piece in what may sound like an acceptable manner, but may have incorrect bowings, bad posture, and wrong fingerings. The mother may be so glad to hear the piece played that she may overlook the quality of the performance.

If the child does learn incorrect bowings and fingerings, it's very difficult to undo this learning. I know first-hand how difficult it is to restrain enthusiasm for playing the next piece! We want the child to be motivated by the music itself, and then we're caught putting on the brakes so that the child will learn it properly.

Are you unable to curb your child's enthusiasm to play straight through pieces? (Actually, some parents say they don't like to stop their children because they're afraid they'll suppress their desire to play). If deterring your child seems to cause a great battle, why not say that he can play straight through as a reward for having practiced carefully on certain passages? If it's a review piece, you can tell him to go ahead and play straight through the piece, but you should give him one point to observe and report to you on that point after he finishes.

45

PRACTICE

It is possible to play on the violin what sounds like a creditable performance of Twinkle with a poor bow hold and a poor violin hold. Oftentimes a parent may become annoyed with a teacher, calling the teacher 'too fussy' because of her insistence on correct violin and bow holds. The performance sounds reasonably good to the parent. She may not think the position is all that important since the child can play. It should be understood, however, that a consistent bad posture and bad bow hold will certainly severely limit the child's growth.

I like to show students and parents that I can play a reasonable-sounding version of Twinkle holding the bow in my fist and holding the violin very low with a slumped hand, but that I simply cannot play a reasonable-sounding version of the last movement of the Mendelssohn Concerto with the same poor position.

"See", I exclaimed to one little boy, "When I hold the violin and bow this badly I can still play Twinkle but I can't possibly play this concerto by Mendelssohn. I'm asking you to be careful with the way you hold the violin and bow so that later you'll be able to play all kinds of advanced pieces like this one." My demonstration backfired as he complained, "But I don't want to learn to play that piece! It's way too hard!"

The Terminal Case

Those who have been present at workshops we've given around the country have probably heard the phrase used by Bill to describe students who are allowed to proceed without the necessary attention to basic posture and position. He calls them 'terminal cases'. Although they may be able to give a seemingly acceptable performance of the easy pieces they will never be able to progress through the more advanced literature. Their study has a built-in termination point. When this is understood, it is easier for students and parents to accept the teacher's zealous attention to details.

Parents See the Difference

A teacher told me that one group c   ning pianists had been quite slow to acquire the necessar   the Twinkle variations.

46

Beth, one of the group, had begun to play very well and progress quickly after almost a year and a half of study. Her posture, hand position and tone were all excellent.

"*My husband was transferred to another city so I assigned my students to other teachers in our area. Two weeks after the assignment Beth's mother phoned me. 'I wonder if you could assign us to another teacher. Let me explain why. Yesterday one of Beth's neighborhood friends came to our home. Since we knew that she had been taking Suzuki piano lessons from the teacher you assigned to us, we asked her to play for us. She'd had only a few lessons and she was playing all of the Twinkle variations! Her posture was awful, her hand position terrible, and the tone was not good. Now I know why we stayed on Twinkle so long, although at the time I really wondered whether it was necessary. I can see that Beth has a really solid foundation. She's gained so much confidence because of it, too. We want to continue that way so we hope you can find us a teacher who will work that carefully with us.' I was sorry that I had made a mistake assigning that teacher, but I was delighted to hear that this formerly skeptical mother could see and hear the difference that a slow, careful beginning can make.*"

Sometimes, through situations like this, it becomes obvious to parents that the teacher's insistence on going 'side-ways' until the seemingly simple habits are acquired is the best insurance for future growth.

Relationship of Practice to Performance

According to a well-established psychological principle, movements practiced slowly will transfer to a rapid continuous performance in direct proportion to the extent that the movements made in performance resemble those of practice. This is not so much of a problem in the early years as it is with advanced students.

A specific problem for violinists is rapid shifting. When they practice these shifts slowly, they must be very careful to practice them with the same motions they will use when they play up to tempo. So many students, when they shift rapidly, adopt a different hand position from the one they used for slow practice. No wonder they are insecure about fast passages!

PRACTICE

Judith was always quite attentive to details of practice. I felt comfortable leaving her to do her own repetitions while I looked in on Tim or worked with Michael in the next room. I could hear her carefully going over the passages we had discussed.

As she became more advanced, however, I realized that she needed to become even more aware of what Gallwey calls "increasingly minute muscle and energy sensations in the body". She was working on a passage in thirds. "Judith," I said, "if you're not careful about your arm position here, you can practice this passage over and over again and never feel secure when you play it fast."

At first she was not particular about what she was doing, but after a week or so of practice she realized that she wasn't building up any security. Then she began to observe her arm position carefully. This was a turning point for her. After this, she became increasingly aware of the need for her practice conditions to be as closely related as possible to her conditions of performance.

David was amazed at his freedom and accuracy in the performance of keyboard jumps after I reminded him that during his slow practice he should visualize the jump, pinpoint the target and move slowly and rhythmically in the shape of a rainbow to the second note without stopping before contact. *That last instruction was the most important one. It meant that the practice movements would resemble those of performance. There is no time in most musical performance to stop —* "to be sure" — *before playing the second note of a jump. Logically then, this stop must not be present in practice.*

"That's so much easier!" David said as he demonstrated a jump up to tempo with confidence.

Parents and students who are aware of this important relationship between practice and performance can save much time and frustration during the years of study.

Mother—Assistant Teacher

I often suggest to teachers, in order for them to aid parents as much as possible with home practice, that they make remarks like the following to beginners: "Alice, I'm asking your mother to be my assistant teacher during your home lessons. I'm asking her to write down everything I want you to do at home, and to try to follow my instructions as carefully as she can. It's a great help for me to have your mother's assistance. I expect you to do what she asks at home as carefully as you do for me in my studio."

I've even introduced the mother to the child as home teacher. The children always laugh at this because it seems so absurd to them. "John, I want you to meet Mrs. Brown, my assistant teacher in your home. Oh, I know she's your mother! I just wanted you to be sure to know that she is also my assistant. She's going to do the best job for me that she can. I know that you'll give her the same fine attention you give me. You and I are both lucky to have your mother's help. You'll learn so much easier and faster this way."

You can enlist your teacher's aid in getting your child to practice every day. Suzuki says, "Have your teacher ask your child how he practices at home. If you are trying to get your child to practice before going out to play after school, request your teacher to ask your child to practice every day at that hour before playing and add, 'Mark it down every day you do this, and report back to me at the next lesson'. This can be said quite casually. From this the child will feel a stronger sense of obligation to the teacher."

For beginners it might be helpful not to use the word 'practice' at all. "Let's play the piano for a while". I like the way many Japanese refer to home practice as home lessons. Since the mother has been identified as the assistant teacher at home, this makes sense. It should cause the child to expect the home lesson to resemble the lesson at the teacher's studio. Then the mother could say to the teacher, with the child present, "We are both going to try hard to make our home lessons as good as the lessons here".

Attitude of the Learner

The child should have the intention of improving his performance each time he practices. We should try to convince him that each good practice session adds to the whole. Children often do not believe that when they are in the early stages of a learning situation. They have only a vague feeling about what their practice will accomplish.

PRACTICE

"Every little bit of good practice helps you to program your inner computer", you can remind them. "Remember when you couldn't even play 'taka-taka'? Now it's easy for you. After you work hard on a new piece that at first seems really difficult, it will become one of your 'easy' pieces. Try to remember that when you practice."

Child's Attitude Toward Teacher

One of the most powerful factors in motivating a child to practice is the child's desire to please the teacher. You as a parent should take advantage of this by showing your respect for the teacher and cultivating respect for the teacher in your child. The more your child respects and admires his teacher, the more he will want to work for her. I like the way Suzuki puts it: "Accumulate a debt in the child's heart which urges him to practice."

Remarks about the teacher's expectations should be phrased in a positive manner. They should not put the child in the position of having to produce or be a failure. "Mrs. Evans is really happy when you show that you have worked for her. Teachers try not to show it, but they are disappointed when their students don't practice well. If Mrs. Evans knows you've tried your best, even if you make mistakes, she'll be pleased." Children need to understand that teachers are pleased mostly by the efforts of their students.

At a party we staged for them, our students were shown what it's like to be the teacher of a non-cooperative student. They played a few pieces together and then sat down in a circle. An older student, her identity concealed behind a clown's mask and costume, came in for a lesson. "Who wants to give the clown a lesson?" I asked. Little red-haired Monica, all of five years old, rushed forward eagerly. "O.K., Monica. The clown wants you to teach him how to play 'taka-taka stop-stop' on the E string, but first you have to put him in the proper playing position."

Monica pushed and pulled at the clown, adjusting his arms as she kept instructing: "Hold the violin like this under your chin. This is the way you should hold your bow. Don't slump your left hand." She then stepped back to survey her handiwork before she gave the order to start playing. The clown immediately slumped out of position. "No, no," exclaimed Monica, hurrying to set everything right. Again the clown fell into a bad position. Monica's voice rose, "Please hold the violin and bow the way I show you!" After her next adjustment, the clown again slumped out of position. Monica made one more attempt, only to meet with the same response. Suddenly she stamped her foot. "I quit!" she said, turning on her heel and returning to her seat.

If Your Child Loves to Practice

There are some children who fall in love with the violin, even very small children. They will practice for three or four hours a day without any coercion. American parents hearing the Japanese tour group are continually amazed at the very rapid progress these children have made. Here are some revealing quotes from mothers whose children advanced very rapidly at an early age: "A friend played the violin at kindergarten graduation. My daughter came home and said she wanted to play the violin no matter what!" "My nephew enrolled for lessons. Our daughter saw him and insisted on doing it herself." "My daughter saw her friend's lessons and asked and asked to join. She insisted for a month." "My daughter envied the violin of a friend who was taking lessons. She craved the violin so much that a friend gave her a violin as a toy."

When we read of the famous concert artists we often encounter the same stories concerning their early interest in the violin. Several begged for a violin at the age of three.

Supervision of Practice

If our child loves to play so much that there is never any need to urge him to practice, we are fortunate in having most of the battle won. We should rejoice at not having to devote any energy toward motivation, but we still have a great responsibility to see that the practice is worthwhile. The quality of our supervision of practice is critical and can save the child untold hours of remedial work.

Concert violinist Franco Gulli stated, "Each day my father would practice with me one hour. I never practiced the wrong way, and was thus able to achieve much more than the average talented child who struggles by himself."

Elmar Oliveira, a recent winner of the Tchaikowsky Competition, had an older brother who taught him how to practice correctly. Of this he said, "I think it is of vital importance that a young performer have someone to supervise his daily practice. No single thing is more important than the quality of one's practice."

Suzuki declares again and again that his approach is not calculated to produce concert artists, but still the method is closely akin to the approach taken by parents whose children did become famous concert artists, particularly in the involvement of an active parent, relative, or close friend who supervised the daily practice of the very young student. In this regard, it has been said that talent is common but favorable environment is not.

So, whether our child loves to practice or not, we still have the responsibility to see that the practice is fruitful. Higher levels of skill are not reached by mere mindless repetitions or half-hearted performances, Mednick (1964) notes. Monotonous repetition does not increase skill; it seems only to make lower-level performance more automatic, or reinforces mediocrity.

If Your Child Does Not Like to Practice

If your child does not like to practice, all is not lost. Even among the concert artists we find those who admit they were forced to practice when young. Pinchas Zuckerman, one of today's front-rank violinists, said, "My father forced me to practice three to four hours a day. I would much rather have been outside playing."

Nathan Milstein, great Russian violinist, praised his mother for forcing him to play. "I started to play the violin not because I was drawn to it, but because my mother forced me to. I was attracted to music. I wanted to hear it and make it. My mother sensed my affinity and made me practice regularly. Only when I progressed to feel the music itself in my playing did I practice eagerly and willingly."

We have seen the following happen many times. Children are attracted to the Suzuki program when they see other children perform, but when they find that practice is necessary for them to be able to play like the others, their initial enthusiasm often wanes. As they practice and become more proficient, however, their motivation increases.

If we parents feel that motivation always precedes action and wait around until our child is in the mood to practice, he may never learn to play. Dr. David Burns, psychiatrist, in his book "Feeling Good" states that we should not put the cart before the horse. "Motivation does not usually come first, action does. You have to prime the pump. Then you will begin to get motivated and the fluids will flow spontaneously."

So many parents have told us, "After they've gotten started practicing, they really get involved. It's not as difficult to keep them going as it is to get them started." Dr. Burns put it this way: "First comes action, then motivation, which produces more action."

A great majority of the Japanese children who did not like to practice and whose mothers sought help from Suzuki and his teachers, developed their potential quite successfully in spite of this problem.

Suzuki told parents who complained that they had a hard time getting their children to practice, "Don't be the kind of parents who insist on the immediate progress of their child. Relax, with a determination to make your child great. It's all right to be slow. Handle it so your child enjoys it. Try to motivate him so that he will try to improve on his own initiative. If you have difficulties with practice, try to create a change of attitude gradually."

I for one am happy to see how much sympathy Suzuki has for parents who have trouble with their children's practice. He is always optimistic, feeling that sooner or later the child's attitude, as fostered by a loving parent, will change for the better.

Here's an example of the realistic advice he gave a troubled mother whose child would not practice with her. (This is an illustration of the manner in which Suzuki puts the child first, even, in this case, above his own method!) He advised the mother, "Let the boy practice by himself. Say to him, 'Mother will be in the next room listening'. Of course the child practicing by himself will not do so well. You should tell his teacher that you are trying to create a desire to practice, and ask the teacher to show your child how to practice every detail. Wait for your child to ask before you assist him at home."

PRACTICE

It is Suzuki's hope in this case that the boy will eventually change his attitude as he realizes that he does much better practicing with his mother's help. Many parents have found that it is a good idea to announce an approaching practice session so that the child has a chance to wind up whatever he's doing at the moment. We should also alert him not to get involved in something that will take a lot of time and will have to be interrupted by the practice period.

The Stalling Child

What do we do when the child stalls and stalls? If we have enough time, we can ride it out and come out ahead, but what do we do when we have only thirty minutes and our child will not start on time? Suzuki says again and again to his mothers, "Don't scold!" So what do we do?

Looking over many years on my successes and failures in handling this kind of situation, I feel that both the child and I were winners when I didn't lose my temper or cause the child to become very angry. An older child may be able to get some effective practice done after an angry exchange, but not a young child. I've seen children practice while their tears flowed, both in Japan and in our home, but I'm not sure much was accomplished during those sessions.

Persistent firmness generally works. The first rule is that the child should not be permitted to do anything else while he is stalling. The staller should be restricted to the practice place. We shouldn't call repeatedly, "Please come to practice now." We noticed that Japanese parents didn't waste a lot of energy calling their children repeatedly. If a small one didn't come right away, the mother went and picked him up.

Teachers or parents who have not experienced this kind of frustrating behavior don't realize how painful it can be. You feel as though you are in a no-win situation. If you press the child too hard, he may break down and get nothing accomplished. On the other hand, if you're too lenient, he may extend the stalling throughout the entire practice session. We've found help in the fact that children who don't want to start practicing also don't enjoy a whole session of sitting at the piano stalling. Most will resign themselves to practice as the lesser of two evils.

I think the important thing for us parents to remember is that we should not sink to immature, childish behavior. We must remind ourselves that our immediate goal is to guide our child through some meaningful practice that we both should enjoy. Even if only ten minutes of the thirty was meaningful practice, we have achieved something. Our son David at times used a highly developed technique of stalling, the kind of stalling that would drive a busy mother crazy! Connie asked me to sit with him at the piano on several of these occasions. I used to feel good about the times I could outwait him, even though he might have settled down to work only during those last ten minutes. Here we should repeat Suzuki's advice: "Try to effect a change of attitude gradually."

Boredom

"Most small children like repetition", Suzuki insists. "It is the adult who shows his boredom or displeasure and communicates it to the child. 'She is bored with this piece', a parent will say, not realizing the influence this remark has on the child's attitude."

I've said this to parents who've remonstrated with me, insisting that that wasn't true in their case, that their children were actually bored while the parents were not. Whatever the cause for their expressions of boredom, I have seen some very young children with a well-developed capacity for boredom, a condition that saddens me.

In order to prevent or lessen boredom in our children, we need to work at it all the time, not just at music practice. We need to help increase our children's awareness of the countless beautiful and interesting things, happenings, and people that surround us throughout life. Remember Robert Louis Stevenson's famous lines:

"The world is so full of a number of things, I'm sure we should all be as happy as kings!"

Young children are naturally open to the wonder of everything in their environment, so when Michael started Montessori school at the age of two and a half, he was fascinated by the shapes he'd learned to recognize at school. Whenever he discovered a triangle, square, or parallelogram in his surroundings he exploded with excitement! I remember that I wore a hound's tooth checked wool skirt one day and as

PRACTICE

I walked along with Michael I noticed that he kept looking at my skirt.
Suddenly his eyes lit up. "Parallelogram!" he sang out as he pointed to
the pattern in the material. Sure enough, there it was—a small but quite
distinct parallelogram!

Unfortunately he was not so excited by toilet training. By this time I
was not so excited by it either, having lived through three other boys who
had helped me to understand that there should be no rush. The job would
be accomplished when maturation dictated. . . a little like Suzuki. . .
"Provide the environment and wait." So I was encouraging but not
pushing Michael in this endeavor.

One summer afternoon during Michael's naptime I was occupied in
the kitchen. I perked up my ears when I heard an excited call from the
bathroom and ran to share in the joy of his supposed accomplishment.
There was Michael—standing in front of the commode. "Look, Mommy,
look!" he pointed delightedly at the seat, "an ellipse!"

I remember keenly a trip I made to Atlanta, taking some students
to hear Gregorian Chant sung at a Trappist monastery near there.
One of the students was a geology major. She kept up a running
travelogue as we drove, pointing out to us the changes in the soil and
the general topography as we skirted the Smoky Mountains on our
way to the plains of Georgia. No one slept. It seemed the shortest trip I
had ever made on that familiar road.

Suzuki once said, "When I go in to a room to teach small children, I
stop for a moment so that I can descend to their level of physical
ability, and can rise to their level of childlike wonder and awe."

Our Privilege

As we help our children with their daily practice, we should
remind ourselves that our participation in their growth in music is
not an obligation but a privilege and an honor. We should be happy
that we have a front row seat for this stage of their learning as we
enjoy their daily progress.

I worked extensively with three of our children as they learned to
play the violin. Now they are all grown, and as I write these pages,
many happy experiences come back to me. The struggles and pain
seem much more distant.

We didn't always do the right thing, but then there is no such person, so the psychologists say, as the 'perfect' parent. Neither is there a 'perfect' teacher, or 'perfect' child, and that, of course, boils down to the fact that there is no 'perfect' human being. So no parent should be laden with guilt because he has fallen short of perfection. Still, this doesn't excuse us from trying our best and from making ourselves knowledgeable in all the ways that can help us function as the best parents we can possibly be.

At the foundation of all our efforts must be that most important ingredient—Love. It is love that sees each child as a unique person made in the image and likeness of God. It is love that works to help that individual become all that he can be.

"The greatest good that we can do for others is not just to share our riches with them but to reveal their riches to themselves." Anon.

Additional material on practice will be found in the following chapters on Concentration and Coordination of Mind and Body.

The question is not what you look at
But what you see.

Thoreau

We do not stumble over mountains
but over molehills.

Confucius

The most glorious moments in your life are not the so-called days of success but rather those days where out of dejection and despair you feel rise in you a challenge to life, and the promise of future accomplishments.

Flaubert

Concentration

Webster gives the word 'focus' as the synonym for 'concentrate', calling concentration "directing of the attention, or of the mental faculties, toward a single task or object". From our own personal experience we know that there are different levels of concentration, from merely paying attention to complete absorption.

Directing our attention, or paying attention, requires a certain amount of self-discipline. We have to restrict our sensory input to the object or task at hand. As we become more interested in the object of our concentration, less and less effort is needed to maintain attention. We experience the highest state of concentration when we are totally absorbed in whatever we are doing or observing. It is this last state that is exemplified in superior athletes or superior performers in any field.

We recently heard an interview with the winning Olympic discus thrower, Al Oerter, who has become a legend in his own time. "When I am out there in the event", he said, "I'm not aware of anything around me, the noise, the crowd, or even the place that I am in."

Zen philosophy states it simply this way, "When we sleep, we sleep; when we walk, we walk; when we eat, we eat; when we study, we study."

Japanese Children

On my first visit to Japan with a group of American teachers, all of us marveled at the total absorption that we saw displayed by the young children. Whether they were performing or taking lessons, they gave undivided attention to the task of playing. "What is the secret of their concentration?" we questioned each other. Never had we seen anything like this in children at this early age.

Perhaps the secret is the age-old influence of Zen philosophy on the Japanese culture, an influence that is still nurturing the Japanese children. Experienced observers like John Kendall have commented that the cultural environment as a whole is a strong contributing factor to the marvelous examples of superb concentration shown by the little Suzuki musicians. We came to see the great value Suzuki teachers and parents placed on the ability to concentrate and the persistent efforts they made to help the children achieve it.

Living in Matsumoto with our family, we became part of the society. We saw exceptions to the rule, but came away with the strong impression that many more Japanese children, particularly those in families involved in the Talent Education movement, seemed to be 'centered', or were able to focus more easily and for longer periods of time, than their Western counterparts. This impression has not changed but has been reinforced as we continue to work with children throughout the U.S., and in Canada, Venezuela, Switzerland, England, and Australia.

Many of the Japanese children are adaptable to long periods of concentration and practice, and yet these same children are as child-like and playful as all well-adjusted children should be. They don't go about with long faces or act like miniature adults. We saw no anti-social 'book-wormish' types who were set apart from their contemporaries. American families who've had the opportunity to play host to the tour groups of Japanese children have been delighted to see them behave off-stage merely as happy, carefree children.

In Knoxville in 1970 the entire group visited our home, and recently in 1982 they again visited us in Boulder. They had planned to visit Pike's Peak for a sight-seeing tour on their free day, but snow and ice had forced a cancellation of their plans. Since they had planned a picnic, we suggested that they come to our house in the country, with its open view of the mountains and ample room for the children to play.

When they arrived they scattered in all directions. Some jumped on the trampoline, some picked up frisbees, and others played ping-pong. There was joyous laughter coming from all directions.

Miss Yuko Mori, the senior teacher who led the tour, had insisted that the children bring their violins for a practice session, so after lunch the violins were brought out. They all lined up and, at a signal from Miss Mori, began to play with complete absorption. What a beautiful example of their ability to change focus quickly and completely!

CONCENTRATION

Children Respond to Challenge

We also had a marvelous opportunity to see the children concentrate in an unfamiliar learning situation. Mori-sensei had asked Bill to work with the children on the last movement of the Mendelssohn Concerto which they were playing in unison. He made some suggestions on bowing technique that they adopted and practiced with great intensity. After the half-hour coaching session, he asked if they'd like to play a musical game. They agreed eagerly.

It was a tricky game. A piece was chosen. Each child was assigned one pitch from that piece. They then performed it, with each child playing only her own pitch as it occurred in the melody. It sounds easy, but isn't. Although quite a few mistakes were made, they laughingly kept trying until the piece was finished. When Bill sat down, they clamored for another piece. In spite of errors in the second piece, they kept playing and at the end asked for a third piece! They obviously enjoyed the challenge even though it was difficult.

Developing Attention in Beginners

Capturing the attention of the beginner before going on was considered of vital importance by the Japanese teachers. They told us that some of their beginners came in totally inattentive and that it was only with great persistence that they were able to affect a change in the behavior of those students.

It is our responsibility as teachers and parents to help children with the first step toward concentration, that is, paying attention, by giving them specific instructions to follow.

Haruko Kataoka has often told this story of a four-year-old beginning piano student who was unable to follow her instructions for a correct bow. "Teaching the child to bow correctly is the very first step in developing the ability to listen, to pay attention, and to follow the instructions of the teacher. This boy was unable to bow correctly. Lesson after lesson passed, and still he did not listen and do what I asked him to do. I could not let him begin to study music until he accomplished this first step. How could he learn a much more difficult task if he could not

61

CONCENTRATION

perform this simple one? And so he continued to come for lessons for six months. Then he was finally ready."
When we revisited Matsumoto again in 1973, I questioned Mrs. Kataoka about this student. "He is playing well, although his progress has been somewhat slow", she answered.
I have always marveled at the understanding shown by the mother of this boy. Obviously she respected the teacher's judgment in placing such a high value on the ability to pay attention or she certainly would not have returned week after week to a music lesson that involved no music! Could this incident have occurred in our culture? Do we value such growth enough to persist in nurturing it until it is accomplished? We need to ask these questions of ourselves.

Lesson Environment

Japanese teachers, discussing the environment of the lesson, stated that the behavior of the older children, witnessed by the beginners, was perhaps the strongest positive influence on most of the beginners. This is another illustration of Suzuki's contention that environment is extremely important. "When in Rome . . ."
When I first began teaching, I did most of my teaching in my home studio. I tried to keep material for quiet activities accessible: paper for drawing, crayons and pencils and books, with a low round table that was the center for these activities. At the outset, however, not only did the children talk, but the parents talked out loud to the children and to each other, distracting the student who was being given a lesson.
I firmly but pleasantly made our needs known. "Please don't talk out loud during lessons. When you talk, whisper or speak very quietly. When you take your lesson you will want others to be quiet so that you can concentrate. Try to be as thoughtful of others."
Soon the children were coming in, finding something quiet to do, and settling down until it was their turn to take their lesson. As new students would join us, I rarely had to say anything about this anymore. They would see and feel the quiet environment and conform to it. Similarly, the concentration of the older children on their bows and on their physical and mental preparation for performance set the stage for

the younger children. When the younger ones were required to pay attention to those details, they had precedent for such behavior. Most benefited greatly from it.

With very small children, one can play suitable games to develop their ability to pay attention to, and carry out, specific instructions. The game of "Simon Says" may be used for this purpose. This game is described in detail at the end of the chapter.

Instructions for preparedness for playing the instrument can be used in this game. These should be specific and should always be given in the same order and with the same words. Such a series of instructions will demonstrate the importance of preparedness to the child. They will also help the child acquire the habit of preparedness. It is good to be firm with the beginner, not allowing her to go on to the following step until the next order is given. Countless times we saw young Japanese children wait for their teacher to say 'hai' (o.k., proceed) before they moved.

Paying attention to short specific instructions is not as difficult as maintaining attention as one performs a piece or practices a passage. We need to help our children develop interest which will sustain their attention for longer periods of time.

Studying and Reporting

Most of us who have had school-age children have read articles or books on "How to Help Your Child Study". Again and again we've seen students urged to question themselves on what they have read. "Read a chapter, then close the book and tell yourself what you've just read" is common advice. Some researchers have said that students profit more from time divided between studying and reporting what they've studied than from time spent exclusively on studying.

We ourselves know from experience how much more careful attention we pay when we know we are going to be asked to repeat what we've just read, heard, or experienced. And yet many of us don't expect to be able to recall things easily after only one viewing or hearing. Take listening to directions, for instance. Don't we, as we listen to complex directions, often give up in the middle because we don't expect to remember them and know we'll have to ask for all of the directions to be repeated? But then, of course, we expect our children, however small, to listen to and remember instructions! I have had numerous occasions to witness the high abilities for immediate recall demonstrated by elementary school children who were having fun. Our university string quartet gave a great number of concerts in schools. Our concerts followed the same format used by musicians throughout the country until I came across this Suzuki-inspired idea to challenge the children and spur their attention to the highest.

At the beginning of the concert, after introducing the players and demonstrating the instruments, I called out to the children, "When composers write melodies for us, these melodies are like people in a story. They keep coming back. The composer knows we won't remember them if he writes them only once. The pieces we're going to play for you today all have some pretty important melodies. You'll know they're important because you'll hear them again and again.

"We want you to listen carefully for these important musical characters because we're going to play a game with you at the end of the concert. After we finish our program, we're going to play a group of melodies for you. Some of them will come from this concert, others will not. When you hear one you recognize from this concert, yell 'yes!', but if not, yell 'no!'. We know that you all have fine memories and will enjoy this game."

The children's attention was wonderful to observe. At the end of the concert, they filled the hall with 'no!' and 'yes!' invariably at the correct time. Of course for the melodies they had not heard I chose ones that were quite far removed from the ones they had. The teachers said the children really enjoyed the game, and felt quite proud of themselves recalling a theme from a Haydn quartet they'd heard only once.

Capturing Attention of College Students

Having taught college students for over thirty years, I know how many listen to lectures, take notes carefully, but have the attitude "I'll learn this later". I used to call them highly skilled recording secretaries. "Why don't you actively try to remember as much as you can the first time round?" I asked. I assured them they would get better and better at it and that it would save them hours of time.

One day, as I was teaching a music-appreciation class, I decided to let them see what their abilities were for immediate recall. I announced at the beginning of the class, "I am going to give a short talk on the sonata form and its use in sonatas, symphonies, concertos and chamber works. I know that this is all new material, but it hangs together pretty well. Don't take any notes. Just listen closely. Ask questions if you don't understand any points. I'll go over the material several times. At the end of the talk I'll give you a quiz on what I've just covered."

There was a chorus of complaints! "You mean we have to learn this stuff right now? No chance for study or review? What if we can't learn that fast? We've never had to do this before, why now? I just can't do it."

I assured them that I expected all of them to get one hundred percent since they would be paying extraordinary attention and there would be no lapse of time for forgetting! After the students quieted down, there was a remarkable change in their attitude. They listened intently and interrupted frequently with questions. One boy couldn't stand the pressure. I was told later that he was secretly scratching terms down on the cuff of his shirt! I gave the quiz, and they did very well which surprised them but not me. I told them they could count the grade if they wished, that I had no desire to hold anything against those who had remained in a state of shock.

Afterwards, one of the best students in the class came up to say, "What a marvelous experiment! I just realized how many hours I waste each week in my lecture courses. I've been what you called a skilled recording secretary. If I learned more in class, I would need to study less, and then would have more time for bridge!"

Many of the students lingered after class, stating that they hadn't realized how minimal their attention had been and how pleased they were to see how well they had responded to the challenge. None, however, wanted me to repeat that kind of class very often! "We just haven't developed the habit of paying attention that long and that intensely!"

CONCENTRATION

Non-judgmental Observations

Timothy Gallwey, in his superb book "Inner Tennis", makes a great point of dealing with anxiety and boredom, recommending what he calls non-judgmental awareness for motivation to sustain people in practice. He developed a number of very clever ideas designed to keep the player's eye on the ball.

We've been working on a similar train of thought to create and sustain children's interest in repetitious practice.

I question the children to get them in the mood for focusing their minds on various things. I start with external objects in the room. "Let's look at this chair. Notice its color, size, shape, position in the room. Is it heavy? Is it comfortable?" If I'm working with small children I don't keep them looking at the chair for very long. I know there's not much they can observe. I move around the room, selecting several more objects for the same kind of focus.

My next move is to the child's body. "Look at your left hand. Notice its size, its shape, the skin, the bone structure, etc. Now close your eyes. Close your fists tightly, then relax your hand. Notice how different it feels. Now move your mind to your feet. Feel the soles of your feet where they touch the floor."

Youngsters enjoy body awareness even though some of them can't feel or observe anything at the beginning. One shouldn't give up if this happens but just come back to it later.

The goal is to increase the child's powers of observation of what he does and what he feels. We should work to make them interested in this kind of awareness. We ourselves can become fascinated with it — fascinated at how sensitive and observant we can become!

If a student knows that she is going to be asked to report what she has observed, she will be much more observant of what she does than if she had just been asked to play. We need to request specific reports from her, but we don't want these reports to be judgmental . . . "That was good" or "That was bad". If we allow value judgments, they will pre-

dominate and we'll get little or no specific information. We won't know
what, if anything, she has observed.

A child who has always been very self-critical will say "That was
bad" after a creditable rendition while a child notoriously tolerant of
her own errors will say "That was great!" after poor playing. Neither of
these comments is worth anything.

Not only should we discourage the child from making value judgments, but we should develop the ability to make simple specific
requests. "Watch your bow" infers that the beginner should draw
short bow strokes and keep the bow straight. I find it much more
effective to request, "Please watch how your bow moves straight and
remains between the tapes. If it should happen to move past the tapes,
please tell me after you've finished playing whether it moved above or
below the tapes".

So many times I have had this request followed by a near-perfect
performance. Why? Simply because the student was involved.

Occasionally one encounters a student who will bow far past the
tapes, then say to you, "I saw the bow stay within the tapes". I would
counter with this: "Oh, I didn't see it quite that way. Would you please
play it again and give special attention to the lower tape? Remember,
I'm not asking you to play it perfectly. I just wanted to know if you
could see what your arm was doing. It may not be doing what you
know it should do."

Cindy's Improvement

For weeks five-year-old Cindy had been encouraged and reminded
by me at her lessons and by her mother during practice, to keep the first
joints of her fingers firm. Nothing seemed to be accomplished. Soon
afterward I decided to try observation and feedback at her lesson. I
listened and watched her play "Lightly Row", a review piece, with the
same collapsed joints and concave fingers that had been obvious for so
long. When she finished I said, "Cindy, let's try a new game. I'd like you
to play the first line of "Lightly Row" for me again. Watch your fingers
as you play. When you finish tell me what you saw. Did your fingers
collapse and look like this? (I demonstrated playing with collapsed,
concave joints.) Or did they look like this? (I demonstrated with firm

slightly curved joints.) Now you can play the first line and tell me what you saw your fingers do . . . did they collapse or did they stay firm?" Cindy proceeded to play, fingers firm and curved slightly throughout the entire line! "What did you see?" I questioned as she finished. "My fingers stayed firm," she answered, beaming. "Right! That was great! Now let's do the second line the same way. Watch your fingers again and tell me what you saw." Line after line was performed with the same firm finger position. Naturally this same sequence had to be repeated again and again during practice at home, the mother always asking for observation and verbal response, but after enough repetitions a good habit was born - in half the time required by the usual persistent reminders!*

Tommy's Success

At a workshop I was giving a short lesson to a four-year-old boy who had just completed all of the Twinkle variations. I asked his mother to work with him a few minutes while I watched, after which I intended to make suggestions that I hoped might be helpful.

The little fellow proceeded to play the first variation of Twinkle, quite well I thought, but his bow did keep slipping over the fingerboard. Each time this happened his mother said, "Watch it, Tommy. Your bow's slipping over the fingerboard." He dutifully pulled the bow back without stopping. This happened again and again. It seemed that his mother was talking continuously throughout the performance. After he finished, his mother turned to me and said, "You see the problem we're having. Tommy holds the violin up nicely, his left hand position is good, he plays in tune, his bow strokes are short, he plays quickly with spirit, but he just can't seem to keep the bow midway between the bridge and fingerboard. Please work with him."

I complimented Tommy on the positive aspects of his performance that his mother had just enumerated. "Let's play a game, Tommy. Please play that Twinkle variation again. This time neither your mother nor I will say anything at all to help you. But I'm going to ask you to stop playing if you notice your bow moving out over the fingerboard. Don't play one extra bow stroke. As soon as you see it move, you stop. This way we'll see how well you notice the movement of your bow."

Tommy nodded eagerly and began to play. He finished the whole variation without the bow once sliding over the fingerboard! His mother was both delighted and astonished. Tommy was overjoyed by his success and our joyous reactions.

Later I explained to his mother that I felt that he had not been in the habit of feeling much personal responsibility for his bow's motions. He had been waiting for her to tell him when he was off and then he would move the bow back. This time he was totally responsible yet felt no particular pressure to perform since I had not directed him to keep the bow in the right place but asked him merely to observe its motion. This was easy for him to do. He enjoyed it and did well.

Something similar takes place when we drive a car down the highway. We don't command ourselves, "Stay in the proper lane!" We merely ask our eyes to notice when we start to move out of the lane and to send corrective messages to our hands to move the steering wheel. Have you ever noticed all the tiny motions you keep making with the steering wheel without any conscious thought? You wouldn't do well at all if you consciously took over, telling yourself repeatedly to stay in the lane. Try it some time. You'll be surprised how tense you become. On the other hand, you also wouldn't do well if your eyes didn't notice the car's motion because you were looking at the mountains in the distance. Don't try this.

Once I was working with a college student who was studying the Bach Chaconne. I was trying to help her bring out the bass notes in chordal passages so that the harmonies would be clearly heard. Again and again I asked her to bring out the bass . . . to no avail. She had an ingrained habit of playing chords differently. Finally I thought what I had been doing with my young Suzuki students. "Carol, please play that passage again for me. This time listen to the resonance of the bass notes. Observe the beautiful sonorities produced by the vibrations of the lower strings. Don't pay attention to the upper sounds. Just focus on the rich bass." Even though I expected improvement, I was still astonished by the difference in her playing! I began to realize that adults were no different from small children in this regard.

We parents and teachers should make it a habit of noticing the power of the spoken word. What may seem like a slight difference in wording may produce surprising results.

I can think back on the countless times I said to students, "Watch your bow!" Watching the bow can become very boring to a child. How many keep the eyes on the bow for just a few seconds, then allow the eyes to stare out into space or worse yet look all around the room? Or how many keep watching the bow as it wanders all over the place?

Now I use an entirely different approach that invariably produces much more satisfying results. "Please keep your eye on the bow to see how nicely it stays between the tapes. If for some reason your arm doesn't obey your directions or gets mixed up and the bow moves past the tapes, let me know after you stop exactly what the bow did." This request implies that the bow will move correctly and that if it doesn't, it wasn't the child's fault but a lack of muscular control.

I like to bring the child over to my side so that both of us can observe together how the child's fingers, hands, and arms learn to play. I remember a reading expert saying that some children will not try to learn to read because they do not want to subject themselves to the teacher's power to correct them or to declare them wrong or inferior. The kind of approach I'm suggesting here does not put the child on the spot. It minimizes our power to correct them.

Children like to 'pass the buck' of responsibility as well as we adults do. It's great to hear a child say, "My second finger never wants to go down in the right place", rather than, "I can never play that right." If your child starts with the latter accusation, try to shift her to the first which is less personal. "Your second finger keeps forgetting that it needs to be next to the first in this minuet. I think that's because it's been so friendly with the third finger for so long. Please play that part again. Let's watch that second finger. Maybe if he knows we're watching, he'll remember where he's supposed to go this time."

Asking the child to perform with eyes closed is an effective way to develop body awareness. You might say to your child, "Close your eyes and I will draw the bow straight, keeping it between the tapes. Notice how it feels when I do this. Keep your eyes closed. Now you draw the bow. Did it feel the same? Do you think the bow stayed between the tapes?"

We have found in our teaching that this kind of questioning draws the student from merely paying attention to interested *attention and then to the highest state of concentration - that of being totally absorbed in what he is doing. And he is relaxed as he moves through this process. Gallwey says, "Calmness and interest are two of the qualities of mind which make it so easy for a child to learn."*

By your careful attention during lessons you will be able to carry out the observation and questioning during practice at home that is directly based on the teacher's assignments. Those details may deal with bowing, posture, finger, hand and arm position, tone, dynamics, rhythm, balance of melody and accompaniment for pianists, keeping eyes focused, etc.

When you first begin such involvement and request the student's own feedback, there will often be no response. If you get that blank look or an "I don't know" answer, your response should be "Oh, I guess you forgot to watch and listen! Let's do it again. This time you'll remember to watch and listen and be able to tell me what you saw and heard." Try not to back down and give an answer unless the child seems to be emotionally upset or looks alarmed by being expected to produce an answer. In that case you might want to pursue another tack and come back to it later. If it does not seem that serious, a good positive encouraging response might be, "Sometimes this is hard to do when you first try, but soon you'll be able to tell me what you saw or heard every time you practice something."

This is such an effective tool for productive practice and maximum learning that the effort expended to accomplish it is far outweighed by the results.

CONCENTRATION

A Game to Develop Attention

Since we are trying to help the young child develop concentration and attention, the game of "Simon Says" is a good one. This may be used as a relaxing interlude during a practice session or preceding practice. Specific requests that relate to the instrument being learned or the hands and fingers as they relate to that instrument can be helpful and can be alternated with general requests.

The parent gives a request for an action which is to be followed only if the request begins with the words "Simon Says. . .". Sample requests might be:

Simon Says . . .

> *hold up your right hand*
> *wiggle your left hand (right hand)*
> *clap your hands three times*
> *wiggle your right hand second finger*
> *touch your thumbs together (second fingers, third fingers, etc.)*
> *turn around*
> *jump up and down four times*

Touch your toes. (This request would not be followed by action because it was not preceded by "Simon Says".)

The object, of course, is not to get caught! This requires attentive listening. It is a good idea to set a certain number of requests that the child can expect. "I will give you ten things to do. I think you can listen so well that you will not get caught. Remember, only do the things if I say "Simon Says" to do them." At the end congratulate her on how well she listened. As the child becomes more attentive the number of commands may be increased.

This game may also be played with a group of children. The child who responds to a request without the "Simon Says" prefix is considered 'out of the game'.

*Well done is better
Than well said.*

Benjamin Franklin

The routine followed by the family of Felix Mendelssohn might seem slightly severe by modern standards. The children rose at five in the morning and began lessons with a tutor immediately after breakfast. For relaxation they read serious books, took lessons in drawing and painting, went for long strenuous rides on horseback, and practiced their music. The siblings plus Felix seemed to thrive on this rigid discipline. They were not docile or cowed by it. They simply used their energies seriously and followed the tradition of the family.

Coordination of Mind & Body

One clue to the concentration we saw in the Japanese Suzuki children came when Suzuki referred cryptically to the principle of 'keeping one point'. "From early times," Suzuki explained to his teachers, "martial arts teachers have explained how to be relaxed and yet centered, ready for instantaneous action. At lessons, if we ask students who are tense in their shoulders and arms to focus strength in the area of their center of gravity, their 'one point', we will find that their shoulders and arms relax." Aikido practitioners speak of the center of gravity Suzuki refers to here as an imaginary point in the person's lower abdomen several inches below the navel.

Suzuki also has written that physical ability and mental ability are correlated. Zen writers state that the mind and body are one, that a calm mind and clear vision are attained in a quiet body, and that only the quiet and focussing mind can perceive the ticking of a clock or produce an exquisite tone on a musical instrument.

We were given an impressive introductory demonstration of these ideas quite through serendipity. We were waiting in the Seattle airport on a pleasant day in July, 1973, about to leave for a month's return visit to Japan, when an announcement came that our plane's departure would be delayed for two hours.

Mihoko Hirata, a Suzuki teacher whom we'd met in Japan, had just introduced us to her husband, an aikido instructor and Suzuki teacher. We expressed impatience at the delay so Mr. Hirata set out to entertain us.

"Let me show you something interesting," he said, turning to a little girl standing next to his wife. "Mari-chan, I want Mr. Starr to pick you up. Please let him." I reached down and picked her up with little effort.

"Now, Mari-chan, please come over here. I want to tell you something that I don't want Mr. Starr to hear." He took her a little distance away and whispered something in her ear. She nodded solemnly and returned to stand in front of me.

"Now please lift her again," he requested. Casually I reached down to pick her up. I was shocked to find that I was unable to lift her at all! I repositioned myself to get a firmer grip around her waist and only then was I able, with considerable effort, to raise her feet off the floor. She seemed to be three times as heavy as before but didn't seem to be resisting me at all!

Mr. Hirata laughed at my consternation. "Mari-chan is a very good student!" The little girl laughed and ran off to tell her mother what she had just done. "What on earth did you tell her to do?" I asked in amazement.

"When I spoke to her the first time, you heard me ask her to let you pick her up. Before you lifted her the second time, I asked her not to resist you but to think of the underside of her feet, to imagine that all the weight of her body was going down through her feet into the earth, and to keep thinking all of her weight down as you were trying to pick her up. Obviously, she did this very well as you did have great trouble in lifting her. This shows the wonderful power of the coordination of the mind and body."

"Let me give you another example using yourself as the model. This is called the 'unbendable arm'. First, extend your arm and tense it, attempting to make it unbendable. Now I'll try to bend it up toward your shoulder."

Hirata then put one hand on my upper arm and with the other hand began to push my forearm up toward my shoulder. My arm trembled violently as I tried my best to keep him from bending it. He bent it anyway in spite of my great effort.

"Now", Hirata instructed, "I will show you how to make your arm unbendable without your using any physical effort, but rather using the coordination of mind and body. Hold your arm out straight as before, but instead of tensing it, imagine that your arm is a water hose through which water is streaming toward a fire in your neighbor's house. As I try to bend your arm as before, don't try to resist me but keep thinking of the fact that the water rushing through your arm is putting out the fire in your neighbor's house."

I conjured up the scene. In my mind I saw the burning house and the water rushing through my arm and suppressing the fire before it could spread. Hirata then tried to bend my arm. It remained straight. Surprisingly, I felt no muscular tension as he applied more and more force to my arm.

"Actually," explained Hirata, "the picture I gave you is the one we use with children. I could have asked you to imagine that the power of your spirit was rushing through your arm and out from your fingertips into limitless space. This would have worked as well, but since this was your first time I wanted to stimulate your imagination as effectively as possible. An experienced student of aikido need only ask his arm to remain straight."

These demonstrations seem almost magical examples of the power engendered in us when the mind and body are coordinated. Together with others we later learned, they make a great impression on children and illustrate the fact that this kind of mind-body coordination can produce almost unbelievable results.

The unbendable arm demonstration is most effective if both of the people involved are of similar strength, but I like to ask the child to be the one with the unbendable arm in order to give her added confidence in her potential. I use Hirata's water-hose picture since children respond well to it. Most of the times I've done this the child maintains an unbendable arm. I apply force very gradually, and usually stop after I've reached the same amount I expended the first time when the child was trying to resist. I compliment the child on the wonderful way her mind and body work together.

Many observers who've not seen this demonstration before simply think that less force is being applied the second time. At this point, I often ask the skeptical observer to try to bend the child's arm. That person can then experience the strange sensation of feeling great strength in the child who shows no apparent exertion. I do have to warn certain skeptics not to apply excessive force on the child's arm, or not to apply force suddenly. Either of these actions could distract the child from her visualization of the water hose and the burning house.

When doing this with an older child, we might try Hirata's alternate suggestion, asking the child to relax completely and then imagine that the power of her spirit is rushing through her arm into endless space. Practitioners of aikido call this 'Extending Ki', a principle of the coordination of mind and body.

Suzuki often uses the term 'life force' in talking about the wonderful potentialities of children. When aikido masters refer to 'Ki', I think of it as related to the life force that Suzuki mentions. In extending one's Ki, one must think and believe that the power of her spirit is being projected outward from herself with a positive and vigorous thrust.

After our encounter with Hirata in the Seattle airport, we invited him to one of our institutes in Knoxville where he accomplished wonders working with the children's postures. He first explained the four basic principles to unify mind and body:

1) Keep one point
2) Relax completely
3) Keep weight underside
4) Extend Ki

He told us that these principles overlapped and that any one of them would suffice. "These are four approaches to the same goal. One may work better for some than the others. Certain individuals may at first need several."

Hirata's success with Brad, a slack teenager, was astonishing. I almost didn't recognize the boy whose renovated posture made him look like Heifetz! At first, Hirata told Brad, "Keep one point. This means to coordinate your mind and body by settling your mind at a single spot in your lower abdomen. Don't tense your abdomen. Just put your mind at your one point, which is your center of gravity a few inches below your navel."

To help him with this, he gave him another principle of Ki. "Put your weight underside, or think all of your weight down." Brad at this time was standing with the violin in rest position. "The weight of all objects naturally falls underside. The only time this is not true with the human body is when it is tense."

A third request followed. "Relax completely. Do this as you continue to stand straight. Many people are confused about the state of relaxation, thinking that the body should be slack. They conceive relaxation as a pleasant and weak state and think that it is necessary to revert to tension when action is required." Hirata later told us that if he had asked Brad to relax first he might have slumped more than usual, but after being instructed to keep his one point and think his weight down, he found that he was already relaxed.

Since Brad had been accustomed to bad posture for some time and had been used to daydreaming while he played, he found himself slipping easily into his old posture as his mind drifted away. He had trouble keeping his one point and thinking his weight down. "I've never thought this way before!" he exclaimed. Hirata had to play a few more games with him before he was able to put his mind in one place and keep it there.

The first game was the unbendable arm which Brad did rather well the first time. Then Hirata directed, "Please walk by me. As you walk, think of something behind you." As he passed, Hirata put out his arm to stop him. He stopped him easily. "Now," he added, "please walk by me again, only this time think about going directly over to that wall at the other side of the room." Again he put out his arm to stop him. This time Brad continued without stopping and actually carried Hirata on with him! "Ah, now you see that you can put your mind where you want it and your body reacts accordingly!"

"Now put your violin and bow in playing position. Keep one point and think all of your weight underside. Your teacher has told you to apply arm weight to the bow to get a big tone. To apply this arm weight without force, think of the underside of your right elbow." Hirata then tried to lift the elbow. It was very heavy.

After doing this preparation routine several times, Brad was finally ready to play. Hirata assured him, "As you play you needn't keep thinking about your one point or your weight down. As long as you are absorbed in your playing, you will be holding your one point and your posture will be good. Being absorbed in your playing means to watch and feel your fingers, hands and arms move, to listen to the music you are playing, to sing along with your playing. There are so many aspects of your playing that can absorb your attention. Go ahead and play the Bach concerto. I will check to see if you remain absorbed in your performance."

After he had played a while, Hirata came up from behind him and pulled backward gently on his right shoulder. He was immovable. "If your mind had left your playing, it would have been easy for me to turn you around by pulling on your shoulder."

Piano students at the institute also benefited from Hirata's instruction. He demonstrated the unbendable arm, and asked them to walk, thinking at first behind them, then ahead.

As each student assumed a sitting position on the piano bench, Hirata would question her, "Are you going to play the piano? Yes? Then you must play the piano and not think about TV, or playing outside, or eating ice cream!" He told them that so many times we play the piano only with our bodies while our minds are thinking thoughts of other things. Then we are not really playing the piano.

He went on to explain about 'keeping one point' and 'thinking weight down'. Postures improved almost immediately. Slouching and slumping positions gave way to firm straight backs that showed no tension. "Now if you keep your thoughts on the music when you play, you will always have a good posture and no one will ever be able to move you off balance. When our minds and bodies work together as partners, we are able to do any task beautifully."

I like to use these exercises in group lessons. I say nothing about the one point to very small children, but rather state the principle, "Think all of your weight down", which seems easier for them to visualize than "think your weight underside". I occasionally embellish this to stimulate the children's imaginations, asking, "Imagine that while you are standing straight, you are getting heavier and heavier, that all of your weight is going down to the soles of your feet and then down into the earth!"

As they stand, I walk around behind them pulling on their right shoulders to see how solid they are. I tell them in advance what I'm going to do, saying, "Don't resist me by pressing back. Just keep thinking your weight down and you'll be solid."

I've asked the parents to watch the children closely as I call out, "Now stop thinking about your weight down and think about going out to lunch or out to play." Parents have repeatedly noticed that many of the children start to move and sway as they change the direction of their minds. When I pull on their right shoulders, I have to be very careful. They can be turned very easily. Some almost fall down. I practice this with the children before I ask them to play. As they prepare to play, I say, "Please think all of your weight down after you place your violins and bows up in playing position. Think how heavy your bow elbow is. This will help you produce a beautiful tone. When you play, watch and listen to yourself play. Just play the music with all your heart. As you are playing, I'm going to walk around behind each of you and pull backward on your right shoulder. If your mind and heart have left the music, I will be able to turn you around easily."

Children are usually able to remain focussed on their playing for short pieces. If a child complains, "But I don't know what to think about when I play", we must give her specific suggestions that will help her maintain her concentration. We must first train her to watch, feel, and listen to her playing, develop her powers of observation, and her awareness of what she is doing.

There is no better example of coordination of mind and body than that demonstrated by an infant totally absorbed in trying to pick up something in her hand for the first time. Coordination of mind and body is always a fascinating thing to see. How enjoyable it is to watch the superb athlete in top form, the great musician producing a beautiful performance, or our own children totally absorbed in their playing!

A Game for Quieting the Mind and Body

Because the quieting of the mind and body are so important for the beginner we might use a version of Montessori's "Silence Game" to accomplish that purpose in a pleasant way. This may be done before practice, when diversion or relaxation is needed during practice, or at any desirable time during the day.

The parent sits in a comfortable, relaxed position and asks the child to assume a similar pose. The comments that are necessary should be brief, quiet and followed by stillness. "I am going to ask you to close your eyes and listen. Listen to the sounds you hear in this room . . . in rooms around us . . . outside. After a while I will quietly ask you to open your eyes very, very slowly, and we will talk about what you heard. Now make yourself comfortable, close your eyes and listen to the quietness and the sounds around you."

At first the time period should be short, then extended to longer periods as the child becomes capable of greater control and quietness.

Actually the parent could use this game in its original form with all siblings in the family. After the same preparation as above, and after the children's eyes are closed, the adult tells them in a whisper that a soft voice will call their name. The parent then moves quietly to a spot behind each child in turn and in a slow, drawn-out manner, calls each one by name. Each child opens his eyes, rises and follows the parent's beckoning gesture walking around the room. This is a kind of meditative experience.

A Game for Body Awareness

Since the children need to know the number names of their fingers as they are used on their particular instrument we can use a finger number game that will also promote body awareness.

Invite the child to hold his hand upright with fingers extended. Touch each finger, saying aloud the number name. (Remember: For violinists the index finger will be 'one', for pianists, the thumb is 'one'. This can be confusing to a child who plays both instruments, a good reason why the lessons on different instruments should not be started at the same time!) If children are quick to identify numbered fingers, invite them to close their eyes, keeping the upright hand in place with fingers still extended. Now softly touch the tip of the finger, quietly asking them to tell you the number of the finger you have touched.

At first this can be done one hand at a time, then with both hands together. Children who know 'right' and 'left' can be questioned by prefacing the number with 'right hand' or 'left hand'.

Doing this requires a physical 'feel' for finger placement as well as concentrated attention.

Talent is a species of vigor.

        Hoffer

I dwell in possiblity.

        Dickenson

The notes I handle no better than many pianists
But the pauses between the notes —
Ah, that is where the art resides!

        Artur Schnabel

Relaxation, Affirmations, Visualizations

Aids to a Positive Mental Attitude

"I think I can, I think I can, I think I can", said The Little Engine That Could. Our children loved that story. We all did. We strained with the little engine and heaved a sigh of relief when it succeeded and went over the top. I hope that story is still around to entertain *and* encourage children. Our oldest children, Kathleen and Teresa, recalled it at the same moment not long ago as we stood near the ruins of the small train station on the top of spectacular Boreas Pass in Colorado. How did that train long ago make that torturous journey over the mountains? In Fairplay, a fascinating, restored Western town, we read an old newspaper account of the train carrying a circus over the mountains through Boreas Pass, just like The Little Engine That Could!

We know that The Little Engine was able to go over the mountain because of its oft-repeated "I think I can", which then became "I thought I could". It visualized itself reaching the top. It kept affirming the possibility of success. Since it could not think two opposing thoughts at the same time, negative thoughts were not possible. It acted as though it were impossible to fail! This is the attitude we should help our children cultivate!

For whatever reason, perhaps it is the human condition, negative thoughts about oneself recur with persistent frequency in many, many people. Suzuki feels that the child learning to play a musical instrument is particularly vulnerable. "Not being able to play is the child's natural condition", he has said. "Since this is so, it often follows that the child thinks he cannot learn to play." We parents, therefore, are confronted with the challenge of helping our children build a healthy, positive mental attitude toward themselves, their potential, and in fact toward all of life.

RELAXATION, AFFIRMATIONS, VISUALIZATIONS

Mind Over Matter

In recent years, much has been written about mental attitudes affecting performance in all areas of life. The sports world is turning more and more to the psychologist to help the athlete. Doctors are becoming more sensitive to the power of imagination in effecting healing. The business world studies means of assisting employees with their mental attitudes. People in all of these areas are finding new ways to help individuals develop, maintain, and strengthen positive mental attitudes. Relaxation techniques, visualization techniques, and the formulation and repeated use of affirmations are finding increased use in these fields. With these techniques it is believed that mental attitudes can be changed by individuals themselves, and as a consequence, they can improve their performance.

Jack Nicklaus's remarks concerning his use of visualizations are well known to golf enthusiasts. He practices these visualizations with careful attention to every minute detail.

Arnold Schwartzenegger states, "As long as the mind can envision the fact that you can do something, you can do it, as long as you believe one hundred per cent. It's mind over matter. The body will follow through. It happens every time I close my eyes before I lift a heavy weight. I imagine it. I do it."

Bonnie Harmon, world champion shooter, declared, "My mental preparation consists primarily of a technique I call 'visualization', a technique consisting of formulating a mental picture of what I want to accomplish."

Betty Wanz, Olympic consultant, describing a self-regulatory program for athletes, writes, "Specific muscle tension-relaxation training is followed by a combination of muscle relaxation, deep-regular-smooth breathing, the use of stimulus words, and imagery. Athletes are asked to concentrate on certain words or phrases by repeating them silently to themselves. Words such as *warm, serene, calm,* and *confident* are used to achieve the desired psychophysiological state".

Richard Suinn, Olympic psychologist, uses what he calls "visuomotor behavior rehearsal" with athletes. "The method can be divided simply into three steps: relaxation, the practice of visualization, and the use of visualization for strengthening psychological or motor skills".

Vernon Ball, world champion backgammon player, prepared his own tape recording of relaxation guides, visualizations, and affirmations. He used it once a day for thirty days prior to his winning the world's backgammon championship.

We could go on and on citing examples of these techniques being used to shape mental attitudes to enhance performance. The tremendous power of the imagination as it affects our behavior and our growth is only beginning to be recognized. Those of us who work with children should become familiar with these techniques. It's not at all difficult for us to learn to guide our children into using these techniques effectively, techniques that we now know are used by athletes all over the world. In a sense, isn't the musician also an athlete? And don't we want to utilize all the aids we can in assisting our children?

Affirmations and Relaxation

Affirmations are positive declarations about one's self or about one's performance of an activity. If repeated often enough while a person is in a relaxed state, affirmations can help build positive attitudes and a sense of self-worth. Properly used, affirmations also effectively erase negative thoughts and feelings.

In order for affirmations to be the most effective, it is necessary for the person saying them to relax the body and quiet the mind before beginning the recitation. Barbara Brown, the biofeedback researcher, states, "To date we have learned that deep relaxation can vastly improve health, but perhaps more challenging is the finding that profound muscle relaxation can lead to startling changes in awareness and states of consciousness."

Richard Suinn, who has worked with Olympic athletes, writes, "I have been extremely impressed by the quality of imagery that is possible after deep muscle relaxation. This imagery is more than visual. It is also tactile, auditory, emotional, and muscular".

Relaxation should always precede the use of affirmations and visualizations. Perhaps the most common relaxation technique used by physical educators and sports psychologists is some form of

RELAXATION, AFFIRMATIONS, VISUALIZATIONS

Edmund Jacobson's progressive muscle relaxation, a procedure they find most effective psychologically and physiologically. Progressive relaxation involves tensing and relaxing various muscle groups throughout the body, one after another.

At Home Relaxation and Affirmations

Below you will find a sample procedure that you may wish to use with your child. Study it and make yourself comfortable with it before you do it together. Naturally, you may make any variations you wish as long as they are in harmony with the goal of the exercise, which is to provide an environment that allows the maximum effect from the use of the affirmations that follow.

You may wish to use the following introductory remarks:

"We're going to do an exercise that will help us to relax our bodies and minds. Many fine athletes do this to help them play better basketball, football, baseball, tennis or golf. This will help you to feel good no matter what you're doing.

"The exercise involves tightening up all of our muscles from toe to head, one part of our body at a time. Then when we relax those muscles we'll know what it feels like to be relaxed. We won't get tired because our muscles are tense all the time. By relaxing all of our muscles we can become calm even when someone or something has made us feel scared or upset. If we have an exam at school, if we're playing a solo on a program, or even if we have an appointment at the dentist, we can still relax and be calm. When we have relaxed all our muscles, our minds will become calm.

"Now, let's begin. First, you may lie down on the floor or sit in a comfortable position." (It is really best for the child to lie down because deep diaphragm breathing is easier and more natural in this position.)

"We're going to take some slow, deep breaths. Picture your chest as a balloon that fills with air when you breathe in and gets flat and empty when you breathe out. This will help. You'll see your stomach push out as you breathe in and then become flat when you empty your lungs of air. If you put your hands on your stomach, your hands should move up and down as you breathe in and out. Let's repeat this slowly a few times . . . breathe in through your nose - breathe out through your mouth, or

we sometimes say . . . inhale - exhale . . . that means the same thing."
We're then ready to do our progressive muscle relaxation. Fortu-
nately, children enjoy these exercises. Most do them quite well the very
first time.
"Let's close our eyes now and begin to relax our whole body. First,
think about your toes and the bones and muscles inside. Tighten your
toes. Curl them as tightly as possible. Hold them that way while I count
slowly to five . . . 1 - 2 - 3 - 4 - 5. Good. Now relax them completely. Let
them go. See how good this feels! (This observation by the child is very
important.) We always feel good when we can relax."
In sequence you should continue the same procedure with 1) the feet
2) legs 3) abdomen and lower torso 4) chest and back 5) arms and hands
6) neck and head.
As your child becomes accustomed to this relaxation exercise, she
will be able to tense and relax all the muscles at once. The goal is to make
the individual really aware of what it means to be relaxed. Many
children (and adults, too!) think they are relaxed when they still exhibit
tension in a number of muscles. Athletes who have done this progressive
relaxation exercise many, many times, eventually can become physi-
cally and mentally relaxed within seconds. They bypass the tension
portion completely because they know what it is like to be totally
relaxed, and they are able to scan their body quickly searching for
tension areas.
Now is the time to read the positive affirmations to the child and ask
her to repeat them in a very quiet voice.
Below you will find a list of affirmations to use as a guide. Pick and
choose those which will fit your situation, and then create your own.
Certainly there will be a need to tailor-make affirmations for your
unique child and her needs. It is best, perhaps, to use only eight or ten
during one session.

Affirmations

1. I like myself.
2. God made me. I am a very special person.
3. There is no one just like me.
4. My body is a wonderful creation.

5. My body takes care of me without my direction.
6. I must eat the right foods, and give my body enough rest so that it will be healthy and strong.
7. I want to learn about the world around me.
8. Music is a wonderful gift from God to all of us.
9. Music makes our lives more beautiful.
10. Music is not 'alive' until it is played.
11. I want to learn to play music on the (piano, violin, cello, etc.)
12. I am thankful that my teacher and parents are helping me to learn to play music on the (piano, violin, cello, etc.)
13. When I play music I bring it "to life."
14. I am thankful for all the great composers who have written beautiful music.
15. To play well I know that I must practice each day.
16. Practice is easy when I want to learn.
17. When I practice well I learn easily and play better and better.
18. Each day as I practice I play better and better.
19. Good practice helps me to enjoy my playing.
20. Before I start to practice I relax and quietly prepare my mind and body to learn.
21. I can relax easily.
22. To relax, I take slow, deep breaths and think quiet, calming thoughts.
23. To relax I think that my body is heavy. I feel all of my weight going down.
24. As I practice I watch and listen to what I am doing.
25. Practicing music trains my arms and fingers to work well.
26. I send clear messages to my arms and fingers when I practice so that they will know what to do.
27. My eyes watch and my ears listen to tell me how to practice correctly.
28. At my lessons I listen to what my teacher asks me to do when I practice at home.
29. I listen to my recordings everyday so that I will know when I play correctly.

30. When I was small and learning to walk I fell down many times and always got up to try again.
31. It is all right to make mistakes as we are learning.
32. We learn from our mistakes.
33. I believe that I can learn easily and well.
34. When I believe that I can do it, I can do anything that I try to do.
35. I have a good memory. It grows better each day as I use it.
36. I remember everything that I learn.
37. I remember easily what my teacher asks me to do.
38. I remember easily all the pieces I have learned.
39. The music I have learned is stored in my mind, and I can remember it whenever I want to.
40. I will be thankful and happy about each new thing I learn.
41. Each time I play music I know I am doing something very important.
42. I give the gift of music to people when I play for them.
43. I can make people happy by playing music for them.
44. I am calm and relaxed when I play for people.
45. I am peaceful and quiet inside and have control of my thoughts and feelings.
46. I thank my teacher for helping me to learn.
47. I thank my parents for everything they do for me, helping me to grow into a fine person.
48. I hope that all children will learn to play music beautifully.
49. I hope that all students and parents will love and enjoy music.
50. I will be kind to everyone.
51. I will do kind, thoughtful things for my family and everyone I meet.
52. I will help to make my home happy by being thoughtful of others.
53. I will try to make others happy, and then I will be happy, too.

After a period of affirmation, ask the child to open her eyes very slowly. It is always best to return slowly to regular activity so that the maximum effect from the affirmations can be realized. At the conclusion of the affirmations, you might say, "Now I'm going to count slowly to five. When I say 'five', please open your eyes very slowly. Stand up and stretch. Now you're all ready to proceed."

Visualizations

"Visualization", writes Vernon Ball, world backgammon champion, "is nothing more than using your imagination to produce life-like full-color images of your choice on your mental screen."
Suinn suggests that if we visualize a positive goal so vividly as to make it real, and think of it in terms of an accomplished fact, we will also experience winning feelings - self-confidence, courage, and faith that success is attainable. Since we are now aware that the mind does not differentiate between vividly imagined and actual experience, we can develop a powerful imagination as a confidence-building tool! We can create our own experiences of success in our minds.

Children may be guided to do visualizations at home on a regular basis, or some weeks before a scheduled solo performance, preparing them for a pleasant positive experience when they perform. Visualizing the details of an enjoyable performance paves the way for a successful real-life musical experience. This visualization may include the appreciative audience smiling and clapping, the teacher helping the student get ready at the piano, the encouraging pat on the back, the nice sound of the music, the smooth feeling of the piano keys, the well-practiced fingers doing their job with ease.

Again, relaxing and quieting the mind is necessary before visualization, so the relaxation exercise above may be used, or any variation you may find useful. After the relaxation preparation you may, in a quiet, gentle voice, guide the visualization as follows.

"Let's keep our eyes closed and make our own movie inside our head. It will be a movie about us . . . we'll watch ourselves just like in a regular movie except that we will make our own pictures in our imagination. (Pause for a moment, then begin.) Let's walk out the back door. What a beautiful afternoon it is! Is it cold enough for a coat? Yes, even though the sun is warm it is still cold and you're wearing your green jacket over the red shirt and navy corduroy pants that you like so much. You're opening the back door of the car, getting in and scooting to the

other side because Jim is behind you. (If the child plays an instrument that she carries, go through the details of which hand it is carried in and where it is put in the car.) Daddy comes around the car to get in the driver's seat, and I get in next to him."

Now relate details in the environment, and the reactions and feelings surrounding them . . . driving fast or slow, waving to friends in another car, finding close parking space, walking to the building, teacher smiling and greeting students, sitting with parents in the second row, walking to the front, calm and relaxed but excited and eager to play, feeling good inside, bowing, sitting or standing quietly in rest position as you get ready to play, placing fingers on keyboard or putting instrument in position, feeling warm hands, watching fingers move smoothly over the keys or fingerboard, etc., listening to beautiful tone, finishing piece, smiling faces in the audience, teacher saying "Very beautiful".

Go on to add any pleasant details that may be pertinent. This would also be an opportune time to add a few affirmations.

It must be remembered that all of the visualizations must be done in very vivid detail - inner feelings, seeing, hearing, touching, and even smelling should be a part of them. The visualizer should feel as though she is actually going through the experience of performance. The more vivid the imagination the more effective is the visualization.

According to a well-established psychological principle, a skill learned or practiced in one situation will transfer to a new situation in direct proportion to the extent that the new situation resembles the one in which the practice takes place. Fortunately, the mind and nervous system also respond well to visualized performances to the extent that they resemble the real performance. This is the reason why this kind of visualization can be so helpful in preparing the child for actual performance. We have found this to be particularly helpful with adolescents.

Here's an account of visualization being used with surprising results with our son David, then eight. David had been playing piano for three years when he asked if he could study violin, too. We weren't too keen on this since it meant more commitment in an already crowded schedule, but I decided to start him myself. After a few weeks he began to rebel against double practice periods and it was the violin that suffered. He had progressed slowly up past 'Perpetual Motion' when summer arrived, and off I went to a round of workshops. We expected David to keep the piano going through the summer but I decided to let the violin ride and see if he expressed any interest in resuming study in the fall. Nothing was said for weeks after he started school. Then one day, out of the blue, he asked, "Whatever happened to my violin?" And so it was that we got out the violin and prepared for the first lesson in four months. I had been reading about the unusual results obtained through visualization, so I decided to use it with David to see if we could shorten the return to his past playing ability.

"David, let's play a game before you pick up the violin." I then asked him to sit comfortably in a chair and close his eyes. We went through a short form of progressive relaxation of his muscles. We had already done this before, so he was quite capable of doing it quickly.

"Now, David, I want you to go with me on an exciting trip down into your subconscious mind. Right back of your eyes I want you to imagine a heavy door. Open the door, and you will see a flight of ten steps leading to a large room below. Let's count the ten steps as we go down slowly. One, two, etc. . . . Now look around the room. It's filled with computers humming away, and file cases. Those computers are running your heart, your breathing, everything that goes on in your body automatically. Over in those file cases is stored everything you've ever learned. Let's find the file case that says 'music' on it. There . . . the second drawer says 'violin' on it. Open it and find the computer card that says 'Perpetual Motion'. There it is! It has on it all the instructions for your fingers, arms, muscles, and nerves. All of it is recorded in detail. So you don't have to try to remember how to play 'Perpetual Motion'. Your body already knows. You just have to let it play. Put the card in that computer next to the file case. When you go back upstairs, pick up the violin and put the bow on the string. The computer will be directing everything automatically. Let's go back upstairs slowly, and count the steps up as we go."

David opened his eyes shortly after leaving his subconscious mind's room. He picked up the violin, and then proceeded to play

'Perpetual Motion' better than he had before the four month layoff! In fact, the level of performance was so high that Connie, in the next room, thought I was demonstrating for him! I forgot myself and yelled, "Wow! That was great! I didn't know you'd do it that well! Connie, come and hear David play 'Perpetual Motion' just as though he'd been practicing every day for the last four months!"

Here I made a serious error. I should have shown enthusiasm for his performance, but not so much surprise. After what I told him, didn't we both believe it possible? Anyway, my remarks put David on the spot and broke the magic spell. He played falteringly for Connie. Afterward I wished I had said, "Great, David! That's just what we both expected to happen. It shows what you can do if you trust your mind."

(I'm writing this seven years later. David read it over my shoulder and remembered details that I omitted in this account, among them the fact that the stairs were heavily carpeted!)

Another Form of Relaxation Using Visualization

The following relaxation technique can be used without going through the progressive relaxation sequence if the child possesses a naturally calm and quiet personality, or it may be done after having practiced the progressive relaxation sequence for a period of time with satisfactory results.

Getting the child settled comfortably as before, ask her to breathe slowly and deeply a few times, and then proceed as below.

"I've found a beautiful colored picture of a mountain lake that I want you to see. The water is so blue, so still, there's not even a little ripple in it. Can you see the fluffy white clouds and the bright blue sky reflected on it? Now let's close our eyes and see this picture on a screen like a TV set inside our head. See the lake, the still mirror-like surface, the mountains, the fluffy clouds? Our minds are still and quiet like that lake. Let's say this together: 'I am relaxed, peaceful and quiet. My mind is like that lake, quiet, still and peaceful. (It is best if this can be repeated aloud quietly several times in a kind of sing-song rhythm. Also choose a key word that can be repeated in a quiet voice three to five

times during the relaxation - a word like peaceful, quiet, calm, etc.)
Obviously, you may choose a picture of your own choice, the only
prerequisite being that it must conjure up feelings of quietness and
calmness. It would be good to change the picture at intervals if you do
this regularly.

Relaxation During Practice

"Relax, Mary Ann! You're not even breathing! Put your shoulders
down! Relax!"
A well-meaning parent may observe that a child has built up tension
during practice and want to help her to release it so that she may
practice effectively. Yet we know that a person who is tense cannot be
forced to relax by the request or command to "relax". Instead, a few
things you might ask your child to do are listed below. You may wish to
use all of them or only one as the situation indicates.
  1. *Stop for a moment to take a few slow, deep breaths.*
  2. *Let the arms hang loosely at the sides. Shake the hands vigorously*
     for about 30 seconds.
  3. *Use the tense-relax method with back, arms and hands.*
  4. *Sit quietly, eyes closed, saying aloud two or three times, "I am*
     peaceful and quiet inside and have control of my thoughts and
     feelings".
This short but helpful relaxation need not consume a great deal of
time, perhaps 5 minutes maximum, but the time is well worth it.

Relaxation Before a Performance

Because I believed so much in the benefits of relaxation, I decided to
experiment with my students during the time preceding a solo pro-
gram. I asked the parents to bring all the students fifteen minutes early
and leave them with me. We met in the band room which had a carpet on
the floor. The parents returned to the auditorium and seated them-
selves, saving a seat for their child. I waited until all the children
had arrived.
"I'd like you all to sit in a very comfortable position. You may sit on
the floor or on a chair. Just be sure you are comfortable enough to stay

that way for a while without having to move. Now I'd like you to close your eyes and take a few slow deeps breaths to help you relax and quiet yourselves." (At this point there were a few giggles and whispers to which I responded that anyone who did not think they could be quiet while we did this relaxation could go back to the hall and wait for us. No one left. I think they were afraid that they'd miss something!) "Ready? All right . . . breathe in slowly through your nose, then breathe out slowly through your mouth. Again, breathe in . . . breathe out . . . Please do this a couple of times by yourself. (I allowed time for them to do this on their own.)

"Now I'm going to read a sentence for you and after I do I will give you time to repeat it to yourself silently before I read the next sentence. Just keep your eyes closed, listen to each sentence, and repeat it slowly to yourself."

At this point I chose affirmations from the preceding list. When the affirmations were completed I proceeded to say, "Now, very, very slowly open your eyes. We'll walk very quietly into the hall. Find your parents and sit with them until it's your turn to play."

The procession into the hall was amazing. There was almost no conversation. It was as though they were in a trance. It was obvious from the performances of the children that they all benefited from the relaxation and affirmations. They showed poise, centered behavior, and made no impetuous starts.

This group of children ranged in age from five to fifteen. Age seemed to be of no significance. Afterward, one of the children said, "Mrs. Starr, I really liked the way you hypnotized us!" Just to alleviate any parents' fears, I thought I'd better explain what had gone on in our private sessions behind those closed doors! At any rate, after they heard the performances the parents indicated they liked it, too.

Relaxation for Pre-teens and Teens

Michael, from the age of 5, had always been completely relaxed when he walked onto the stage to perform, acting as though he were walking down the street with very little on his mind. Until he was twelve. Then after a performance of "La Folia" he came offstage with tears in his eyes. "I was so nervous! I couldn't believe it. I've never felt that way before."

Many parents observe this phenomenon. The age of self-awareness, the painful self-awareness of the growing adult, rears its head during these years, and what before brought no thought of anxiety or fear suddenly takes on a whole series of new feelings. Previously discussed relaxation, affirmations and visualizations can be used effectively with children this age, with affirmations and visualizations especially appropriate to them. Below are some suggestions. You may add some of your own.

1. I believe in myself, in my ability to grow and learn.
2. I am growing in confidence everyday.
3. My memory continues to improve each day as I am getting older.
4. My ability to play and perform improves as I am growing up.
5. As I grow up, I continue to enjoy playing the (violin, piano, etc.)
6. Each day as I am growing up I practice and play better and better.
7. When I was small, I enjoyed playing for people and I continue to enjoy it now that I am older.
8. I continue to be calm and relaxed when I play for people.
9. Since I am playing more advanced music now, I enjoy practicing and playing more than ever before.
10. While my body is growing and developing I am helping my mind and spirit to grow by learning and playing music.

The principles of aikido may also be used both for this age and for smaller children. These are presented in the chapter on the Coordination of Mind and Body.

Relaxation at Lessons

It was obvious that Mark, age 5, needed some help to be able to settle down during his lesson. His mother and I had discussed his behavior in situations outside of the music lesson - kindergarten, church, and home. She was concerned, as I was, that it seemed difficult for him to be attentive for even a short period of time. We discussed food, the possibility of allergy, and his sleeping habits, without being able to pinpoint the cause of his tension.

Because the family had moved to a nearby town, Mark was forced to change his lesson schedule and he was, for a limited period of time, taking his lesson alone instead of with the group with which he had started. Since he would not be embarrassed by the presence of the other children I decided to try a 'pre-lesson' relaxation.

"Mark, would you please lie down on the floor?"

He looked at me incredulously, "What for?"

"We're going to play a game. Close your eyes, relax and get very comfortable. Put your hands right here." He grinned as I placed his hands on his abdomen. "Now very slowly breathe in through your nose. Breathe in, try to hold it while I count to 5, then let out all the air."

We did this a few times. Then I went through the 'tense-relax' routine, but instead of isolating each part of the body, we tensed the entire body at one time.

"Tense up your body. Tighten up everything - your fists, your shoulders, neck, legs, feet - everything as tight as you can. Tighter! Hold it until I count to 3. 1 - 2 - 3. Now relax. Doesn't that feel great? Just lie there quietly, keeping your eyes closed and enjoying how good it feels. Think of yourself floating on a magic rug - floating, floating through the air."

After a few minutes I suggested, 'Very, very slowly now, open your eyes and stretch. S-t-r-e-t-c-h and then get up. Now we'll get up on the piano bench and begin your lesson."

After that when Mark walked in the door of the studio he'd ask, "Am I going to lie down on the floor again?"

We didn't do that at every lesson, but many times after we'd started a lesson without it I wished that I had taken the time to help him relax. There was definite improvement in his attention and retention when we spent those few minutes on relaxation.

Actually if you feel that your child could benefit from even a shorter version of this before a lesson, you can do this at home before leaving for the lesson or in the car if your schedule is tight. The prone position is helpful but certainly not necessary for a quick, effective relaxation. You might find the list from "Relaxation During Practice" helpful if time is short.

RELAXATION, AFFIRMATIONS, VISUALIZATIONS

Adult - Parent Affirmations

Thus far we have related the use of relaxation, affirmations and visualizations to your children, who are Suzuki students, but these techniques can be just as helpful to parents in the midst of an active family life. Very few adults can say there is no area in their lives that couldn't use some positive reinforcement. I would tend to be suspicious of the person who did, because most of us have a complex composite of strengths and weaknesses, of confidence and insecurity, of desire for change and inflexibility. After we'd given a talk on these techniques to a group of parents one was heard to say, "Those ideas sound great, but it's hard for me to believe they'd work in my family. I guess I'm too old to change". There is nothing more detrimental to a full life than the feeling that because we are 'adults', we have 'arrived' - that there is no need to go on searching and expanding, or that it is impossible to change 'at our age'. That is my definition of being 'old' - and it can come at age twenty, age eighty . . . or never.

See what the addition of a 'food for the spirit' break can do for you each day.

Here are a few suggestions. You'll be able to formulate your own, unique to your needs. Some of them are the same as the ones given for your children. No offense . . . some needs are universal. Again, we believe that eight or ten of the affirmations at a time will be most helpful.

1. I like myself.
2. Despite my weaknesses and deficiencies, I am a worthwhile person with many good qualitites and valuable assets.
3. I am not a perfect parent. There are no perfect parents!
4. I do not have a perfect child. There are no perfect children.
5. I am a worthwhile (father, mother) who is understanding and capable of intelligent and compassionate parenting.
6. I am always open to new ideas and ways to become a better person, and therefore a more effective parent.
7. I love my children, and I want to show them that love by my actions as well as my words.
8. I will find quality time to spend with my child (children) each day.

9. I will try never to be too busy to listen to what my children want to share with me or talk over with me.

10. When my children want to talk to me about something, I will give them my undivided attention.

11. When my children talk to me, I will remember the importance of eye contact.

12. I will find every opportunity to give a reassuring pat or a spontaneous hug to my children, realizing the importance of physical contact in the expression of my love for them.

13. If I cannot stop my activity to listen when my children come to talk to me, I will explain this if it is not urgent, and make a definite time to listen to them as soon as I'm free.

14. I have confidence in my ability to grow, to reinforce those areas in my personality where I feel inadequate or shaky.

15. When stress and tension make me feel uptight I will stop for a moment to relax, repeating "I am calm" until I regain my composure.

16. I am peaceful and quiet within and have control of my thoughts and emotions.

17. I look at all problems as challenges for which to find solutions.

18. I am excited by new situations and find facing them exhilarating.

19. I like to learn new skills and acquire new knowledge.

20. Learning new skills and acquiring new knowledge helps me to understand the learning process that my children are experiencing.

21. I like to take time to "smell the flowers" and enjoy the beauty of of nature all around us.

22. Life is exciting, and I look forward to each day, wondering what wonderful things will happen today.

23. I greet each day with a thankful heart.

24. I am thankful for my healthy mind and body.

25. I am thankful that I can hear music and the voices of the ones I love.

26. I am thankful for my children, their many gifts and talents and their love.

27. I am happy in my role as a parent. The responsibility is great but the rewards are greater.

28. Working with my child while he learns to play the (violin, piano etc.) is a joy filled time for me.

29. I must always remember that enthusiasm and a sense of humor are the best environment for the enjoyment of learning.

30. I like to help my child relax and enjoy learning to play music.

31. When practice time becomes difficult, I remember to remain calm and keep the proper perspective.

32. I can improve! I can grow! I can change!

Nothing great was ever achieved
Without enthusiasm.

Emerson

The parents of Richard Rodgers, half of the famous Rodgers and Hammerstein team, loved musical comedy and attended each new one as it made its appearance. The following evenings were spent in their living room singing and playing the entire score from opening to finale. Richard, born in 1902, was exposed to these family concerts from infancy. At four he picked out one finger versions of the songs he heard—at six he taught himself to play with both hands—at ten he made up his own tunes—and at twelve he scarcely left the piano to eat and go to school. In an interview he joyfully said, "What I'm doing today is what I have wanted to do all my life!"

Motivating The Young Child

"How do you help mothers awaken in their children the desire to play violin?" "How do you help the child to enjoy practicing the violin?" These are questions frequently asked Suzuki in Japan and America. After more than thirty years of experience teaching small children, Suzuki still regards the problem of motivation as *the* principal problem for parents and teachers.

An often overlooked aspect of the mother-tongue education is the awakening of the desire to speak as a result of the environment of the young child. The importance of the role of listening to records for the development of musical sensitivity oftentimes overshadows the effect of listening on motivation. "The baby cannot speak at birth, but in his everyday environment he hears his mother and father speak, and gradually begins his desire to speak," says Suzuki, who tries to follow the same path of motivation in his violin instruction program.

In his book, *Nurtured by Love*, Suzuki describes what he feels is the ideal way to begin instruction:

"Although we accept infants, at first we do not have them play the violin. First, we teach the mother to play one piece so that she will be a good teacher at home. As for the child, we first have him simply listen at home to a record of the piece he will be learning. Children are really educated in the home, so in order that the child will have good posture and practice properly at home, it is necessary for the parent to have first-hand experience. The correct education of the child depends on this. Until the parent can play one piece, the child does not play at all. This principle is very important indeed, because although the parent may want him to do so, the three or four year old child has no desire to learn the violin. The idea is to get the child to say, "I want to play, too", so the first piece is played every day on the phonograph, and in the studio he just watches the other childen (and his mother) having their lessons. The proper environment is created for the child. The mother, moreover, both at home and in the studio, plays on a small violin more suited to the child. The child will naturally before

102

long take the violin away from his mother, thinking, "I want to play, too". He knows the tune already. The other children are having fun; he wants to join in the fun. We have caused him to acquire this desire.

"This situation having been created, lessons are led up to in the following order. First the parent asks, "Would you like to play the violin, too?" The answer is "Yes!" "You will practice hard?" "Yes". "All right, let's ask the teacher if you can join in next time". This always succeeds. What a thrill the first private lesson always is! "I did it, too," the child boasts. "Now I can play with the other children". Parents who understand children make fine teachers. In the studio there are private lessons and group lessons. Parents who do not understand children think they are paying for the private lessons and that the group lessons are just recreation periods. So although they make sure that their children attend the private lessons, they often fail to bring them to the group lessons. But the fact is that what the children enjoy most is the group playing. They play with children who are more advanced than they are; the influence is enormous, and is marvelous for their training. This is real talent education".

Suzuki feels that the three-year-old is most desirous of pleasing the mother and therefore regards this as the best starting age. However, by no means all of the mothers wanting to register their children for lessons bring three-year-olds as beginners. "Do you turn older children away?" "What is the oldest child you accept as a beginner?" These questions are often directed to Suzuki. "No age limit", he replies. "I say to mothers of older children, 'Let us start today before the child is older!' "

Although teaching the mother first is generally accepted as being the ideal way for a beginner to start in Talent Education, for one reason or another not all Talent Education teachers do this. Some are content that the mother knows how to teach the child at home. If the child is older than three, the desire to imitate the mother may be overshadowed by the desire to be independent. An any age, Suzuki has found it normal that the child wants to please the parents and teacher. The child expects his parents to be vitally interested in what he is doing, and wants praise for his successful development. In Japan often the whole family shows great interest in the child's violin playing.

When we made a short summer visit to Japan a few years ago I had the opportunity to visit Misako Yanagida and observe piano lessons in her studio. Misako has accompanied the tour group a number of times and is a fine pianist. At the time we lived in Japan she was still a 'kenkyusei'—a student—but on this visit she already had a large class of students in Tokyo.

It was at the lesson of a three-year-old girl, a potential student, that I first saw the effective teaching of a mother and the ideal reactions of the child. Misako sensei was working with the mother, and the small child spent almost the entire time beside the mother's chair, watching intently everything that the mother was doing. She was not just standing there, lost in her own thought. She was obviously aware of and interested in what was happening. It was the perfect example of that 'ideal' way we had heard so much about.

Praise

In a lesson for a beginning three-year-old, Suzuki was heard to say 'umai' (good) after every effort the child made. He never said, "No, that is not good", but only "Good. Can you do this better? Let's try again." He urges the mother also to praise the child at every step. Many mothers withhold praise if the child does badly thinking that if they then praise the child, he will not know when he is doing well and when he isn't. Suzuki explains that there can be degrees of praise and that it is better to be silent than to be critical. In most cases, the ingenious mother can find something worthwhile to call to the child's attention. "That tone was better". "You remembered all the notes." "You held your violin higher". "Your bow hold was good". If the teacher and mother are guiding the child properly they need not worry about a little undeserved praise. "Very good. Can you do better?" is the basic Suzuki formula.

Suzuki is quoted from a videotape interview:

"In Japan, some mothers never say 'very good'. I say to mother, "Please say 'Very good. you can play well, but can you play much better?' 'Yes, I can'. With pieces that are already known, mother and teacher must ask for them again and again asking for better tone, better intonation, and better tempo. Gradually we can make ability from repetition of pieces that are known by the child".

The review of known pieces makes it possible to reach a high level of excellence that is truly deserving of praise and hence is a motivational factor. If the child knows a piece but continues to work to refine it in all ways, a praise response is natural and the student enjoys well-deserved attention.

Attitude of Parent and Teacher

Suzuki was asked about patient perseverance in the mother and teacher. "Patience is not necessary. We don't need patience. While the child is learning to speak his mother-tongue the parent doesn't feel he needs patience. Everyone enjoys the child's learning. My teaching is my leisure time. Children play at lessons. Nice time for children and nice time for mother and teacher. I watch what point I can bring to the child's attention. Patience is not necessary. Mothers should enjoy each step as children learn. Beginners grow so slowly, same as mother-tongue education".

Suzuki is by no means the only teacher in Talent Education who thoroughly enjoys teaching small children. I felt the spirit of enjoyment while watching a number of teachers at work. This spirit was contagious. Many of the children and mothers seemed to be enjoying themselves. Mothers often moved to the rhythm of the music. I was surprised to find mothers of advanced children enjoying the behavior and actions of very small beginners learning 'Twinkle'.

Recently, at a summer institute, a six-year-old girl was performing extremely well in one of the afternoon programs. I was so completely captivated by the actions of her mother who was sitting in the front row that I must admit I didn't give full attention to the performance. The mother was leaning forward, almost out of her seat, extended hands holding a small cassette tape recorder, her body swaying in time to the music, while her beaming face had an almost ecstatic expression! There was no doubt that the child felt those wonderful vibrations that came to her from that spot!—and would certainly feel that music was a glorious part of life!

Home Concerts

Suzuki urges each mother to stage weekly home concerts for the father to be shown the child's progress. These concerts can be scheduled at the beginning of instruction even before the child can perform anything. Many mothers have made this a real event, making small stages or platforms out of boxes for these concerts. At first, the child walks up onto the 'stage' with his violin tucked under his arm and his bow in his hand. After facing the father, he bows solemnly and then leaves the stage. He has shown the father how well he can hold the violin 'at rest'. In the early months when the progress is very slow as the teacher and mother are trying to prepare the child's posture and bow hold properly, the weekly home concert can be quite an incentive for the child. Every small step forward is noticed and applauded.

Private Lessons

Suzuki finds that the private lessons provide a great deal of motivation if the teacher really loves children and enjoys teaching them. The private lesson is always a public affair in Talent Education. Suzuki says that the child should always watch lessons of other children. He considers this environment essential, observing that the child learns from the advanced students possibly more than he does directly from his teacher.

Suzuki expresses considerable sympathy for the teacher just starting a program. "This is so difficult, without the environment of the advanced children to inspire the beginners. When I started in Matsumoto 24 years ago, it was very difficult because of the limited environment of the private lessons. We had at first only six children playing 'Twinkle', taking turns playing on our only small violin! Beginning teachers should expect the beginning year of their program to be the most difficult. Even the second year, their older students will help them teach the new beginners."

In a typical Talent Education private lesson the studio is filled with mothers and children who wait patiently watching private lessons of other students.

"I saw in America", Suzuki commented, "sometimes only one child and one mother alone with the teacher in the studio. This is a very bad environment. Perhaps the child's progress is very slow and the desire to play is very weak. If the mother says, 'You must study', then the child plays only for the mother, not for himself, but if the child sees other children play every week in lessons, he will want to play as they do. Mother and child must stay and watch other children. Advanced children also play in the room. Mothers watch everything. Children enjoy playing for others and enjoy watching others play."

Early Participation in Concerts

Early participation in concerts is a fine motivating force for beginners, Suzuki believes, not only in the home concert, but also in public recitals and concerts. I witnessed a charming demonstration of this idea of early participation at a prefectural concert performed by over four hundred students. Immediately after intermission, members of the audience hurried quickly to their seats to see the beginners bow. The children came on stage solemnly, violins under their right arms and bows clutched in their fingers. After they had been lined up, a chord was played on the piano, and they bowed, staring out at the audience which responded with resounding applause. They then ran happily off the stage. Some had come sixty miles by train for this event!

Concerts and Recitals

Beginners are always taken to concerts and recitals of the more advanced children. They are much more stimulated by the playing of their peers than by adult performances. "In Matsumoto now we have many advanced small children," says Suzuki. "When beginners attend concerts, we find they learn more rapidly than children of the same age years ago before we had such a favorable environment."

Concert deportment is important. The Talent Education concerts in Japan are rather relaxed affairs, obviously given primarily for the children on the stage and in the audience. Children are not kept absolutely quiet throughout the performance. If the mother is always scolding a child, insisting that he not move or make a sound, he will

107

regard the concerts as unpleasant affairs. Naturally, there must be a happy medium. The children cannot be allowed free rein but the atmosphere should not be too repressive. If most of the members of the audience are reasonably attentive, the majority of the children will conform fairly well. Of course, concert behavior is a problem but not one to be solved by the parents forcing 'adult' attention and behavior on a small child. If the child is sufficiently praised for reasonable behavior and attends concerts with some regularity, his deportment will most likely become satisfactory.

Parents should always realize that even a seemingly indifferent child is absorbing more than seems possible. Eiko Suzuki, (no relation to Mr. Suzuki) is one of Suzuki's fine adult students and now a teacher in Talent Education. She began her study of violin at the age of two. Once in her fourth year her parents took her to a violin recital given by a visiting soloist. The little girl did not sit still one minute, but constantly annoyed her father by climbing all over the seat and watching the audience throughout much of the program. The father thought the evening a total loss until several months later when Eiko recognized a sonata being played over the radio as having been on that recital program months earlier. Her incredulous father had to find a concert program to verify her statement before he believed his little daughter who had seemed so inattentive that evening.

Graduation

To increase motivation in the young children, Suzuki has created a system of "graduations" throughout Talent Education in Japan. Talent Education youngsters from all over Japan send tapes to Suzuki to qualify for "graduation" from one level of difficulty to the next. This means that Suzuki listens to approximately one thousand tapes every year. All of the children graduate, and all are rated "excellent" or better by Suzuki!

At the end of the student's selection, Suzuki records comments and advice for improvement. Not all of these remarks deal with technique, tone, or musical sensitivity. For instance, graduates progressing on to the Bach Concerto in A Minor have been given words of advice that must have received warm welcomes in Japanese households.

"Now you are going to play great concertos of Mozart and Bach, and you must try to catch the heart of Bach and Mozart in their music. You must practice every day to catch the feelings of others without words. Look at your mother and father. Can you see how they feel? Try to see when your mother needs your help—before she asks. Then it is too late. If you practice every day, watching not to harm anyone by what you say, and also trying to catch how they feel, then you will develop sensitivity toward the feelings of others. Perhaps later you will also catch the heart of Bach and Mozart in their music."

Suzuki receives many letters from mothers expressing their gratitude to him for these words of advice to their children.

Some Suzuki teachers in the West give pins or certificates to students in recognition of their graduation to another level. These are usually presented at the recital at which the children have performed their graduation pieces.

Institutes and Workshops

Each summer several thousand children are given a heady dose of motivation at numerous institutes being offered in many different localities. The first institute, patterned after Suzuki's summer schools in Japan, was given in 1971 at the University of Wisconsin in Stevens Point, Wisconsin under the direction of Margery Aber. It proved so successful that institutes similar to it began to be offered all over the world where Suzuki music instruction was offered.

Private lessons, group lessons, student and faculty recitals, group, chamber and orchestral concerts, lectures, panel discussions, theory instruction, and related offerings crowd the schedules of most of the institutes. The children are kept busy but at the same time have enjoyable social contact with peers who are interested in musical pursuits. Many parents value this motivation as much as that resulting from the actual instruction involved.

Some families plan their vacations to coincide with institute dates. If all the children in the family are playing instruments and can participate in the program and both mother and father enjoy spending their vacation in this way it can be a great experience. To be that, it must be a unanimous choice . . . everyone must be happy about such a decision.

If you haven't participated in an institute and feel that you could include one in your family vacation plans, ask your teacher about information on institutes in your area or in areas of the country you'd like to visit. You'll be pleasantly surprised by the motivation they provide. Parents have told us that institutes have helped improve the home practice situation for months!

More and more Suzuki programs are offering weekend workshops throughout the school year that are patterned after the week-long summer institutes. Guest faculty are brought in, and sometimes students from adjacent communities are invited. At any rate, these workshops are highly motivational and are also reported to have a salutary effect on home practice. It is not so difficult to fit these workshops into the family schedule, and yet teachers often lament the fact that not enough parents take advantage of these opportunities to stimulate their children musically. It's not that the teachers don't have enough enrollment to finance the workshop; it's that the teachers know how much the children benefit by their participation.

Teacher-Parent Cooperation

The teacher and mother should discuss the problem of motivation together frequently, suggests Suzuki, considering ways to influence the child. The mother and teacher should be very sensitive to the state of mind of the child. Suzuki does not believe that the correct way is to force the child to practice every day. The highest degree of ingenuity and creative imagination must be brought into play to create the most favorable environment for the child.

Happy is he who has the power
To gather wisdom from a flower.

Medieval Saying

Love comforteth like sunshine after rain.

Shakespeare

Although Franz Liszt was not yet big enough for his feet to touch the floor, he would sit at the piano and play all of the melodies that he had heard his father play before him.

111

Motivating The High School Student

As Suzuki students become older, many parents and teachers become concerned about their continuing Suzuki study throughout high school. The aids to motivation that they have been using don't seem to work as well as when the children were younger. They find that motivating the high school student is quite different from motivating the young student. People are confronted with these questions: How can we make our Suzuki programs more attractive to our high school students? How can we motivate them to continue lessons and practice whether they stay in the Suzuki program or not?

The High School Student in Japan

If we look to Japan for guidance, we find that the structure of Talent Education there provides little motivational impetus for the high school student. Suzuki's program is primarily oriented toward capturing and sustaining the interest of the very young child. We all know with what phenomenal success this has been done. However, the percentage of Suzuki-trained students in Japan who continue to take private lessons and participate in Suzuki concert and recital programs throughout high school is not large.

I was once accosted in Japan by an American teacher who was disturbed by this fact. "Why doesn't Suzuki concern himself more with the older student?" he asked. "What can he do?" was my response. I then explained that most Suzuki students come from families who are not only interested in their children's Suzuki music education but also have a great deal of interest in their children's academic achievements. Many of these parents want their children to attend college.

In Japan entrance into college is extremely competitive. And this competition starts early. Middle school students must pass tests to enter the regional high school which prepares them for college entrance examinations. These high school exams require a great deal of study, consequently limiting or eliminating time for practice. This pressure causes many of the students to stop taking lessons. Others continue with less and less time allocated to practice. Those who continue studying and do maintain a rigorous practice schedule are the minority who are very advanced and are orientated toward a performance career or are planning to become Suzuki teachers.

The fact that there are so few outlets for performance in orchestra, solo, or chamber music also contributes to a lessening of interest. There are hardly any orchestras in school or college. String players are not motivated to continue repeating the Suzuki literature in group concerts year after year. We saw evidence of this when we noticed, in big group lessons, some of the high school students we knew slipping out of the hall when they reached the easier pieces.

I don't think that thoughts of regret cross the minds of many of these students or their parents. I met a young man who had been a member of Suzuki's original tour group and who was then studying medicine. "Do you play the violin anymore?" I asked. "No," he replied. "Do you wish you could?" "Not really, but I did enjoy it very much when I was a boy. It was a wonderful education for me."

I really think that many Japanese parents feel that their children's education via Suzuki instruction can come to a natural close as their children enter high school. They see the mission accomplished. Recalling the following words of Suzuki, they feel that they have fulfilled an important parental obligation toward their children's total education: "The greatest duty and joy given to us adults is the privilege of developing our children's potentialities and of educating desirable human beings with beautiful harmonious minds and high sensitivity. I believe sensitivity and love toward music and art are very important things to all people whether they are politicians, scientists, businessmen or laborers. They are the things that make our lives rich."

Western Teachers Look Ahead

Teachers and parents in other countries are reluctant to see their students drop out in their high school years. They want the children to participate in music in high school and they see a great number of opportunities for performance available to adults who are skilled amateurs. Youth, college, and community orchestras are open to string players of ability, and opportunities for chamber music also exist.

I have come to know first-hand the regrets felt by many college students who had dropped their study of a musical instrument in earlier years. During the period in which I taught music appreciation to college students, I accumulated over three thousand responses to questionnaires regarding their own musical training and background. Well over half of these students indicated that they had studied music as a child, had disliked practicing, had quit studying and then later had found themselves wishing very strongly that they could play a musical instrument. They also wished that their parents had had the fortitude to keep them at it!

Interestingly, a similar reaction comes from Japan in this story told by a Japanese mother. Her son had been a Suzuki student for a number of years. When he reached the age of thirteen, his complaints about practice rose to such heights that his parents allowed him to quit studying the violin.

Some years later, at college in Nagoya, he roomed with a boy who played cello in the college orchestra (one of the few such groups outside of the music schools in Japan). He went with his roommate to several rehearsals during which the orchestra was practicing Brahms' First Symphony. Captivated by the music of Brahms, he wished that he were playing in the orchestra. At home on a school holiday, he accosted his mother. "I used to play the violin when I was a little boy. Why didn't I continue taking lessons?" "You don't remember?" his astonished mother replied. "You behaved so badly when we asked you to practice that we gave in to your wishes and let you drop the violin." The mother could scarcely believe his following retort: "You should have known better than to have paid attention to a thirteen-year-old!"

Last year during a teacher-training session in Memphis one of the young participants told her own story after we discussed the subject of parents forcing their children to continue the study of music. She said that during her early high school years she told her parents she wanted to stop studying piano. They agreed that when she finished high school that would be fine but until then they wanted her to continue. "After that I became really excited about music and—well—here I am, studying to make a career of playing and teaching." It was a great testimony! As in Bill's story, our children don't always really want us to take their requests seriously. That's what so hard about being a parent—knowing when to stand fast and when to give in!

How to Make Our Suzuki Program More Attractive to the High School Student

First of all, the group lesson itself can provide motivation IF its format is tailored especially for these students. It should not involve much repetitive playing of the Suzuki literature but should reflect innovative programming. Included might be: 1) sight-reading training 2) study of orchestral techniques 3) solo presentations 4) study of advanced techniques not covered in the Suzuki literature 5) learning fiddle tunes and popular songs to be played as solos or in groups for entertainment.

If it is not possible to have a group lesson of this kind especially for high school students, those students should be excused from regular attendance at group lessons. If your child does not attend group lessons regularly for this reason, he should be expected to participate in important group concerts and in recitals as soloist. If he is reluctant to cooperate, you should point out to him that he is fortunate to be in a position to give something back to a program from which he has received so much.

Suzuki programs need high school students as role models for the younger children. Both the younger students and their parents are excited and motivated by hearing the older advanced students perform solos in recital. And what a thrill it is to a small group of children who have been rehearsing the Fiocco "Allegro" in group lessons to have five high school students join them at the concert to perform this piece!

Solo Repertoire Can Motivate

More variety in the music given the high school student can make his practice more enjoyable. Short solos that he can play in church or at social functions will be attractive to learn. Most of the music in the Suzuki books is drawn from the Baroque and Classical periods of music. Music from the Romantic period is usually greeted with open arms at this time.

Parents have heard that the Suzuki literature provides too limited training for students who want to progress into very advanced solo literature, or who want to become skilled orchestral or chamber players. Most teachers in the West have found this to be true, and are supplementing the advanced Suzuki pieces with scales, etudes, reading material, orchestral excerpts, and solos drawn from periods other than those covered in the Suzuki books. As I point out in the chapter, "Orchestral Experience", be sure your teacher is giving your child practical experience in reading music. Etudes are fine for this purpose.

Broadening the solo horizon with a variety of styles of music is one way of stimulating the pianist's interest. There are those who are satisfied by getting into the romantic idiom. Others are excited about ragtime or musical comedy. Jazz interest can grow out of chordal knowledge from theory study and can result in easy jazz improvisation and playing by ear. There are numerous possibilities. Discuss them with your teacher and your child. It's a kind of uncharted course, but can provide some exciting new interests in the same field!

The Strolling Violinist

A number of our students in Knoxville learned a group of popular pieces to prepare themselves for opportunities to appear as strolling violinists. Several of them were able to earn money playing for parties, receptions, and at restaurants.

The students enjoyed the attention they received when performing, but especially so when it came from their peers! Two of them played for several banquets at their high school and were always well received. They were able to play some of the Suzuki pieces as well as the more conventional dinner music selections.

Our son, Tim, began to play weekends at the Hyatt Regency Hotel when he was fifteen. He and a friend who played accordion performed there together for three years. They had memorized about a dozen songs before they auditioned for the job, and kept adding songs that were requested by the diners.

Incidentally, the song most frequently requested was "Somewhere My Love" from "Dr. Zhivago". I arranged a harmonized version for a group of our Suzuki students to close an evening program they gave at a local country club. They brought down the house playing it with the rhythm section of the dance band. The club showed its appreciation by donating a large sum to our scholarship fund.

Orchestras and Ensembles

Students' participation in orchestras generally provides excellent motivation to continue playing, but doesn't necessarily induce home practice on the solo lesson material. Teachers should use the orchestra music to develop the student's technique. (You will find more on orchestras in the chapter, "Orchestral Experience".)

Students who play in a small ensemble with some of their friends find this a delightful experience. Ask your teacher's help in starting a small ensemble in which your child can play. Duos, trios, and quartets often find places to perform. It's nice to see students enjoying sharing these musical experiences with their friends.

We talk about duets, trios, all kinds of chamber music in the reading chapter. Reading is, of course, a prerequisite for this kind of enjoyment. It's true that the music can be 'worked out' but the reading ability decides whether it is more a chore or an enjoyable experience. Developing the reading skill is also a side-benefit of ensemble playing but, paradoxically, an elementary reading facility is required to motivate further action along these lines.

117

Opportunities for the pianist to work with others is limited, so it is very important to pursue and encourage students in this area. There is valuable social enjoyment but there is also the growth of ability to listen and fit with other parts—a sensitivity that is often undeveloped in the pianist who hasn't had the opportunity to spread his wings this way. A new feeling of excitement often accompanies this new experience and with it the desire to explore more!

There are numerous institutes that are incorporating chamber music for teens into their schedules. Look into that for your pianists if you're attending one.

The Pianist as an Accompanist

The pianist can be in great demand as an accompanist as soon as reading ability is established, and he shows that he is sensitive to what goes on in the solo spot.

Opportunities are numerous. The Suzuki pianist can accompany other Suzuki instrumentalists or instrumentalists outside of the fold. There are always choral groups in schools that welcome competent accompanists. Sunday school classes are another outlet. I, and some of my contemporaries, started doing this at a very young age and continued all through high school.

Although an accompanist is usually considered in a background role, if he is capable he will have much enjoyment and a definite feeling of being needed! He may even be able to earn money from his services—a definite motivational source!

Attendance at Concerts of Artists

Live performances by outstanding performers can have a tremendous impact on students. I was a late beginner, starting my study of the violin as I turned thirteen. After a year and a half of study I had the marvelous opportunity of hearing the celebrated American violinist, Albert Spalding, in recital at Bethany College in nearby Lindsborg, Kansas.

My father got us front row seats. I still remember the magic of that afternoon! Spalding's beautiful tone, with his marvelously expressive vibrato, enthralled me! I ran back at intermission and knocked on the door of his dressing room. "Excuse me for bothering you, Mr. Spalding," I hurried to say, "but I'm trying to develop my vibrato. I'm learning so much watching and listening to you today that I wondered if you would please play the slow movement of the Bruch Concerto so that I would have more opportunity to observe your vibrato. It's so beautiful!"

Spalding was very kind. He didn't think my suggestion was appropriate for an encore but he did choose a slow piece to play, and afterwords encouraged me in my work.

I took home, in my head, a sound movie of his playing and played it again and again as I worked on my vibrato. My teacher, for whom the violin was a second instrument, was delighted for me to have this aid.

Today, with so many families having videocassette players, many parents are recording performances by concert artists for their children to see again and again. Researchers in sports have found that people perform better after watching an expert in action. We parents should give our children opportunities to hear both live performances and those on TV. These performances both motivate and teach our children.

During my high school years I remember being as enamoured of the great concert pianists I heard in almost the same way as many kids today are about rock stars! (Well, I guess that's a bit of an exaggeration—I didn't do any crying, swooning, or fainting at the sight of them!) I did cut out publicity clippings I found in the newspaper and kept a scrapbook of programs, autographs, tickets and paraphenalia related to them. And why shouldn't the teen-age tendency to give adulation to the famous be channeled to these representatives of classical music?

Actually there are instances where a few concert artists have captivated the collective public eye. Van Cliburn, when he won the Tschaikowsky piano competition, became a kind of idol. Eugene Fodor, who like Van Cliburn is young and handsome, has attracted a youthful following not otherwise too interested in classical music. Itzhak Perlman is widely known because of his articulate charm. These people's lives are accessible to the young musician of today because of TV and other media coverage. Why not encourage a kind of involvement that makes classical music more alive and pertinent to young lives?

Solo Appearances

Parents and teachers should work with the student to find opportunities for performance. Numerous occasions for me to perform as soloist in my hometown of Concordia, Kansas provided me with strong motivation to practice during my high school years. I played often at churches, local clubs, banquets, high school functions, hospitals and nursing homes. During my last three years of high school, I averaged over thirty performances per year. Although I was never paid—those were the last years of the depression—I felt fortunate to have that many opportunities to play in public. Kind expressions of gratitude from many people gave me the feeling that I was really contributing a service to the community.

I'll never forget my first performance on our high school assembly program. A freshman, I was clad in knickers that had gone out of style but were hand-me-downs from an older brother! ("They're in perfectly good condition," my mother insisted.) The students of the high school in our town had not had much contact with classical music. I was apprehensive about their reception, but my teacher assured me they would enjoy my playing.

That was an afternoon of shocks. My first shock came when I looked around the curtain and saw the hall crowded with noisy students, with the football team sprawled in the front rows! I almost had to be pushed out on stage.

Fortunately, my teacher had given me a piece (a Sarabande whose composer I've forgotten) that she thought would have an immediate appeal because of its bravura style. It began with several dramatic chords. After the polite applause, I took a deep breath and said to myself, "I'm really going to sock into this!"

The second shock came after my final chord. The students broke into tumultuous applause accompanied by shouts and whistles! I had greatly underestimated my audience, an audience that welcomed me back again and again throughout those four years. I was able to play all kinds of music for them, even solo Bach! The enthusiastic support of those students remains with me today almost half a century later.

These performances in high school included my shortest solo, a performance of approximately one minute in length! I was playing on the commencement program, with my younger sister Virginia at the piano. We had played only a half minute or so when I heard her fumbling with the familiar accompaniment. Glancing over my shoulder, I saw her point to her music. The entire four-page middle section of the piano part was missing! Only the first and last pages were on the piano. I could see my part at the top of the last page so I slipped into that passage and on we went for another thirty seconds or so. Then it was over! I'm sure the audience was astonished by the brevity of that rendition!

Like Bill, I did a lot of performing during high school years— church, school, and clubs. In small towns, clubs are always looking for free entertainment. The fact that it was gratis didn't affect my feeling of importance one bit.

I even had a somewhat regular schedule of personal appearances. Our next door neighbor loved music. He played a bit himself. Whenever they entertained guests I would be summoned to come and play for them.

When kids of high school age are given the chance to perform often for appreciative audiences they realize that what they are doing is not just between them and their instrument. Their skill has a social value. It is an appreciated contribution to the enjoyment of others.

Setting the Stage for Continued Study

If we have been nurturing independence in our children for some time, assisting them to develop their powers of observation and to become fascinated with the learning process that unfolds within them, we have done the best we can to prepare them for continuing study on their own. If they enjoy both practice and performance, the battle is won. No matter how much parents encourage, persuade, cajole, bribe or force their teenager to practice, ultimately the student must want to continue if he is to keep playing. And his desire to play must be strong enough to overcome the pressures of school work and of other interests that may arise.

Some parents, when faced with children who want to quit, make a pact with them to continue study until they finish high school, hoping that, once over that hurdle, they will continue into adulthood. In fact, it is easier for all concerned if this pact is made in earlier years before the commitment is felt so keenly by the student!

All is Not Lost if They Quit

Even if you are not able to keep your children playing their instruments, don't feel that those years of study were a waste of time. Reflect on Suzuki's words addressed to Japanese parents quoted earlier in this chapter. And when you read the chapter, "Life-Enriching Benefits of Suzuki Study", you will notice that you and your children have already shared many of these benefits even if they decide not to continue their study.

During high school years Japanese students who are not interested in a career in music usually do terminate their study. And, as Bill has said, few of them seem to have any regrets.

The important thing to realize is that most of them had been able to develop their talent to a high degree before they stopped. That is quite different from the student who has barely skimmed the surface in his study.

Perhaps we might try to view accomplishments with a different perspective. In a particular period of time we may work hard on a specific skill with seriousness and strong intent of purpose, developing it to a high degree, after which it can be continued as an avocational or 'side' activity. Then another goal may be given first place in time and effort until it has reached the level where it also can be considered functional. I think it is the word 'quit' that sounds like a final loss of some kind. Actually, it is only the termination of active study. For the person who has used that study well the benefits will continue to enrich the life of which it was a part—for a lifetime.

Judith, Michael, Bill, Connie, and Tim in family
performance on stage of Shiminkan in Matsumoto.

Judith, Bill, Jr., and Michael in performance at Stevens Point.

(Photo by Montzka.)

Teresa and Kathleen in the tokonoma (place of beauty) of our first Matsumoto house.

Greg with Yamashita-sensei's baby.

Dr. Suzuki and Tim at Dr. Suzuki's birthday party in the Talent Education Institute in Matsumoto. Hiroko Iritani Driver is in the background.

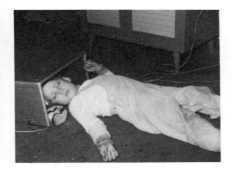

Timmy asleep with the detachable speaker over his head — probably listening (?) to Mahler!

Michael, Greg, David, Bill, and Bill, Jr., walking from Shiminkan to Talent Education Kaikan.

Posted announcement of Suzuki's students in recital, in the basement of the Talent Education Institute in Matsumoto.

Japanese classmate with Michael in the Talent Education Kindergarten in Matsumoto.

Greg in background, David, and Kaoru Tomita after Christmas dinner in our Matsumoto home.

Judith and Bill, Jr., with the display of family shoes in the entry hall of our home in Matsumoto.

In heaven it is always autumn
His mercies are ever in their maturity.

John Donne

The famous Hungarian pianist and composer, Bela Bartok, tells of hearing his mother's piano playing during his infancy. His mother noticed that one particular piece caught his interest and he sat nodding his head and smiling even though he was one year and a half. Soon after he took her to the piano and shook his head 'no' until she repeated that same piece again. By the time he was four he played forty songs by memory.

Listening

As is evident from everything Suzuki has written or said about Talent Education, an underlying principle is that the child's musical education, insofar as the development of his ear is concerned, should parallel the manner in which he acquired his mother tongue. Young children have an uncanny aptitude for recognizing and later reproducing delicate nuances of spoken languages. Suzuki believes and has demonstrated through his teaching that a young child can develop, in the same manner, a highly discriminating musical ear. Much repetitive listening is necessary, just as it is in the acquisition of the mother tongue.

Suzuki feels that the child's musical education should start shortly after birth, with the baby being exposed to repeated playings of a single selection of music. In his *Outline of Talent Education Method*, he writes: "If I let a newborn baby listen to classical music, for example, a Brandenburg Concerto or Tschaikowsky Serenade or a Beethoven quartet, I choose one movement from such classics and let the baby listen to the same tune every day. In about five months time the baby will memorize this melody. If you do not believe this, please try it yourself.

"It is very easy to test whether the infant has memorized the melody or not. To relate one of my experiences: A certain friend of ours had a baby. At that time its sister was six years old and she would practice the first movement of Vivaldi's G Minor Concerto every day. I visited their home when the baby was five months old. The baby was in a good mood and in its mother's arms. So I decided on the test. I played Bach's Minuetto. The baby looked happy. In between I switched to the first movement of Vivaldi, which the baby was always hearing. At the first three notes, the baby moved his whole body in time with the music and looked much happier. He clearly distinguished these two melodies.

"We should try to let babies listen to good music and to nurture a good music sense as early as possible.

124

"Let me here explain how a nightingale is trained to sing well. If we catch a very young, wild nightingale in the spring and put a good-voiced nightingale beside it for about 30 days, the throat of the baby nightingale changes so that it will be able to sing like its teacher. By changing the surroundings, the wild bird will change in order to fit the new situation. If we use a gramophone to train a nightingale, the bird will sing accordingly—even imitating the sound of the needle going over the surface of the record.

"Almost the same may be said of human beings. Children listen to the pronouncing of words by their parents and their vocal chords adjust themselves physiologically to make the same kind of pronunciation as their parents. The pronunciation of English by a Japanese child and an American child is different. This is because the physical adjustment has not been made by the Japanese child.

"To give a bad example: If a nightingale that sings poorly is kept close to a young nightingale for some time, the young bird will learn to sing poorly. This is one basic rule.

"From my tests of twenty years, I have found that young children who have been given a chance to listen to good music acquire a good sense of music—just like naturally being accustomed to their mother tongue. We should realize that even a child of six has been receiving education for six years. From a musical point of view, the child can be educated by good music, bad music, or no music at all."

When — How

Listening should be established as a daily habit. The child need not be forced to sit down and listen to the recording. He can listen while doing something else. The child easily absorbs the sounds without seeming to be paying any attention to the music. In spite of the fact that Suzuki constantly preaches the importance of much listening, he still finds it difficult to convince some mothers. He remarks that the most effective statement he can make and one that does seem to impress mothers is that THE YOUNG CHILD'S RATE OF PROGRESS IS DIRECTLY DEPENDENT UPON THE AMOUNT OF LISTENING HE DOES. Many students who have been exposed to saturation listening learn new music almost automatically. Their fingers seem to find the right notes without thought.

Some Japanese mothers combine music listening with daily breakfast, and others play recordings as the child lies in bed before going to sleep. Mothers who find that mechanical problems are often the biggest hindrance to the establishment of a daily routine make tape recordings of the song with several repetitions on the tape. Thus they can play a single tape without having the interminable changes that call them from their work. Some use "endless" cassette tapes that repeat continuously. One ingenious mother made a cassette tape recording, then strapped a small cassette recorder to the back of her little girl who then was able to listen while playing in the sandbox in the garden!

The child should not only listen to recordings of the pieces that he is studying, but also to recordings of the pieces that he will study in the future. Some parents make tapes of a whole book of selections which include future works and review. An advanced student may enjoy listening to the earlier pieces for review to help him keep them in his memory for group lessons and concerts.

It is very important that the more advanced student listen to the new pieces well in advance of his study of these pieces. This will save him and the teacher much time as he learns new pieces. One Talent Education teacher asked his students to listen to the Seitz Concerto #5, in Book IV, for six months before starting to learn to play the piece. These same students then played this Seitz movement well after only two weeks of practice.

Adults should understand, Suzuki warns, that the child will not tire of the recordings as an adult might. The small child loves familiar sounds, but if he hears a parent complain about the repetitions of the recording, he may adopt the attitude of the parent and his musical training will be stunted.

Joy of Listening

Long before we encountered Suzuki, we found that our children did not tire of hearing familiar music, and I don't mean just nursery songs which they loved to hear again and again when they were very small. As we introduced them to new music, they often would take a fancy to one particular selection and listen to it hundreds of times. We let them

use the phonograph and records themselves, asking them to be reason-
ably careful. They did take care, but the records were nonetheless worn
out. That didn't bother us, because we saw the children making the
music their own.

When Gregory and Teresa were four and five, I brought home a
recording of Schubert songs sung beautifully by Gerard Souzay. I
wanted them to know this wonderful music, so I chose the 'Erl King'
to introduce these songs to them. This is a dramatic song about a sick
child being carried by his father on horseback while death appears to
him as a ghost.

It became a great favorite of theirs. They listened to it so many
times they memorized the entire German text. One day Connie heard
them singing it together as they rode around and around outside on
the whirligig.

They were also drawn to some of the other songs but not to that
extent. Gregory liked 'The Wanderer' because of the uplifting change
in the music at the end when the disconsolate wanderer recalls his
homeland with great joy. In fact, Gregory used to place the needle
near the end of the song so he would hear only the change to the bright
ending! "I just want to hear the part where he gets happy," Greg
explained.

They all used music for jumping. Kathleen rode for many hours on
her wooden red horse to the music of the 'Nutcracker Suite', and
Timmy and Judith practically wore out a couch jumping up and
down in rhythm to the last movement of Schubert's C Major Symphony. I tried to suggest another piece in the same tempo. "No,
Daddy! We want this record again!"

We ended up by getting phonographs for the bedrooms. The phono-
graph in Timmy's room had detachable speakers, one of which he
placed over his head 'to get close to the music'. He looked like a creature
from outer space lying there with Tchaikowsky's Piano Concerto pour-
ing out of his head! Or the Mahler Fourth Symphony which was another
favorite at that time.

When I picked Timmy up at kindergarten at noon one day, he
excitedly told me that the teacher had asked them to bring their favorite
record the following day for "Show and Tell". "And I'm going to take my
Mahler!" I gulped - this was one of those moments of decision. We were

so happy that he loved this music. How could we tell him that there was a possibility that this might not be acceptable? We decided to say nothing.

Timmy took the record for three days, reporting each day when he came home, "The teacher didn't have time." He finally gave up. We tried to ease his hurt by murmuring about its length and the lack of time.

Looking back as more experienced parents, we feel that we should have accompanied Timmy to school the day he took the record, explained his love of this music to the teacher, and offered to talk about the music to the other children — a kind of mini-music appreciation class for mini-listeners. In this way, we could have given Timmy our loving support and at the same time possibly opened a musical door for the other children.

Need for Listening Continues

Listening to the recordings of the literature remains important throughout the training of the child. The advanced student may have to listen quite carefully to distinguish the delicate nuances in a performance of a selection such as the second movement of the Bach Concerto in A Minor. Some children listen to such recordings with the music before them.

Advanced students should be encouraged to listen to several recordings of the same work by different artists. They will find it intriguing to hear the variety in interpretations, although they are often surprised that artists' conceptions of a work may differ widely. We should ask them which performance they like and why. This should make them more keenly aware of the elements that make a superior performance. It should also make them more mindful of their own playing and help them develop a healthy musical sensitivity.

Many of the Japanese homes are quite small, and so the mother hears the recording as often as the child. This makes her role as assistant teacher easier as she is well equipped to help the child because she knows exactly how the piece should sound, and can easily tell when her child is playing a wrong note or playing out of tune.

In summation, Suzuki believes that not only will the child's ear be well trained by listening, but that he will be motivated to want to play the music he hears. Also, the student who has all the music memorized will be able to give all of his attention to the problems of playing the instrument. He will not be distracted by reading notes or trying to recall the next note. Suzuki thinks it is invaluable for the child to develop his musical memory, and to become accustomed to performing without notes.

Parents need to fill a child's bucket of self-esteem so high that the rest of the world can't poke enough holes in it to drain it dry.

Price

The sweetest of all sounds is praise.

Xenophon

To love anyone is to hope in him always. From the moment at which we begin to judge anyone, to limit our confidence in him, from the moment at which we identify— pigeon-hole—him, and so reduce him to that identity, we cease to love him, and he ceases to be able to become better. We must dare to love in a world that does not know how to love.

Anonymous

The Lesson:
Before, During, After

The Boy Scout motto, "Be Prepared", speaks succinctly of the value of preparation in any activity. We could also quote a few Starr versions of proverbs that support the same premise: "An ounce of preparation is worth a pound of remedial work". . . "One piece in the head is worth two on the page". . . "Where there's practice, there's hope". . . "All's well that is worked out well". . . "When all else fails, practice".

The First Lesson

Psychologists tell us that we can save the child apprehension and discomfiture by preparing her for new experiences. Even adults are apprehensive when faced with a totally new situation. It helps so much to be familiar with some aspects of the new experience. For this reason it is good for the parent and child to observe lessons of other children for some time before actually beginning their own lessons.

"This afternoon we are going to visit a music teacher who will be giving some boys and girls piano lessons", mother tells Sally. "We're going to sit quietly and listen. If you want to ask or tell me something, please whisper so that we don't disturb the lessons of the other children. You may take a coloring book and crayons or one of your other books to look at quietly while we are there".

In this way the child may observe without any pressure. She learns that quietness is expected and she absorbs the mood of the environment. When she is ready to go for her own first lesson, she will be at home in the studio.

Practice

The first and most important preparation for the lesson is good practice of the assigned material. Naturally the student is going to look forward to her lesson if she feels confident in her practice and is eager to share her accomplishment with her teacher. Everyone enjoys doing a task for which she has prepared with both time and effort. There is the pride and joy of feeling, "I can do this very well".

Most children don't volunteer for practice. I can remember an idealistic soul enthusiastically approaching me with, "Oh, it must be wonderful to be in your family! I can just imagine your children coming to your bedside in the mornings, saying, 'Please, Mommy and Daddy, may we practice now?' Oh, it must be wonderful?" I didn't have the heart to congratulate this lady on her fertile imagination. I'm glad she never had to face reality with a visit to our home! She would have been disillusioned.

There are isolated cases where this kind of thing might happen, however. I know, because I happened to be that kind of child myself. I had decided quite early in life that I wanted to be a pianist, much to the displeasure of a businesslike great uncle who tried his best to discourage me from such an unrealistic and impractical endeavor. I had very romantic ideas about sacrifice and achievement, and I decided that I would get up each morning at five or five-thirty to practice. The house was cold and it was dark outside. These were wonderful props supporting my sacrificial feeling. There was no doubt in my mind that I would become a great concert pianist. . . . Wasn't I suffering like the great musicians I'd read about? I practiced each morning until seven o'clock and then prepared for school. I actually loved to practice!

I was too young to be sensitive to the fact that since the grand piano was at the foot of the stairs, the sound must have been loud and clear in the bedrooms on the second floor. Although my parents and grandparents rose at six o'clock, they never did more than make feeble attempts to suggest a later time for my practice: "Couldn't you wait to start practicing at six?". . . "Aren't you too cold to practice?". . . "You could wait until Daddy fires the furnace at six".

This went on for years. Can you imagine their last hour of morning sleep being interrupted all during that time? In retrospect I am grateful for their tolerance and encouragement.

Although most children don't volunteer for practice, most also don't like to go to lessons unprepared. If circumstances have prevented your child from normal practice for that week, explain to the

teacher that she hasn't practiced because:
1. You couldn't work with her because you were too busy.
2. She was too busy at school, or with sports activities, or drama.
3. You had house guests.

Explanations can eliminate grief for all of you. The child will be less fearful of exposing her unpreparedness to the teacher's scrutiny. She can feel that he will understand and not be too displeased by her lack of progress.

If she hasn't practiced because she refused to do so, inform the teacher before the lesson, preferably by telephone, certainly not in front of the child. You will want to enlist your teacher's aid in helping you with the problems.

Daily Practice Record

Keeping a daily practice record is a great non-judgmental tool, especially with the reluctant student. Both the parent and child benefit from seeing just how much time is *really* spent in practice. At the same time, the record provides an objective, non-verbal report to the teacher. He can immediately evaluate the child's work and be more helpful with his guidance. It's easy to understand why a child is not progressing if her practice is minimal. If she is practicing what should be an adequate amount of time and is still not moving at a normal pace, she may need help in learning how to practice efficiently and effectively. If the teacher is knowledgeable about the student's practice habits, he can give her that help.

Relaxation and Quiet Time

Running in from a high-powered game of soccer, Jason heard the screech of brakes as Mom turned into the driveway. She had worried during the whole trip home that she wouldn't make it in time for Jason's violin lesson. Now he was whisked into a tension-filled car for the hurried trip to the music studio. No parking place! (The bane of Suzuki mothers!) "Get out and run in while I find a place to park. We're late! Run!", mother screamed. Thus Jason entered the studio with less than normal composure.

There are days when such a scenario may be unavoidable. We've all had them. But planning and preparation should be done to reduce the number of these occurrences. There is no chance that a child can do her best work under that kind of tension. How much better it is to plan for the lesson in the following manner.

After a short shopping trip, mother picks up Judy at the door of her school. She knows that if she picks her up on music lesson days instead of letting her ride the bus, they will have time for a snack and short relaxation period before leaving for the lesson. "After you've washed your hands, come and have an apple, peanut butter sandwich and milk", mother says as they walk into the house. Following the snack, there is time for a short relaxation, affirmation, or visualization session. With plenty of time to spare, they leave home for the trip to the teacher's studio. They find a parking place and go in without any feeling of hurry.

It's obvious that Judy is in a position to gain more from her lesson than Jason. Preparing and planning ahead for the pre-lesson time yields a worthwhile result. You will see the difference and so will the teacher!

Snack Time or Snafu Time

In this book's chapter on nutrition, we talk about the effect that poor food choices for pre-lesson snacks can have on the quality of the lesson. We won't go into that again here except to say that it is extremely important that parents take this seriously, and many do. Enough is known about the effect of certain foods (or perhaps we should say non-foods) on the behavior and personality of the human being to make us think about and evaluate our own eating habits. We should ask this question: "Do our eating habits contribute constructively to the health of our minds and bodies?" With that in mind, we should choose our foods accordingly. Foods should build health, not just satisfy taste buds.

Enjoy Your Child's Learning

"This is Tuesday! You have a piano lesson this afternoon, Tammy. I just love Tuesdays for that reason, don't you? It's such a joy for me to

hear you play, and I like to hear the other children play, too. Don't you just love Mr. Bridges? He's always so cheerful and helpful. He really shows how much he loves music. You know, when I go to your lessons I forget about anything that's bothering me. I just relax and listen. It's like a short vacation for me."

Compare this scene with the following one.

"Oh, no! This is Tuesday! Jeff, you're supposed to have your piano lesson today. I don't have time to do that! How will I ever manage to get everything done today when I have to spend all that time taking you and sitting through your lesson? I wish you could go on alone, but your teacher insists I have to be there. What a burden! I wish we could skip this week. I don't see what harm it would do. Well, I guess I'll just have to manage it. What a mess!"

Children will respond to joy or resentment, and their own values and attitudes will be formed from that input. It isn't hard to know which of the above children will value and enjoy his or her music learning, is it? Suzuki again and again urges his mothers in Japan to enjoy all of the steps of their child's learning. "The mother should enjoy, then the child will also enjoy."

Don't Put Your Child on the Spot

Doug was a very conscientious seven-year-old. In fact, I had the feeling that he was putting too much pressure on himself, and because of that I tried to ease the burden by not being too demanding of him. Unfortunately, his mother was not aware of this. She had stars in her eyes about his future and tended to push too intensely. Arriving for a lesson, Doug would bow and settle himself on the bench while his mother would say, "Now Doug, show Mrs. Starr how well you can play that piece you practiced so hard this week. Play it just like you did at home. Mrs. Starr, you should have heard him! It was just beautiful. he can really play it. Show her, Doug, show Mrs. Starr how much you accomplished this week!"

And then, guess what happened! . . . Doug's performance sounded as though he hadn't practiced at all! With the pressure to 'show' what a great performance he could give, he crumbled. Heralding too high expectations may place too much responsibility on the child's

shoulders. He may fear that he can't live up to them.
Not all children will respond this way, but it's always best not to put
any child on the spot to produce. Every child wants to do well, but he
may want to give up if he feels that adults around him are expecting too
much from him and that he has a good chance of failing.
If a child knows he has practiced well he will be anxious to show the
teacher what he's accomplished. Let that incentive carry him through.
There may be no need of other reinforcement.

Respect For the Teacher

Your child will benefit greatly from your obvious respect for her
teacher, and she should understand why you have that respect. As a
skilled professional who is dedicated, knowledgeable, and interested
in each student, a good teacher is deserving of respect. The more
highly regarded the teacher is in your child's eyes, the easier it will be
for you to help her carry out the teacher's instructions. You have a lot
to gain by helping to nurture respect for the teacher in your child.

If at any time you cannot sincerely feel this way toward a teacher,
it is best to change your situation. Your feelings will speak loudly to
the child and to the teacher. No good work can be done in that
situation. Choose your teacher carefully and then back him one
hundred per cent!

During the Lesson

Teachers like parents to remember these points concerning
lessons:

FIRST. Give the lesson your undivided attention. No needlework,
no magazines or books to read, and no letters to write, please. If you
must bring a younger sibling who is constantly expecting your attention, try to enlist the aid of some of the other parents in attendance to
watch him during your child's lesson. If that is unsatisfactory, it
would be best to find someone with whom you could leave him for a
short time. Of course, if he or she plays well alone and doesn't distract
you during your child's lesson, by all means bring him along. You're
giving him a head start with listening and absorbing the lesson
environment.

SECOND. Bring a notebook in which to write the teacher's assignment and comments, or bring a casette tape recorder and record the lesson. If you do the latter you will have an accurate record of the entire lesson to refer to during the week. It will eliminate any argument about what the teacher said or didn't say. Any question on the assignment can be settled by referring to the tape.

THIRD. Remember that during lessons "silence is golden". We teachers often want to remind mothers that they have the children all week but we have them for only one short period of time. It really is very difficult for a child to get suggestions or directions from two people at the same time. "Whom shall I listen to?" wonders the child. In the case of the piano student, I always feel as though he's squeezed between parent and teacher and can certainly feel pressure when both are giving him instructions. I know how difficult it is to keep from making comments or inserting a suggestion now and then, but it is best to leave this to the teacher at lesson time. Your child will function better and so will the teacher.

FOURTH. Be aware that negative body language is as disturbing as spoken comments. Your child's mistakes may trigger all kinds of body responses you may not be aware of. You may shift position in your chair, take a deep breath, sigh, shuffle your feet, or fold your arms. Any of these tell the child that you noticed her error, are disturbed, or disapprove of what she's done. If this is a regular occurrence the child will soon be more attentive to your actions than to her work, waiting for your response to every mistake.

Many times we can eliminate our negative behavior by just becoming aware of what we're doing. Recently, David commented on my tone of voice. He said that my voice tended to change, becoming tense and tight, when I gave him a lesson or supervised some of his practice. I realized he was right and am trying to catch myself when I hear this happening. I've asked him to tell me if he notices a change at any time during our work together. It should be possible for me to eliminate this fault with his help.

FIFTH. Do ask questions of your teacher if you need clarification of anything that transpires during the lesson. This is one time that talking is not only permissible, it is encouraged! Don't worry about appearing ignorant. Only smart people question what they don't understand. Any good teacher will welcome the interest you show by questioning, so question away!

After the Lesson

Your reactions and comments after the lesson can be very helpful to your child. This is a very good time to review what happened during the lesson. Asking pertinent questions of the student helps you to determine how observant and attentive he was. If you do this regularly, your child will be motivated to observe well and remember what she observed so that she can talk about it with you. This need not take on the appearance of an inquisition, but can be done in a casual manner with you inserting comments and observations of your own. The discussion should certainly not be too detailed or involved so that the child feels intimidated.

Most of all, I am delighted when I hear a parent comment positively on anything that can qualify for praise, whether it be paying attention, listening and trying to do what the teacher asks, being respectful of the teacher, or being pleasant and cooperative. If the time after lessons is remembered as happy and supportive, the student will want to return for more. Pleasant conditioning like this places music study in an atmosphere of joy.

The principle of perfect parenting is simple to express
Err, and err, and err again, but less, and less, and less.
                                                    Piet Heim

            Dreary, rainy days
            Children screaming everywhere
            Patience! Stay with me!
                                Judith Starr

    The mother of Bevery Sills, the famous opera star, had an
intense passion for music, especially for the opera. All day
long she played records. By the time she was seven, Beverly
had memorized the twenty-two arias from a collection of old
Galli-Curci records—old seventy-eights—that she had heard
daily throughout those early childhood years.

The Self-Image

"*An individual's self-concept is the core of his personality. It affects every aspect of human behavior: ability to learn, capacity to grow and change, choice of friends, mates and careers. It's no exaggeration to say that a positive self-image is the best possible preparation for success in life,*" says Dr. Joyce Brothers, well-known psychologist and author.

"*I know of no single factor that more greatly affects our ability to learn and perform well than the image we have of ourselves,*" writes Timothy Gallwey in his superb book, "*Inner Tennis*".

Since every parent wants to raise his child in the way that will provide her with this positive self-image, it's important that we know what actions and interplay with our children will lead to this growth. Although love is essential to the development of psychological health, Bruno Bettelheim, the well-known psychologist says, "*Love is not enough.*" We must understand how the needs and the best interests of our children can be satisfied. It isn't enough to have "*common sense*", it isn't enough to rely on our own childhood experiences. Do you remember some of the things your parents did to you during your childhood or teen years that were so distasteful to you? And do you remember how you vowed that you would never do anything like that to your children? Then you found yourself acting in those same ways that had been repugnant to you. Learned responses take conscious effort to erase.

We have come to realize in our own parenting that we didn't always "*know best*", that some of our common sense didn't prove sufficient, that trying to learn and grow more lovingly sensitive to the needs and best interests of our children was the only way to becoming more effective parents.

Not all children are able to verbalize their needs, but our youngest son, David, was articulate and to the point. (Perhaps being the youngest child in a large family provided the necessary motivation!) From the time that his vocabulary allowed him to express his feelings he would come to us and get our immediate attention with one simple phrase — "*I want you!*" No interpretation or speculation was necessary on our part to know David's needs. We were most thankful for his help.

140

Yes, I Can!

If a child feels that she has an open-ended potential, that anything is possible, that the deciding factor is her desire, application and persistence, then life is a great adventure, not a threatening unknown.

Unfortunately, the words "I can't" are a staple in many people's thinking. The word "can't" is very potent. In itself it is just a symbol, but if you believe it and give it substance, it becomes reality, a very powerful force that stops the user dead in her tracks. The only antidote is "Yes, I can!" used daily and often. This becomes like an "Open Sesame!" . . . unleashing and unshackling mind and body.

If children approach a learning task with the handicap of a poor self-image, feeling defeated before they start, it's as though they're trying to run a race while dragging a ball and chain. To accomplish growth we have to be able to believe that we *can* grow!

One summer I was teaching at a Suzuki institute and had three thirteen-year-old girls in a small class. When I found that all three were in need of work on their vibratos, I decided to spend all of the class time on vibrato development. We tried many different approaches to vibrato, exercises that I demonstrated, then asked each girl to try in turn. They watched each other and me closely. I felt we were really getting somewhere as they started to improve slowly. On the third day, I received quite a shock. I was playing, passing closely in front of each girl while demonstrating a 'finished' vibrato that was perhaps too removed from the exercises we had been doing. "In the future you'll be able to vibrate this way," I said. "Do you think you'll be able to do just as well as I'm doing?" "Nope," said the first. The second replied, "I don't think so." Noting my incredulous look, the third girl backed off from a flat "No" by merely shrugging her shoulders.

"But how can you get a better vibrato if you don't believe you can do it?" I exclaimed. Grabbing my violin in my right hand, I tried to demonstrate a vibrato with that untrained hand. Of course, I couldn't do it. My vibrations were as stiff and jerky as theirs. "See! My right hands looks like yours. I'm not able to vibrate with it because I wasn't born with a natural ability to vibrate with either hand. I can vibrate easily with my left hand only because I developed that ability with persistent practice. "I'm absolutely convinced that you three girls can all do as well. Of course, it won't work if you are convinced that you CAN'T! No matter what your teacher does to teach you, you will never have a beautiful vibrato *if you don't believe you can!"*

Parental-Family Responsibility

"Self-concept — who we are — we learn mostly from our family. This is why the family has an enormous responsibility. The most important thing in the world is that you make yourself the greatest, grandest, most wonderful, loving person in the world because this is what you are going to be giving to your children." This is what Leo Buscaglia has to say in *"Living, Loving & Learning"* about the family's influence on the self-concept of the child.

Stanley Coopersmith, associate professor of psychology at the University of California, studied 1738 normal middle-class boys and their families. The study began in the pre-adolescent period and followed through to manhood. He compared homes and childhood influences of the boys who had the highest self esteem with those of the boys having a much lower sense of self-worth. Three important characteristics were evident.

1. High esteem children were clearly more loved and appreciated at home. Parental love was deep and genuine. The children were the object of the parents' pride and interest.
2. High esteem children had homes which fostered a more strict approach to discipline. During the latter part of the study it was found that the most successful, independent young men had come from homes that demanded strictest accountability and responsibility. Permissiveness in homes of lower esteem children created insecurity and dependence. Having no rules made children more likely to feel that no one cared enough to get involved.
3. High esteem children had homes characterized by democracy and openness. When boundaries for behavior were established there was

freedom for individual personalities to grow and develop. They could express themselves without fear of ridicule. There was an overall atmosphere marked by acceptance and emotional safety.

Developing Attitudes of Self-Respect and Adequacy

"Parents seldom recognize how significant their verbal interactions with children are," say Dr. Don Dinkmeyer and Gary McKay in "Raising a Responsible Child." "The parent has considerable capacity and countless opportunities to build the child's feelings of self-respect and adequacy by indicating his pleasure in any accomplishment or effort the child makes." If a child faces a particularly difficult task, the best preparation the parent can give is to leave her with the attitude that the parent believes "You can do it". Then even if the child is not completely successful, the parent should make sure that the child knows that she has not slipped in the parents' estimation.

Even if parents attend athletic events, contests, or recitals where the child isn't completely successful, a supportive attitude should be shown:

I was really pleased to be there and to be your parent.

I am so glad that you played.

Even though everything didn't come off as you had hoped, I think it was a very good effort.

I can see that you made a lot of progress since last time.

I'm really proud of your hard work and good attitude.

Since feelings about self-worth are more difficult to change than physical performance scores, Suzuki's programming is very gradual so that small successes are planned. "Children like what they can do", Suzuki with his great insight often repeats. They like what they can do, as we all do, because of the wonderful feelings of self-worth that accompany an accomplishment, no matter how small.

What Did I Say!?!

With the child standing beside them, parents often discuss her weaknesses and shortcomings as though she were deaf, dumb, and blind. She doesn't seem to be listening, but maybe the child is smart enough to pretend *not to listen so that she can avoid embarrassment, or maybe she blocks out the words to avoid being hurt.*

In a class of four beginners, Janet, age 4, was progressing at a slower pace then the others. The children came at the same hour. Of course each had his individual lesson. This provided the environment for motivation that Suzuki suggests.

As the class was preparing to leave, Janet's mother stopped to talk to me. "Janet is very slow in catching on to new things. Her brother is so quick in everything he does, but Janet just seems to take a long time before she understands." Janet was standing at her elbow.

I wanted to protest. "Do you really think that Janet doesn't hear what you're saying? Do you realize that right now the word "slow" is probably being added to her inner descriptive file?"

Instead I tried to counter her negative remarks with positive ones. "Janet is a very attentive little girl. I like the way she listens and watches when I play for her. She always waits until I give her the signal to begin. Her bow and her posture at the keyboard are very good. I'm very happy to have her as a student."

Psychologists have observed that children do hear what is being said about them and most often will latch on to the key word or words and store them away for future use. What's the key word in the above conversation? Right - "slow". From that moment on (it's possible and probable that Janet has heard this before, of course) she has another piece to put in her image picture . . . "I am slow".

In "Your Child is Dying to Learn", Richard Gariepy says, "A vital fact with which parents must be acquainted is that your child is going to evaluate himself: he wants to know about himself and will come to some conclusion. He can only rely on what other people say and do, and on his interpretation of it."

Interpretations Vary

It is true that each unique human being will react differently to the same input, so we can't always be sure that what we say will have a negative result. This is where interpretation comes in. To some, a critical or negative evaluation will be a challenge to work and show what they can do. To others, it will be the trigger to give up, to rationalize failure.

An interesting story is told of twins who had an alcoholic father. Psychologists traced their paths in later life to see how their individual lives had progressed. One of the young men was an alcoholic like his father, the other a teetotaler. The remarkable thing was that when each was questioned as to the reason for his choice of life style, irrespective of the other each gave the same answer, "What would you expect with a father like mine?"

In spite of the unpredictable effect that our words might have, we must be always aware that casual, evaluative remarks about a child's qualifications are helping her to form her picture of herself. "He's good in English but doesn't have an aptitude for math". . . "She's just plain sloppy and always will be " . . . "She's so forgetful she'd leave her head behind if it weren't attached to her" . . . "Betsy isn't good at any sport" . . . "John will never learn to be responsible". Often we wonder why these comments and predictions become reality. Considering that this is the material we give the child to build the human being she is to become, it shouldn't be hard to understand.

Maybe all of us ought to remind ourselves everyday of something we often tell our children — "If you can't say something good, don't say anything!"

Erasing the Negative Self-Image

If a child states that she is stupid, ugly, or bad, there is nothing that we can say or do that will change that evaluation immediately. "A person's ingrained opinion of himself resists direct attempts at alteration," writes Dr. Haim Ginott in "Between Parent and Child". "As one child said to his father, 'I know you mean well, Dad, but I'm not that stupid to take your word that I'm bright!' If a child expresses a negative view of himself, our denials and protests only bring forth a stronger declaration of his convictions." Our best bet then is to show him that we understand the feelings that cause him to believe these things about himself.

Betty: I'm so dumb. I can't learn pieces as fast as Ann.

Parent: You really think that you're not smart? You really feel that way?

Betty: You said it!

Parent: That makes you hurt inside, doesn't it?

Betty: Yes. A lot.

Parent: If you feel that way you're probably scared when you go to your lesson. You feel that your teacher will be disappointed that you haven't done enough, so you can't even play the part you've learned. Solo programs are probably embarrassing because the other kids you started with are playing pieces beyond yours. Well, Betty, I think you're a fine, capable person and I'm proud of you. It isn't how fast you learn, it's how well you play, and I'm proud of you and your work. Your opinion is quite different, but it doesn't change my opinion or my belief in you.

If parents have established a loving relationship with their children over a period of time, this kind of dialogue should sow some questioning doubts in the child's mind about her own conclusions.

Sometimes negative meaning may be given to what was meant to be a positive praising comment. A neighboring family had experienced the birth of an abnormal baby and had lived through the agony and pain of seeing a frail, sickly child deteriorate until she died at the age of two and a half years. Their next child, born three years later, was a lovely baby — a healthy and robust little girl with a beautifully formed body. One evening as the father was bathing the two year old child, he looked at her strong, sound body and remembering past experience, commented with admiration, "What a sturdy little girl you are!" Years later, as a teenager that girl told her parents, "You know, I have never felt very feminine or graceful. I've always thought of myself as the "sturdy" girl that Daddy told me I was when I was small."

Praise and the Self-Image

"You do not spoil your child or make him conceited by giving him genuine admiration and adulation", says Dr. Richard Robertiello in his book, "Hold Them Very Close, Then Let Them Go." "As a matter of fact the more of this you feel for him and express to him, the better self-image he will acquire."

Although we all recognize the human need of approval and praise, the way we frame our words of praise is of utmost importance to a child if she is to draw a realistic conclusion about her personality. Dr. Haim Ginott in "Between Parent and Child" says we should provide the child with "words like a magic canvas on which the child can't help but paint a positive picture of himself."

It is possible to give compliments that are ego-debasing instead of ego-building. "You are such an angel!" "What a wonderful boy!" These are the kinds of comments that make children squirm because they are wise enough to sense that they are being "buttered up" and insulted to think that the adult considers them stupid enough to be taken in. The child believes that the adult can't think of anything *really* good to say.

Instead, compliments that are specifically related to an accomplishment or effort are ways of giving the child realistic recognition of her abilities.

As an example, Bill, age 9 years, had volunteered to clean up the basement. He stacked up scattered boxes, rearranged and hung up tools on the peg board, threw away accumulated trash and swept the entire floor. When his mother came home she was obviously delighted.

"That basement was so messy I didn't think it could be cleaned up without a weeks work. There was so much trash and so many scattered boxes and tools that I thought it would be a mighty big job."

Bill replied, "I did it in 4 hours."

"It's so clean now, I think I'll come down here once a day just to enjoy looking at it! You did a fine thorough cleaning."

"I really like the way it looks", Bill beamed.

"So do I. Thank you very much, son," Mom said as she put her arm around his shoulder.

"You're welcome, Mom. It was kinda fun."

Can you imagine Bill's sense of pride in a job well done? He probably can't wait until his father comes home so that he can share his accomplishment and once again receive genuine appreciation and praise.

Music and Praise

Praise given a child who is studying music can also fall into the same desirable and undesirable categories. If we dwell on exaggerated generalized evaluations this can be embarrassing and uncomfortable. "You are the best musician I've ever heard." "Nobody's fingers can fly as fast as yours!" "I don't think anyone can play that better." Instead, the praise that focuses on accomplishment or effort is believable and acceptable. "That was very good practice this morning. You were attentive and careful." "That sixteenth note passage is very clear and rhythmical since you've worked on it." "You've learned an entire page today! Congratulations!" "What a beautiful tone you have in that melody!"

In response to our words of appreciation and praise for her efforts, the child draws positive conclusions about herself which she makes a permanent part of her self-image. These conclusions repeated internally by the child greatly determine her good opinion of herself and her world.

To sum it up, we need to remember that effective praise does not generalize. It recognizes specific good efforts, comments on and expresses gratitude for jobs well done, values achievements and creative ability. By its very nature it encourages and motivates the recipient.

Unconditional Love!

In a TV interview some time ago, John McKay, a great football coach at the University of Southern California was asked about his son's athletic talent. John, Jr. was a successful player on his dad's team. Coach McKay was asked to comment on the pride he must feel at his son's accomplishments on the field.

"Yes, I'm pleased that John had a good season last year. He does a fine job and I *am* proud of him. But I would be just as proud if he had never played the game at all."

Coach McKay is telling John that his human worth does not depend upon his ability to play football. If the next season brings failure and disappointment, John will not lose the respect of his father. His father's love is not dependent upon his performance. It would be nice if all parents could transmit this feeling to their children.

"The foundation of a solid relationship with our child is unconditional love," writes Dr. Ross Campbell in his book, "How to Really Love Your Child." "Only that type of love relationship can assure a child's growth to his full and total potential. If I only love my children when they meet my requirements or expectations, they will feel incompetent. They will believe it fruitless to do their best because it is never enough. Insecurity, anxiety, and low self-esteem will plague them and will be constant hindrances in their emotional and behavioral growth."

Campbell is quick to point out that no parent can successfully achieve this ideal one hundred percent of the time, but that shouldn't prevent us from being aware of its importance and constantly work toward that ideal.

As a parent and teacher, I have become increasingly aware of the consequences of conditional love. Our youngest child, David, has an exuberant personality and enthusiasm in abundance which is often a hindrance to serious focused attention. After a particularly trying practice time at the piano, I found myself withholding my love and attention to show my disapproval. "Mom, will you rub my back tonight?" David called from his bed later in the evening. "No, I'm too tired", I answered coldly. I was tempted not to answer at all! And guess what I found? . . . that David learned to use those same tactics on me in return! When I refused a request of his, he would withold his love from me . . . resist my hugs, avert my eye contact, or just fail to answer me. I had to face the fact that he learned well what I had taught him!

A few years ago I had an application for lessons from parents of a four year old girl and made arrangements for a meeting with them after a program. When the door opened, I saw, with some dismay, a sad looking mother with drooping eyes that 'cried', a down-turned mouth and a general look that said "Woe is me." The father behind her projected an unapproachable air of importance, stiff postured and humorless. "Jenny has been tested and found to be of genius capability", he pontificated. (Years ago when we were taking applications for a new Montessori class, I was astounded at the mumber of calls that started with "My Sara or my Tommy is far above average intelligence for his/her age." I always wondered where the 'average' children were with whom they were being compared!) And then I met Jenny, a darling little girl who realized how much her "smartness" meant to her parents. She had already learned to play games. When ever we came to something that she couldn't execute instantly, she pulled out her protective device . . . an attitude that said "I couldn't care less about this so why should I bother? It's not important to me." She felt that her parents' love depended upon her ability to be tops in all her efforts. Would anyone want to jeopardize that position? If she could feel that they loved her because she existed, because she was their daughter, because she was invaluable as a human being created by God, she would be able to chance it. She would be free to try and fail because she could always come back to loving arms.

Responsibility

The confidence and worthwhile feelings that accompany the child's acceptance of responsibility are worth the parental efforts. Actually children begin to enjoy being responsible. After all, it's very pleasant to be more independent, to learn new social skills, and to gain adult approval.

Here are a few suggestions for helping your child in his growth.

1. The child should be allowed to perform tasks that he can do for himself. Even though the results do not match adult standards, remember the product is not as important as the effort.
2. Training time must be relaxed. No time limits should be felt. Be sure you have enough time to allow him to work at his own pace.
3. Make a request, not a demand. Remember how you feel when someone tells you what to do instead of asking you. Children should be treated with the same consideration that adult relationships require.
4. Let natural and logical consequences occur. If the child refuses to perform a task that is his responsibility, and his alone, he must be allowed to experience the consequences. It is the parents' duty to stop talking, withdraw from conflict, and wait.

He deserves Paradise
Who makes his companions laugh.
                                    The Koran

The only worry for parents should be to bring up their children as noble human beings. That is sufficient. If this is not their greatest hope, in the end the child may take a road contrary to their expectations. Your child plays very well. We must try to make him splendid in mind and heart also.
                                    Shinichi Suzuki

Home Environment for Growth

Of all the gifts we can give our children the most far-reaching one is the positive environment we provide daily in our homes. Parents who show great love for music or exhibit great excitement and enthusiasm for any activity often find their children caught up by that emotional eagerness into the same pursuits. Suzuki's idea, right? The child is motivated by the obvious enjoyment of those around him.

In "A Touch of Wonder", a beautiful little book by Arthur Gordon, he says, "The easiest door to open for a child, usually, is one that leads to something you love yourself. All teachers (parents) know this. And all good teachers (parents) know the ultimate reward: the marvelous moment when the spark you are breathing on bursts into a flame that henceforth will burn brightly on its own."

If your children can feel and hear, both verbally and non-verbally, that you are excited by the possibilities for new growth and new opportunities in your own lives, they will catch your feelings and will be ready to embrace whatever challenges come into theirs. You are really living if each new day is begun with an anticipation that questions, "What new exciting things are in store for me today? I can't wait to find out! In some things I'll suceed, in others, I might fail, but they will be learning and growing experiences, no matter what the outcome."

Again Arthur Gordon says, "The real purpose, then, of trying to open doors for children is not to divert them or amuse ourselves; it is to build eager, outgoing attitudes toward the demanding and complicated business of living. This surely, is the most valuable legacy we can pass on to the next generation."

Encouragement Versus Pushing

I have often suggested to parents that they learn a new skill, preferably to play a musical instrument, during the time that their child is learning also. Have you ever heard that famous Indian quote, "Do not criticize another man until you have walked a mile in his moccasins"? Walking even a half mile in your child's moccasins can be helpful. Our three daughters had learned to play recorders and enjoyed playing together. After Kathleen and Teresa had left home, Judith encouraged me to learn so she could have someone to play duets with her. I decided that I could spare fifteen minutes a day to practice, which made my progress a bit slow!

Judith walked in the kitchen holding her recorder two weeks after I'd started. "I've heard you practicing and you sound pretty good. Will you play a few of those simple duets with me . . . you know, the ones at the beginning of the book?"

"I'll try, but you'll have to be patient and be satisfied to do only those simple ones. I don't feel secure beyond the first ten pages."

We set up the stand in the music room and started on page one. After finishing page five, I was realy enjoying my accomplishment. "This is fun! Thanks for encouraging me to play."

"I knew you'd like it, Mom. Do you think we could try that last one a little faster?"

"I really don't think I can. That was just about my limit."

"You can do it, Mom, I know you can. Let's just try it anyway. I'll bet you'll do it easily."

We tried — and I didn't do it easily. The increased speed was just enough to confuse me because my responses had not yet become automatic.

"C'mon, Mom, let's try it once more. I'm sure you can do it," Judith repeated.

I stamped my foot. "No, I can't — not yet. Give me time to absorb what I've learned." Then I laughed and shook my head. "Just think how many times I've done this to you children, not accepting your own wise evaluation of where you were — always pushing for a little more."

The moral of the story is — if you want to be a more understanding, supportive parent to your child who is studying music, engage in the same activity yourself. You'll be more respectful of his feelings.

Expressions of Love — Eye Contact, Physical Contact

We can never find too many ways to express our love for our children. A child who is secure in the love of his parents, who knows beyond a doubt that this love is always there, is free to live fully.

"Eye contact—looking directly into the eyes of the child—and physical contact are both pleasant ways of giving a child the love that he so desperately needs," says Dr. Ross Campbell in "How To Really Love Your Child." If these ways of showing love are incorporated into our daily encounters with our children we will be able to meet their emotional needs.

Eye contact is often used by parents only when a child has accomplished some task that makes the parent proud. More often, eye contact is reserved for criticism or disapproval. If this is done habitually, although a young child may respond with obedience and docility, as he grows older resentment and anger will become the response. Making a habit of eye contact when your child talks to you or needs a reassuring glance is a worthwhile effort.

Naturally, the type of physical contact will vary with the age of the child. A young child, boy or girl, loves to be cuddled, kissed and hugged. Later, at seven or eight, children may want more rugged physical contact, wrestling, bear hugs, playful hitting. If the family has always engaged in a lot of physical affection throughout the early years, even adolescents do not reject those overtures which they have come to accept as natural expressions of those who care.

Our children, both boys and girls, were always demanding that Daddy play "sleeping dragon", a game he'd concocted during their early years. Daddy would lie down on the floor pretending to be asleep while they would courageously venture toward him, very, very quietly, sometimes daring to touch him, all the while knowing that at any moment he might suddenly grab them, growling and holding them in his grasp as they struggled to escape! Often he would have two or three of them in his power and then they would try to help one another to get free. This was a rather strenuous game for the "sleeping dragon". Even though at times it seemed to get a bit violent and I was tempted to stop it, I never did, and now I'm glad! It was a delightful way for them to fill their 'emotional tank' as Dr. Campbell puts it.

It is natural, too, for the Suzuki teacher and parent, to have eye contact and physical contact with the child who is taking a lesson or practicing. We, as teachers, are physically close to the young child when we teach individual lessons. As we direct and encourage them we maintain eye contact. It is the same with the parent during practice. Students will have their fingers placed correctly, their posture adjusted, their bow hold shaped, arm and hand movements patterned by the teacher or parent. Piano teachers and parents have the added opportunity of extra physical contact with beginners when they sit on the child's right, encircling the child with their left arm as they play the accompanying bass part to the melody. Most of the time children will welcome that kind of closeness and relax in the enclosed arm. Some students, though, will try to free themselves from the teacher's grasp as she prepares their hand for playing. This, perhaps, should be an obvious sign to the parent that the child should experience more physical affection at home. It does not mean that he doesn't want it . . . only that it has not been a part of his environment and he is unaccustomed to it. This awareness may be helpful to the entire family.

By caring for the child's emotional needs we are building security and confidence. Then the child is free to learn, to accept any learning experience as a welcome challenge. He is free to become the best that is in him.

A Sense of Humor!

The parent with that quick smile and sense of humor knows that most every situation can be dealt with more easily and more effectively when it can be viewed with a less than life-or-death manner.

In our partnership, I have always been the one with the too serious outlook. Bill has a way of sticking his chin out and assuming a kind of crackly voice and dialect that has forced many determined sad sacks in our family—including me—to laugh when we didn't want to! There's nothing more disgusting than finding yourself laughing when you really wanted to hold your austere, steely demeanor to impress people with the gravity of the situation! Now that I am alone with him and David, I haven't a chance to keep a straight face under any circumstances! (In spite of my complaints, I've been grateful over the years for that ever present sense of humor!)

A sense of humor is good for your health, too. Anger and its companion emotions are detrimental physically as well as emotionally. So keep smiling!

The Single Parent

There is no doubt that there are too many demands on the single parent who does not have the support system inherent in a partnership. The single parent who has a job allowing him to be home when he is needed is most fortunate. It is such an important priority that if at all possible, careerwise and financially, it should be a prerequisite for a choice of job. The part-time or seasonal job, of course, can fill this need perfectly.

Your parenting role should be the basis of your planning and decision. "How can I have enough quality time with my children? How can I be sure that by my scheduling I will transmit to them that they are a most important part of my life? How can I arrange to 'be there' when they need me for physical or emotional reasons?"

One busy single mother was always consulting her calendar when her children questioned her, "Mom, can we go shopping on Saturday afternoon?" "Will you take us to the show Friday night?" Her answer was, "Sorry, I have a previous engagement" or "No, I'm scheduled for an important meeting that evening." One day after a similar dialogue, her son replied, "Mom, aren't we important enough to be on your calendar, too?"

Even if you can't spend a couple of hours a day practicing with your child, if you consider the musical education of your child important, your involvement in Suzuki training can be a great respite and delight for both of you.

The Working Mother

There are now seventeen million women with children—more than half of all mothers in our country—who are working. We can say with assurance that the working mother is a permanent part of our social structure. Whether the decision to work has been made because of financial need or because of emotional need really doesn't matter.

156

In the past in our society, the child had the almost constant attention of the mother and father during his infancy, almost to the exclusion of anyone else. In this age of working mothers and busy fathers this is no longer true. When we realize that the early relationships are of such vital importance in the child's initial understanding of himself, we parents must take very seriously the choice of people and places that he will be exposed to in child care situations. The attitudes and reactions of parents and child care professionals are absorbed by the child and put into his computer for use later in his total evaluation of himself.

Recently I came across a book that I feel could be truly beneficial for all woman cast in this dual role. Called "Working Mothers" by Kay Kuzma, a working mother herself, it is filled with suggestions of all kinds for using time wisely and making sure that the quality of parenting will not be sacrificed. It addresses the most pressing problems— "Making the Most of Your Time Together, The Problems of Never Enough Time, Solving Job and Family Conflicts, Guilt, Illness and Fatigue, Meeting Personal and Family Needs" and many more.

I actually feel that there are working mothers who do a better job of mothering than some of their stay-at-home counterparts. A mother can remain at home and yet not give her children enough time or attention while the working mother tends to feel the need to plan more wisely to allow special areas of time specifically for her mothering job. So as with all problem situations, it's not the existence of the problem that matters it's how we see it and solve it that counts.

Actually your child's Suzuki involvement can fulfill some of that quality time. You can make the lessons and practice an oasis of enjoyment in the midst of inevitable bustling activity. Remember, music soothes the savage beast, so let it relax you and your child with the same soothing but valuable rewards!

TV or Not TV

Although there are families who have refused to let the TV set move into their homes and their lives, most families have accepted its presence for better or worse. Controversy continues to rage as to its value, its detrimental effect on the physical and emotional lives of our children, and its general long-range effect on our society.

My own personal feeling is similar to my feelings on good nutrition. It's not only an issue of right or wrong, good or bad. It's mostly that filling your stomach or your mind with something of little value means there is no room for more worthwhile or nutritious substances. Not many people would invite undesirable characters to come in their front door and spend hours in their living room as guests. Neither should they be allowed to enter your living room or family room via the TV screen. We believe that parents should take an active part in planning and controlling TV viewing in the family. We have a duty to shield our children from a diet of sex and violence presented as acceptable ingredients of living.

When the hours of TV viewing are over what has been gained that is of lasting value? Those same hours spent learning a skill, exercising the imagination by reading or engaging in creative crafts and active sports, builds capability and strength of minds and bodies.

What are the physical liabilites of too much TV? For one thing, a lack of physical exercise. A report in Time magazine called "Those Tired Children" (Nov. '64) told of pediatricians at two Air Force Bases who were puzzled by a large group of children, ages 3 to 12, complaining of headaches, loss of sleep, chronic fatigue upset stomachs and vomiting. All of them were found to be TV addicts, watching three to six hours on weekdays, six to nine hours on weekends. When TV was forbidden and the rule was observed the symptoms disappeared. Those who did not obey the rule retained the symptoms.

TV is a great baby-sitter, if your requirements are just keeping the children occupied and out of your hair. But there is a price to pay. Our children are being fed a menu of Madison Ave. cleverness that builds desire for anything and everything that the market can produce to make dollars for its creators. This advertising is mixed with raw violence and murder that's dished up hour after hour with no redeeming features—neither originality nor artistic value.

TV has its place. There are some excellent educational and entertaining programs. Yet if it runs your home and your life, you'd better take a second look at your priorities. At one time we allowed no TV at all on school nights and a maximum of 2 or 3 hours on weekends if there was something of value. Now David watches "Leave It to Beaver" while he snacks after school. We feel this is a pleasant recreational interlude between the school day and resumption of homework or practice.

I've never been able to accept a Saturday morning filled with cartoon watching. Watching a cartoon is OK but hours and hours of it?! I don't think that should be a sacred commitment. So many times I have heard parents complain because of Saturday morning group scheduling . . . "But they'll miss cartoons!" I would think they would be glad for a substitute activity.

In the past we were told to guide our childrens' reading to the tales of great men and women in history, in every field, so that they would have instilled in them the fine qualities of character present in those great people. This is comparable to Suzuki's desire to have children hear and play the music of the great masters so that their hearts may become sensitive to great beauty and their lives may be enriched by such association. If we believe in this influence, how can we now expose our children to evil derelicts, insensitive criminals, and immoral lifestyles as though this will have no effect whatsoever on their thinking and their lives? It doesn't seem to make much sense.

Learning to play a musical instrument and practicing during those hours that might be passively spent sitting in front of the TV screen is a positive substitute, not just a time consuming activity. It's a good choice to make.

Please Treat Me Like a Perfect Stranger!

One evening as David and I were practicing following an afternoon of teaching, I realized that my voice was getting strained and tense. David turned to me, "Mom, how come you sound so different when you're working with your students then you do when you're working with me?" Out of the mouth of babes comes the reckoning with truth! Of course, I sounded different. I rarely become impatient or tense with my students, but often my own children didn't fare so well.

Turning it around, I once heard the story of the parent who, after enduring the grunt and run stage for some time, asked his teenager, "Please, just treat me like a perfect stranger."

159

Perhaps in many cases our own children would prefer to be treated as our neighbor's or friend's children. If we're honest we have to admit that they probably have a just criticism. Does familiarity have to breed irritation and impatience? Not really, if we are aware of the tendency to 'let down our hair' in family situations we can make the effort to eliminate it. It's worth a try.

To See Ourselves . . .

Suzuki advises mothers, "With your own child, please try to use the same expression, feeling, and language that you would use with others' children."

Our tone of voice, the words we use, and our facial expressions all reflect our inner attitude which to be the most effective, should be one of joy. Sometimes we try to disguise our real feelings rather than try to change our inner attitudes. Even when we use the correct words, our facial expressions may be disturbing to a child. And when we scold, our facial expression may become really frightening!

One Easter Sunday morning we had gathered the children outside for some home movies while they were dressed in their Easter finery. They kept running around enjoying the beauty of the morning and I was impatiently giving orders. "Get together so that I can take some pictures before you get those clothes dirty. Come on, Gregory, don't run over there! Kathy and Teresa, come back over to the porch. Now stay there for a minute." By the time I took the pictures the fake smiles were not very convincing!

"This camera is making a strange sound", I said irritably. Turning the camera around to see if the shutter was working properly, I pressed the trigger to start the camera. The shutter seemed to be working. I also noticed the red light was on indicating that there was no more film.

Two weeks later the film came back, and we settled down for an evening of the latest home movies. It was then that I found I was wrong about the last roll of film. There had been some film left even though the red light was on. Following the shots of the children, looking subdued but dutifully pleasant, a huge frightening face filled the screen! With one voice they yelled, "That's you Daddy! That's just

how you looked!"
We rarely have the opportunity to see ourselves when we are
scolding. Most of us wouldn't like what we saw. I know I didn't!

Traditions

*Those of you who know "Fiddler on the Roof" have heard the great
song, "Tradition". Although the rigidity of tradition is questioned in it,
there is still a feeling of its value . . . of belonging, of meaning, of
history.*

*Large families have a way of setting up traditions naturally. Our
most extensive ones surround the Christmas season, beginning with the
four week Advent season preceding Christmas. These have persisted
through the years as a wonderful ribbon of continuity. When the older
children come home bringing their spouses, they love to share these
family activities with the new members. Even the things that they have
admitted they disliked they still don't want to abolish—like having
tomato soup and grilled cheese sandwiches for Christmas Eve supper!
"Don't change it, Mom. We've always done it that way."*

*Tradition is important to the family sense of history—past and
future. As children grow older, these constantly renewed memories give
them a feeling of the importance of that history.*

*None of the events have to be elaborate or time taking—just a way of
doing something that is "our family's" special way. You can incorporate musical activities into your festivities—a special piece of music, a
special song, a home concert, or even bringing together a larger group to
play together. You can be sure that your children will value those efforts
even after they have established their own traditions for their own
families.*

Sharing Hospitality

*We like to instill in our music students the feeling that they are
giving a unique gift to others when they perform music. There are ways
that families, too, can share their unique love and community with
others outside that is good for children to experience.*

*During our older childrens' early years we were able to share our
hospitality with many of the foreign students at our university. It*

161

actually started because of our musical programs at international functions through which we were introduced to many of these students. Our children had many opportunities to meet and develop lasting friendships with people from Africa, Iraq, Malta, Costa Rica, Bolivia, England, Phillipines, Taiwan, and Venezuela. Many of these students liked music and were extremely appreciative of impromptu concerts at our home.

While our children felt that they made a vital contribution to the family hospitality, they knew that they were the recipients of much more. They gained understanding and knowledge of other peoples and cultures first hand. One of our dearly beloved friends, an Iraqi lawyer and political scientist, who returned to Baghdad because of family illness never returned to the U.S. He was shot in a political reprisal. We'll never forget him—he enriched our lives by his presence.

The Arabic students loved to hear Bill play the Monti "Czardas" and would clap, sing, and dance with great enthusiasm throughout the performance.

All of our guests haven't been foreign students, of course. For children to grow 'outward' they need to be encouraged to open their hearts and help their parents share the warmth of music and home.

Don't part with your illusions
When they are gone you may still exist
But you will have ceased to live.
                              Mark Twain

I will sing to the Lord all my life,
Make music to my God while I live.
                              Psalm 103

In Vienna during the period that Franz Shubert was a child, it was not unusual for families to make music together in the evenings. The Shubert family sang the latest songs, played the latest waltzes, string quartets, and often joined with other families to do larger more serious works. By the time Franz was ten he had outgrown his violin teacher and was sent to the local choirmaster who taught him piano, organ, violin, singing, and music theory.

Family Lifestyles

It is often said in Japan that the 'only' child or the 'one-child' family has the best environment for success in Suzuki's Talent Education method. It is true that quite a few of the outstanding students in Japan were 'only' children. Of course, that statement didn't do much to encourage the Starr family, since there was no way to retrace our steps and qualify!

A family's lifestyle does have a significant bearing on the accomplishments of children. An only child who has no sibling interference or distraction, whose time at home is spent mostly in the company of adults, has quite a different environment from the child who has brothers and sisters, or even one brother or sister. The mother's and father's attention need not be divided. The mother with one child may have the opportunity, if she wishes, to spend all of her free time working or playing with this one child. If she does not have a job outside of the home, she should have adequate time for maintaining the home and family plus pursuing some interests of her own. This makes a more calm, relaxed mother and consequently, a more calm and relaxed family atmosphere.

Parent Priorities

If I had the opportunity to re-live my life, knowing what I do now, I would take a second look at my own personal commitments during the time that our children were small. During the years of my children's infancy and early childhood, I would have curtailed my outside activities. (I know that in my case that would have involved many years, but in a smaller family of two children who are close in age, that would be only a matter of a few years.) I don't mean that the mother should be cloistered at home every minute, but her top priority should be her mothering. My teaching, accompanying, playing in a string quartet and the local symphony took too much time away from my children. . . in my case not from my husband, of course, because most of the time we were working together professionally.

164

I remember one unforgettable experience when our second daughter, Teresa was three years old. I was preparing the Grieg Concerto for a performance with the Knoxville Symphony, so as the concert date neared I was practicing many hours a day. Teresa was a very outgoing, animated little girl who communicated her feelings openly. Naptime was over and Teresa came into the living room as I sat down at the piano. She threw herself on the floor beside me, kicked and screamed, "No prac'ice, Mommy, NO PRAC'ICE! NO PRAC'ICE!" I didn't need an interpreter to know her feelings. She felt cheated of my time and attention, and she felt it strongly!

Every privilege carries with it a responsibility. The privilege of having loving, happy, well-adjusted children makes time demands upon both mother and father. There are necessary sacrifices to make, as with all worthwhile goals and activities.

Evaluate your own feelings. Do you think you give your child enough of yourself? Or do you assuage your guilt feelings by giving your child everything else and letting others give him love and attention and keep him busy?

Perhaps most of all we need a change of attitude toward child rearing. Being a parent is perhaps the most important job in the world . . . building and nurturing the human person is certainly more important than building a bridge or a skyscraper or even writing a great piece of literature. We are helping to form the future creator of those buildings, the painter of those masterpieces, and the composer of those compositions. In that way we are helping to mold the future.

Children's Priorities

All parents want to give their children all the benefits that exist in abundance in our society. Yet we simply can't succumb to the fear that our children will not be "fulfilled" or "well-rounded" if they are not exposed to every available stimulation in the academic and social environment. Flitting from one activity to another and remaining mediocre in all destroys a good self-image and causes inner conflict. Children are robbed of the wonderful 'high' that comes from working hard, learning and accomplishing in depth in one field of activity. To do something well, while using all one's resources and abilities, builds true happiness and confidence. Then the person can say with conviction, "I like myself!"

When a child comes to a parent asking to participate in some sport or lessons, it would be a good time to explain to the child what his responsibility will be. Often the child is soon over the first flush of "something new" and the daily routine of work and sameness is not so desirable. If the parent has explained the child's obligations beforehand, it is easier to again remind him of those obligations. Perhaps in the future, because of his experience, the child as well as the parent will be able to weigh the time and effort that an added activity will require and make knowledgeable decisions that benefit *both* parent and child.

Evaluating your children's activities as to priorities is very important to their futures. First, you must know your child. What are his physical needs? Is he active, needing ample physical play and outdoor activity? What are the needs for sleep?. . .eating habits, etc. In other words does a heavy schedule interfere with getting to sleep or eating properly? Some children show obvious results of over extended activities. These are easy to observe, but the child who internalizes the stress is more difficult to see. It is a known fact that ulcers, a stress disease, as well as mental illness, have increased in the early childhood years. Dr. Ross Campbell, well-known psychiatrist, says that the age of children needing psychiatric help has plummeted to six and seven years of age where in the past it was mostly needed by pre-teens and teens. Too much pressure is a contributing factor to this alarming trend.

Physical Activity

A good balance of physical and mental activity is important. Suzuki has spoken so often of the importance of physical development that produces quick, facile movement. We parents of Suzuki students should be especially sensitive to this important facet of our child's growth and pick extracurricular activities that offer such opportunities. In making decisions on childrens' schedules, try to balance dancing, skating, gymnastics, or a team sport with musical pursuits.

The child who is well coordinated physically should excel in both areas.

Michael was four when he attended the Talent Education kindergarten in Japan. One diminuitive little girl, Reiko, appointed herself as Michael's guardian. Although Michael was a head taller than Reiko, she was his constant guide and companion. Numerous slides and snapshots show them standing together, hand in hand! But one thing bothered Michael . . . Reiko could jump rope, fast and without faltering, while the rope got tangled in Michael's feet after one hesitant jump. Our combination cook, interpreter and friend, Mikiko, found this disturbing also and decided to accompany him to school to survey the problem. She found that what Michael said was true. With Mikiko's help and much effort Michael improved.

Our next oldest son, Billy, Jr., attended first grade at Genshi Elementary School, about a block away from our house in Matsumoto. On his first report card there appeared a comment on his "clumsiness". It was obvious that this was considered important to his overall performance in school. Calisthenics were a daily activity, done each morning on the school playground to the strains of the Colonel Bogey March played over loud speakers. From our house we could hear it loud and clear! His last report card had this comment on it: "Billy has improved in physical activities. He is no longer clumsy."

Not only children, but Japanese adults consider physical activity important to overall performance. This summer (1983) while we were in Matsumoto for the International Conference, we looked down from our hotel window on a construction site below. It was early morning and work had not yet begun, but in the open area adjacent to the new building the workers were lined up in front of a gentleman who was leading them through vigorous calisthenics. Years before when we had lived in Matsumoto we had noticed that during lunch hour business employees played ball or exercised. What a much more stimulating way to prepare for a full day or an afternoon of work than to linger lethargically over a second cup of coffee or dessert!

Musical Activity

It has been said, and we firmly agree, that a regular practice time should be established, and the practicing should be done at that same time each day. But in many families—ours included—that was an impossibility. If we tried to establish an after school time for our pianists, that could be done on only two days of the week because I taught on the others and the piano was not available. If an after dinner time seemed desirable we were reminded that swimming took place on two weeknights. Other irregularities kept popping up in parents' or childrens' schedules. A half hour in the morning for part of the practice was least in danger of being superseded . . . unless activities of the night before made the early rising time not feasible!

Sound familiar? Even if you don't have as many children as we did, you are still able to identify with scheduling problems, I'm sure.

I can say that our year in Japan was much less hectic and so wonderful for me because of help with shopping and the cooking of meals. I was able to spend more time with the children and even practice some myself, which I hadn't done with any regularity for quite a few years. The cold winter evenings were spent together huddled near the kerosene stoves, reading, talking or writing letters. I even had time to knit scarves and mittens for everyone! I often said that my "culture shock" was greatest upon our return to the States!

In spite of the problems, priorities do have to be established within the framework of your own unique family's lifestyle. If you consider that music education is important in your child's life, some sacrifices have to be made by both parent and child. Parents must be prepared to give time and effort to support and guide the child's musical growth, an inherent part of Suzuki philosophy. The parent may need to terminate some personal pursuits to be available for practice time . . . but it needs to be done willingly and pleasantly, without the "I'm doing this all for you when I'd rather be doing something else" expression on the face and in body language. If you don't enjoy it, don't expect the child to enjoy it. He gets the message clearly.

Plan and Persevere

Some parents seem to feel that a child should have every spare minute filled. So poor Mary or Kevin goes to dancing on Monday, skating on Tuesday, drama on Wednesday, crafts on Thursday and music lesson on Friday. Personally, we believe there should be some unscheduled time, time left for 'doing nothing', 'day-dreaming'! The spirit as well as the mind and body needs the nourishment that comes from quiet moments.

Family lifestyles do differ. . . in myriads of ways. The important decisions must be made to complement and enrich each unique family unit. Do you really want to pursue the course of Suzuki training enough to reevaluate and adjust your time priorities where necessary, and help your child do the same? If you answer affirmatively, be firm and persistent in your pursuit, so that your child and you will have a rewarding and worthwhile experience. They will thank you in a few years, and you will thank God that you had the foresight to participate in such a life enriching opportunity!

Health and cheerfulness mutually beget each other.
Joseph Addison

There is no duty we so under-rate
As the duty of being happy.
Robert Louis Stevenson

Humanity is fortunate
Because no man is unhappy
Except by his own fault.
Seneca

Sibling Rivalry

The Grass is Greener

Mom and Dad had been vacationing for two weeks in Hawaii. On the day they were to leave for home they spent many hours exploring toy and gift shops searching for presents to take home to John and Jim, their six-year-old twin sons. The agonizing decision resulted in identical T shirts, white with a green surfer on green waves, "Hawaii" printed in green script letters across the top.

Mom and Dad were barely out of the car when both boys flew out of the front door to greet them. The boys took turns hugging each parent and after the luggage was carried in, they all sat down in the kitchen for a snack. "Oh, yes", Dad said as he suddenly pushed his chair away from the table, "before we listen to you tell us all about what you did while we were away, we have something we want to give you". When Dad returned he carried the two packages. "We thought you might like these". Both parents smiled expectantly as the boys ripped open the packages. There was a moment's hesitation - then John dropped his shirt and grabbed Jim's. "I want his!" he spouted with vehemence.

A Place in the Sun

It isn't too difficult to understand the basis of sibling rivalry. Each human being needs her own place "in the sun", and so every child needs to feel that she is getting a fair share of those loving sun's rays provided by her parents. "Am I really as important to them as Jim is? . . . Do they really love me as much as they love John? . . . Why did Daddy play two games with Jim and only one with me?"

Of course, the child who has brothers or sisters is confronted daily with having to share and be satisfied with a portion of her parents' time and attention. The only child may confront a similar situation if a parent or parents are involved with a career or hobby that swallows the time she feels rightfully belongs to her.

171

Plan Activities to Avoid Natural Conflict

Because of this very sensitive area in childrens' lives it is certainly best to plan activities that will not provide ground for such feelings. For that reason in the music study area there are a few simple guidelines to help you plan realistically to try to avoid the natural conflicts that may occur.

1. Children in the same family should be encouraged to study different instruments whenever possible.
2. If children in the same family do have the desire to play the same instrument and cannot be dissuaded, their starting times should be staggered, i.e. one child should begin a year or two before the other, or might study with a different teacher.
3. Parents (and teachers, too, of course) should avoid comparison. Statements such as "I wish you'd practice as much as . . . be as enthusiastic as . . . learn as fast as . . ." only provide fertile ground for resentment and hateful feelings toward the person to whom they are being compared. If it's a family member, that's disastrous.
4. If at all feasible, the choice of the instrument (which you have already narrowed down beforehand) should be discussed with the child. She should know that her thoughts and feelings are worth considering. At the same time, guidance as to the wisdom of her choice should be given.

Peace or Strife

Even the most conscientious parents who provide adequate time and attention for their children are often disturbed by the lack of peace in family life. "Perhaps the most important idea (for parents) is to give up any Utopian ideal that you may have of a household of children getting along nicely with each other without fighting," says the Gesell Institute's book on "Child Behavior". It is somewhat comforting to know that your children are not abnormal, or that you are not bad parents.

Since I was an only child who felt deprived because I had no brothers or sisters, Bill's tales of life in a family of six children sounded like heaven to me who had felt so alone in a world of adults. Of course, he never embellished the reminiscences with any of the realism of bickering, disagreements, or just plain fighting. I honestly don't think he remembered them as being a part of it. God is good in this way as in so many others. We seem to forget the unpleasant things that surround an otherwise pleasant occasion. So my version of idyllic family life was nurtured. Why should children fight at all? If the home were filled with love and caring, if they loved each other, why? I visualized our future home in a daily setting of peace with enthusiastic activity. It took years for Bill to convince me that anything else could be normal! Yet, it is one thing to recognize the inevitability of occasional bickering and fighting and another to try to do something about it so that daily family life may be more tranquil.

This Too Shall Pass

As we mentioned above in reference to music study, planning ahead with alternatives when we can see situations coming that would be sure to cause conflict is one way to avoid explosive situations. It's really worth the effort. And then there is a most comforting thought that has soothed my distraught mind often at times such as these . . . "This, too, shall pass". And it does. With children advancing in age the teasing, bickering, squabbling and wrestling all become a thing of the past.

Now that we have grown children who with their diverse personalities have provided us with experiences of all kinds, we can comfortingly offer consolation to other parents because we have seen and are experiencing that "calm after the storm". In our family, Teresa and Gregory, our second and third children, were like dynamite and match to each other . . . the role of dynamite and match alternating between them! The fact that they were only a year apart in age may have contributed to the problem. Today, as our oldest children have become young adults, we observe with joy the new dimensions of loving relationships that are evident in the family network. And it is our turn to forget the struggle of those earlier days . . . and when we do remember, to agree wholeheartedly that it was all worth it!

Write on your hearts
That everyday is the best day of the year.
Emerson

Even before they learned to read or write, Jerome Kern and his brother began to study the piano. His mother's love of music and her devotion to the piano inspired in her sons the love of good music. During later years Jerome remembered with nostalgia the little impromptu concerts which he, his mother and his brother often gave in the family living room.

Nutrition

Does It Matter What We Eat?

Today more and more people are thinking about the kind of food they eat and the effect that it has on their bodies and minds. They are realizing that it is illogical to carefully maintain a car with high quality gasoline and motor oil and not consider the quality of the food they eat to maintain the much more complex human being.

Sometimes we need personal experiences to make us aware of our nutritional needs. At the time when our three oldest children were five, three, and two, my own personal world seemed to be falling apart. I loved my family dearly. I had three beautiful, normal, healthy children and a thoughtful, loving husband who was supportive and encouraging. I couldn't understand why I felt so drained physically and mentally. I was exhausted much of the time. The mid-morning of each day would find me shaky and dizzy. Feeding lunch to the children was a tremendous effort. My only goal was to get them down for a nap, so that I could lie down to rest.

My activities, shopping and household chores were often done in a 'fog'. The voices of people talking to me sounded as though they were coming from a distant planet. Naturally, you can imagine that I began to wonder about my mental health. However, I rationalized that this was probably the natural state of affairs for a mother with small children who kept busy professionally.

Sometime later, Betty Newell, a dear caring friend and fellow symphony violist, presented me with a book by the famous pioneer nutritionist, Adele Davis. Tactfully she told me that she had noticed how tired we had been looking during symphony rehearsals, and she hoped this might help. Feeling as badly as I did, I started reading the book voraciously. Here I found that all of my symptoms pointed to hypoglycemia, or low blood sugar. I began to eliminate sugar and multiply protein intake in our diet. This was the turning point in the health of our family.

NUTRITION

Needless to say, I don't claim to be an expert in the field of nutrition, but I have been so happy with my own and our family's great improvement in mental and physical health that I've wanted to share our story with others. For years our medical expenses have been so low that we have been unable to qualify for any medical deductions on our income tax! That's not bad for a family of ten! It must mean that we're doing something right!

Food Affects Behavior

We are hearing with increasing frequency about hyperactivity, allergies, and the inability to concentrate. We have been told of the harmful effects of junk foods and sugar, and yet most children, and teenagers in particular, are downing gallons of carbonated sweet drinks. One pediatrician observed that the record among his patients was 98 gallons of cola in two months! Younger children are drinking more of the powdered sweet drinks and the 'fruit drinks' which many mothers use as inexpensive substitutes for real fruit juices. The labels on these drinks state "10% fruit juice" and the two top ingredients, listed in order of highest content, are water and sugar.

Dr. Derrick Lonsdale, who heads the biochemical genetics section at the Cleveland Clinic's Center for Children and Youth, says that some behavior accepted as typical of teenagers might be symptoms of what has popularly become known as the "junk food phenomenon". "I think it's going unrecognized. It's being treated as neurosis, nervousness, plain bullheadedness, or 'It's his personality, you know. He's growing up.' " Dr. Lonsdale believes that this approach to diet is changing the balance of neurological transmission which is the hallmark of the function of the brain and the central nervous system. "It means", emphasizes Dr. Lonsdale, "that the quality and quantity of nutrition can change your behavior. That's the bottom line!"

Sugar—A Danger Zone

Children and adults, too, have allowed themselves to be educated to a great extent by those who produce food for profit. Where do our children hear about the merits of the latest sugary cereals? From the ads on TV that are aimed directly at them. And many parents, even though they actually know better, go ahead and buy the products because they can't stand the pressure! That is just what the big commercial interests are counting on.

Consumer Reports, March 1978, in the article "Too Much Sugar", points out that much of the food industry operates on the assumption that the consumer has three taste preferences - sweet, sweeter and sweetest. For that reason we find sugar in table salt, hot dogs, most cold meats, toothpaste, catsup, creamers, soft drinks, peanut butter, yogurt, salad dressings, and baby foods. In fact, I recently learned that if catsup is made without sugar the label must read "imitation catsup"! Sugar is everywhere, as we realize when we start reading labels on the food products we buy. Remember that the first ingredient on the label is the chief ingredient in the product, and the others are listed in the order of their prominence.

The late Senator Hubert Humphrey, before the Senate Select Committee on Nutrition in the U.S. Senate, stated, "Having undergone surgery recently for cancer, the more I read about this the more I could literally weep over my dietary habits over the years. The evidence is there on sugar. The evidence you present is unmistakeable scientific evidence, but how do you compete against an ad on television?"

In his book, "Feed Your Kids Right", Dr. Lendon Smith, a former Clinical Professor of Pediatrics at the University of Oregon Medical School and a member of the American Academy of Pediatrics says, "Some mothers are afraid to take a strong stand on sound family nutrition because they are afraid that their children will not love them if they don't provide sweet foods".

Research Proves Effects of Sugar

The research of numerous biochemists and physicians documents the harmful effects of excessive sugar ingestion. All conscious bodily activity is initiated in the cerebral cortex of the brain and in order to adequately function it needs a constant flow of glucose. An imbalance of blood sugar can cause the cortex to respond to stimuli with bizarre behavior. Complex foods which produce a gradual breakdown into glucose provide the steady, even flow required by the cortex and the entire body. In contrast, when there is an intake of refined sugar, the pancreas responds with over-production of insulin to metabolize it and the blood sugar level falls suddenly and drastically. A sensitive person can become anti-social, depressed, or may have a variety of psychosomatic symptoms. This is called "the roller coaster" syndrome because the subject usually eats something sweet to make him feel better, and the whole sequence starts all over again! It is estimated that 50% of the American people are afflicted with this condition . . . a great number of children among them, of course.

A study published in March 1981 was done by two University of Michigan scientists on the total sugar intake of 657 randomly selected children, five to twelve years of age. The study found that these children were consuming on the average of 134 grams (about 1/4 pound) of sugar per day. Some of the children studied were using as much as 280 grams (1/2 pound) a day! This came mostly from sweetened beverages, cakes, cookies, pies and other desserts and fruit juices.

Learning and Diet

An article called "Why Johnny Can't Learn - A Surprising Answer" by Lawrence Galton, cited a study made at the New York Institute for Child Development. Of 265 hyperkinetic children (children who have an abnormal amount of uncontrollable muscular movement often resulting in inability to concentrate or learn) who were tested for glucose-tolerance, 74% showed abnormalities. In other words, high sugar and refined carbohydrate intake stimulated the insulin production that causes blood sugar to plummet and produce the behavior associated with hyperkinetic children. The Institute's multi-faceted treatment of these children included six high protein feedings a day, reduced intake of sweets and refined carbohydrates and as much as possible the elimination of artificial colors and flavors from their diet.

"I've taught in schools from ghetto to upperclass and seen the behavior dysfunction when children came in at 8 a.m. munching on a candy bar or doughnut and sipping a cola", says Mary Ann Pickard in the preface to her cookbook "Feasting Naturally". "And sending them off with a sugary breakfast cereal, white toast and jelly with a pre-sweetened Vit. C drink is no better! No wonder the discipline situation in our schools is such a nightmare!"

Sweet Holidays—Sour Aftermath

So many times teachers and parents are aware of the problems in concentration and personality that occur at the time of holidays, birthday parties, and similar breaks from routine. We often have chalked it up to excitement, but it is wise to try to understand why these deviations occur. If we do, we can try to do something about the kind of food the children consume during those holiday celebrations.

"Too many sweets can turn some usually agreeable children into monsters at home and in school. Many children simply cannot handle the over-large doses of sugar in Halloween candy, for instance. Too much sugar can cause irritability, disruptive behavior, decreased attention span and loss of concentration. Parents and teachers have told us they dread this post-Halloween period. There are arguments and fights at home, and classes the next day are virtually unmanageable, with children agitated and restless", says Dr. Jerome Vogel, medical director of the New York Institute for Child Development. This Institute for Child Development has dealt with more than 3,000 children with learning problems. They have found over the years since 1968, when their non-profit institute was founded, that nutrition can play a major role in many learning and behavioral problems.

Hidden Additives

In 1975 Dr. Ben Feingold, a California pediatrician and allergist, outlined a diet for children who were considered to have symptoms of hyperactivity. It has since received nationwide attention and the testimonies of parents who have been given hope and help after years of frustration testify to its effectiveness in a large percentage of cases. This diet forbids all foods that contain certain dyes and other additives as well as foods that are rich in salicylates. (Salicylates are a group of compounds related to salicylic acid in their basic structure and are present in a number of fruits, and vegetables, as well as beverages and medications.) Eighty-five percent of the food not permitted in this diet is in the category of high sugar. Chemical additives found to be so destructive to childrens' behavior are found in largest amounts in junk foods. And junk foods include the following: candy and candy bars, all cookies, all packaged desserts and beverages such as puddings, gelatins, instant drinks, all soft drinks, most "convenience" foods in packages (muffins, biscuits, cookies, cakes), all ice creams, except those which specify on the label that they do not contain any additives. All of these foods, if bought at the supermarket, are likely to be loaded with dyes, synthetic flavorings, preservatives, thickeners, surface active agents, sequestrants, stabilizers, starch modifiers, texturizers, binders, anti-caking agents and on and on and on. These are the hidden additives that can do so much damage.

What About Adults?

Children are not the only ones affected by additives and the consumption of sugar. Numerous adults have experimented with the elimination of these offending foods and found that their health improved significantly. If you suspect that you might benefit from such a regime why not try it? Things like frequent headaches, chronic fatigue, and a lack of general vitality are often attributable to diet. There's really nothing to lose except a bit of effort, and there could be a lot to gain!

After discussing this together, Bill and I decided to analyze our food intake to see if we were inadvertently getting more than we meant to have of these additives and sugar. First, we don't buy refined sugar, but instead use honey and fructose (fruit sugar) when we need sweeteners. We use honey at the table and honey and fructose in baking and occasional desserts. Sometimes critics equate honey and fructose with refined sugar, saying all sugar is alike. Naturally we should not ingest large amounts of any sugars. However, you will remember that earlier in this chapter we compared the body's reaction to complex foods which produce a gradual breakdown into glucose, allowing a steady even flow to the brain and body, to the body's reaction to refined sugar which needs no breaking down. With refined sugar the pancreas responds with an overproduction of insulin to metabolize it all at once, thereby causing the blood sugar to fall drastically immediately afterward because it has been instantaneously metabolized. Both honey and fructose are complex foods which produce the gradual breakdown.

Second, we buy no packaged foods, no sugar cereals, no soft drinks or Koolaid type drinks. Our shopping consists mostly of fresh fruits and vegetables, real fruit juices, whole grain breads, flours, and cereals, natural cheeses, and snack foods such as chips without preservatives that are purchased at health food stores. To the statement that these foods are more expensive, I would answer that if their volume would increase, the prices would go down. As it is, we would rather spend money on preventative measures for health than pay for medical treatment that will try to repair the damage caused by poor nutrition. This reminds me of a statement I heard recently about the value of exercise, "If you don't take time to exercise, you'll take time later for illness". I think the same could be said about diet. if you don't spend money on foods that build health, you will spend it later on medical care. Nature has a way of balancing the books and somehow she can never be fooled!

School Lunches—Nutrition in Action

In the Fulton County Schools of Atlanta, Georgia, Sara Sloan is a one woman dynamo who has completely revised the eating habits of the schools where she is Director of Food and Nutrition Programs. The program, in existence since 1976, is called "Nutra", the Natural Program. It features natural whole foods, low in fat and salt with no artificial coloring, additives, preservatives, or refined carbohydrates. She schedules workshops to educate teachers, parents, and children, has "mini" Nutrition Time in the classroom, and nutrition blurbs on the school intercom. Walking through the halls in her schools you would hear . . . "Try the "real thing" - See the pot of grass (sprouts) in the cafeteria. Interested in growing your own? Contact our cafeteria manager" or "Are you a Hot Fudge Sundae? You are what you eat. Is your behavior pattern like a hot fudge sundae - Smooth and creamy and sometimes bittersweet? Sugary snacks create mood swings and put you in an energy slump. Hardboiled eggs, fruit, seeds, nuts, cheese, yogurt, kefir, tofu give you more bounce per ounce for feeling fit energy".

And has her program been successful? The increased student participation in the school lunch program attests to that - an increase from 61% to 87%. This is the first school system in the nation with a program eliminating refined sugar in school meals for children. "The success of the Nutra Program has proven", Ms. Sloan says, "that when children are educated and involved in growing, preparing and cooking food, they will eat those foods even if the food is new and unfamiliar".

Courage to be Different

For quite a few years now our family has been "different" in our eating habits. At certain ages the children have suffered some ridicule for this, and we've tried to be sympathetic and supportive while educating them to the reasons behind our diet. Generally speaking, they have been cooperative and open minded, and it has been pleasing to see their spirit of acceptance.

When David, our youngest son, was in fourth grade, he had one particular lunchroom antagonist who eagerly waited each day as David opened his lunch box to see what "yuky, weird" thing would be exposed to his scrutiny. Of course, he was quick to call everybody's attention to "what David brought today"! One particular object of examination was a bag of green pepper sticks. For some reason nobody had ever eaten raw green pepper sticks before—they smelled and looked weird! Alfalfa sprouts on sandwiches were also a novelty, but David discovered a new tactic. He asked people if they wanted to taste them. One morning as I prepared his lunch, he came into the kitchen. "Mom", he said, "Can you put more sprouts in a sandwich bag? Lots of the kids are asking me for them, and I don't have enough for myself and them, too". My 'hallelujahs' had to remain silent.

One of our older sons, Bill, Jr., an architecture student who is spending this school year ('82-'83) studying at Waseda University in

Tokyo, Japan, lived in a dorm during his freshman year at Cornell. The following year he moved into a house with ten other students who divided household and cooking chores. Many of them were vegetarians and most of them were serious about a diet of natural and whole foods.

During the Christmas vacation in the middle of that year we were talking about what kind of meals they had prepared. "It's really strange", he said. "Most of the kids haven't had a lot of the food at home that they're cooking and eating now. I think they feel as though they've discovered something "different" by themselves—almost like a kind of rebellion. But when they ask me if I've tasted some of the things they make, I always say 'Sure, we have that at home'. They say they want to meet you, because you sound like such neat parents". Fortunately, Bill has not felt the need to rebel in any other way to make up for our not providing him with this harmless outlet!

So don't be afraid to help your children by educating and providing them with food that builds instead of destroys. If you can weather the storms and stick to your convictions in this as in other important areas, you will probably qualify in their book as "neat" parents!

The Tide Changes

All in all, we have been heartened over the years to see the changes in the eating habits of a large percentage of the people in our range of contact. Years ago receptions given after recitals at the University of Tennessee used to consist of the usual sweet punch, cakes and cookies. In the past few years, however, the Sigma Alpha Iota music sorority girls have been serving fruit juices, cheeses, raw vegetables and dip, and whole grain crackers and chips. These have been consumed with enthusiasm!

When Suzuki came to our campus in 1981, his visit attracted 800 youngsters and their parents from all over the Southeast. At this time the SAI music sorority under the direction of Mary Ann Goodwin, then a Suzuki teacher trainee, decided to fill a dual purpose by providing good wholesome food and drinks for the children while at the same time raising funds for their group. They didn't realize how popular their offerings would be. They were swamped! Within a short period of time their total inventory was sold out! Many of the parents came to thank them for their thoughtfulness. It was only after they closed down their booth that the soft drink vendors were able to do much business.

Nutritional Snacks

Suzuki teachers really appreciate working with children who are attentive and relaxed during their lessons. Many teachers have noticed improvement in the children's behavior at lessons after they have requested that parents try to provide good nutritious snacks before lesson time. Here is a helpful list you might wish to consult.

Acceptable snacks: Fruit or real fruit drinks, milk, popcorn, nuts, cheeses, peanut butter, whole grain crackers or chips without additives.

Taboo snacks: Cokes and all soft drinks that contain caffeine, sugared drink mixes, ice cream, candy or candy bars, cookies, cake.

With a little planning the elimination of sugary and additive filled foods can be accomplished. Try it—you'll like it!—and you'll especially like what it does for your children.

Parents' Nutritional Needs

Adults, as well as children, have nutritional needs which, if not satisfied, can lead to inability to cope with the physical and emotional stresses of parenthood - or of any other occupation for that matter. Parents cannot say "Do as I say, not as I do" and consider it good advice. A recent television spot shows a mother eating "junk food" as she sadly delivers a lecture. "Kids just don't eat right. You tell them what's good for them, but they just won't listen!" she says as she munches away.

"Your ability to handle anger is influenced by many things, most of which have nothing to do with the actions of your teenager", says Dr. Ross Campbell in his book "How to Really Love Your Teenager." "One of these is your physical condition. Are you eating foods that will help you feel your best? Most authorities consider breakfast the most important meal of the day. What you eat for breakfast pretty well determines

how you feel the rest of the day." Too much carbohydrate and not enough protein and bulk are common errors in the diet that usually produce a lack of energy later in the day and cause people to indulge in stimulants, such as coffee and soft drinks containing caffeine. "Caffeine has differing effects on people", continues Dr. Campbell, "but none of them aid the emotional stability and calmness you need to deal effectively with your teenager."

What a difference it makes when we can get up in the morning feeling alive and capable of accepting a new day's challenges! Most people today are leading tremendously busy, stress-filled lives - a very good reason for making sure that bodies and minds are receiving the nutrients they need to cope with these demands.

The ads on TV seem to take it for granted that various aches and pains are a normal part of everyday life. Perhaps because of this we accept less than good health as though that's the way "everybody" feels. To feel alive and alert, with clear heads and a 'get-up and go' feeling is every human beings' rightful heritage. Why should we settle for less? Adults who exercise, who eat foods chosen for good nutrition as well as taste, are better able to live their lives effectively in every dimension - family, work, and play.

No act of kindness
No matter how small
Is ever wasted.

            Aesop

If only I may grow;
Firmer, simpler ·
Quieter, warmer.

            Dag Hammarskjold

If the day and night are such that you greet them with joy, and life emits a fragrance like flowers and sweet-scented herbs—is more starry, more immortal—that is your success. All nature is your congratulation.

            Thoreau

Reading Music

When your child goes to school, or sometimes even before, he learns to read the language he has been speaking for a number of years. We consider this the natural sequence of development. Why then should there be so much controversy over the child who learns to play music before he learns the written symbols for musical language?

I can remember the consternation of a piano teacher whom my mother had chosen to be my first teacher. In the course of the introductory conversation my mother mentioned that I had been playing by ear, picking up tunes that I'd heard her play and some from the radio. With great seriousness the teacher replied, "Thank goodness you're starting her lessons now. If she went on playing by ear without learning to read music it could be a great handicap later on." I don't remember questioning her about that dire prognosis. We thought of her as the expert and her opinion was accepted without question. This outmoded thinking is responsible for the concern over the delay in music reading which is a normal part of Suzuki training.

First of all let me inform you that the number of traditionally trained music students—especially pianists—who are excellent sight-readers of music are very few. Reading music at sight, which is comparable to what we do with language when we pick up a book, is generally a very poorly developed skill.

Many of us don't realize that there was only the crudest form of musical notation in existence until the medieval period. People learned by imitating those with whom they had personal contact. For that reason improvisation and composition were considered in everyone's capability. Musicians were not captives of the printed page, and it was no sin to play "by ear" something you'd heard someone else play. If you have read biographies of well-known performing artists who were prodigies in their day, you will note that most grew up in an atmosphere permeated by music. Mothers or fathers, or both, were either amateur or professional musicians and the children were surrounded by the sound of music. The outcome? They just began to play!

William Primrose, the famous violist, in his autobiography, "Walk on the North side" recounts, "As an infant I often sat on the floor with a wooden stick in each hand—one, of course, represented the violin and the other the bow—and copied my father's movements as he played. When he, relishing my enthusiasm, bought and placed a quartersized violin in my eager hands in 1908, I began at once really to play."

A few years ago I invited a local teacher into my studio to look at a video tape of a program of young Japanese pianists that had been made during our stay in Japan. She had shown some slight interest in knowing what the Suzuki method was all about. I felt that seeing these young children perform so beautifully was an impressive introduction. After a five-year-old girl finished the Gigue of the B Flat Partita by Bach (the last piece in Book IV) I turned off the tape. There was a moment of silence. "Can they read music?" she questioned coldly.

My jaw dropped! Could anyone not be emotionally excited by this child, this infant, reaching such a high level of musical ability? What difference did it make whether she could read? Did that change this exciting experience?

When an infant displays an impressive vocabulary, is able to verbalize thoughts and feelings coherently or memorizes a poem, who discounts that ability by questioning, "Can he read?" Instead, we are delighted by such a display of ability. Where then have we gotten off the track in recognizing the development of musical language?

Reading Music—An Invaluable Skill

Lest you think that we do not consider music reading important, we want to state right here that the preceding paragraphs are presented only to accentuate the validity of Suzuki's mother-tongue method. "Speak first—read later." "Play first—read later."

Just as we consider the reading of language an absolute necessity for the whole human being, so we consider the reading of music a necessity for the musician—professional or amateur.

Two Kinds of Reading

It is important that we clarify here the two kinds of music reading. First: the child is reading music when he knows and can identify musical symbols, names and locations of notes on the staff, kinds of notes and their values, clef signs, time signatures, rests, etc. With this knowledge he should be able to work out and learn new music. Second: a child is 'sight-reading' music when he can look at the musical page and can play what is written there in the proper location with the proper rhythmic structure at the proper tempo. He can literally 'at sight' bring the music to life, translating symbols in the music as conceived by the composer. There is no study involved, except perhaps a superficial 'looking over' what is on the page. It is performed at the moment it is seen. Hence, the term 'sight-reading'. This is the skill we want to develop.

In an introduction to a sight-reading book, Sir Ernest MacMillan has this to say. "While good sight-reading is obviously essential to a would-be-professional-musician, it is no less important to the amateur. Indeed it stands to reason that, when a student has given up the idea of a musical career HIS MAINTAINING OR DROPPING AN INTEREST IN MUSIC AS A HOBBY WILL DEPEND IN ALMOST EXACT PROPORTION ON HIS ABILITY TO READ AT SIGHT. If he has nothing to play but the few pieces he has learned in his days of music study and no time to practice new ones his interest will soon pall, whereas the good sight-reader may keep his interest alive with almost unlimited new material, even though he never brings his playing to a stage of technical excellence fit for public performance." That says in a nutshell exactly what we feel about the place of music reading in the training of young musicians.

Music Reading is a Psycho-Motor Task

In the realm of language it is a natural thing to expect that when one knows the letters of the alphabet, their sounds, and the words that combinations of letters produce, the ability to 'sight-read' will follow. We expect only the beginning reader to struggle with a kind of working-out process—slowly sounding out words, stumbling and hesitating, making not much understandable sense out of what is being read. (I remember lying with David on his bed after dinner when he was in the first grade, listening to him laboriously sound out a new word and then repeat the phrase or sentence to make sense out of it after he knew the word! It was exciting to see the evolution from that stage into the stage of proficiency.)

Yet reading music is different. It involves a physical response to a mental stimulus—a new physical skill. In reading language our responses are already learned. We don't have to teach our vocal chords to make the sounds of the letters and words.

Studies on Reading Music

Robert G. Petzold advanced the idea that effectiveness in music reading is hindered in the early stages of instrumental training because of the concern with developing control over the instrument rather than with the musical notation. He felt that one of the significant problems contributing to poor music reading has been the lack of musical experiences before a student begins to learn to read music.

J. Watson pointed out the need of a music vocabulary by stating, "So in learning to read music as in learning to read language we must build a vocabulary based on direct experience."

What great recommendations for Suzuki training! The Suzuki student has had much direct experience with music before he learns to read the language.

When Do We Begin to Read?

Although we have said in the previous section that many activities can be done that prepare and preview music reading, we do not believe that actual music reading from the page should be done by pianists during the study of Book I. Until the important goals of Book I—focused attention, good posture, position and tone, firm fingers and rhythmic feeling—are well established for that stage of development, reading should not be considered. Generally speaking, we feel that all students need the experience of learning and reviewing all of the pieces of Book I before beginning to read. Exceptions may occur, but I think they are rare. An older child who learns very quickly and has easily formed all the correct attitudes and habits may be considered an exception. It may be feasible to begin reading sooner with a child like this. Our judgment must be based on the accomplishment of the above goals.

If the child begs to begin reading, parents need to explain the reasons for the delay. The desire to read can motivate the child to learn to play!

Your response could be, "Sandy, your teacher wants us to be sure that you are set in all of your good habits before we start looking at the music. If you always pay very good attention and listen to what she says and to what you are doing, if you have good posture, good hand position and firm fingers, if you play with a beautiful tone and good rhythm on all the pieces in Book I, we will be able to begin reading. Let's work on these things as we practice each day and then it won't be long. That will be really exciting, don't you think?"

I agree that the violinist also should not begin to read music until his basic technique is well established. Students usually take all of Book I to learn to play with good posture, a good bow hold, correct left hand position and finger action, and straight, firm bow strokes. This is a place where overlearning is especially needed. Reading music demands so much of the learner that he will not be able to devote much attention to his basic technique. If this technique is not well set, it will deteriorate as he neglects it to learn to read.

Once I taught a college string methods class by rote. These students were wind, brass, and percussion players who were required to learn basic string techniques. The head of the music education department had agreed to allow me to teach the class by the Suzuki method, but had insisted that I should also make the students acquainted with the elementary string methods that were in current use in the public schools. They were to play through several of the beginning books during the semester.

After six weeks of rote instruction to which the class responded enthusiastically, I brought in copies of one of the method books for the students to read through. Before they began to play, I emphasized the importance of maintaining good posture and fine tone.

You ought to have seen the reaction of the class to the introduction of reading! "I'm not ready!" exclaimed a fine clarinetist. "We're not either!" the others protested. "But you already know how to read music," I remonstrated. "What's so difficult?"

"Of course we can read the music! We're just not ready to take any of our attention away from our playing. We still need to watch our bows and our fingers."

This was a conscientious group. They had grown used to working for a good tone and good intonation, and felt that it was impossible to continue to do so if they had to give even a minimum of attention to reading. We finally compromised by alternating rote playing and reading music.

It was surprising how much the tone quality changed for the better each time we returned to rote playing. If combining playing and reading was difficult for these young adult musicians, one can see how difficult it could be for the young beginner whose basic technique is not set.

Getting Ready to Read

During the study of Book I there are many concepts and symbols that can be introduced to the student. Children consider learning these fun, so they can be done during rest periods in practice sessions or at lessons, if the teacher wishes. Your teacher may discuss her ideas about this with you.

Pianists can be introduced to the "high and low", "up and down" concepts of the keyboard, and the names of the keys. They can also learn the names of the notes on the staff, learn the alphabet backwards, recognize rhythmic groups of twos and threes when heard, clap the beat to recognize the durations of quarter, half, whole, and dotted half notes, and learn to recognize clef signs, flats, sharps, etc.

Answer any questions children might ask about how certain things look on the printed page by showing it to them. When the teacher asks for specific attention to some points in the piece . . . accents, crescendos, diminuendos, staccato, etc., point to them on the page during practice at home. Casually comment that they will see these often when they learn to read music.

Practicing Reading

Once the Suzuki student has begun to read music it is necessary to practice it every day as a part of the regular practice period. At first this reading period will be short but gradually it should become twenty minutes to a half hour of the practice session.

Music educator J. Fisher supports daily reading practice with this statement, "Real understanding of musical notation involves consistent day to day attention to the symbols and practice in their use."

We are all aware that "knowing" is not enough to accomplish a skill. It's the "doing", the actual experience using our knowledge, that teaches us to be skillful. The practice of using the musical symbols learned is the deciding factor in becoming an accomplished music reader.

Practice, of course, must be specific to a particular skill. This should be remembered when the time spent on theory and games is considered "reading" exercise. These activities may provide necessary background knowledge but they do not substitute for actual reading experience.

A new skill must be done regularly and often for one to become proficient in it. For that reason music reading practice shouldn't be considered an adjunct to practice but a part of it. Be sure both your child and you understand that.

Sight and Vision—Its Relation to Music Reading

Children are given school eye examinations at regular intervals using the familiar Snellen chart. This chart dates from around the time of the Civil War and was designed mostly to test children's ability to see the school blackboard. This examination measures only visual acuity, or clarity and sharpness of sight. Sight is the mere ability to see, the eye's response to light shining into it. Vision, on the other hand, is the result of the child's ability to interpret and understand the information that comes to him through his eyes. This is a learned process. Children may have 20/20 eye sight or even better and still have critical vision problems that interfere with school work and hence music reading.

A child learns visual skills just as he learns to walk and talk. Children who are restricted in play pens and walkers are prevented from having the crawling and creeping experiences that provide a range of movement and normal development patterns. Children who don't creep long enough or who are restricted in their physical exploration of the environment frequently move into life with a disability. It is a handicap that may never be exposed during physical or eye examinations.

Since a child must first learn to team the two halves of his body together before he can team his two eyes, so he must first learn to control the large gross muscles before he can control the fine muscles of his eyes. For that reason, balance boards, walk rails and jumping boards or trampolines plus crawling and creeping are an important part of vision training.

Here are clues that might indicate a possible need for vision therapy:

1. Blurred vision, double vision, words running together.

2. Reversals when reading—was for saw, on for no, etc.

3. Reversals when writing—b for d, p for q, etc.

4. Transposition of letters and numbers—12 for 21, etc.

5. Loss of place when reading, line to line and word to word.

6. Use of finger to maintain place.

7. Holding book too close.

8. Omitting small words.

9. Confusing small words.

10. Short attention span.

11. Daydreaming in class.

12. Poor handwriting.

13. Clumsiness on playground or at home.

If your child's performance is not up to his potential, if verbal ability far exceeds visual learning ability, you can suspect a vision problem. Observations from teachers—or from you—that the child "is lazy", "doesn't try", "could do better if he exerted more effort", point to the possibility of a vision problem. Even surly, hostile or belligerent behavior may be an indication of visual/perception dysfunction.

Optometrists in vision development suggest examination by the age of three so that any problems or lack of development can be found and corrected before school attendance. Of course, it's never too late to try to correct a later discovered problem.

I became interested in this because of observing the great number of students (not Suzuki students but general music students) who had difficulty reading music. The possiblity that vision problems might be causing some of these difficulties intrigued me.

Some astonishing figures will show the prevalence of this handicap. In one study, 1 out of 4 students were shown to have significant reading deficiencies. Seventeen million school children are achieving much below their potential with ten percent so severely handicapped that they are literally unable to learn. The Commission of Education ran a study called Project 100,000 with the U.S. Armed Forces and found 68.2% of the young men fell below grade 7 in reading and academic ability.

If you even slightly suspect your child might need this kind of help, seek out a vision therapist in your area. (For more information write: College of Optometrists in Vision Development: P.O. Box 285, Chula Vista, CA 92012.)

A Good Reading Environment

1. Young children need optimal visibility when beginning to read music. Large notes and symbols and good lighting are absolutely necessary for success.

2. Children show very slow rate of progress in early stages of sensory-motor learning. Knowing this, be very patient and understanding of the long period of time they need for accomplishment.

3. Children must repeat each new learning step many, many times to absorb it. Give them that opportunity. Inspire them to do it. Watch with cheerful feelings and encouragement.

4. Children must make each new step automatic before learning something new. Being aware of this, don't be eager to get on with new things. Be sure the step you're working on is automatic before you begin another.

Keep these things in mind and help your teacher by giving her your observations on the progress your child displays at home. That way you can knowledgeably work together on the reading study schedule.

Parents, Want to Learn to Read Music?

If you don't know how to read music, why not start now? You will be a much more understanding home teacher if you do. There's nothing like learning a new skill to put you in a more empathetic, supportive role with another new learner. Learning something new keeps your mind sharp, alert and young! Your child will enjoy and appreciate your efforts, too—both because you are open to doing new things and because it makes for greater understanding between you. Besides, if you try it, you might like it!

Importance of Attitude

Reading music is a complex activity and the supportive attitude of the parent can mean a great deal to the learning student.

Parents' positive help, when needed, is most important at the early stage of reading. Avoid statements like: "You played a wrong note", "That whole line was wrong", "Can't you see the difference between a line and a space note?", "You know that interval! Why did you play a third instead of a second?. . . a D instead of an E?" Allow the child to read the pattern, the line or the phrase without stopping even if he makes mistakes. Then, instead of pointing out and correcting the error, say, "I think you made some changes there. There were some notes different from those that are written. Please play it again. I think you'll see them and play it as written this time." If errors still persist, narrow the field. "There was something different in the second measure." Should the student still not play correctly, question, "What is this note? (interval, kind of note, etc.) What should it be? What did you play?" In this way the student is made aware of his mistakes and learns from them because he has been helped to focus on them and make his own correction.

One teacher said, "The most important thing is learning to read music is believing that you can." Our positive attitudes as parents and teachers can help build that belief in our children.

Encourage Your Child to Read

It is an unpleasant adjustment for some children to return to the feeling of being a beginner again when they start to read music. The familiar routine of listening and being guided by the parent is much more comfortable than having to put forth their own effort to make sense of the printed page.

Yet, as we said before, reading music is a valuable skill for any student. The amateur musician's future with music depends upon it. The professional must have it highly developed or many opportunities are unavailable to him.

There are many highly proficient musical performers whose reading skill is very poor. That is similar to the actor learning to recite Shakespeare beautifully with all meaningful inflection and convincing rhetoric, but being unable to read the daily newspaper or a book on a second grade reading level! The limitations are obvious.

It is not very desirable for a musician to stay in the rote-learning category. Sometimes the student needs to have this lack of options pointed out to him to give him the incentive to make the effort to learn to read. There is always hesitation on venturing into new territory. Help him take the step.

The secret of education
Lies in respecting the student.
                    Emerson

Young Bedrich Smetana, the Bohemian composer, thought the sound of his father's violin was a permanent part of his environment. For recreation in the evenings the family would often make music together. Bedrich was three when his father showed him how to handle a violin and keep time to music. By the time he was four he'd mastered the fundamentals of the violin—at five he started the piano, and at six made his first public appearance.

Your Child's Instrument

Is a Good Piano Necessary for the Beginning Student?

Your four-year-old Nancy is ready to start Suzuki piano lessons. You are eager to have her begin but the purchase of a piano does not have top priority on your acquisition list. "Since pianos are so expensive and we don't really know whether Nancy will continue, let's just get an old used piano that won't cost much," you say. "Later we can invest in a better one after we find out whether she's really interested. The one I found sounds like a piano in the Blue Lounge Bar. The keys keep sticking, and pedals don't work, but we'll get it fixed. It will have to do for now."

You, mother, want to learn to sew and your husband agrees that the purchase of a sewing machine can be considered. "But", he says, "since we don't know whether your interest in sewing will continue, I think we should buy this old 1909 Singer advertised in the paper. I called the owner. She says it runs but is temperamental at times. The stitches are irregular and don't seem to respond to the setting knob. The motor makes a funny noise but we'll get it fixed. It will have to do for now."

Can you imagine that any interest you might have in sewing will be nurtured by a broken down machine? What fine garment could be made by a machine of this kind? At your sewing lessons, you would be shown the intricacies of many creative items, but what happens when you try to duplicate them on your antique machine at home? And how long do you expect your interest to continue under those circumstances?

At Nancy's lessons she will be given guidance and stimulation to play with a beautiful sound. If she has a piano at home on which this is impossible to achieve, what will happen to her interest? Frustration and unpleasant sounds do not provide for continued interest and motivation to learn to play.

We all know that we cannot do any job well if we have inferior tools. A musical instrument is the tool of the musician, young or old. The young musician with a poor instrument will probably not persevere to become an old musician. It just isn't a very enjoyable, satisfying or desirable experience when no amount of careful practice can bring beautiful results.

Choosing a Piano

When your child is beginning lessons and you do not own a piano, or if you are wondering whether your piano is adequate, consult your teacher. It is to her advantage that your child has a good instrument at home. She will be glad to advise you. Sometimes you may find an estate or moving family that is selling a used instrument. In this case, you will really need your teacher's expert advice, plus the advice of a technician who could give you an estimate of the amount of work needed to put the piano in good shape.

In most cities there are piano stores who rent pianos with the agreement that the rental fee will apply to the purchase price should you decide to buy later. This may be your best solution because it provides you access to a decent instrument without your making a sizeable financial commitment at the outset of your child's training.

Musical Instrument Versus Furniture

Try to keep in mind that this piano is to function primarily as a musical instrument and not as a piece of furniture. It is fine if the style of the case and woodgrain compliment your decor, but that should be a secondary consideration. Naturally, if you are going to have it in a living room setting, you are not going to want a monstrosity that looks like it came from Dracula's castle, but if you must make some compromise, let it be in the furniture category, not the instrumental one!

Naturally, it would be nice if every piano student could have a nine-foot concert grand to begin on but this is not feasible, space-wise or financially, for most people. I would like to put thumbs down on the spinet-style piano that has been so popular because its appearance is so 'romantic'. Inasmuch as the sounding board on the spinet is very short, the bass register tones sound like dull 'thuds'. The upright grand is a better choice because the sounding board extends up behind the music rack and gives the lower register more tonal resonance. The baby grand has the best potential but of course its price is much higher than the upright grand.

Care and Maintenance of Your Piano

Your teacher will be glad to refer you to a good piano technician so that you can keep your instrument in good playing condition.

During the winter months a humidifier may be needed because of the heat in the house. A humidistat to measure the humidity in the room may be purchased inexpensively. It is best to keep the humidity level around 40%. In certain areas of the country, as in Tennessee, it is necessary to have a dehumidifier in the summer if the room is not air conditioned. Too much moisture may cause the keys to stick. On the other hand, an atmosphere that is too dry may cause the sounding board to dry out and crack.

It is best to locate the piano on an inside wall because of the ease of maintaining an even temperature there. Care of the instrument should not be the only consideration for its location. Keep in mind that the location of the piano may also affect the child's attitude toward daily practice. If the instrument is stuck down in a far-off corner of the basement away from all normal human interaction, that is not a pleasant environment for practice. Neither should the piano be placed in proximity to the TV set, or a play area. Whenever possible, these factors should be considered.

It is best to have the piano tuned regularly every six months if normal conditions prevail. Remember that the ears we're trying to develop become very sensitive to out-of-tune sounds! Sometimes parents are astounded when the child complains "that note doesn't sound right" when they themselves don't notice any difference at all. This is just another example of the marvelous sensitivity and hearing ability of children.

Since most of the new piano keys are topped with plastic, they don't need as much care as did the ivory keys. (At least we can be happy that pianists are not contributing to the demise of the elephant anymore!) It is still best to keep the piano keys clean with a soft, damp cloth. No soap should be necessary and excessive wetness should be avoided for obvious reasons.

It is true that pianos are a major investment, but with time for investigation and the expert help of your teacher and a technician, you should be able to find an instrument that will satisfy the needs of your child and your budget.

Choosing a String Instrument

Fortunately, finding a suitable small instrument for the beginning string player is not nearly the undertaking parents have with the young pianist. You should follow the guidance of your teacher with regard to the purchase of the small instruments, either new or used. Most teachers are very helpful in this matter. They want your child to have a fine instrument in good condition, and they will help to see that this is so.

When your child arrives at the need for a full-size violin or cello, you will have to continue relying on your teacher's advice. A better instrument will generally be easier for your child to play and will be an aid to the production of a better tone, but there are limits to this. I don't think there's any reason to give a child a violin from which he can draw only a fraction of the quality and quantity of sound it possesses. So much depends on the player. An admirer of Jascha Heifetz exclaimed after a concert, "Mr. Heifetz, your violin has a glorious tone!" Heiftez bent an ear toward the violin resting in its open case. "I don't hear anything", he replied.

At the full-size stage, I think an instrument should be bought for its tone and appearance rather than the name of the maker. Unfortunately, as one moves to a better instrument to get an appreciable difference in the tone quality, one has to spend quite a bit more money.

Some children are motivated to practice more by the fact that they have just acquired a new (to them) instrument. Some may even feel obligated to practice more when they know there has been a considerable outlay of family funds for their instrument!

I think the time to consider a major investment for a string instrument is at college entrance. The most important factors influencing the price of the instrument would of course be the family's finances and the serious intent of the student. I remember being shown a magnificent violin, worth at least $30,000, that had been given to a high school girl of indifferent ability. Oh, she was thrilled by its value but was unable to appreciate its tonal possibilities because she could not produce a good tone on the instrument. I didn't feel so badly later after I heard that the violin was given her by her multimillionaire grandfather. Who knows, perhaps today she is practicing like a fiend!

Choosing a Bow

Small bows, like the small instruments, are fairly standardized in quality and price. Your child will most probably have gotten his first bow with the violin, and will continue to get a bow with each larger-size violin. Even the first full-size violin may come with a bow and case.

When your teacher feels that your child should have a better bow, follow her guidance if family finances permit. As the student becomes more advanced, the bow he uses becomes more important. A bad bow may have a strong negative effect on a student's growth, more than most parents realize. I see more hopeless bows than I do hopeless violins!

Care and Maintenance of String Instruments

When your child receives his first instrument, your teacher will give both of you instructions regarding care and maintenance of the violin and bow. Your child should form the habit of taking great care of these from the beginning. This is part of the preparation for practice and lessons. Periodically, you should ask your teacher to let you know how the violin and bow are faring. Are you putting enough rosin, or too much, on the bow? Does the bow need rehairing? Should you replace the strings? Is the bridge all right? We teachers need to be reminded of these things. We know better, but sometimes we forget to keep a constant check on these matters.

Parents need to know that even with the best of care, under normal use string instruments need adjustments and repairs. With fine instruments, this may run into several hundreds of dollars at times, but not every year. String players usually spend more money keeping fine old instruments maintained than they do modern instruments, although these also suffer from lack of attention over a period of time.

Prices

You may be disappointed that there are no price guidelines given here. If we were to do so, our information would be out of date by the time this book is printed. We remember, with nostalgia, buying a fine half-size violin in Matsumoto for Judith in 1968 for $28! And that included bow and case. In this era of rising prices, parents whose children study string instruments may be consoled by the fact that their instruments, if well-cared for, are also appreciating in value!

Where there is great love
There are always miracles.

Willa Cather

"*From the day I was born I heard music*", so said Serge Prokofiev, the famous Russian composer pianist. As soon as he could balance himself on the piano stool next to his mother, she let him be a part of her daily practice. Soon she began to give him short lessons—never exceeding twenty minutes. When he was five and a half he picked out the notes of his first tunes, playing them over and over again.

Finding and Choosing a Teacher

During the past few years our mailbox has been the recipient of many letters from anxious parents who are moving to a new area, or from equally anxious Suzuki teachers whose students are moving. Both parents and teachers want to be sure that their students find a competent Suzuki teacher.

Unless we've had the opportunity to work with a teacher personally, or have heard or worked with his students, or know a close colleague who has had that opportunity and recommends him on that basis, we find it difficult to give a recommendation that is of much value. We can only suggest that those inquiring search the directory of the Suzuki Association of the Americas for names of teachers in the new location, or write the SAA for the files on teachers in the area. You should do the same. If the teachers have registered their work with the SAA, you will be able to see what kind of training and experience they have had. If you have a choice of teachers, no matter what training and experience is indicated, you will want to observe the teachers at work before you decide who might be the best for your child.

Since Suzuki teachers should be accustomed to having observers during lessons, the process should not be too difficult. Call each teacher, explain that you are interested in the Suzuki method for your child and that you and your child would like to attend some lessons and programs. Our advice to parents has been: if a teacher doesn't allow observation visits, cross that teacher off your list.

When you attend the lessons of a prospective teacher, observe the relationships between teacher and child, and teacher and parent. Does the teacher make sure that the parent knows what the goals are for home practice? Is the atmosphere pleasant and relaxed? Does the teacher expect and receive respectful attention? Is there a good balance between concentrated work and good humor? Are the teacher's comments supportive and encouraging even when necessary corrections are made? Does the teacher show a grasp of the basic technical problems, and demonstrate how they can be solved? To questions such as these, add prerequisites important to you. Remember that the game-playing good-humored, entertaining teacher might not be the best choice unless these qualities are balanced by the expertise of a well-trained teaching musician.

Don't be fooled into believing that 'anyone can teach Suzuki'. It's fine if one loves children, praises and encourages them, provides listening opportunities and uses the Suzuki repertory, but the teacher must also have knowledge of the technique of the instrument. I have had individuals tell me that they thought they could teach their own childen even though they had had little or no musical background. They felt that buying the books and combining the repertory with the Suzuki philosophy that they already knew was all that was necessary.

How would you feel if your child's math teacher walked into the classroom and announced, "Look, kids, this is going to be a great year. I really don't know anything about math . . . I mean I never studied it beyond grade school, but I have a book, and I'll study it along with you". You'd probably call the school office immediately to find out why they had employed a teacher with no math background or expertise to teach math to your child.

You should be just as concerned that your child have a knowledgeable, competent musician as a teacher. It will make a great deal of difference in the development of her abilities. Whether she develops her ability according to her potential or becomes what my husband calls a 'terminal case' depends upon your teacher's expertise. There is no substitute for a competent musician who has embraced the Suzuki approach to musical training. This kind of teacher has the necessary broad background that you should want your child to be given. Don't settle for less. It's an investment that will bring worthwhile results.

If you are moving into an area where there is no Suzuki teacher listed in the SAA directory, that doesn't mean that no Suzuki teacher exists there. It might mean that the teacher has not yet joined SAA, has not kept up membership, or is just a loner! Talk to parents, look in the phone directory, question the music teacher in your child's school, or call the local music stores. If after all that, no names have turned up, investigate the surrounding towns or cities. Many parents drive long distances to provide a teacher for their children. At one time families came from Illinois, Kentucky, Georgia, and North Carolina to our studio in Knoxville.

If your search reaches a dead end, rethink your problem. If your child has finished Book 2 and is reading music adequately for that stage of development, you are in good shape. You can look for a competent teacher who is sympathetic and open to the Suzuki concepts. This is very important! Some traditional teachers seem to be hell-bent on proving the Suzuki approach won't and can't work. If you team up with such a teacher inadvertently, head for the nearest door immediately. That kind of relationship can only end in unhappiness for you and your child. If your child is not yet reading and you want her to continue study in the Suzuki style, you might try to interest a resident, reputable, well-trained teacher to study and adopt Suzuki principles with your child.

Changing Teachers

Some parents feel that because their child's teacher is particularly adept at working with very young children, that same teacher cannot teach advanced literature. There is no basis for such an assumption. Rather, the teacher's training and experience will have a great bearing on his being successful with teaching your child on an advanced level. It is not necessary for the teacher to have all of the literature under his fingers ready for performance, but it is extremely helpful if the teacher has played the music your child is to study, or music of comparable difficulty.

The most advanced performer in the community, however, may not be the best teacher for your child. He may not be able to communicate well, may not have a supportive personality, and may not be able to diagnose your child's particular problems and guide her accordingly.

A case like the following is unfortunate. An excellent Suzuki teacher, who had yet not had any students past Book VIII, had taught a young girl to play very well in Book VI. A nearby college brought in a nationally-known violinist to perform a recital and conduct a weekend of master classes for students of all ages. This particular girl made a great impression him. "Your daughter plays beautifully," he said to her mother. "May I suggest to you that she be given the best instruction available in this area?" No mention was made of the superior instruction that had brought this girl to that position of excellence!

The mother, gathering that he was recommending a new teacher, dropped the Suzuki teacher at once, and enrolled her daughter with the violin teacher at that college who was known as a fine performer but was not generally regarded by his peers as a good teacher.

This mother's precipitate action hurt the Suzuki teacher's reputation with the other parents. They began to think that she was not capable of teaching on a more advanced level. And the little girl floundered under her new instructor who was particularly inept at working with a young, precocious child. In this case, I knew the capabilities of the Suzuki teacher, and felt that it would have been better for all concerned if the girl had remained with her teacher who was certainly qualified to teach the little girl through Book X.

I had a delightful eleven-year-old girl in a master class at an institute this summer. She played beautifully and responded well but seemed depressed about something. I asked her teacher if she knew what was bothering her. "Yes, I know, and it depresses me too," said the teacher. "Her father thinks she's too good to continue as a Suzuki student, so he's starting her with another teacher after this institute. He let her attend it as her farewell to the Suzuki world. She still cries when she thinks of losing her association with her friends at group lessons, and also when she thinks of stopping her lessons with me. I told her she could come to group lessons whenever she wanted, that she would always be welcome. Still, she's pretty upset."

This was another case in which the teacher happened to be well qualified for continuing the child's musical education. I felt that the change of teachers could have been justifiably and profitably delayed for two or three years. If the girl had been with her Suzuki teacher for a number of years, which she had not, the teacher's effectiveness might have diminished. Length of study with one teacher may be a factor contributing to the desirability of change, but again, it may not.

I am not suggesting that the child should not change teachers under any circumstances, but that such a change should be well thought out. If you are truly convinced that your child has outgrown her teacher, and you have arrived at that conclusion after much deliberation, try to effect the change as smoothly and tactfully as possible. If you or your child, however, are suffering from a personality conflict with your child's teacher, and you don't think there's much chance of change for the better, of course you should terminate the relationship without undue delay.

In all cases involving a change of teachers, I advise parents to weigh as objectively as possible all the pros and cons of the situation before taking any action. A hasty decision should be avoided.

Institute Environment

Parents often come away from institutes confused about the true worth of their child's teacher. Institute directors try their best to hire fine teachers but this doesn't mean that your teacher is automatically inferior to all of the institute teachers. If you have seen, at an institute, teaching that seems to you superior to that of your teacher's, and you feel that your teacher is capable of equalling it, you might discuss this privately with your teacher. If you hear remarks that contradict the way your child has been taught, try to talk to the institute teacher about it, and also discuss it with your teacher. You may still be confused but at least you have tried to clarify the situation. Your teacher may be wrong, the institute teacher may be wrong, or they may both be right, since, even in Suzuki teaching, many paths may lead to Rome. Don't assume without question that your teacher is wrong.

Under no circumstances should you automatically accept, as Bill has said, the fact that your home teacher is deficient because of what you observe at institutes or workshops. Unless you are a well-schooled instrumentalist yourself, you will have to question, study, and spend time and effort to wisely evaluate your situation before forming an opinion or taking an action.

A situation was called to my attention recently by an excellent teacher, a well-qualified teacher trainer, a teacher whose work I have admired for some time, who had sent some of her students to a summer institute. The institute teacher had questioned the parent about who the child's home teacher was, then made some deprecating remark about the quality of teaching and actually said, "She's been taught all wrong!" This, in front of the student as well as those observing! Naturally, the parent went home, told the teacher they were quitting and recited the above encounter as the reason.

Of course, first of all, no matter what the status of the student's performance, no temporary institute teacher ethically has a right to demolish the reputation of the home teacher. How does he know what that child has been told at home and how many times it has been repeated with no results?! The correct procedure would be to talk to the mother alone after class, question her, and then perhaps make suggestions or merely understand the differences. From that a positive outcome might have resulted. If this was an erroneous evaluation, which it must have been in this case, we can only suspect that the institute teacher saw validity in only his way of teaching and was not open to the thought that there could be variations of any kind. This is sometimes dangerous thinking and you would be wise to approach this kind of encounter with caution. Bolting to another teacher is not the answer . . . the grass is not always greener!

Fun and Games or Joy and Enthusiasm

I've heard parents complain that institute teachers are more entertaining than the teacher at home. Parents should realize the situation confronting the institute teacher. Because of the difficulty of making much impact on a child in four or five fifteen-minute lessons, and because there are often observers in the room, he may resort to entertaining the child and parent with games. These games may be all right in themselves, but not at all suitable as a steady diet week after week and would not be used by that institute teacher with his own students at home. We remember being surprised to see Suzuki using so few games with his private students.

211

FINDING AND CHOOSING A TEACHER

There is a prevalent but mistaken idea circulating in our Western adaptation of the Suzuki method that Suzuki training has game playing and 'fun' activity as its central core. We are seeing more and more efforts being focused on the production of games to cover every aspect of music learning.

Somewhere along the line our Western minds have been led to believe that all work and learning must be sugar-coated or disguised—kind of like a bitter pill that must be swallowed but is fundamentally good for you. Only if we camouflage learning will it be accepted, we are saying.

One teacher who watched video tapes of some Japanese piano lessons commented, "There certainly doesn't seem to be much fun involved. They just seem to be constantly working hard." That's true, I suppose, if you consider all work as drudgery and discount the joy of accomplishment. It is true that private lessons in Japan are not made up of 'fun and games'. If a creative teacher finds a way to approach a problem with a kind of game, he will certainly use it. Suzuki himself is quite a playful fellow and will often entertain with creative, functional games at group lessons, but private (one on one) lessons are basically working periods devoid of 'entertainment' for entertainment's sake. The secret of education, Suzuki says, is to approach music or any learning without a strict, formal attitude, but with joy and enthusiasm from the teacher. Then the child will 'catch' that joyful spirit and will develop a skill that will bring him happiness.

When you are evaluating a teacher, look for loving care of the child coupled with high standards for every level of performance. Your child should be consistently challenged to produce the best of which she is capable. It is possible for this to be done in an atmosphere of love and encouragement.

One kind word
Can warm
Three winter months.
Japanese Proverb

Be like the bird
That pausing in her flight
Awhile on boughs too slight,
Feels them give way beneath her
And yet sings,
Knowing that she has wings.
Victor Hugo

The ends of the earth stand in awe at the sight of your
wonders, the lands of sunrise and sunset you fill with your joy!
Psalm 65

Orchestral Experience

School Orchestras

What should you do when your Suzuki-trained violinist or cellist enters the fourth grade and wants to join the orchestra and play with her friends, or when the school orchestra director asks your child to join? (Most public school programs start at the fourth grade.)

I think the first thing you should do is to discuss the whole subject, pros and cons, with your child's Suzuki teacher. If your teacher knows the public school string teacher or knows of his work and personality, you are fortunate. If not, either of you can inquire about the quality of the program and the instructor. Ask other parents, other music teachers, attend the orchestra's programs, or ask to look in on a class. More and more public school string teachers are Suzuki-oriented and have their own programs in earlier grades. Your child might then have no problem with adaptation.

You must realize that no matter how competent the string teacher may be, it is still very difficult to teach, in the same class, beginners and youngsters who've had several years of Suzuki training. The string teacher is in a far worse situation than the first grade teacher whose entering class contains children who already read well. That teacher can give separate reading assignments and the readers can progress at different rates, but the orchestra players are all supposed to play the same thing at the same time!

Some public school teachers become very defensive when confronted with such a situation. They are afraid of the Suzuki student becoming bored, and possibly disruptive, or acting in an arrogant manner toward the beginners. Frankly, I think it's almost unimagineable that a child who has had several years of study would not become bored sitting in a class with youngsters who were being taught to play their very first notes! If your child has had no previous reading experience, reading the notes might occupy her for some time, but since reading progresses very slowly at the beginning, this might not prove enough of a challenge.

You might discuss these possible alternatives with your teacher and the school teacher:

1) your child be placed in the more advanced orchestra if she, as a fourth grader, doesn't feel out of place playing with sixth graders.

2) your child attend only those classes immediately prior to a concert.

3) your child volunteer to play viola so that she will also be, in a sense, a beginner. Knowledge of the viola clef will be very helpful later.

If none of these are acceptable to all concerned, you might want to keep your child out of the orchestral program until the sixth grade when the other youngsters have become fairly proficient. This is often the best solution. If you do decide on this course, don't let your child join a more advanced orchestra without sufficient music-reading preparation.

Music Reading Important

Our son, Tim, coming back from studying with Suzuki in Japan, went into a junior high orchestra without any previous orchestral experience and with very little training in music reading. He had been almost nine when he started studying violin in our then-new Suzuki program. Although he listened to the recordings faithfully, he did use the music to help learn the fingerings and bowings. I mistakenly thought he was developing the ability to read music, and had decided to start reading instruction at the level of Book IV. At that time we left for Japan and the whole business was postponed.

Tim was shocked when he auditioned for seating in the school orchestra. Everyone seemed to know that he was the best violinist in the school, but the orchestra director, after hearing his attempts to sight read music, put him on the last stand of the third violins! (I really felt and still feel guilty about this, but it did make me keenly conscious of the student's need for everyday experience in reading.)

Tim was concertmaster of the orchestra by Christmas. When I told him I was sorry that I had not prepared him earlier, he said, "Well, anyway, it's a lot easier to learn to read music than it is to learn to play the violin."

215

Be sure your teacher helps your child develop sight reading skills. I don't mean just acquiring theoretical knowledge, nor learning a new piece from the music, but actually developing the ability to sight read music she has never heard. Group lessons provide opportunities for more advanced students to sight read in an ensemble setting, and should be used for that purpose in addition to rehearsing Suzuki literature in unison, or teaching supplementary material using music. Also, the student should be sight reading material daily at home. Etudes are fine for this purpose.

If your child goes into the beginning orchestra, indoctrinate her with the proper attitude. She shouldn't feel superior to a classmate who is a beginner at age nine or ten, who isn't studying privately, and if she does practice at home, practices without parental help!

You may be concerned that your child, playing with beginners in a group situation, will be exposed to a great deal of really bad intonation and will lose her own sensitivity to correct intonation. Being subjected to bad intonation may be painful, but shouldn't be detrimental if the teacher keeps the child's attention on intonation in her own practice. The student should be careful to keep her reaction to bad intonation to herself, or quickly become the most unpopular student in the orchestra!

Despite all of the problems mentioned above, I feel that there can be many advantages to the student's participation in the school orchestra and that the disadvantages can be averted or minimized. School orchestras provide students pleasant sociability with boys and girls in their own school who have similar interests and may provide some exciting musical experiences that are highly motivational. Through affiliation with school orchestras, the student will have the opportunity to participate in music festivals, solo and ensemble competitions, and regional and all-state honors orchestras. The regional and all-state orchestras are especially attractive in that they may provide your student the thrill of playing, for the first time, major compositions in an orchestra with a very large string section. These orchestras usually rehearse intensively for only a few days before a concert. The students are given the music well in advance.

216

Youth Orchestras

In this category I'm placing all of the orchestras, no matter who sponsors them, that draw their personnel from more than one school and rehearse on a regular basis. Players are usually accepted by audition. These orchestras usually play music more difficult than the school orchestras since they have a bigger pool of players from which to draw their members. Their membership commonly consists of the better players from a number of school orchestras.

Parents often take pride in their children getting into youth orchestras at an early age, but getting in one of these orchestras too early may be detrimental to the child's musical development. Occasionally the conductor or someone managing the youth orchestra will approach you or your child directly and invite her to play in the orchestra. This is flattering, but I would respond by thanking the person and saying that I wanted to discuss the matter with my child's teacher. The teacher will know or should find out what kind of orchestral training the student would be getting in the youth orchestra, and whether your child is ready for that kind of experience. I wouldn't be writing all of this about youth orchestras if I hadn't had personal experience in this field and if I hadn't heard so many Suzuki teachers lament the fact that their fine students often got too heavily involved in orchestras too early.

Parents must realize that it's very difficult for a string player to hear what she's doing in a large orchestra. Too much orchestral playing too soon may cause your child's basic technique to deteriorate. I feel that youth orchestras should be the province of high school students to whom the social aspect is most helpful, and who are mature enough to withstand certain disadvantageous aspects that may arise.

For instance, youth orchestra directors, and sometimes school orchestra directors, may program music that is far too difficult for many of the string players. "Oh well, the difficult string passages will all be covered by the brass anyway", is a line of reasoning one often encounters. This kind of thinking doesn't help the youthful string player's feeling of self-worth or her integrity as a member of the orchestra. Students are sometimes bewildered when they hear loud applause for their orchestral performances when they know that only two or three of the players in their sections could even come close to playing the part correctly. They don't realize that the audience actually couldn't hear all of the mistakes and forgave the ones they did hear because "they were just kids playing". Suzuki students who have been challenged to play as well in groups as they do as soloists find this particularly disturbing.

It is true that many of the difficult string passages are covered up by the brass and percussion. Experienced players know in advance which passages won't be heard and so they go easy on practicing those passages. They know how to 'fake', how to make a reasonable stab at playing the passage without damaging the effect of the whole. This 'cover' provided by the other sections of the orchestra enables many non-professional and semi-professional orchestras to perform acceptably music that is too difficult for many of their string players. However, in top professional orchestras, all of the string players are expected to play all of the notes that it is humanly possible to play. In fact, professional orchestras require string players who audition to play some of the most difficult passages from the orchestral literature. Of course, at these solo auditions there is no 'cover' whatsoever!

If your child is complaining that the music is far too difficult for her, you and she should talk with her teacher. The teacher may not be in any position to make suggestions regarding programming to the orchestra director (most conductors regard this as their exclusive province), although some teachers have been known to warn conductors that if they continue to program music the teacher feels is far too difficult for his students, he may encourage the parents to withdraw their children from the orchestra.

Studying Orchestral Music

No matter if the music is difficult or easy, your child should be in the habit of showing her teacher all of the orchestral music she is playing. The teacher should be asked to incorporate into the lesson orchestral parts for which the child would benefit by the teacher's assistance. Some teachers are understandably reluctant to spend time on orchestral parts, but I feel that if the student is going to play the music anyway, and often with many repetitions, it's better for the teacher to provide guidance so that the student won't be playing incorrectly. Even simple orchestra parts may present problems, often in bowing, that the student has not encountered in the Suzuki literature.

If it's just an occasional piece that contains passages that are really too difficult for your child at that time, your teacher can help the child 'fake' the passages. As I said above, this is an important part of orchestral experience.

If teachers are encouraged to look at orchestral music with a fresh eye, and ask themselves, "How can I make this easy for my student?", they may come up with new fingerings that make the music much easier to play. We teachers need to be reminded of this: what may be the best for us might not be the best for our students at their level. I used to give fingerings that I liked, then I began to look at the music with the goal of finding the easiest fingering possible for my students. With that kind of approach I came upon some innovative fingerings that made the music much easier. Oftentimes, the choice of fingering may be the determining factor in whether or not the child can play the passage.

I know how crowded the lesson can become if time is devoted to orchestra parts, but I put other material aside if the student really needs help. I remember preparing Missy for an audition for the all-state orchestra. The music included the finale of the Shostakovitch Fifth Symphony which was quite difficult for her but not impossible. I dispensed with all of the other music she was studying so that we could go over the Shostakovitch with careful attention to details. She practiced the part as carefully as she had her solo work. Missy was striving to be concert mistress, and did succeed in getting the second chair even though she had had very little orchestral experience. She gained appreciably from the time we spent on that music. I used the material to develop her technique. Would it have been better if I had continued to cover only her solo pieces in the lessons, and left her to fend for herself with the Shostakovitch? I believe that a sloppy performance in orchestra would have damaged her technique as well as her morale.

Advanced Student

What if your child progresses so rapidly that she is very far ahead of all the other players in the area? Should she enter or remain in the school or youth orchestra if the music is far too simple for her? It may be obvious that she is wasting her time insofar as her own development is concerned, and yet you and she may feel that she has a responsibility to participate in the musical scene of the community. This is a difficult decision to make. If the student is interested in becoming a professional musician, it would probably be better for her to give top priority to her own development, and go to an orchestral camp in the summer for a higher-level orchestral experience.

Auditions for Seating

Discrimination against Suzuki students, taking place at auditions for seating in orchestras, used to be fairly common and still surfaces occasionally. Children should be prepared for the human element that is present in these decisions. Unfairness, favoritism, and discrimination are hard for any child to take, but even more difficult for the Suzuki child who has been trained in a loving, protective, noncompetitive environment. We parents need to be sensitive to our children's feelings and give them the support they need when and if difficulties arise.

No matter how hard one tries to explain to students that auditions for seating may produce some unusual results, it is still quite a shock to the students to see a player whom everyone knows is inferior sitting in the first chair. A girl we knew was complaining to her father about an obvious injustice in seating. "Daddy, it's just not fair!" Her father replied, "Carol, whoever said that life was fair?"

Orchestras Provide Motivation

I hope that your child will have many pleasant experiences in orchestra. Playing a symphony by Tchaikowsky, Beethoven, or Brahms can be very exciting, and playing that symphony with one's friends even more so. Orchestras can provide marvelous motivation, and often do at a time when the student really needs it. Remember, Suzuki initiated his group lessons to provide motivation from the thrill of performance with a large group.

Parents have told us that their children would have dropped the violin or cello if it had not been for the stimulation given by their orchestra. If your child's teacher recommends a particular kind of orchestral experience for her, you should try your best to get her in that orchestra and then give her all the support she needs to continue. You should feel fortunate if fine orchestral experience is within the reach of your son or daughter! As Suzuki says, "Your child will benefit by contact with the minds of the great composers through their music."

May the blessing of light be on you —
Light without and light within.

Old Irish Blessing

Nothing is worth more than this day.

Goethe

No love or friendship can ever cross our path
Without affecting us in some way forever.

Francois Mauriac

Competition—Contests

Competition

"Struggle to win over others" and "a contest between rivals" are the phrases used by Webster to define competition. It is obvious that these phrases are out of place in the Suzuki milieu which de-emphasizes competition as a means to motivate children to practice. Rather, Suzuki hopes that children will be motivated by hearing fine performances of older children and by wanting to play the beautiful pieces that lie ahead.

"How beautifully Mikiko plays! I want to play like she does. I must practice hard so that I will be able to play that well." "That Bach Double Concerto sounds so exciting! I can hardly wait until I play it!" These are the remarks Suzuki likes to hear from children.

Suzuki believes that children benefit from an environment in which they are motivated to play the same music together. His desire is that the environment will be one of contagious enthusiasm. This is one of the reasons his program offers so many opportunities for children and parents to observe the work of other children. Group lessons, frequent solo recitals, and observations of others' lessons are offered to create stimulation but there can be a negative side when parents and children, seeing one child progressing more rapidly than another, are demoralized rather than stimulated. It is often this constant comparative evaluation that causes otherwise understanding parents to push their children ahead and seek a quantitative goal rather than a qualitative one — how many pieces are played rather than how *well* they are played.

We need to remind our children regularly that the proper goal is to play every piece as well as possible as one progresses, and not to race sloppily through as many pieces as possible in the shortest time. Suzuki calls this the "horse-race mentality"!

Often children meeting for the first time at a workshop or institute will ask each other, "What is your last piece?" "I'm in Book IV", is a reply that may demoralize a child who may be much older and yet is only playing through Book III. The first question is never followed up, nor is additional information ever given. I've never yet heard a child say, "I'm in Book IV but I have a lot of problems to overcome", and then enumerate his shortcomings!

Remember! Different Rates of Maturation

In order to offset a possible negative reaction to our observations of other children's progress, we parents need to remind ourselves continually that all children have a different rate of maturation in all fields of endeavor. We also need to ask ourselves questions such as these:

Does my child practice as much and as well as possible?

Does our family life style help him to practice regularly?

Have I been the most helpful home teacher?

Am I willing to give more of my time and energy to help John progress as fast as the other children?

Is my family life more complicated than Mrs. Jones's whose only child progresses so rapidly?

Am I willing to admit that my priorities are different from Mrs. Smiths?

Am I proud of John's interests in many things, but am not happy to settle for less than the best in music even though he cannot spend enough time practicing because of so many other activities?

Can I be satisfied that Susan is making fine progress and enjoying her violin even though she's not one of the best students?

Ambivalence

Even if we have decided that our child's musical development is not one of our top priorities, it is still not easy at times to watch other children move ahead of ours.

When I watched David play soccer, I used to be bothered by two boys who were more skillful players. Even when I found that they spent hours practicing in their back yard, had started playing at age five, and that their father loved soccer, watched it on TV and talked soccer to his children much of the time, I still had a hard time when I watched a game. I liked soccer, was glad that David was playing well and improving, but I would still have liked David to have been the top man on the team even though he spent little time practicing, and didn't have my wholehearted commitment of time, energy and enthusiasm.

I had to face my own irrational attitude when I realized that I was like many of the parents I was exhorting to work more with their children. I liked our children to participate in sports but at the same time wanted their participation to be 'reasonable'. Yet at game time I forgot all this and wanted them to be the best!

Secure and Free

In our chapter on "Sibling Rivalry" we discussed the ever-present competition in daily family life. There is also competition in school, in sports, even in social situations, so we can't avoid it no matter what we do. For the child who feels secure in the love and respect of his parents, these forces need not be destructive.

Joy in the Accomplishments of Others

So often in Japan, parents attending group or private lessons would applaud someone else's child when he gave a good performance. Even in the class of teacher trainees at the Institute, students would show delight when another student succeeded in playing well. There was open rejoicing at the success of others.

How difficult, but how wonderful, if a parent can honestly show delight in another child's accomplishment even when that child is surpassing his own. The child has the opportunity to learn a very important lesson from this. "I can rejoice in other's achievements. If I am giving my best efforts to what I am doing, their accomplishments are not a threat to me."

Our aim, as parents and teachers, is to give our children such security in our love, that the competititon present in our social structure will not intimidate them but will be considered as just another life experience.

Contests

In Suzuki's autobiography, he mentions his first very young student, Toshiyo Eto, as having won a contest at age eleven. After Suzuki started his Talent Education program at the end of World War II, however, there are no references to his entering students in contests in Japan. A number of people have criticized Suzuki in this matter, saying that it would have helped the entire movement had he let the 'mainstream' musical world see how magnificently talent was being developed in his program. This may be so, but it would have been inconsistent with Suzuki's statement that he was not trying to produce professional violinists, but rather trying to enrich the lives of many children by developing their capabilities. Suzuki has never encouraged the use of contests and competition as a motivating force in Talent Education.

Contests, however, are a way of life in the professional musical world. It seems that students seeking a professional performance career benefit by having participated in and won a number of contests, but I still think it is better if children do not enter contests too early. They can be very emotionally disturbing. A student can win one contest and not even place in the next. Judges vary in their likes and dislikes.

Early participation in contests should be limited to those contests in which all students are given ratings in categories: I, or Superior, II, or Excellent, etc. Theoretically all students entering could get in the I category. A competition in which only one person gets first place, one gets second, etc., is often more detrimental than developmental. In the first type of contest, the student is usually given constructive comments by the clinician which can be very helpful to the student and teacher.

Contests may provide strong motivation in some children without producing any detrimental side effects. There are children who relish the excitement of a contest. These children are usually those who have practiced long and well and who have confidence in their ability to succeed. Other children may find the anxiety built up in anticipation of a contest neither helpful nor desirable. Even if your child enters only the rating type of contest, be prepared for circumstances you cannot control and give him plenty of encouragement and support if there is a disappointing outcome.

I remember vividly an unhappy experience with a rating contest in my childhood. I was in seventh grade and had been studying with an excellent teacher whom I loved and respected. Virginia Hardacre not only had a personality that radiated enthusiasm and love of music, but she also encouraged her students to listen to recordings of the works they were learning . . . pre Suzuki! I had studied long and hard on the Scherzo in B Flat Minor, by Chopin and had listened to a recording many, many times, absorbing the style and tempo. Although written in 3/4 time, this piece is felt in one beat to the measure as most scherzi are. I had practiced long hours so that I could play it at the proper tempo.

I was involved in a series of contests constructed on a district, state, and national level. If a student received a I rating in the district contest, he went on to the state level. A I rating in the state meant going on to the national. After playing in the district contest I was elated! The clinician, or judge, as we called her, had welcome words of praise and encouragement, so with confidence I went on to the state level. The performance there went very well, and I looked with anticipation at the posted list, sure that my name would be in the I category. It wasn't there!

I hurried to pick up my critique sheet and read, "You play this piece much too fast! It is written in 3/4 time. Don't play it as though it were one beat per measure." I fought back tears of frustration and disappointment. My teacher was incredulous. She investigated the credentials of the clinician and found that he was a band director and wind player. He simply did not know this literature. There obviously were no qualified pianists available for the position, so someone in the vicinity was drafted. Even though I realized the circumstances I could not help but feel "unfaired" against! It is an incident that is still very vivid in my memory . . . yet I don't spend any emotional energy resenting the experience. Because of the loving support of my mother and teacher it was not a devastating one.

Naturally we don't want to shield our children from all risk of disappointment or failure. It is only through varied life experiences that human potential is developed, character is built and maturation accomplished. If a child is secure in the unconditional love surround-

ing him and is not dependent on "being the best" to assure him a sense of self-worth, all of these experiences can be growth producing. Results can then be accepted without the accompaniment of self-doubt. We should help children evaluate the situation . . . not judge themselves. . . . "That clinician was not knowledgeable. He should not have been in that position. His comments did not reflect on my capabilities."

Weigh your child's resiliency, his confidence and his ability to grow with success and learn from defeat. Then when he enters contests or competitions of any kind, support him, guide him, and love him through it all.

Life-Enriching Benefits

Through his "mother-tongue" method Suzuki has committed himself to the happiness of all children, not just fostering musical sensitivity and performing ability, but fine character and sensitive natures. In articles and speeches throughout the world he repeats again and again that adults should appreciate the privilege of helping their children to become "fine human beings with beautiful harmonious minds and high sensitivity."

Suzuki's passionate conviction that all children possess the potential to be trained to acquire superior abilities is obvious in all he says and does. This is his leitmotif, a refrain he never tires of repeating to all who will listen. I believe that the cornerstone of all his success is his ability to convince so many parents of the superior innate potential their children possess.

Self-Concept—Future Success

There are many benefits for both child and parent in the study of music by the Suzuki approach. Robert Singer, prominent American sports psychologist, wrote, "Enriched and varied early childhood experience is a factor leading to the probability of success in a wide range of undertakings." Margaret Robb, authority on motor-skill acquisition, stated, "When a person is successful in learning a skill, his self-concept is enhanced because of his mastery over the task." Again, Singer writes, "Early successes are important to motivation. Satisfaction achieved elevates the level of performance which in turn increases the probability of better performance output." Dr. James Dobson in his book "Hide or Seek" speaks about the need for developing skills early in childhood so that the child will face his teenage years with what he calls "compensatory" skills, skills that give him a feeling of self-worth during difficult growing years. All of these experts support Suzuki's program for children.

Capacity, Enthusiasm and Respect for Work

When we lived in Matsumoto, Billy, then six, went to the first grade at the Genshi School near our home and near Suzuki's Institute. The Japanese teachers there were anxious to talk with us about American schools. One day we were invited to visit the school for a long informal exchange of information. During the discussion a few of the teachers mentioned some Genshi School students who were studying in Suzuki's program, or had graduated from the kindergarten at the Institute. They said that Suzuki students exhibited a great capacity and enthusiasm for work, also a level of concentration far above average. American and other non-Japanese parents have noticed these same attributes in their Suzuki-trained children.

Concentration

The ability to focus the mind, or concentrate, is a great asset in any and all activity. Using music as a vehicle for its development from an early age is ingenious. Almost without our realizing it Suzuki training fosters this growth.

Suzuki talks about the growth of the span of concentration. "When the small child can play all the variations of 'Twinkle' without stopping, he shows that he can concentrate four minutes," Suzuki says. His teachers gradually draw the children into longer and longer lessons, and then the parents are able to increase the practice sessions accordingly. I think it is a wondrous thing to see a small child totally absorbed in making music.

Parents' Growing Interest in How Children Learn

Parents have told us that over the years they have become more aware of their children's learning processes and the problems in all of their learning situations, not just the musical ones. They became more and more interested in what and how their children were learning. This increased interest in turn delighted the children and encouraged them to do better.

Exposure to Greatness

The reading of great literature and the study of great art and music have always been considered important influences on people's lives. Suzuki believes that children should have contact with great minds. He says, "Children are taught by Bach, Handel, Vivaldi, Schumann, Mozart and others." When he sees the music of the great composers becoming a part of the children's lives, he is filled with joy, because this love and appreciation will enrich their entire lives.

Long Range Interest in Music

I have been greatly encouraged when I have met some of our young adult graduates who are no longer playing the violin, greatly encouraged because they have expressed a continuing love of music, of Bach, in particular. A young engineer's fond remembrance of the Double Concerto led him to more of Bach's music. A young newspaperwoman attends symphony concerts regularly, and a young mother looks forward to the time when her baby will play the Bach Double Concerto. In these, as in many more young lives, music has continued and will continue to enrich their existence.

Group Lessons, Concerts, Institutes, Social Occasions

Suzuki's group lessons for violinists are really wonderful social affairs bringing together children with a common interest. As in many urban Suzuki programs, our students came from a number of different areas. The group lessons were often the only time these children saw each other. I always liked to give them a little time to socialize before we started. Once we had a visitor who grew a little impatient as I delayed the beginning of the playing. "Just when does this group lesson start?" she asked rather imperiously. "It has already started," I replied, pointing to the clusters of children animatedly catching up on each other's news. "I like this to be an enjoyable experience. I know that the social aspect motivates attendance."

We should be glad that there are other things children enjoy about lessons, concerts and institutes. Most institute directors try to get feedback from the students and parents about the institute experience. In answer to a query about what they liked best about our institute, a great number of the children mentioned our Olympic-size swimming pool! One boy rated the elevator at the top of his list! Still, quite a few especially liked the informal play-ins in the dorm halls at night before bedtime.

Close Parent-Child Relationship

Suzuki lessons do bring parent and child closer together. Although we must admit this increased contact is not always amicable, it does mean that the parent and child will see more of one another. After these years are over so many parents look back on them with nostalgia, forgetting all the struggles that occurred.

One of our mothers whose children are grown and gone comes back occasionally to a concert or play-in. As she watches and listens to the small children play the familiar tunes she recalls what she now remembers as mostly happy days. I met another of our ex-parents recently. I remembered the many painful struggles she'd had with her bright, charming, but willful daughter. I was surprised to see the wistful look on her face as she recalled her daughter's early study!

Now that our youngest is sixteen, we also have our moments of nostalgia. I can't help but tell parents of young children to enjoy all they can as the children progress. In spite of all the troubles, it is a very special time with many possibilities for joy and pleasure.

Parent Absorption—An Island of Repose

Parents who've become absorbed in their children's lessons and those of other children have repeatedly stated that the lessons were often an island of repose for them, drawing their minds from their many cares. I think the secret to this is the fact that they entered into the spirit of the lessons and became absorbed in what was happening. They found themselves rejoicing when a child could finally play a passage correctly after many trials. They felt themselves awed by the capacities of the children and rooted for them intensely.

Entertainment—Lessons, Concerts, At Home

Lessons and concerts in the Suzuki style are very entertaining. The very young children particularly often say and do humorous things.

One little pianist always clapped for herself after performing in a program. At an institute concert, after the solo and violin soloist were announced, the little boy ran up to Connie at the piano and whispered, "How does it go?" One of my very first four-year-old students who seemed to be paying very close attention to everything I was saying and demonstrating, suddenly interrupted me. "I'm going to the foot doctor right after my lesson," she said very seriously.

One evening at a party at our house in Matsumoto, I was demonstrating a prank that I had played on my younger brother. This boy could sleep through every disturbance imaginable. I would stand beside his bed, serenading him on the violin with my special version of the *Star Spangled Banner*, a version in which every second or third note would be out of tune, followed by a few legitimate measures and then more out of tune notes. I was playing this version for the Suzukis when David, our then eighteen-month-old son, came running in from the other room yelling, "Bad! Bad!" He even tried to pull my bow arm down! Suzuki burst into laughter and said, "See! He knows this is bad because he's heard so much good music at home." Suzuki loved to tell this story all over Japan. It showed, he said, the effects of early listening.

We took a group of youngsters to play after dinner on the terrace of our chancellor's house. During the program, I announced 'Andantino' and then proceeded to start the children playing 'Allegretto'. I realized my mistake when I saw the incredulous look on five-year-old Rita's face. She was bursting to tell me that we were playing the wrong piece, but she dutifully kept on playing. When we finished, however, before the guests had a chance to applaud, she burst out, "That was the wrong piece!" Needless to say that took a bit of explaining!

At a demonstration concert we were giving with just two children, Connie and I were to play some of the easier Suzuki tunes after our children had played their portion of the concert. In the middle of

'Humoresque' I went completely blank and came to a sudden halt. I didn't even hear Connie's cueing me at the piano. "Excuse me", I said, "you must remember that I'm not a Suzuki student!" The next try proved successful, but after the program Michael came running up to me. "You didn't forget. How could you forget a piece that you've heard and played so many times?! I think you did that on purpose to show how Suzuki kids remember things much better." I finally persuaded him that I actually *did* forget. "I wonder what you would have thought if we'd have forgotten like that!" he said.

At one of Denda's group concerts in Nagano, Japan, the audience was amused to see a little boy rush up on stage when the next number was announced, start to play with the others, realize almost immediately that he couldn't play that piece, stop and rush back down off the stage, all in the space of about twenty seconds!

Desire to Play

It wasn't until we went to Japan that we were aware of really early participation in concerts. At a violin solo recital in Matsumoto, we watched a tiny three-year-old make her first solo appearance in public. The teacher was right beside her on the stage, making sure of her posture and bow hold. The teacher placed the bow on the string at the tape, then said, "Taka". The little girl played the rhythm of the first variation of Twinkle vigorously, then, placing the violin in rest position, she took a quick bow. Her pigtails bounced in the air. The audience of parents applauded enthusiastically. She looked up in surprise, then hurriedly repositioned her violin and played her encore, a repeat of the Twinkle rhythm!

Most parents who studied an instrument in childhood can remember how they feared playing for people, so the eagerness of Suzuki students in wanting to play is quite astounding to them. Parents have complained that when they have guests, the children want to perform a whole book of pieces—complained while at the same time were proud! A similar thing occurs after piano play-ins. There is often a scuffle among those who want to play more of their pieces at the piano. Many times during programs the children will ask if they may add

234

another piece to their performance. That's a truly impressive side-effect!

Projected Adult Activity

The adult who as a child has developed his musical proficiency to a high level will be able to continue it as a hobby or avocation during his adult years if he does not choose it as a career.

Even though I chose music as a profession there have been periods during my life when practice was impossible. Because of what Bill calls "musical money in the bank", my return to playing was not difficult. The years of three and four hours of daily practice during childhood and adolescence, and later extensive practice in music school, built a strong foundation that could be brought out of hibernation.

The amateur musician can do the same if he has developed musical skills to a high level by practicing well through childhood and the teens. In this way music remains a vital part of his life always.

Poise and Self-confidence

Recently some of our Suzuki students participated in an area solo recital in which traditional as well as Suzuki students performed. Before the Suzuki students began to play they bowed quite naturally, adjusted the stool, and paused for mental preparation before they placed their hands on the keyboard. Their generally impressive behavior presented a picture of poise, grace and composure, quite a contrast to the impetuous way many children approach the keyboard.

Ann, a little piano student, demonstrated a wonderful example of composure during a spring recital. She began Mozart's "Arietta", reached the end of the first line and blanked out. Instead of showing signs of panic—the fumbling and chaotic searching that is often the hallmark of a situation like this—she quietly returned her hands to her lap and repeated her preparation again. She began once more only to reach the same impasse. I was sitting close to her, so I whispered, "Would you like me to help you?" "Yes", she whispered in return. I went up behind her, and played pianissimo past the part she had missed.

She smiled, started again and played a fine performance from begin-ning to end. This was an excellent example of the kind of poise and self-confidence that is evident within the child who is a Suzuki student. Afterward I thanked her for her wonderful recovery and told her how proud I was of her performance.

Respect of Peers

Peer attention during school years comes mainly from participa-tion in sports. The fact that music performers can gain the respect and admiration of their contemporaries may seem unlikely to those who haven't seen it, but it is possible.

Our Judith, 10, was asked to perform a violin solo on a school assembly program. She was in the fifth grade and a bit skeptical about her reception from her peers. Bach's A Minor Concerto was her choice because she knew it well, not because it was a hit parade selection! Her performance was filled with vitality. There was such excitement in her playing that the kids in the audience were caught up in it. When she finished, they clapped with so much enthusiasm and for such a long time that the adults were all amazed. This demonstrated that even young children recognize exciting accom-plishment in their peers.

Many Suzuki students have been surprised at the attention they have gotten from students and teachers when they have played at their schools. One mother reported that after her child played for her class, she received so many compliments that she said to her mother incredulously, "Gosh, I didn't know I was *that* good!"

Memory Development

Memory is the necessary ingredient of all learning, although not long ago educators de-emphasized its importance, giving higher priority to the development of creative thought. Why should they be mutually exclusive? I think creative thought must have stored mate-rial to give it substance. We must have input before we can have output!

The Talent Education kindergarten's emphasis on, for one thing, memorization of the Japanese poem, the haiku, gives the very young child the memory exercise that helps generate his later success in school, in all subjects at all levels.

The growth of memory capabilities is also present in Suzuki music study. Again and again stories are told with incredulity about children who memorize orchestra parts after several playings, or who learn a book or two of music in fantastically short periods of time.

On an afternoon recital, a student string quartet was to perform a movement of a Haydn quartet. The second violinist, as she walked into the room, gave a horrified gasp. "I've forgotten my music!" There was no time to return home for it, and no other copy was available. "Do you think you could remember your part?" the cellist asked. "I'll try." It was quite a demonstration, especially for the adult musicians present. The quartet performed with no problem. The little 'absent-minded' musician was not 'absent-minded' at all. She was very 'present-minded' as she played her part from memory!

The memory develops and grows with use. Suzuki training provides fertile ground for its flowering.

Playing Together

Making music together is one of the greatest joys for the amateur as well as the professional musician. The Suzuki string player has wonderful experiences in playing with others in group lessons. Later he can participate in orchestras and in chamber groups. Even his solos are ensemble experiences because an accompanist is usually required.

The pianist is not so fortunate. As soon as he can read music well, however, he can play duets and accompany on an elementary level. Later, he too will be able to participate in chamber groups, usually with string players.

Musicians feel that ensemble playing makes the musician. One cannot go one's own merry way, (as pianists often do) but must listen to all the other parts as they relate to the whole. Aside from the enjoyment involved, ensemble playing develops sensitivity and maturity in the musician.

A Chance to Give

Many Suzuki students have had the opportunity to experience the joy of giving happiness to people outside of their own families. Students have many opportunities to perform as soloists and in groups but one of the most gratifying is playing for senior citizens in nursing and retirement homes. In Knoxville, our Suzuki students played at regular intervals during the year for a nursing home. The staff said that the turnout for these programs was larger and more enthusiastic than for any other program presented there. The appreciative smiling faces, the sincere compliments, the loving gestures of the audience gave the children a joyful experience—that of being able to give something unique and special to someone.

Benefits for Parents

When we enroll one or more of our children in Suzuki study, we are putting ourselves and our children into a position wherein all may accrue many benefits, quite a number of them not directly related to developing the ability to play well. We will learn much about music, about our children, how skills are acquired, the tremendous effect of the environment on the learning process, and the importance of a healthy self-image in ourselves as well as our children.

Watching the changing attitudes of parents and teachers toward children, I wonder if Suzuki might not have had an ulterior motive aside from "the happiness of all children". Perhaps it could have been "for the character formation of all parents and teachers."

Suzuki has generated for the world the birth of belief in the potential greatness of each small child and the joy of nurturing that seed of greatness. The growth of love and the gratitude and respect for the gifts that God has bestowed on all of us make life the exciting adventure it should be. It is this celebration of life that is the magnet that draws people of all nations and creeds to Suzuki and his Talent Education. It is for this that we, parents and teachers, now and in the future, shall be eternally grateful to him.

GENERAL BIBLIOGRAPHY

Ball, Vernon. *Alpha Backgammon.* New York: William Morrow, 1980.

Billings, Helen K. *A Priceless Educational Advantage.* Ft. Lauderdale, Florida: Helen K. Billings Foundation, 1976.

Briggs, Dorothy Corkille. *Your Child's Self-Esteem.* New York: Doubleday, 1975.

Brown, Barbara. *New Mind, New Body.* New York: Harper and Row, 1974.

Buscaglia, Leo. *Living, Loving, and Learning.* New York: Ballentine Books, 1982.

Carton, Lonnie. *Raise Your Kids Right.* New York: Putnam, 1980.

Campbell, Ross. *How to Really Love Your Child.* Wheaton, Ill: Victor Books, 1977.

Campbell, Ross. *How to Really Love Your Teenager.* Wheaton, Ill: Victor Books, 1981.

Cook, Clifford A. *Suzuki Education in Action.* New York: Exposition Press, 1970.

Cratty, Bryant J. *Psychology and Physical Activity.* Englewood Cliffs, N.J.: Prentice-Hall, 1968.

Cratty, Bryant J. *Psychomotor Behavior in Education and Sport.* Springfield, Ill.: Charles Thomas, 1974.

Dechant, Emerald V. *Improving the Teaching of Reading.* Englewood Cliffs, N.J.: Prentice-Hall, 1964.

Dobson, James. *Hide or Seek.* Old Tappan, N.J.: Fleming H. Revell, 1974.

Dobson, James. *The Strong-Willed Child.* Wheaton, Ill.: Tyndale House, 1978.

Dolch, E. W. *Psychology and Teaching of Reading.* Champaign, Ill.: The Garrard Press, 1951.

Gallwey, W. Timothy. *Inner Tennis.* New York: Random House, 1976.

Ginott, Haim. *Between Parent and Child.* New York: MacMillan, 1965.

Gordon, Arthur. *A Touch of Wonder.* Old Tappan, N.J.: Fleming H. Revell, 1974.

Green, Elmer and Alyce. *Beyond Biofeedback.* New York: Dell Publishing Co., 1977.

Hart, Hornell. *Autoconditioning.* Englewood Cliffs, N.J.: Prentice-Hall, 1956.

Holding, Dennis H. *Human Skills.* New York: J. Wiley, 1981.

Kataoka, Eiko and Masayoshi, editors. *Talent Education Journal.* St. Louis, 1979.

Kohl, Herbert R. *Reading, How to*. New York: Dutton, 1973.

Kuzma, Kay. *Working Mothers*. New York: Rawson, Wade Publishers, 1980.

Lawther, John Dobson. *Learning of Physical Skills*. Englewood Cliffs, N.J.: Prentice-Hall, 1968.

Lawther, John Dobson. *Sports Psychology*. Englewood Cliffs, N.J.: Prentice-Hall, 1972.

Maltz, Maxwell. *The Magic Power of Self-Image Psychology*. Englewood Cliffs, N.J.: Prentice-Hall, 1964.

Mednick, Sarnoff A. *Learning*. Englewood Cliffs, N.J.: Prentice-Hall, 1964.

Montessori, Maria. *What You Should Know About Your Child*. India: Kalakshetra Publications, 1961.

Mursell, J. L. *Music Education: Principles and Programs*. New York: Silver Burdette, 1956.

Oxendine, Joseph. *Psychology of Motor Learning*. New York: Appleton-Century Crofts, 1968.

Petzold, Robert G. *The Perception of Music Symbols in Music Reading by Normal Children and Children Gifted Musically*. Journal of Experimental Education 28:272, June, 1960.

Robb, Margaret. *The Dynamics of Motor-Skill Acquisition*. Englewood Cliffs, N.J.: Prentice-Hall, 1972.

Rosenthal, Robert, and Jacobson, Lenore. *Pygmalion in the Classroom*. New York: Holt, Rinehart, and Winston, 1968.

Schultz, Johannes, and Luthe, Wolfgang. *Autogenic Training: Psychophysiologic Approach in Psychotherapy*. New York: Grune and Stratton, 1959.

Singer, Robert N. *The Psychomotor Domain*. Washington: Gryphon House, 1972.

Starr, William J. *The Suzuki Violinist*, Secaucus, NJ: Summy-Birchard Inc. 1976

Suinn, Richard J., editor. *Psychology in Sports*. Minneapolis: Burgess, 1980.

Suzuki, Shinichi. *Nurtured by Love*. New York: Exposition Press, 1969.

Tinker, Miles. *Bases for Effective Reading*. Minneapolis: U. of Minnesota Press, 1965.

Tohei, Koichi. *Book of Ki*. Tokyo: Japan Publications, 1976.

Wiener, Norbert. *Cybernetics*. Cambridge: M.I.T. Press, 1965.

Westrup, J.A., and Harrison, F.L. *Notation*. The New College Encyclopedia of Music. New York: W.W. Norton, 1960.

NUTRITIONAL BIBLIOGRAPHY

Abrahmson, E.M., M.D., and Pezet, A.W. *Body, Mind & Sugar*. New York: Avon Books, 1951.

Davis, Adelle. *Let's Eat Right to Keep Fit*. New York: Harcourt Brace Jovanovich, Inc., 1954.

Dufty, William. *Sugar Blues*. Radnor, Pa.: Chilton Book Co., 1975.

Feingold, Ben F., and Helene S. *The Feingold Cookbook for Hyperactive Children*. New York: Random House, 1979.

Kinderlehrer, Jane. *Confessions of a Sneaky Organic Cook*. Emmaus, Pa.: Rodale Press, Inc., 1971.

Pickard, Mary Ann. *Feasting Naturally*. Lenexa, Kansas: Cookbook Publishers, Inc., 1979.

Pickard, Mary Ann. *Feasting Naturally From Your Own Recipes*. Lenexa, Kansas: Cookbook Publishers, Inc., 1981.

Pickard, Mary Ann. *Feasting Naturally With Our Friends*. Lenexa, Kansas: Cookbook Publishers, Inc., 1982.

Sloan, Sara. *A Guide for Nutra Lunches and Natural Foods*. Atlanta: SOS Printing, 1977.

Smith, Lendon H., M.D. *Improving Your Child's Behavior Chemistry*. Englewood Cliffs, N.J.: Prentice-Hall, 1976.

Smith, Lendon H., M.D. *Feed Your Kinds Right*. New York: Dell, 1979.

APPENDIX

Publications in the Suzuki field by Kingston Ellis Press.

Audiocasette tapes:

SUZUKI SPEAKS TO PARENTS

This is a conversation between Shinichi Suzuki and William Starr made in Suzuki's studio in Matsumoto in 1969.

GIVE YOUR CHILD A PRICELESS EDUCATIONAL ADVANTAGE AT HOME, FREE

This tape, made by Dr. Billings herself, is a digest of her book of the same title.

Books:

THE SUZUKI VIOLINIST by William Starr

Already a classic, this guide for teachers and parents is used in the Americas, Europe, and Australia. Teachers have found this book an invaluable aid and continue to recommend it enthusiastically to parents of their students.

THE MUSIC ROAD, BOOKS 1 AND 2 by Constance Starr

An antidote to "Why Johnny Can't Read - Music". These volumes provide the same repetition and review to develop music reading skills that the Suzuki student has already employed in learning to perform the Suzuki repertoire.

TWENTY-SIX COMPOSERS TEACH THE VIOLINIST
by William Starr

A book of excerpts from solo, chamber and orchestral literature supplementing the Suzuki books at the Book VI level. Carefully compiled and edited, the material covers a great range of technical problems.

Our plans went like this: Chloe would get a job at the perfume counter in Debenhams. I'd get a job in the café on the top floor, or failing that, Woolworths—who Chloe said would take anyone. We'd save up our money, and then we'd rent a flat. She'd progress to the make-up counter, or the VIP personal shopper's lounge.

The flat was going to have a balcony because Chloe didn't think it was hygienic to smoke inside, and I wanted to get a rabbit. We'd be good about paying the rent and the bills, but we'd spend the rest of our money on skirts and beads and blue bottles of alcohol in nightclubs. We'd have wallpaper like her mother's but we were going to draw it ourselves so it'd be limited edition and worth a bundle. We'd have ashtrays made out of pink glass, and dream-catchers in the windows. We were going to eat Arctic Roll whenever we felt like it, and watch Leonardo DiCaprio in *Titanic* and *Romeo and Juliet* every night. I never got a job at a cafe, and I never tried Woolworths. I clean the shopping centre. And Chloe never got to grow up at all.